ESPN

SPORTSCENTURY

ESPN
SportsCentury

INTRODUCTION BY DAVID HALBERSTAM
FOREWORD BY CHRIS BERMAN
EDITED BY MICHAEL MacCAMBRIDGE

DESIGN DIRECTORS:

Walter Bernard and Milton Glaser

ART DIRECTOR:

Irene Vandervoort

CONTRIBUTING DESIGNER:

Nancy Eising

PICTURE RESEARCH:

Kristine Gentile Smith

CHAPTER OPENING PHOTOGRAPHY:

Matthew Klein

PREVIOUS PAGES

Title Page.
Ebbets Field,
October 1947, the
World Series.

The Sultan.
The Yankees'
Babe Ruth swinging
for the fences at
the Polo Grounds,
1921.

Sudden Death.
Johnny Unitas
of the Colts passing
in the late stages
of the 1958 NFL
Championship game.

The Showdown.
Lew Alcindor
and Elvin Hayes at
the opening tip
of the UCLA-
Houston game,
January 1968.

Victory.
Bobby Orr
celebrates after
scoring the goal
that gives the
Boston Bruins the
1970 NHL title.

Touchdown.
Johnny Rodgers
scoring on punt
return in Nebraska-
Oklahoma "Game of
the Century," in
Norman, Okla.,1971.

The Thrilla.
Muhammad Ali
and Joe Frazier
slug it out during
their third bout,
Manila, The
Philippines, 1975.

 **General Motors**
We would like to acknowledge the support of General Motors and its divisions (Buick, Cadillac, Chevrolet, GMC Truck, Oldsmobile, Pontiac/GM, Saturn, AC Delco and DirecTV) to the SportsCentury project.

Library of Congress Cataloging-in-Publication Data

ESPN sportscentury / introduction by David Halberstam ;
    foreword by Chris Berman ; edited by Michael MacCambridge. -- 1st ed.
        p.   cm.
    ISBN 0-7868-6471-0
    1. Sports--United States--History--20th century.
    I. MacCambridge, Michael. II. ESPN (TV network)
    GV583.E76   1999
    796'.0973--dc21   99-27715
                        CIP

FIRST EDITION
10 9 8 7 6 5 4 3 2 1

FOREWORD

By Chris Berman

FOR THE PAST 20 YEARS, or score, as Abraham Lincoln would have termed it, it has been our privilege at ESPN to chronicle the nation's sporting events. In the following pages we get the distinct pleasure of increasing our focus five-fold as we look back at a century of sports and the individuals that made these 100 years so special.

When the year 1900 arrived, we as a nation were just as close to the presidency of Thomas Jefferson as we were to that of William Jefferson Clinton. We were much closer to the Civil War than we were to the civil rights movement.

At this, the turn of the 21st Century, we can traverse the country by air in under six hours, watch countless games from all over the nation by satellite, and get instant information on the Internet. Alan Shepherd has long since hit a golf ball on the moon.

At the turn of the 20th Century, there were no planes and precious few cars. We moved by train, horse or foot. There was no TV and, for all practical purposes, no radio. We got our news by reading the newspaper or by word of mouth. So much has happened over these 100 years that it could be argued that no century has ever seen as much technological change.

If there has been any constant in the 1900s, it has been sports and our fascination with it. We have always marveled at those who run the fastest, jump the highest, and hit the hardest—with one's fists, and, as team sports developed, with a bat or with shoulder pads.

Sure, the athletes evolve, but in those sports which span the century, no matter how things change, they remain the same. In baseball, Babe Ruth became Mark McGwire, Lou Gehrig became Cal Ripken, Ty Cobb became Pete Rose, and Walter Johnson became Nolan Ryan. In boxing, Jack Johnson became Jack Dempsey, who became Joe Louis, who became Muhammad Ali. Sugar Ray Robinson became Sugar Ray Leonard. In the Olympics, Jim Thorpe became Jesse Owens, who became Carl Lewis. In golf, Bobby Jones became Arnold Palmer and Jack Nicklaus, who became Tiger Woods, maybe. In football, in many ways, Red Grange became Jim Brown.

Don Hutson became Jerry Rice. Even in horse racing, Man o' War became Secretariat.

In great athletes we see those attributes which we ourselves can only hope to emulate. Who wouldn't want to possess the sheer joy of competition of the Babe, Ali, Willie Mays, Joe Namath, Magic Johnson, Michael Jordan, Bobby Orr, or for that matter, the Harlem Globetrotters? Who wouldn't want the quiet elegance of Joe DiMaggio, Hank Aaron, Joe Montana, Wayne Gretzky, Kareem Abdul-Jabbar or Chris Evert? Who wouldn't want the dogged determination of Ted Williams, Johnny Unitas, Bill Russell, Maurice Richard, Ben Hogan, or Billie Jean King? Who wouldn't want the longevity of Lou Gehrig, Gordie Howe, George Blanda, or Al Oerter? Who wouldn't want the courage of Jackie Robinson?

Sports in this century have often been way ahead of society. When Robinson broke baseball's color barrier in 1947, he was eight years ahead of Rosa Parks, and 16 years ahead of Martin Luther King's "I Have a Dream" speech. In fact, you could argue that when it came to civil rights, sports helped spur on social change, and certainly heightened public awareness. Three great black heavyweight champions—Jack Johnson, Joe Louis, and Muhammad Ali—are proof. Jesse Owens at the 1936 Olympics gave probably the strongest statement of all, but in the Sixties, Arthur Ashe's winning at Forest Hills, and Texas Western beating Kentucky for the college basketball championship, sent messages home loud and clear.

One of America's beauties is that it is truly a melting pot. So, too, is sports. As we approach the 21st Century, where else can you find *anything* that knows no socioeconomic boundaries? Athletes, and certainly sports fans, are men and women, old and young, white and black. A millionaire and someone on welfare could have an intelligent discussion about yesterday's ballgame. Try that with any other subject.

One hundred years from now, when we get to do this again, I'm sure that the passion for sports will still be special. It will have to go a long way, though, to top what we've seen these past 100 years.

EDITOR'S NOTE

By Michael MacCambridge

THERE ARE SPORTS FANS OUT THERE still angry about Don Denkinger's call in Game 6 of the 1985 World Series. People who insist even today that Frank Gifford had enough for a first down late in regulation of the 1958 NFL title game. Groups dedicated to the proposition that Bill Mazeroski or Otis Taylor ought to be in one Hall of Fame or another. And 80 years after Babe Ruth was sold to the Yankees, kids in Boston still grow up hearing about The Curse.

In other words, serious sports fans have memories with tusks. And so a book like this—which presumes to honor the century's greatest athletes, best teams, biggest games, and most unforgettable moments—is destined to start more arguments than it settles.

But the arguments are worth having because the world of sports, in a real sense, is *about* memory. Babe Ruth resonates in Yankee Stadium even today. A cellar-dwelling Celtic team is all the sadder for the championship banners hanging overhead, even if the place where they won those banners is gone.

The end of the century serves as an irresistible lure for cataloging memories. ESPN, as part of its SportsCentury celebration, convened a panel of 48 respected writers, commentators, historians and observers to select the 100 greatest athletes of the century. This is a task both thankless and fascinating. Even within a single sport, picking the 100 best athletes requires tricky relative judgments of different eras and styles and strategies. But to expand the universe to select the best from among all sports invites the sort of endless apples vs. oranges arguments for which barstools were made. Should Sam Snead be here instead of Greg Maddux? (I think so.) Should Bob Beamon be here rather than Bronko Nagurski? (Depends on your criteria.) Should Henry Armstrong be here rather than John Elway? (*Hell*, no.) And where's Marion Motley?

The full lineup of the 100 greatest athletes appears here, for the first time; though if you want to find out the order in which the panel ranked them, you'll have to continue tuning into ESPN's weekly SportsCentury countdown.

We've used that group of 100 athletes as the beginning of a wider-ranging exploration of the century in sports. So while this book carries the SportsCentury name, it is not a commemorative, but rather an independent companion volume to the series, providing a different perspective.

It begins with "A Dynasty in the Making," David Halberstam's essay about what sports meant to this country in the 20th Century, exploring the way these games and athletes occupied an increasingly central role in American popular culture.

The core of the book comes in 10 essays by a superb lineup of writers, each of whom was asked to write about the athlete who best defined a particular decade of the century. This is an intentionally provocative, open-ended question, offering 10 more arguments in waiting. We chose Bill Russell rather than, say, Jim Brown as the defining athlete of the '60s. We went with Pete Rose as a better reflection of the '80s than Wayne Gretzky. But Brown and Gretzky get their due in this book, as do all of the 100 athletes named by the ESPN panel, each of which—save the "defining athletes" featured in the longer essays—is profiled in a short biographical sketch.

Complementing these profiles are a set of 10 Playbooks, providing context for each decade. These sections include a round-up of the most memorable games, matches and tournaments of the decade; a chart of champions in every major team sport; profiles of important coaches and off-the-field influences; even a "time capsule" for each decade, showing how sports intersected with the world at large.

The result is not a formal history of sports over the past 100 years, but it does present several diverse dimensions of sports in this country, and tells a larger story in its own right. To begin with Gerald Early's essay on Jack Johnson and read through to Nelson George's assessment of Michael Jordan is to trace the arc that American sports traveled during the 20th Century.

And, it is hoped, to get a better sense of why sports played such a significant part of the American Century.

A Dynasty in the Making

A century of astonishing growth—from Kitty Hawk to cyberspace—elevated the United States
to the role of preeminent global superpower. Along the way, a country that had always worked hard
learned to play hard as well. Sports moved from the margins of daily life toward a central role
in the civic culture, the games becoming a microcosm of the American experience itself. Sports provided
much of the glue that kept a diverse patchwork of races and cultures together. And illuminated
the way Americans saw themselves, and tried to make themselves better.

AMERICA ENTERED THE NEW CENTURY on the very threshold of becoming a great power. Barely more than a century old, it was already moving at an astonishing rate from agrarian to industrial society, and from rural to urban society. With a population of roughly 70 million, the nation was becoming urbanized at an accelerating rate; indeed tensions between the new immigrants who lived in the cities and were often Catholic, and people who were nativists, that is the older stock Americans who lived in more rural areas, would dominate the country's politics for the first third of a century.

More than a third of the population made their living from farming. The pace of life was slow; for every 1,000 Americans, there were only 18 telephones, most of these in businesses. No one spoke of disposable income or the entertainment share of the take-home dollar—take-home dollars were too scarce. Sports, both amateur and professional, had a limited importance; ordinary people lacked the time to play them, and more important, the time and money to watch them.

But the country would become the most dynamic society in the world. In a century of stunning advances in technology, no country was so systematically on the cutting edge like America, not only in inventing new and critical scientific breakthroughs, but in bringing them to market as devices to be enjoyed by simple working citizens. If there was one great American revolution, created by hundreds of smaller inventions, it was a revolution which created the good life for ordinary working men and women. It was a revolution which in sum made the worst kind of physical labor less harsh, paid workers a fairer share for their labor, gave them a decent wage, and allowed them not only great

personal dignity and economic independence with an increased amount of disposable income, but more leisure time. How America spent both that leisure time and disposable income—the rise of an entertainment society and its effect upon the world of sports—would be one of the most dramatic by-products of what was often called the American Century.

By the end of the century, it had become America the affluent, a place where ordinary families owned two and sometimes three cars, one and sometimes two houses, took long, expensive vacations, and spent a vast amount of the GNP on the search for pleasure. In the process—in part because of its wealth, in part because of the direction the new technology took it—America had morphed itself from a grim, often joyless, rather Calvinist society to a modern mass-production industrial society. By the Sixties, it changed again, into a communications society, to finally, by the end of the century, an entertainment society in which images replaced print as a principal means of communication.

In all of this change sports—amateur and particularly professional—would be among the main beneficiaries. By 1998, America's most famous athlete, Michael Jordan, a young black man from North Carolina, made some $78 million dollars a year in salary and endorsements, and certain professional sports franchises, like the New York Yankees and the Dallas Cowboys, were said to be worth close to a billion dollars.

Rarely had the beginning of a century in one nation seemed so distant from the end of the same century. In January 1900 the country was barely a generation removed from a bitter and exceedingly violent civil war, yet from that war were the beginnings of American power, dynamism and industrialism first fashioned.

But that was yet to come. If the Civil War had been fought to end slavery, then there was in the Reconstruction era, as the true political price of reunion emerged, a resurgence of racism, slavery replaced by legal racism, and fierce continued suppression of

Coming-out Party: As the country's wealth grew, its formality waned. Gray-flannel men gave way to rabid, demonstrative rooters, many of whom seemed to be competing with the game itself for the camera's attention.

1908: Lewis Hine's photograph of boys playing stickball in a Boston alley.
It wasn't just the games that changed...

the children of slaves. If, in Lincoln's phrase, a house divided against itself cannot stand, then America as the century began was neither a house divided nor a house unified. In the new century, one of the great struggles played out would be that of black Americans struggling for full citizenship. And no arena would showcase this battle in a series of stunning and often bitterly divisive increments, or reflect the true talents of black America more clearly, than the world of sports.

THE CENTURY WOULD BEGIN with what was virtually a national attempt to limit the possibilities of a great black fighter, Jack Johnson, because he was considered uppity and was far too often seen with white women. Special laws were passed as a means of entrapping Johnson and ending his right to be seen as the heavyweight champion of the world. It was just the beginning. The struggle of blacks in the century ahead would be an ongoing source of national tension and debate.

But for those who weren't bound by race (or gender), the country was still a land of promise, the place where the past could be shed and a man could start anew. America offered the concept of hope—if not for yourself, for your children, the place where in one generation change could be wrought. The most telling comment on that American ideal came when I. I. Rabi, the distinguished scientist, won the Nobel Prize for physics. A reporter interviewed him that day and asked him what he thought. "I think that in the old country I would have been a tailor," he answered.

No one would illustrate that unique American social fluidity more than most of the best-known athletes of the century, each with their own very American drive to excel. Babe Ruth, born of a troubled, shaky family. Joe DiMaggio and Johnny Unitas, each the son of immigrants. Muhammad Ali and Michael Jordan, descendants of slaves who would become special American icons. All of them were in different ways driven by the unique forces which created America—the combination of prejudice inflicted

on those who had gone before them, and yet the belief that in the lives of their children things would get better. More, the world of sports offered the ideal arena for new Americans, or black Americans whose forebears had been suppressed by racism, to show their strengths and their talents. Only the U.S. military was in any way nearly as democratic a venue.

America was, of course, almost without knowing it, a favored nation. The quality and energy and passion of its immigrant citizens and the part they were to play in the successes of the coming century were not to be underestimated: They were to become inventors, scientists, workers, farmers and exceptional citizens. "Give me your tired, and wretched and poor," Senator Daniel Patrick Moynihan once said, ironically mocking the words taken from Emma Lazarus and engraved on the Statue of Liberty, then adding himself, "Some wretched, some poor." What Moynihan meant, of course, was that America was getting the cream of the crop, though when they had first arrived they did not look like the cream of the crop—all they carried were their hopes and ambitions, and their desire to be not just Americans but good Americans.

This explosion of affluence and power and confidence connected directly, it would turn out, to the world of sports; more, the world of sports would serve as an almost ideal window through which to watch the profound changes taking place elsewhere in the society. Was the country more confident, more affluent, and did its citizens have more leisure time? Then they would show it by becoming more addicted to their games.

No one signified the coming of power quite like Babe Ruth. He changed the very nature of sports. He was five years old when the century began (or at least he so believed, since it was also possible that he was four years old). Because his deeds were so awesome, particularly when measured against the existing dimensions of what passed for power, his name was almost immediately turned into an adjective. Long drives, more than half a century after he played his last game, are said to be Ruthian. He was

1996: ...it was also the people playing.
Young girls in a junior soccer league, watched over by swing voters.

the perfect figure about whom to create a vast assortment of myths and legends, some of them true, some of them not, though it meant little if they were true or not, because the ones which had been made up seemed just as true as those which could more readily be documented.

RUTH WAS BIG, JOYOUS AND SEEMINGLY CAREFREE. Rules were made to be broken—he had spent much of his childhood in an orphanage not because his parents were dead but because they could not control him. That sense of him, as a kind of all-American Peck's Bad Boy, seemed to endear him to many of his fellow citizens, more trapped by all kinds of rules in their lives than he was in his. If editorial writers on occasion thundered against his childlike and occasionally boorish behavior, the same antics seemed to charm millions of ordinary American sports fans.

He brought drama to everything he did. He was not just a great athlete, he was a show, fun even when he struck out. He became a phenomenon. Ordinary people longed to read about him. The outrages he committed socially were the outrages of the common man, the ordinary American catapulted to an elite world by his athletic success, but unspoiled in his heart. After he had signed for $80,000, a salary greater than that of President Herbert Hoover, and a reporter questioned him about it, he had said, "Why not? I had a better year than he did." When he met Marshall Foch, the commander of the French forces during World War I, he had said, "I suppose you were in the war."

If Ruth was the most egalitarian of sports heroes, then this was the most democratic of lands, the nation where mass production—and a new kind of economic democracy that went with it—was born. It was not by chance that the new century was perfectly designed for America, and indeed was often known as the American Century. That was a partial misnomer. In truth, it was the Oil Century, as the Japanese intellectual Naohiro Amaya called it, for it was a century in which gas-driven machines would

replace coal-driven machines, with an explosive increase in productivity. In the oil century productivity flowered; it could generate products enough for everyone—not just for the handful of rich. The oil culture because of the nature of the fuel created vastly more wealth, a wealth so great that it was shared by ordinary people. And of all the industrialized nations poised for the start of a new era, America, with its rich indigenous oil deposits, was uniquely well–positioned for the new age.

In the oil culture, because oil produced so much more in the way of goods, the workers became prosperous, too. The oil century produced, it would soon become clear, workers who would become consumers; and the more they consumed, the more they created work for others. It was the dawning of a culture in which ordinary people achieved not merely middle-class status, but an elemental social dignity which had in the past been reserved for a tiny number of people. This was an American invention—a nation with something new, a mass middle class. The citizens in this new society gained dignity, confidence, leisure time and, in time, disposable income. That alone was to have a profound effect on the rise and the obsession with sports in the century ahead.

If there was one key figure who represented American genius in the first half of the century, and gave a sense of what America was to be—a mass-driven society with mass-produced goods, all those forces which would make America an economic superpower—it was the first Henry Ford. He was the architect of the most powerful of American ideas which drove the century and made American economic democracy unique—the worker as consumer. He brought the concept of mass production to its height with his River Rouge plant, and turned the auto from an item available only to the rich into something that all Americans could own. In time he came to love the assembly line—the true diamond in his eye—more than the car itself.

Almost from the start, sensing that his workers were his real customers, he began to put most of his energy into what was his production line, to build more cars faster, to meet the unparal-

23

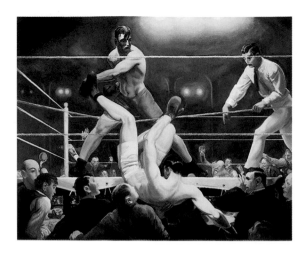

1923: George Bellows' classic painting of
Firpo sending Dempsey through the ropes.

leled demand, and at the same time to keep reducing its price. Because the car was already so simple and well–designed there was not much to tinker with in the car itself, he poured most of his energies and his special genius into the production line.

The cars poured off the line, soon more than a million a year. The speed of manufacture meant he was selling that many more cars per year and could cut the price per car accordingly. Ford loved making a car that benefited working people. "Every time I lower the price of a car $1," he said, "I can get 1,000 new customers." In its early incarnation, in the 1910-11 fiscal year, the Model T had cost $780; a year later with the production ascending in amazing increments, the price had dropped to $690 and then to $600, and on the eve of World War I, it was down to $260. What he had wrought was the beginning of a revolution—the good life for the common man.

And so early in this century America became a vastly more dynamic, vastly less class-dominated, infinitely more open society than competing nations. Its people were busy; they were on the move, driving all the time now, it seemed, prosperous, and ever more confident. Its love of sports became a parallel force. The more confident and affluent Americans were, the more they became sports nuts. In addition, other inventions were taking place which would not only bind America together more as a nation, but make sports an ever more important part of the fabric of the society.

It was not just the games themselves that were about to change and become more important. It was the delivery system—the coming of modern broadcasting, first radio, then network television, and then satellite television—which was going to change the way Americans felt about sports; for the new, more modern delivery system was about to make the games more accessible (and thus more important) and make the athletes themselves infinitely more famous, and soon, infinitely wealthier. In the beginning, there was radio. It would help usher in what became known as the Golden Age of Sport. In 1923 the Yankees defeated the Giants in the World Series in six games. Ruth hit three home

runs, was walked constantly and scored eight times. It was a noteworthy series, not the least of all because it was the first time the World Series was broadcast across the country on radio. The principal voice at the microphone was that of a young man named Graham McNamee, and the fact that this was broadcast to millions of Americans made the Babe's fame—and the importance of sport within the culture—that much greater.

For it was not just the game itself which was changing, it was the amplification system in a country so vast, which for the first time was becoming linked as one by a new and powerful broadcasting system. On a vast, sprawling land mass where the connection of ordinary people to each other had often been tenuous, big-time sports, broadcast to the entire nation at one time, giving the nation shared icons, was to prove immensely important. It was not just a shared moment of entertainment, though that was critical in the rise of the popularity of sports, but it was to be an important part of the connecting tissue of the society, arguably more important in a country so large where the population was so ethnically diverse—and new—than it might have been in a smaller country with one dominating strain of ethnicity. Sports in some way united America and bound Americans to each other as other aspects of national life did not—it offered a common thread, and in time a common obsession. Americans who did not know each other could find community and commonality by talking of their mutual sports heroes.

ALMOST OVERNIGHT GRAHAM McNAMEE became a major cultural figure. In January 1927 he worked the first true national sports hookup, broadcasting the Rose Bowl game. He did every World Series game from 1923 through 1934. He covered the first political conventions broadcast live. On the occasion of Lindbergh's triumphant inaugural flight to Paris, the voice that most Americans heard the news from was that of McNamee. He was very good at what he did. "The father of broadcasting," the

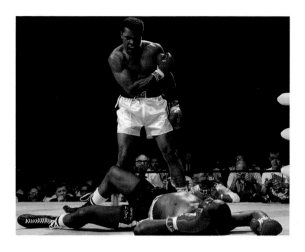

1965: Neil Leifer's classic shot
of the snarling Ali standing over the prone Liston.

distinguished broadcaster Red Barber called him. In the early days of broadcasting, there were no radio booths. So the announcers had to work in an open stadium and do their work in the most primitive of all possible settings. McNamee, Barber noted, "walked into the stadium, sat down…and told the nation what it was waiting to hear and had never heard before…told them about 10 different sports. I concentrated on two—baseball and football—and I thought I had my hands full…. His sign-off was distinctive: 'This is Graham McNamee speaking. Good night, all.'"

Thus was the audience increased, and thus was sports made more important. Americans by means of radio could now monitor its sports heroes as never before. Events in the world of sports seemed to be ever more important and hold the attention of the public that much more. The resulting popularity of sports was amazing, as was the resilience of its appeal throughout the Depression. On the eve of World War II, baseball seemed to be poised at a level of almost unique preeminence. The 1941 season was a historic one: Joe DiMaggio hit in 56 consecutive games and Ted Williams hit .406. Soon both were in the service, and baseball, like other sports, went on essentially a four-year vacation.

If World War I had been the first act of America's emergence as a world power, World War II would be the defining act. If there had been fears in America on the eve of the entry of the United States into the war that a democracy might not be able to stand up to powerful totalitarian military powers, those fears soon proved completely invalid: Rarely had a democratic society's power been so brilliantly mobilized. America rose to true superpower status during the war; its industrial base, secure from enemy attack because of the two oceans, became the arsenal of democracy. When the war was over America stood alone, rich in a world which was poor. The change in the balance of power had taken place with a startling swiftness.

For the war changed the balance of power in the world with a certain finality: In Europe the old powers had been bled white by two wars; America, by contrast, had been brought kicking and screaming to the zenith of its power. No bombs had fallen on America; its losses—roughly 350,000 men on two fronts—were slight in comparison with other nations.

All of these factors had given the nation a startling boost in affluence, household by household, and equally important, a critical increase in personal confidence. Not only had America as a nation played a decisive part in the war, not only had it been, in contrast to most wars, considered a good war, but millions of Americans, whose professional careers might in an earlier part of the century have been proscribed by class, had left their small towns, had learned that they could lead men, and now had a chance to continue their careers through the G.I. Bill. If one of the things which distinguished America from the old world was its concept of social fluidity—the fact that in only one generation ordinary citizens could rise significantly above the level attained by their parents—then nothing made that concept more muscular than the G.I. Bill.

IN THE POSTWAR ERA America had to face the domestic consequences of its own wartime rhetoric. For the war had generated its own powerful propaganda, that of the democracies taking on two totalitarian powers, Germany and Japan, and in the case of Germany a racist, genocidal nation. But there were important domestic consequences to that. If America was the driving force of a new, more democratic world, then it was still a nation divided racially, not just in the South, where feudal laws imposed state-sanctioned legal and political racism, but in the North as well, its major professional sports events still lily white. In the courts a large number of cases trying to end the doctrine of separate but equal were working their way to the Supreme Court. But it would be the world of sports that became the most important postwar laboratory of racial change and where black Americans finally got their first true chance at showing their real talents. That their sports were segregated was

The Twenties: The World Series comes to radio; NBC's Graham McNamee interviews Babe Ruth between innings.

singularly unjust, and no one knew this better than the professional baseball players themselves. For they often barnstormed with black players from the Negro League after the season, and they knew exactly how good the black ballplayers were, that only racial prejudice prevented them from playing.

JACKIE ROBINSON, whose terrible responsibility it was to be the first, the man in the test tube, his abilities and conduct to be scrutinized by an entire nation—was nothing less than history's man. He was a superb athlete, strong, quick, and wildly competitive. He had been a four-sport star at UCLA before he played professional baseball, and he could probably have played professionally in three major sports. Before he entered the service in World War II, though professional basketball and football were still quite embryonic in the West, he played with semi-pro teams in both.

He brought with him a rare on-field and off-field intelligence, and exceptional mental discipline and toughness of mind, an ability to restrain himself despite extreme provocation (and control his hair-trigger temper). He resisted, as he promised he would, the temptation to lash back for a long time despite the constant taunts of fans and opposing players. "Mr. Rickey, what do you want?" he had asked the Brooklyn Dodger boss at their fateful first meeting. "Do you want a player with guts enough to fight back?" "I want a player," Rickey had answered memorably, "with guts enough not to fight back." He might rage inside, but he remained true to the challenge offered him by Rickey. Throughout his career, Robinson remained aware that the spotlight was always on him, and that the challenge to excel on field and behave with dignity off it was singular in his case. Few Americans were ever subjected to such relentless scrutiny in so public a manner; it is doubtful if any of his fellow citizens ever endured such relentless pressure with such sustained excellence.

If American society, in the oddly pious-but-shrewd incarnation of Branch Rickey, was looking for the perfect candidate to undergo so withering a test as being the first black to play in the major leagues, then it could not have done better than Jackie Robinson. He was intelligent, purposeful, resourceful, modern; he played at a brilliant level, and he did not back down when taunted racially. He was fast and strong: clothed in his loose-fitting baseball uniform, he did not look particularly powerful, but there is one photo from those days of him alongside Joe Louis, both men stripped to the waist, where Robinson looks every bit as muscled and powerful as the heavyweight champion. Above all, Robinson was nothing if not a man. Everything about him demanded respect. He had played in endless integrated games as a collegian, and he had no illusion, as many blacks less privileged might have, that white athletes were either smarter or had more natural talent than blacks. White people to him were not people you were supposed to shuffle around who had superior abilities; they were just people, people who because of their skin had gotten a better deal than blacks.

It was a great experiment, and it took place in 1947, seven years before *Brown* v. *Board of Education*. In a way, what Jackie Robinson did, performing in the most public arena in America, was every bit as important as that Supreme Court decision in 1954. His arrival in the big leagues had been the ultimate test on something that most Americans prided themselves on—the fairness of their country, that in this country the playing field was somehow supposed to be fair. In a way it was an experiment which put America itself at a crossroads between two powerful competing national impulses, one impulse reflecting the special darkness of racial prejudice and historic meanness of spirit which had begun with slavery, the other the impulse of idealism and optimism, that a true democracy offered the children of all American citizens a chance to exhibit their full talents and rise to their rightful place. What he was contesting was the worst myths of the past, for in the particular cruelty of the time, America had not merely barred blacks from its professional

The Seventies: Television was ascendant, and the crew of *Monday Night Football* often upstaged the game.

leagues, it had said it was barring them because they were unworthy. Yes, the rationale went in those days, they could run fast, but they lacked guts and heart, and they would fold in the late innings in big games, and, of course, by the way, they were lazy—everybody knew that.

By midseason the argument was over. Robinson was a great player—clearly on his way to becoming rookie of the year. He had brought life and speed and intensity to an otherwise more passive Dodger team. He was an American samurai, the baseball player as warrior, and the other Dodgers became more like him—they were with his arrival much more a warrior team that fought you all the time than they had ever been in the past, and they would remain that way for the duration of his career. As a player no one was more explosive. Pitchers in particular feared him once he was on the base paths because of his explosive initial burst of speed. Years later, the Yankees pitcher Vic Raschi, talking about how he had lost a 1–0 game in the 1949 World Series by giving up a hit to Gil Hodges, said that it was Robinson, bluffing a dash from third toward home, who had beaten him. "I had just never seen anything like him before, a human being who could go from a standing stop to full speed in one step. He did something to me that almost never happened. He broke my concentration, and I paid more attention to him than to Hodges. He beat me more than Hodges."

IF ROBINSON'S STUNNING SUCCESS AGAINST THE MYTHS of the past marked the first great breakthrough of the postwar era, then the second one was driven by technological change. It was the coming of network television and it started as a true national phenomenon roughly a decade after the end of the war. It inaugurated nothing less than another golden age in sports. For in truth the world of sports as the postwar era started actually had two golden ages ahead, both of them driven by technological breakthroughs, the first one wrought by the coming of network television which dramatically boosted football as a sport, especially the professional game, and the second some 25 years later with the coming of satellite transmission, which created the world of cable television and aided all sports, most particularly basketball.

It was the power of an instrument—the power of the camera—which now revolutionized American society. Nothing changed the culture and the habits of Americans more than the coming of television. Television had a kind of greenhouse effect on the society around it: What the camera liked grew and prospered beyond anyone's expectations (often growing too quickly and too large for its own good, of course); what the camera did not like just as quickly withered.

In particular, the camera liked professional football. What the camera caught and savored about football, which radio had always missed, was the speed of the sport, and, above all, the violence. For the camera more than anything else loved action. Football—fast, balletic, often brutal, with its bone-crushing hits—was made to order for the camera. Baseball, with its slow, leisurely pace, a sport which had its roots in an agrarian America where the pace of life was slower, had been perfect for radio, where an announcer could paint a gentle portrait and measure his cadence to the casual pace of the game.

Before the coming of television, professional football was, in comparison to baseball, virtually a minor league; it was a very good game, indeed a connoisseur's game, played by immensely talented athletes before passionate, diehard fans, but it had somehow never quite broken out of its rather narrow place in the sports spectrum. Radio revealed neither the talent nor the fury with which it was played. To the degree that ordinary sports fans committed their time to football on fall weekends—it was on Saturday when they could pick up a Notre Dame or Michigan game on the radio, not Sunday.

Sunday became in the new televised age the day which was set aside in the fall for American males. It introduced the pro game to a vast new audience, and the pro game began to enter the con-

1906: Nap Lajoie and Rube Waddell sell soda pop.

sciousness of average sports fans as never before. Very quickly in the mid to late Fifties, as the country was wired nationally for television, pro football went on a dizzying rise to a point where it began to rival professional baseball as the national sport. In those days not that many people owned sets, and many young American males would agree to meet at a neighborhood bar to watch and eat and drink. The sense of a sport on the rise was obvious—and nowhere was that more obvious than in New York, where the football Giants began to become something new in pro football ranks, media celebrities. Football stars like Frank Gifford, movie-star handsome, were doing commercials (for very little money, mind you), and being welcomed as never before in bars like Toots Shors, where baseball players, fighters and jockeys had held forth. The game was coming of age.

WITH THE COMING OF NETWORK TELEVISION professional football became a truly national game, with a national constituency. A fan did not have to live in Baltimore to be a Unitas or a Colts fan, or for that matter to live in New York to root for the Giants defense led by middle linebacker Sam Huff. Millions of sports fans who cared nothing about Pittsburgh, had never been to the University of Louisville, and had no intention of ever visiting Baltimore turned on their sets on Sunday to watch the daring exploits of a young quarterback from Pittsburgh who had gone to the University of Louisville and now played for the Baltimore Colts. The camera, it turned out, was quite dazzled by Johnny Unitas, the least likely, it would seem, of American media heroes.

In a way his career marked America in a cultural and economic transition. He grew up under the worst hardships inflicted on blue-collar America in the Depression and post-Depression years, living in a home which received almost no protections from the government, and yet he became one of the early celebrities under the gaze of a new and powerful medium which was going to change the nature of the economy and make

part of the society infinitely more glitzy. He knew all too well an America which was tough and poor, and he was largely unmoved by his place in this new America which was more affluent and more celebrity oriented. Unlike Namath (and Ali), who came after him and understood intuitively that in the new sports world created by television, it was always both sport and show, he always thought it was merely sport. His values had been set in that earlier age. Yet Unitas became the first superstar of the new age, the signature player of an old sport amplified by a new and loving medium, the perfect working-class hero for a sport just beginning to leave its working-class roots behind.

To the degree that radio liked football, it loved offensive stars—quarterbacks, running backs and wide receivers. But television was different, it had eyes for the defensive stars as well. Fans loved not only the long passes and the brilliant broken-field runs; they loved the savagery of clean hits. In this new era, living in the media capital of the world, Huff had become the first great national celebrity on defense. CBS did a documentary on him, "The Violent World of Sam Huff," and *Time* magazine put him on the cover. Giants fans cheered more loudly when their defense came on the field than when the offense took over. "Our offensive unit was not highly regarded," Kyle Rote remembered, years later. "When the offensive unit went out on the field, the defense shouted, 'Get in there and hold them.'" Because of that new rivalries developed and flourished: If New York against Baltimore was not necessarily a historic rivalry, then that collision of the Colt offense against the Giant defense, a matchup perhaps without historic roots, was one the knowing fan could readily anticipate.

In 1958, in what was later called the greatest game ever played, Unitas led the Colts to victory in overtime in the championship game against the Giants. He did it with two spectacular long drives, one at the end of regulation, the other in the sudden-death overtime. It was a signature game. Ewbank, not known for his pre-game inspirational speeches, really pushed his

1977: Mean Joe Greene, and the new technology, sells soda pop.

players before the game. "In 14 years," defensive end Gino Marchetti said about pregame pep talks, "I heard 'em all. 'Win for Mother,' 'Win for 'Father,'...'Don't disappoint all those people watching on television.'" Sometimes, Marchetti said, "they even tried to tell you how to act: 'Don't piss in the air with forty million people watching.' But that day Weeb really put it to us. He went up and down the roster, name by name: 'Donovan, they got rid of you—too fat and slow...Ameche, Green Bay didn't want you.' Yeah, he named me, Unitas ... he didn't miss anybody."

On that December day the Colts, because of Unitas, were the favorites, and they took a 14–3 lead. At one point in the third quarter the Colts had a first down on the Giant three, and a chance to put the game away 21–3. But the Giants held and began to turn it around. They came back to take a 17–14 lead in the fourth quarter. With 1:56 on the clock, it was Unitas time. The Colts got the ball back on their 14. Unitas missed on his first two passes, and then he simply took over. He connected on four passes, three of them to Raymond Berry. When the drive was over, the Colts were comfortably poised for the tying field goal on the Giant 13. That drive and a comparable one in the overtime, when the Colts marched for the winning touchdown, were like works of art. "The man was a genius," Huff said later, "I never saw a quarterback that good on those two drives." The Colts were the winners, but when the game was over, the real winner was the game of football itself.

Professional football ascended in popularity like a comet. In 1960, a second league was founded, and its star quarterback Joe Namath, coveted by both leagues because he had star quality, signed for $400,000. In just a few years more, the leagues merged, and played the defining event of America the Superpower in the Super Century, the Super Bowl.

The rise of the nation in the postwar era to this pinnacle was constantly contentious. Isolationist before the war, it was now a leading international power. On the way the debate over race had become ever more barbed. In the early Fifties there had been a

powerful challenge to the existing Jim Crow rules in the South. By the late Sixties, the existing laws had fallen, but the mood of American blacks was changing, and there were constant signs of the powerful alienation just under the surface. The black power movement began to flourish in the late Sixties—its slogan was black is beautiful, and in northern cities, the old religious ties which had been so important to black life in the South had begun to wither. A new movement, that of black Muslims, seemingly threatening to whites—its principal leaders spoke of white people as devils—had taken root among the deeply embittered blacks of the nation's northern cities.

T HAT MEANT THAT A YOUNG MAN named Cassius Clay, who rose to fame as a heavyweight boxer, was to become at once the most dazzling, and the most controversial athlete of his era, a symbol of all the powerful societal forces let loose in the Sixties.

He also in some way understood that television had changed the nature of sports, and no one, it would turn out, was a better entertainer; no one knew better how to hype his own fights. He was, he understood, as much actor as he was fighter, and he was exceptionally skilled at casting not just himself, but his opponents to his specifications. He himself, he liked to proclaim, was beautiful. His opponents were not. Sonny Liston, the most threatening of men until Ali completely defanged him, was too ugly, he boasted, to be the champ.

He was the most volatile of superstars, joyous, talented, angry. Sportswriters, at least the younger ones, loved him, but Madison Avenue avoided him like the plague. He was the perfect figure to illuminate the contradictions of America in the late Sixties, as it surged past mere superpower status, and became even more affluent: Yes, the nation was making great progress in ending age-old racist laws, but no, the progress was never fast. Yes, the country was a bulwark against a totalitarian power in Europe, but yes, too, it had become an anti-revolutionary force fighting on the

wrong side in a war of independence in Asia. He touched all of our fault lines and it was not suprising that attitudes toward him on the part of sportswriters and sports fans tended to divide along generational lines—a reflection of an America which was fighting a war not so much against the Vietnamese, but against itself, a great power with a fractured soul.

Ali was not going to be like Joe Louis, or for that matter Floyd Patterson, the benign black fighter who knew his place, was grateful for his opportunity, was respectful to all in authority around him, no matter how sleazy they were or how tenuous their hold on a position of authority, and watched carefully what he said and did. Ali represented a new and angrier generation of more alienated blacks: A lot of damage had been done over centuries of slavery and neo-slavery, and a lot of anger had been stored up.

In the end he was a marvel, a figure not only of sports but, like Jackie Robinson, though in a different way, of history itself. The day after he became heavyweight champion, he had announced that he was a Muslim and that his name was Muhammad Ali. A few years later, because of the war in Vietnam, he refused induction into the army, citing his religious principles. So it was that he lost his crown—and the ability to fight—for more than three years.

Politically, time worked on his side: By the Seventies, the Muslims were perceived to be less menacing. Dissident, and alienated, certainly, as blacks who lived in the poorer parts of America's cities might feel alienated and dissident, but not that threatening. As for the war in Vietnam, that became something of a badge of honor, that Ali had dissented, and acted upon his dissent; he, it turned out, had paid the price for others on a war which was something of a scar on the national conscience.

In time he regained his crown. Older now, several critical years wasted, he returned, his conscience having been served, to fight better than ever, to demonstrate in his fight with Foreman in Zaire and in three wondrous battles with Joe Frazier his true greatness.

HIS WAS A SOBERING CHALLENGE to America's self-image at a volatile and emotional time. He, the most marginally educated young man, barely able to get through high school (he got his high school degree only because the officials at his school realized that he was going to be the school's most famous product, and that it would shame the school rather than Clay if he did not graduate), had turned out to be right about a war about which the most brilliant national security advisers who had gathered around the President—including the Dean of Harvard college, the former head of the Ford Motor Company, and the former head of the Rockefeller Foundation—had turned out to be wrong. That was sobering, a reminder that America at the height of its affluence and power in this century had lost sight of what its true meaning and purpose was. The arrogance of power, the head of the Senate Foreign Relations Committee, Senator William Fulbright, called it. Ali would never have been able to come up with a phrase like that—instead he simply said, "I ain't got no quarrel with the Vietcong." He had acted upon conscience; the advisors, even when they were later burdened by doubt as the war went forward, had not. He had paid the price for his actions when he was young; they, the architects of this disaster, would pay it when they were older. That, for a nation which in its increasing power had become too prideful, too sure of its value and its rectitude, was a sobering lesson. No wonder, then, by the Nineties he had become something of a beloved national figure.

The success of Ali, the quality of his singular struggles, so much of it political, makes a sharp contrast with that of the final surpassing athlete of this era, Michael Jordan. The two had much in common: Both were supremely talented, both were black, both with their looks, their talent, and their style transcended their sports, appealing to millions of Americans who nominally had little interest in either boxing or basketball.

There the comparisons end, and the Americas they per-

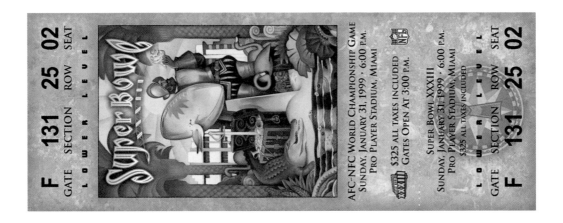

1999: Ticket stub from the century's last Super Bowl.

formed for differ. They are produced by different Americas: Ali by an America which seemingly closed off all of its benefits to a young talented black man from the South, other than the most brutal, primitive road to fame, boxing; Jordan, born in a time which made him a beneficiary of all the modern civil rights struggles. He was born in 1963, a year before Ali as Clay won the heavyweight title. He went to integrated public schools and was able to go on and star at North Carolina, a school which only recently had been closed to black undergraduates and which at the time of his birth still had not fielded a black basketball player on its team. His parents were comfortably middle class, his father by dint of victories in another hard-won battle—that of blacks in the American military. At Carolina Michael received the kind of great education and exceptional coaching that had been denied black athletes in the past.

Jordan was the most charismatic athlete of his era, and he was the best big-game, fourth-quarter player of a generation. He helped carry a team which often in other ways seemed somewhat ordinary to six world championships. He was the perfect figure for the American communications and entertainment society as the century came to a close, the first great athletic superstar of the wired world, arguably the most famous person on the planet. In his last season as a player, he earned some $78 million, $33 million in salary and $45 million in endorsements. It seemed only proper that as the century ended, he was engaged in serious negotiations to buy a large part of an NBA team.

He was a new world prince, graceful, beautiful, but a warrior or samurai nonetheless, and easily recognizable to the rest of the world as such. He arrived, unlike those before him, such as Robinson and Mays and Aaron, in a nation which had begun finally to realize that it was not a white nation, and as much as any other American he was proof that America, in some way, despite all its ethnic and racial divisions, was moving toward the beginning of a universal culture.

He gave the nation nothing less than a new concept of beau-

ty. Not surprisingly, his comfort zone was singularly high. He was gifted, he worked hard, and was beautiful in a nation which was now willing to accept a more complicated definition of beauty. America, after some 30 years of racial turbulence, was delighted to have a gifted young black man who seemed to be smiling back at it. If he endorsed sneakers, millions of Americans bought them, and in time he sold hamburgers and soft drinks and underwear and sunglasses and batteries and a telephone company.

As the century ended, he was known everywhere in the world, for the sport he played, basketball, was easily understandable, and traveled smoothly across borders in a way that American football and baseball did not. For in the new age of inexpensive satellites, America exported not its autos or its machine tools, but its culture—its music, its sports, and finally, the informality of its lifestyle. And Jordan was the most luminescent figure of the new world, his deeds the easiest to comprehend and admire.

IT HAD BEEN, ALL IN ALL, an astonishing century for America. No other country had ever changed so much in so short a time—rising to a position as a monopoly superpower, gaining steadily in power, affluence, and innate self-confidence. In this period much of the change, and the interior struggle, could be witnessed in the world of sports. It was not so much a metaphor for the society as a window on it—the tension, the conflicts, and the constant progress had often taken place first (and been witnessed more widely) in the world of sports. That was true, whether it was the rise of black athletes or the greater independence of the athletes themselves as they enjoyed greater personal freedom. Throughout the century, sports had served as a remarkable reflection of the strengths and weaknesses of the nation—its diversity, its hungers, its excesses, its rank commercialism. But above all the fact that the athletes always seemed to get bigger and stronger and faster, and the games themselves better.

THE 1900s

The century began with an American sporting culture already in place. By 1903, the champions of the established National League and upstart American League played in the first season-ending World's Championship Series. Horse racing and boxing dominated the sports pages. Yet four decades after the Emancipation Proclamation, blacks were still treated as second-class citizens. Onto this stage stepped a flamboyant African-American boxer who embodied in his quest for the heavyweight title the sum of black hopes, and white fears, about the mixing of races.

A Man Out of Time

*It might seem that I, who have devoted nearly all the years of my life to boxing and the severest form of athletic work, who once held the world's heavyweight boxing championship, and who was engaged in more ring contests than any other heavyweight boxer, am stepping out of my role when I presume to turn my attention for the moment to subjects that have no relation to my profession, subjects which in fact are far removed from the stern business of pugilism. But even a boxer must come in contact with life and its many problems. His is a business that permits him to rub against humanity in all its forms; he sees the high and the low spots, and feels the bumps of the rough places and the delight of the smooth ones. When he has lived as I have, **on the edge of two of the greatest eras of world history**, and has, because of the peculiar twists of fate to which I have been subjected, been thrown into all classes of society; when he has felt the stings of life as I have and also gloried in the triumphs that were mine, he comes to know many things that are not in the category of sports and boxing.*

—Jack Johnson, from his autobiography (emphasis added)

ARGUABLY, THE ONLY OTHER BOXER who could make a claim to our attention on the basis of what he thought and what he lived beyond the ring—because what he was beyond his immediate profession was so epochal as to make his presence as an athlete epochal as well—is the man who is most often compared to Jack Johnson: Muhammad Ali.

Johnson, unlike Ali, did not have his title stripped from him, despite his immense public disapproval and his Mann Act conviction in 1913. Johnson won his title in the ring and lost it there. There was a tepid attempt to strip him of the title in 1913 but it went nowhere for lack of support. It was important to whites that a white man win the title back in the ring from Johnson, not gain it through some administrative sanction or censure, such as stripping the title from Johnson, which might be interpreted as being tantamount to whites saying that a white man could not beat Johnson in the ring.

Whether Ali was altogether serious about being approached to play in the film version of Howard Sackler's 1969 play, *The Great White Hope*, a thinly fictionalized version of Johnson's reign as champion, or the people who approached him about it were serious about using a man who had never acted professionally in the lead

PREVIOUS PAGES
Tools of the Trade.
Turn-of-the-century boxing gloves, on display at the International Boxing Hall of Fame.

The Man America Feared. By the middle of the '00s, it was clear that Johnson— 6 feet ¼ inches tall, fighting between 185-221 pounds—was a formidable, unavoidable challenger for the heavyweight title.

role in a major motion picture is difficult to say. It was a common assumption in the late 1960s that there was a similarity, a resonance, a correspondence between Ali's life and Johnson's.

Ali exploited, mythologized this resonance in his autobiography, *The Greatest: My Own Story*. For instance, in his account of his return to the ring in October 1970 to fight Jerry Quarry, a white boxer, after his 3½ year ban because of his draft-dodging conviction, Ali stated that he planned to "dress up like Johnson" and "announce to the Georgia audience that I was dedicating my first fight to him." Ali went on to say that when he saw the stage production of *The Great White Hope*, James Earl Jones, who played the lead in both the play and the film, told him that he based his characterization of Johnson on Ali. Jones emphasized "how Johnson was hounded out of America on trumped-up charges" and how Johnson "was bold and arrogant.... The only way they agreed to allow Johnson to reenter America without being thrown in jail was for him to give up his title and the fix with [Jess] Willard was the result."

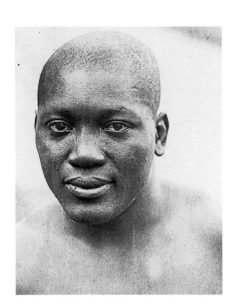

The Champion.
Johnson finally won the title in 1908, knocking out Tommy Burns in 14 rounds in Sydney, Australia.

A LI IS WRONG. The evidence is clear, despite Johnson's claims in his autobiography, that his 1915 fight against Jess Willard in Havana, where he lost the title, was not fixed. As Finis Farr plausibly writes in his biography of Johnson: "There was much indignation at Johnson for concocting this story, and for sticking to it all his life, as he did. Perhaps now we feel a certain pity for Johnson in this matter, showing as it does his pride in the championship, a feeling so intense that he would rather have it thought he had sold the title than that he lost it to a younger, stronger man. It is not to Johnson's credit that he told this tale, but it would be even more to his discredit if it were true; oddly enough, it is in justice to Johnson's memory that we must proceed to prove that he concocted a lie." Moreover, there was no deal with the government to permit him to reenter the United States and not go to prison if he lost the fight. He did not reenter the United States after he lost the fight, and when he finally returned to the United States in 1920, he served his year and a day in federal prison. Not even Attorney General Harry Daughtery, who liked Johnson, could get the ex-champion out of prison a few weeks early. Whenever Johnson negotiated with federal agents during his exile about returning to the United States in exchange for a reduced sentence, they refused to budge. The government also expressed no interest in making a deal for his relinquishment of the title.

But Ali is right in implying or suggesting, as many others have since seen, that Johnson shared much in common with him. Both men were southerners. Both men endured trials in which they were convicted. Both were intensely unpopular during the time of their trials: Ali for joining a religious cult that stressed racial consciousness and racial separation in the age of integration, and Johnson, ironically, for being an integrationist by taking white women as lovers in the age of segregation. Both were outspoken and considered militant or "uppity" for their time. For both, their fights took on symbolic political significance. What is most striking is that both came along during eras of turbulent, convulsive social reform in the United States: Ali during the civil rights era of public demonstrations, bombings, assassinations, and race riots; and Johnson during the progressive era of labor union strife, racial lynchings and riots, assassinations (both presidents Garfield [1881] and McKinley

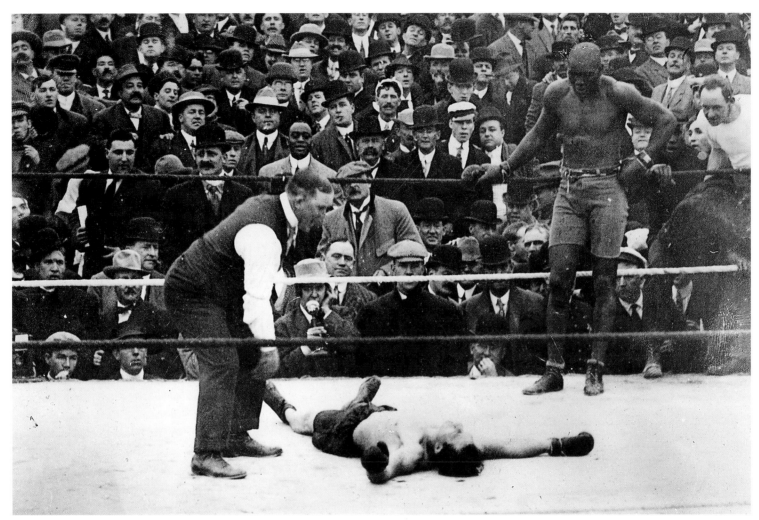

[1901] were murdered during this period), the social gospel, political and social reform to make government more open and responsive, and mass immigration. What is most striking, though, is how the country split in its opinion on Ali, the more conservative, reactionary element opposing Ali and all he stood for while the radical and liberal, social reformist element supported him, even loved and admired him. Johnson faced the difficulty of having to stare down the entire country, as both the reactionary, racist *and* progressive, liberal, reformist elements saw him as a threat to the social order, combining, therefore, to undo him. This difference is crucial to acknowledge if one is to understand the fates of the two men and why Johnson was never truly forgiven or accepted. He was, in the end, if not defeated, certainly contained and reduced.

My mind is constantly on automobiles.
　　—Jack Johnson, during his cross-examination at his Mann Act trial, 1913

Jack Johnson was, according to the white parlance of the period, a "New Negro," that is, a black born after slavery, in the brave, new, conflicted world of laissez-faire capitalism and harsh racist repression. Arthur John "Jack" Johnson was born in Galveston, Texas, on March 31, 1878, one of six children born to Henry and Tiny

Off the Canvas. His 1909 match with middleweight champ Stanley Ketchel was rife with mystery. Ketchel stayed with Johnson for 11 rounds, then knocked him down in the 12th. The enraged champ rose to his feet and quickly connected with a sharp shot to the jaw. He later claimed that the men had been paid to fight to a draw, thereby guaranteeing a rematch.

Johnson. Henry Johnson had been a slave, born in Maryland. He worked as a common laborer, a janitor for a black school. He was apparently physically disabled but he managed to provide for his family, become a homeowner, and keep a steady job. He also managed to make sure that all of his children learned to read and write, even if, as was the case with Jack, they did not go very far in school. As Johnson wrote about growing up in his autobiography: "My home surroundings when a child and growing youth were such that I might have been expected to adopt most any other means of gaining a livelihood other than boxing." Why Johnson became a fighter is a bit of a mystery, although it might be surmised that because Johnson grew up in the tough milieu of black southern working-class life, where being tough was highly valued, becoming a fighter was not a bad trade, and not as disparaged as it might be in more genteel circles. Moreover, there were few occupations open to black men at the time that had either the possibilities for travel or adventure, or the potential to generate income as did boxing. Even a lower-ranked, unheralded black fighter almost certainly made more money than the average black laborer. Finally, getting extensive schooling was difficult in those days, as few areas in the South even had high schools for blacks (most southern whites thought eight years of schooling for blacks was enough). College—even inexpensive black institutions of higher learning—was out of the reach of the average working-class black, and, besides, what sort of occupations, other than preaching and teaching, were open to a black man with a college education? Johnson was by nature a restless man, a seeker of novelty and adventure (his autobiography is one long recitation of fantastic adventures of almost the quality to be found in a boy's novel); neither study nor a rooted domestic life would have suited him. Johnson was also highly individualistic and something of a show-off. I doubt if he could have borne an anonymous life. He seemed incapable of taking orders from a white man, which he would have had to have done had he become a common laborer. Boxing was a perfect form of expression for him, an ideal profession satisfying his need for individual endeavor and autonomy and his wanderlust.

What is even more important is that Johnson was born at the tail end of one of this country's most remarkable reformist eras: Reconstruction. It was in 1877 that Republican presidential candidate Rutherford B. Hayes made a deal for southern support, when the election was so close as to be thrown into the House of Representatives, by promising to remove federal troops from the South, thus effectively ending federal participation in enforcing and protecting the rights of recently emancipated African Americans. From 1865, the end of the Civil War, to 1877, blacks were freed from slavery, made citizens of the United States, granted the right to vote in all the former confederate states, were granted the opportunity to go to school, to serve on juries, to enter into legally binding marriages, to enter into contracts with whites, to testify against whites in a court of law. Legislation was passed to

The Showdown. (Above) Manager George Little, at left, and Johnson close the deal for his fight with Jim Jeffries, seated, far right.

The Survivor. (Right) Though his professional record was 68-10-10, Johnson had in fact fought in dozens of "battles royal," the racist spectacles in which a group of black men fought among themselves until only one was standing.

protect the civil rights of blacks and to prohibit discrimination or segregation in public accommodations. Blacks were elected to public office in many confederate states. The status of southern blacks, nearly all of whom had been slaves, changed rapidly and forever during these years, but not without bloody and determined resistance on the part of southern whites, most of whom opposed nearly all these reforms. The Ku Klux Klan, the oldest terrorist organization in the United States, was launched in Tennessee by Nathan Bedford Forrest, a confederate general and former slave trader, during this era. The white bourbon class, never fully disenfranchised or out of power, worked relentlessly to halt this revolution, which was generally supported only halfheartedly at best by the white population of the country.

JOHNSON WAS BORN WHEN WHITES WERE IN THE PROCESS of assuming complete, ruthless control of southern politics again. From the time of Johnson's birth until he lost the heavyweight title in 1915, the political and social condition of blacks was to erode steadily as the elaborate machinery of segregation was put into place, culminating in the Supreme Court decision of 1883 declaring the Civil Rights Act of 1875 unconstitutional and in the 1896 *Plessy* v. *Ferguson* case, which granted racial segregation constitutional protection, enforced by lynchings, economic peonage, a convict lease system, a police system that kept blacks under control, and an educational system that provided them with an inferior education designed to keep them agrarian laborers or domestics. Education was one of the most important issues of the day debated by blacks, with Booker T. Washington, principal of Tuskegee Institute and the most powerful black political figure of the day, having the ear and access to the purses of whites who controlled philanthropic foundations and educational policy, and W. E. B. Du Bois, Harvard Ph.D. and mover and shaker among the black radicals who were eventually to form the Niagara Movement, which led to the formation of the NAACP, emerging as the leading spokesmen for the two divergent sides: vocational education and the pursuit of economic self-sufficiency in acceptance of the status quo versus academic training and the pursuit of full civil rights in opposition to the status quo.

By the time of the appearance of Du Bois and Washington as major figures in African-American life near the turn of the century, Johnson was already an established prizefighter, learning his craft with pickup fights in the West after having spent his adolescence fighting in battles royal. The battle royal was a common feature of prizefights in the United States at this time: A group of eight or nine black boys, often blindfolded, would be thrown into a ring and forced to slug it out until one was left standing, in some sadistic parody of the Social Darwinist beliefs of the day.

During the latter half of the 1890s, the United States became an imperialist power with pretensions of empire, driven by a vision of Anglo-Saxon dominance over "lesser races," acquiring the Philippines, Cuba, Puerto Rico, and Hawaii. As historian August Meier wrote, "Oriental exclusion, the Southern race system, the New Imperialism, and racist Social Darwinism all combined to give the close of the nineteenth century and the opening of the twentieth an interesting configuration in regard to race relations." What is surprising about Johnson, considering his times, is not his ultimate downfall but that he should ever have risen to the point where he was permitted to fight for the heavyweight title in the first place.

Although there were several first-rate black heavyweight fighters during Johnson's

Mismatch. Johnson dominated
Jeffries throughout the 1910 championship fight, and the ex-champ was
nearly defenseless when Johnson
felled him in the 15th round.

era (Peter Jackson, the most famous and highly regarded, in the 1890s; Sam Langford, Joe Jeanette, and Sam McVey after 1900), none ever fought for the title. The United States became the center of professional boxing in the 1880s, and all the champions before Johnson drew the color line, from John L. Sullivan to Jim Jeffries. There was some unease about interracial fights, period, at this time, regardless of whether they were for the title. As nearly all whites of the period held strong racialist beliefs that they were superior, both mentally and physically, to blacks, the idea of fighting a black in the ring was risky, for if the black should win, the idea of white supremacy was challenged, even effectively rebuked. Moreover, just having a black in the ring with a white suggested a certain social equality that made most whites uncomfortable. There were, however, black champions in some of the lighter weight divisions, such as Joe Gans, George Dixon and Joe Walcott. But the heavyweight title, the most glamorous title in a disreputable and largely illegal but still very popular—even charismatic—intensely masculine sport, was off-limits to blacks.

Boxing as a major sport emerged when the machinery of American popular culture was being put into place: Recorded music, which was to change entirely the way popular music was distributed and sold in the United States, came into being at the turn of the century; the film industry was well established by the time Johnson became a name fighter in the early 1900s; the automobile, perhaps the most mythologized technology associated with popular culture (and which became a passion of Johnson's) also began to make its presence felt; and spectator sports were becoming increasingly popular, with baseball a virtual mania, college football coming onto the scene, and the invention of basketball. There was also track and field, the resurgence of the Olympics, golf, tennis, bicycle racing and race walking. Black participation in sports at the turn of the century was limited, indeed, shut out of baseball by racism; forced out of jockeying for the same reason. Blacks were largely confined to boxing, probably because the means of learning the sport was well within their grasp, and whites did not seem to mind watching them perform it under certain conditions and with certain prescribed outcomes. The racist thinking of the day led many whites to believe that blacks were, in fact, particularly suited for boxing as they supposedly had harder skulls, smaller brains, and tougher skin. Blacks in the ring at the turn of the century came very close to being for whites something like automatons.

With the emergence of spectator sports at the turn of the century came an ideology of the strenuous life and, more important, fair play. As Johnson built a reputation in the early 1900s as a good fighter worthy of a title shot, his cause was championed by such people as Richard K. Fox, publisher of the *National Police Gazette*, the most popular sports newspaper in the country, and President Teddy Roosevelt, an avid sportsman himself. Both of these men believed the racist ideas of their day; indeed, both espoused them in varying forms, but they also thought it was unfair that the color line should be drawn against Johnson, since he was a worthy contender. Moreover, Johnson was well liked by the white writers who covered sports and the white sporting crowd during these days. He was a good, smooth fighter, gregarious, seemingly a bit indolent, and not especially threatening to whites. Although he may have been seeing white women at this time, it was not necessarily a matter of much concern among the "sports."

N THE BLACK AND WHITE SPORTING WORLDS OF THIS ERA, so well described by black writer James Weldon Johnson in his 1912 novel, *The Autobiography of an Ex-Colored Man*, miscegenation was not at all uncommon. White women hung around the black sporting world of athletes, musicians, singers, dancers, gamblers, pimps, prostitutes, and the like, in hopes of finding a black sugar daddy. It is interesting to note that Belle Schreiber, one of Johnson's white girlfriends who testified against him at his 1913 Mann Act trial, had been trained as a stenographer and a typist, and periodically did work of this sort for Johnson. Many women with skills like Schreiber's became prostitutes at the turn of the century. In a good brothel, the work paid better, the people one met were usually more interesting than the normal workaday world, and the work in a brothel often was easier, certainly no more stressful than work outside, where the average working woman had far less protection against sexual harassment or abuse. The sporting world had its stimulants and its thrills. It was in this world that black men formed sexual alliances with white women. George Dixon, the famous black featherweight champion, was married to a white woman. The revered Peter Jackson, in his travels to England, Australia, and San Francisco, almost certainly bedded many as he lived in this world of easy sex. George Walker, of the famed Williams and Walker comedy team, despite being married to his black costar, Ada Overton, had sexual relations with many white chorus girls. So, in the beginning, Johnson's miscegenation, taking place within the context of the sporting world, was not much of a big deal.

Thus, this cultural wedge made by the ideology of fair play, Johnson's likability, and the free-and-easy morality of the sporting world opened the door for his title shot. Another occurrence that helped Johnson was that Jim Jeffries, last of the truly great white heavyweight champions, retired undefeated in 1904 and organized an elimination for his title, eventually won by a mediocre fighter named Marvin Hart, who lost to another mediocre fighter named Tommy Burns. There were virtually no impressive white fighters on the scene, and popular interest in heavyweight fighting waned dramatically. Johnson had clearly emerged as the strongest contender and, for those with business connections to the sport, the sole fighter who could save heavyweight boxing from the doldrums, by the controversy of race if not by an appreciation of his considerable skills. As in any sport operating in a free market, there is a demand for excellence, no matter the source, to bring in customers. A shielded mediocrity simply will not do, after a time. In short, when Tommy Burns fought Johnson for the title in December 1908 in Australia, a big boxing country, he had no choice if he was to make any sort of match that could earn him any future money at all and get him any sort of public notice. Johnson was, without question, the best fighter in the world from 1905 until 1915—indeed, one of the best and most impressive athletes of the time. He beat Burns easily.

Black and White. Much of white America placed their hopes on "Great White Hope" Jim Jeffries, and around the country the buildup to the fight inflamed racial tensions. When Johnson won, it prompted race riots in parts of the country.

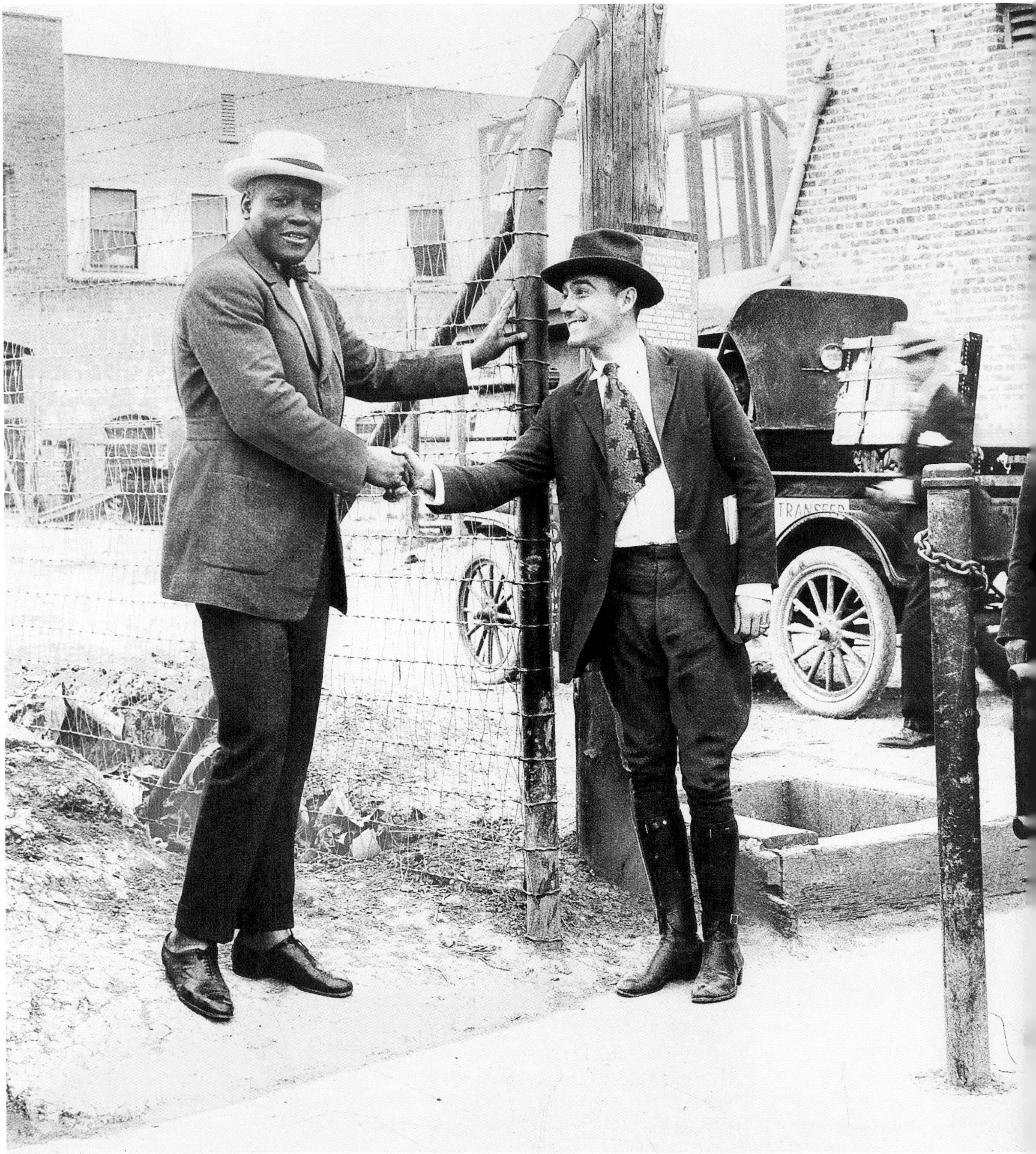
TRANSFER

I Fought the Law.
Moments before his arrest on his Mann Act conviction, Johnson shakes hands with the deputy sheriff of Imperial County, California. When he stepped across the borderline from Mexico into California, he was brought into custody of federal officials.

From the time Johnson beat Jim Jeffries on July 4, 1910, in Reno, Nevada, to retain his title until his return to the United States from exile in July 1920, he lived a very accelerated life, a span of 10 years that would have seemed surreal to any other man, and might have seemed that way to him. He may have wondered in some ways how he survived that time. Why wasn't he murdered by some crazed racist white man thinking that he was performing a public duty by ridding society of a horrible menace? Why wasn't he killed at this point by his reckless driving? Why didn't he, under the stress and pressure of these years, kill himself, either through a direct act of suicide or through the slow destruction of alcoholism, drug addiction, or a nervous breakdown? Despite the public disapproval, no white man ever tried to assassinate him in an act of racial patriotism. Indeed, Johnson, despite the fits of furious hatred that he evoked, was still able for a while to tour as a stage act, as most heavyweight champions did, until the time of his Mann Act indictment in November 1912. He was, for instance, amazingly able to go back on stage by mid-August 1910 after his July knockout of Jeffries, which prompted racial violence in Greenwood, South Carolina; Baltimore; Cincinnati; New Orleans; New York; Pueblo, Colorado; and scores of other cities, usually with whites attacking and killing blacks who seemed to be celebrating Johnson's victory too energetically. Despite an endless stream of speeding tickets, some bad auto accidents, a race against a professional auto racer (Johnson lost by a good distance), Johnson was never seriously hurt in an automobile during these years. Though Johnson loved his drink, he never fell prey to out-of-control use of drugs or stimulants, and though he loved sex with white prostitutes and showgirls, he apparently never contracted venereal disease (or had it cured with medically efficient dispatch). He apparently had an iron constitution, for he was able to recover in good order. He died at the age of 68 in 1946 from injuries sustained in an automobile accident, not from disease or sickness.

AFTER JOHNSON WON THE TITLE FROM BURNS, the cry was heard in the sports world for a "great white hope" to emerge to beat Johnson. This was in good measure thanks to the incendiary prose of Jack London's coverage of that fight for the *San Francisco Call*. Indeed, the cry went out immediately for retired champion Jim Jeffries to return to the ring, the rank of good white heavyweights being thin and Jeffries being considered invincible by the knowing white coves and Corinthians. London not only added an expression to the language that has endured to this day, he crystallized an attitude, a fear on the part of whites of the possibility of black dominance in any competitive activity, especially in the very public arena of sports. High-performance athletes were, by the time of the reign of Johnson, representative men, symbols of a way of life, a cultural practice and a political ideology, a politicized view of biology. And in a racist country, representation meant race. In the context of this thinking, Johnson was a dangerous man to white society. It was not simply because of his penchant for white lovers. Johnson was not hated simply because he was black. If Sam Langford or Joe Jeanette had become champion, they might have been, not lionized, to be sure, but perhaps accepted a bit more easily, if condescendingly, simply because they were not, taken in their entirety, the threatening package that Johnson was. Johnson was hated because through all of his habits taken together—his disdain of, even contempt for, his white opponents in the ring, his preference for

white women, his love of speeding cars, his casual attitude toward morality—*he publicly displayed a lack of respect for white men and their power.* This was unthinkable in the 1900s and 1910s. No wonder Johnson became virtually an enemy of the white state.

Unfortunately for Jeffries, who heeded the calls of race pride and white racial consciousness for his return, came back from a five-year layoff and tried manfully to get himself into shape to beat a man who was at the top of his game as an athlete. He publicly said that he was fighting again to win the title for the white race. He made it clear in the press that he was fighting *as a white man.* In effect, Jeffries, who had drawn the color line during his reign and would not fight Johnson or any other black, was rather doing the same here. Johnson was a mistake and Jeffries was coming out of retirement, not to combat a superb athlete and worthy foe, but to correct an error and set the world right again. For him, it was not a sporting event but a political mission. The fight became the biggest popular culture event, the biggest athletic event in American history up to that time. It also was the richest prizefight in history, with promoter Tex Rickard promising both fighters combined purses of $101,000 (winner getting, not the advertised 75 percent, but 60 percent in fact), and two thirds of the film rights. To Progressive-era reformers, it was obscene. And to think it was merely the notoriety of a Negro having the title that was generating this type of payment to two men—or one man and one half-ape—to engage in 45 rounds of brutality! Sullivan versus Kilrain, Corbett versus Sullivan, Fitzsimmons versus Corbett did not even come close. Johnson, if nothing else, made boxing a crossover, mainstream sport, which Dempsey took advantage of when he won the championship after the first World War.

J

EFFRIES NEVER STOOD A CHANCE except in the fevered imaginations of whites who hoped he would win. He had no shortage of advice from white ex-champions. John L. Sullivan, covering the fight for *The New York Times* (or at least someone who was writing the columns under his name), was in Reno with suggestions for Jeffries, although he could not get near the fighter's camp as ex-champion and Sullivan nemesis Jim Corbett was actually working for Jeffries, trying to help the challenger lose about 80 pounds and shake off five years of ring rust. Jeffries not only had to struggle mightily to get into shape for the fight, he also had to deal with the increasingly unnerving burden of representing the white race and winning the title back as a form of race duty. In the fight itself, Jeffries was completely overmatched. He couldn't even bull or maul Johnson, as most pundits commonly thought he could, because, surprisingly, Johnson turned out to be much stronger than his challenger and moved him as he wished. This was the high point of Johnson's career as a professional fighter. He was not to enjoy another truly impressive title defense during the remaining five years he held the championship. What was to hurt Johnson most financially was Congress's eventual ban on the interstate transportation of the film of the fight (and all fight films, a ban that was not lifted, ironically, until Joe Louis became champion), supposedly for public safety. The ban lessened the worth of a Johnson fight, as a source of revenue for both promoter and fighter was the distribution and exhibition of the film at movie houses.

The 1910s were the most intense years of social reform in the United States since the end of the Civil War, culminating in 1920 with the 18th Amendment, which pro-

A Day at the Races. Johnson lived in high style during his years as champion. Here, he visits the races in Paris, with his first wife, Etta Duryea, who would commit suicide in 1912.

hibited the sale and manufacture of alcoholic beverages. Other federal legislation of this type included the controversial Mann Act of 1910, an attempt to stem the tide of prostitution by prohibiting the transport of women across state lines for immoral purposes. Johnson found himself squeezed between a powerful temperance movement and a national sex morality impulse, thus becoming a perfect scapegoat for reformers, politicians, and law enforcement.

Johnson's real downfall began when, shortly after he opened his Chicago nightclub, Cabaret de Champion, on the night of September 14, 1912, his first white wife, Etta Duryea, despondent about her unhappy marriage to Johnson, blew her brains out in an upstairs room at the nightclub.

During this time, the government had already started investigating the champion, suspecting him of violating the Mann, or White Slavery, Act. At first government agents tried to construct their case around Lucille Cameron, a young white prostitute, who also did stenography work, and who, the government wanted to claim, was kidnapped by Johnson. Cameron, who had been having an affair with Johnson before Etta Duryea committed suicide, was actually in love with the champion and would not cooperate with authorities, but Johnson was arrested for abduction in October 1912, further inflaming an already wildly hostile white public. A case of abduction could never be built because Cameron refused to testify against Johnson.

The Bigger They Are. In April 1915, the champion Johnson lies prone, apparently shielding his eyes from the sun, in the 26th round in his Havana fight against Jess Willard. He would be counted out, ending the reign of the first black heavyweight champion.

When Cameron was finally released from federal custody, she returned to Johnson and they were married on December 4, 1912, *less than three months after the suicide of his first wife*. For the white public, this was the final straw.

TWO DISTINCT IMPRESSIONS EMERGE from the transcript of Johnson's 1913 Mann Act trial. First, that the three white prostitutes, including a young prostitute named Belle Schreiber, whom Johnson was clearly proven to have had as lovers at the same time from 1909 to 1911 were, beneath the sordid details, lonely, outcast women who were desperately seeking both love and material favors from Johnson. Particularly in Schreiber's case, Johnson seems the only man who ever really cared for her, which is not to say he always treated her well, for he surely did not, on many occasions. But he helped her almost every time she needed it and asked him. ("I never really called him up unless it was absolutely necessary," she said in her testimony. "To get money?" asked Johnson's lawyer. "Yes," she responded, "when I was put out.")

The second impression is that of Johnson, who testified at his trial. He was forceful in his testimony, sometimes making unappreciated jokes with the prosecutor and sometimes answering questions even over his own lawyer's objections, such as when he was asked if his October 1909 fight with middleweight champion Stanley Ketchel was fixed. Over his lawyer's objection, Johnson cryptically responded, "They are all crooked."

It was a foregone conclusion that Johnson would be convicted, but it was not a foregone conclusion in his mind that he would be imprisoned for this crime, a decidedly minor offense, if Johnson were truly guilty of it. Johnson became depressed and angry when he was sentenced to a year and a day. He plotted his escape almost immediately. His years in exile were strange, unhappy, surely unfulfilling. The first World War made him superfluous. Europe had more important matters to consider than being entertained by an out-of-shape, black American prizefighter, even if he was the champion.

Johnson should have won the Havana fight against Jess Willard, the huge, clumsy Kansas farmer, to whom he lost the title. But Johnson was woefully out of condition and Willard, moreover, was four years younger than the fading champ. But losing to Willard simply set Johnson drifting again, back to Europe, back to Mexico, without even the renown, limited though it may have been, that the title had bestowed. When he finally returned to the United States in 1920, he was happy to come home.

After he served his time, Johnson did what many smart ex-athletes do: He hustled, by taking advantage of his name and his achievements. He fought exhibitions, told his story in dime museums, exchanged predictions about upcoming championship fights for meals from reporters. This may seem a pathetic end, but there was something of dignity in Johnson, even in his somewhat shabby last years. He continued to drive fast. He continued to marry white women. And while at times he may sound in his autobiography like a gentrified conservative (such as when he rails against jazz, the music of the day: "For my own part, I find my delight, as far as music is concerned, in the splendid compositions of the old masters, who not only wrote music in its highest forms, but who made it live with the reality of life..."), he also gives note to his militancy, such as when he assesses Booker T. Washington and Frederick Douglass: "White people often point to the writings of Booker T. Washington as the best example of a desirable attitude on the part of the colored population. I have never been able to agree with the point of view of Washington, because he has to my

After the Fact. Johnson's later years were spent in a flurry of exhibitions and vaudeville shows. Above, he prepares to enter the ring as a professional wrestler. At right, though he had no formal training as a musician, Johnson often played the bass cello in his vaudeville act.

mind not been altogether frank in the statement of the problem or courageous in the formulation in his solutions to them. On this point, Frederick Douglas' [sic] honest and straight-forward program has had more of an appeal to me, *because he faced the issues without compromising.*" (emphasis added)

There is a curious episode that opens Johnson's autobiography. At the age of 12 he runs away from home to find someone named Steve Brodie, who had jumped off the Brooklyn Bridge and lived to tell about it: "One of my earliest ambitions was rather a strange one, and, like many others of my younger years, bore no relations to the course that eventually marked my life. That ambition was to see Steve Brodie, the man who made himself famous by leaping from the Brooklyn Bridge." After some extensive travel as a stowaway, Johnson arrives in New York. His story continues:

> Once I was in New York, however, I lost no time in hunting up Steve Brodie. I began by asking the first person who would listen to me after I had landed. To this stranger I addressed my eager inquiry.
>
> "Where is Steve Brodie?" I asked excitedly. He did not know, so I went about firing the question at all who would pause long enough to hear me. I did not so much as provide myself with food or shelter, so determined was I to pursue the quest for Brodie. And it was successful—more successful than I had ever anticipated, for I found at least twenty-five Steve Brodies. . . .
>
> Steve Brodies were beginning to fill my life. I met them at every turn. They went by me in long processions. I dreamed of them when I slept, and day after day I met new Steve Brodies.

T IS NOT IMPORTANT WHETHER THE STORY OF THE QUEST is actually true; it reveals, even as a lie, a fantasy, or a literary device, a great deal about the complexity of Johnson's mind, for the whole Brodie episode is an elaboration of the two major themes of his autobiography: thwarting imposture even while suggesting it, and performing stunts on the edge of American culture, in the margins of boxing, of interracial relationships, of international travel among the sporting crowd. There are several vital reasons why Johnson the autobiographer would have been attracted to the figure of Brodie, who may or may not have performed the stunt that he took credit for. First, the very ambiguity that surrounded Brodie's greatest stunt, the possibility that Brodie may have been an impostor, probably intrigued the adult Johnson. Although accounts of Brodie's death-defying leap made on July 23, 1886, made the major newspapers of the day, there were many who doubted that he actually jumped. Not only was Brodie's imposture intriguing but his sex life was also the stuff of 19th-century scandal: He was eventually forced, through public outcry, to marry his fifteen-year-old traveling companion and groupie, Gertrude Lord. Finally, Brodie was one of the few men to fake his own death and consequently to have two obituaries appear in *The New York Times*: in 1899 and 1901. Since Johnson met so many men who claimed to be Steve Brodie when he ran away to New York, we arrive at the complicated instance of the imposture of imposture. Brodie was both a wizard, by virtue of his stunt, and an impostor, by virtue of the possibility that he never performed it in an age when imposture and stunting meld together. Johnson's ostentation in relation to his ring career, his white wives, his adventures in exile, which, according to the book, include bullfighting and espionage, were stunts, to be sure, but Johnson was never an impostor. Johnson did, without question, jump off something higher than the Brooklyn Bridge, and he, unlike many who tried such stunts, lived to tell about it.

HONUS WAGNER
The Best Ever?

Hall of Famers John McGraw and Branch Rickey, whose combined baseball experience extended from before the turn of the century to after the erasure of the color line, both flatly stated that Honus Wagner was the best baseball player they had ever seen.

While Wagner is still regarded as the best shortstop ever to play the position, he was so versatile that McGraw claimed he would have excelled at any position save pitcher. "Wagner is a whole team in himself," he said.

Wagner was one of the original class of five inductees into the Baseball Hall of Fame, but you wouldn't have guessed it by looking at him. The broad-chested and bow-legged Wagner's large and awkward body was seemingly devoid of grace, but what he may have lacked in style points he more than made up for in efficiency. He led NL shortstops in fielding four times, prompting the saying that you could roll a barrel between Wagner's legs—but not a baseball.

Fittingly, Wagner was the first hitter to have his name on a Louisville Slugger. His prodigious hitting feats came in the "dead ball" era when the juice was on the ball, not in it. He collected eight NL batting titles, hitting above .300 for 15 consecutive years, and won six slugging crowns as well. He retired as the all-time major league leader in hits, runs, RBI, steals and total bases while also setting the NL mark for singles, doubles and triples.

Ty Cobb, Wagner's AL counterpart as a hitting machine and terror on the basepaths, was also his rival for the title of baseball's best. But when they met in the 1909 World Series, Wagner had the upper hand. Cobb, 13 years younger than Wagner, boasted, taunted and threatened throughout the Series, while the folksy, easygoing Wagner just went about his business. In the end Wagner led the Pirates to victory, stealing six bases to his two, and, according to legend, finally answered Cobb's taunts with a hard tag to the face that left Cobb with a cut lip and two loose teeth. In the aftermath, Cobb said Wagner was "the only man in the game I can't scare." Cobb's teammate "Wahoo" Sam Crawford simply said, "Wagner is the greatest player who ever lived."

Wagner's work ethic, established as a preteen in the Pennsylvania coal mines, was as rock solid and steadfast as his character. But it was his play ethic, an unabashed and undying love of the game, that made him a fan favorite. "There's not much to being a ballplayer, if you're a ballplayer," he once said. As the best hitter, baserunner and fielder of his era, the genial "Flying Dutchman" soared above all comparison. Almost a century later, McGraw's declaration that "Wagner is just in a class by himself" may still be true. —*Michael Point*

WAGNER: "AN UNABASHED AND UNDYING LOVE OF THE GAME"

YOUNG: A SUPERSTAR IN TWO CENTURIES

CY YOUNG
Trailblazing Cyclone

There's a reason they call it the Cy Young Award. Actually there are 511 reasons, each and every one a pitching victory by a single individual.

If winning is what it's all about, Young, as the winningest pitcher in baseball history, was the best there ever was. As Casey Stengel said, "You can look it up, and when you do, be prepared to find statistical achievements that seem to defy not only logic but human physical capabilities as well."

Young, a superstar in both the 19th (267 wins) and 20th centuries (244 wins), seemed to transcend the normal limitations of the athletic body in general and of the pitching arm in particular. In a similar manner, his success was totally unaffected by the wholesale evolutionary changes of baseball's early years, as he pitched with equal dominance no matter what new rules or styles of play were introduced, serving as a rock of consistency in an era of constant change.

Baseball history and Young went together like a fastball and a curve. He led the AL in wins the first three years of its existence, threw the first pitch in World Series history, pitched the first perfect game of the 20th Century, and generally set the standards of excellence subsequent pitching stars have vainly tried to equal. Young, a five-time 30-game winner, didn't just cross the mythic threshold of 300 wins with ease—he moved further above and beyond it than any pitcher in the history of the game, setting a record that remained unchallenged for the rest of the century. His closest competition, the legendary Walter Johnson, finished 94 wins behind Young's win total of 511, which was 24 greater than those of Hall of Famers Whitey Ford and Bob Gibson *combined*.

In addition to taking the mound more often than anyone in history, Young also finished better more than nine of every 10 starts, establishing a complete games record (749) so unapproachable that the only challengers to come within 200 games of it—Hall of Famers Pud Galvin and Tim Keefe—passed away more than six decades ago.

Denton True Young could set such records because he threw strikes, and he threw them very hard. His nickname, "Cy," was not a shortened form of Cyrus but instead a baseball abbreviation for "Cyclone." As the story goes, it was a tag hung on him by hitters who didn't always see it but did hear his fastball roar by with tornadic intensity.

He was still an effective power pitcher at age 44 but was finally forced into retirement because his middle-aged belly wasn't in as good shape as his ageless and awesome arm. But when he returned to his farm for the final time, Young did so with timeless statistical achievements any two pitching aces would be proud to share. —*Michael Point*

The Unforgiving Hour: Pietri on his last legs, nearing finish line in London.

OLYMPICS

Going the Distance

As a crowd of 100,000 inside London's Olympic Stadium roared, Italy's Dorando Pietri entered the stadium with a big lead in the 1908 Olympic marathon, ahead of American John J. Hayes by more than a minute. But the 22-year-old candy maker from Carpi was clearly fatigued, and after mistakenly turning left onto the track, then correcting himself, his run slowed to a halting, haunted pace. "The man was practically delirious," wrote one reporter. "He staggered along the cinder path like a man in a dream, his gait being neither a walk nor a run, but simply a flounder, with arms shaking and legs tottering."

Around the track, Pietri collapsed three times, only to be helped to his feet by Olympic officials who carried him toward the finish line. Describing the scene later, Sir Arthur Conan Doyle wrote, "It is horrible, yet fascinating, this struggle between a set purpose and an utterly exhausted frame."

As the officials brought the dazed Pietri to his feet the final time, the American Hayes entered the stadium and ran the finishing lap. Hayes finished his run 34 seconds after Pietri lurched across the finish line, but after an American protest that Pietri was obviously unable to finish under his own power, the Italian was disqualified. Hayes finished the race (the first Olympic marathon at the now standard length of 26 miles, 385 yards) in 2 hours, 55 minutes, 18.4 seconds.

It was described by *The New York Times* as "the most thrilling athletic event that has occurred since that marathon race in ancient Greece, where the victor fell at the goal and, with a wave of triumph, died." For his part, Hayes was matter-of-fact in his post-race interview. "I took nothing to eat or drink on the journey," he said. "I think to do so is a great mistake. Before starting I partook of a light luncheon, consisting of two ounces of beef, two slices of toast, and a cup of tea. During the race, I merely bathed my face with Florida water and gargled my throat with brandy."

BASEBALL

1903 World Series

■ After his Pirates had clinched the 1903 National League crown, Pittsburgh owner Barney Dreyfus challenged the Boston Pilgrims, champions of the upstart American League, to a "world's championship series." The Pilgrims accepted, and the first modern World Series, a best-of-nine affair, opened at the Huntington Avenue Baseball Grounds in Boston on October 1. Two of the Pirates' stars—shortstop Honus Wagner and 25-game winner Sam Leever— were playing hurt, and another Pirate, pitcher Ed Doheny, had been hospitalized for mental illness. But the Pirates still opened strong, as Deacon Phillippe won three of the first four games, and Buc third baseman Tommy Leach had seven hits and five RBIs. Then Pilgrim hurlers Cy Young and Bill Dinneen (who together pitched 69 of 71 innings in the series) alternated wins down the stretch as Boston surged, winning the series 5 games to 3. Phillippe pitched well in the clinching eighth game, but Dinneen was sharper, shutting out the Pirates for his third win of the Series.

COLLEGE FOOTBALL

1905 Chicago–Michigan

■ Fielding Yost's Wolverines hadn't lost in his nearly five seasons at the school, a span of 56 games, but when they visited Chicago (before what was then the largest football crowd ever in the Midwest, 25,791), Amos Alonzo Stagg's University of Chicago Maroons were ready for them. In the second half of a scoreless game, Chicago's All-American Walter Eckersall executed a daring fake punt from the Maroon end zone, running out to the 22 for a first down. The gamble not only allowed Chicago to keep the ball, it gave the Maroons a crucial advantage in the battle of field position. In the fourth quarter, Eckersall punted into the Michigan end zone, and Michigan returner Denny Clark chose to run the ball out. He was tackled behind the goal line for a safety, and Chicago vanquished mighty Michigan, 2–0. "We had won on an error of judgment," recalled Stagg later. "And we had been lucky to do it."

BOXING

1906 Joe Gans vs. Battling Nelson

■ Gans became the first native-born black American to win a world boxing title, defeating Frank Erne in 1902 for the world lightweight title. But his most memorable bout came in 1906, when he sought to regain his lightweight belt against Battling Nelson, the "Durable Dane." The fight was held in Goldfield, Nevada, the brainchild of promoter Tex Rickard. The scientific fighter Gans, noted for his superb economy of motion, held the upper hand for much of the way, but couldn't dispose of the tenacious Nelson. Gans knocked Nelson down several times in the first 30 rounds of the fight, and broke his hand with a punch to Nelson's head in the 33rd round. The fight raged on until the 42nd round, when Nelson was disqualified for a low blow. Gans, suffering from the onset of tuberculosis, lost two rematches to Nelson in 1908, and died in 1910, at the age of 35.

Great Performances

■ It was billed as a battle of wits between the New York Giants' pugnacious John McGraw and the Philadelphia Athletics' autocratic Connie Mack. But the 1905 World Series was won on the field, not in the dugout. Christy Mathewson dominated throughout, leading his Giants to a 4 games to 1 defeat of the Athletics. Mathewson threw three complete-game shutouts in six days, allowing just 14 hits and one walk to win Games 1, 3 and 5. The triumph was particularly sweet for McGraw, who'd declined to play the '04 Series.

The Nightmare

■ Late in the taut 1908 pennant race between the Cubs and the Giants, New York's Al Bridwell broke a 1–1 tie in the bottom of the ninth inning at the Polo Grounds with a single that scored Moose McCormick from third. But as fans ran on the field in the celebration that ensued, the Giants' Fred Merkle, who'd been at first base, veered off the basepath and headed toward the Giants' clubhouse behind the centerfield wall. When Cubs second baseman Johnny Evers saw Merkle leaving the field, he called for the ball. After a struggle with fans and Giants' third-base coach Joe McGinnity, Evers recovered a ball (though probably not *the* ball) and stepped on second for the force play, nullifying McCormick's run. An epic rhubarb followed, after which National League president Harry C. Pulliam upheld the umpires' decision to call Merkle out, and ruled that the game would be replayed only if the teams finished tied for the league crown. They did, and the Giants and Cubs met on October 8. Mordecai "Three Finger" Brown, pitching in relief, outdueled Christy Mathewson, 4-2, to give the Cubs the pennant. And the errant base running—quickly termed "Merkle's Boner"—would forever live in infamy.

EDITOR'S NOTE: *All unsigned material in chapters written by the editor, Michael MacCambridge.*

Elis Coming

Yale was the consensus national champion in college football three times during the first decade, winning 100 games, losing just four and tying five. It was the culmination of a 34-year run, beginning in 1876, in which Yale went 315-14-18, and won at least a share of 19 national titles. Howard Jones' 1909 Bulldogs went 10-0, outscoring opponents 209-0. Their defense was so strong that no opponent advanced inside the Yale 28-yard-line during the entire season. Walter Camp placed six of Yale's 11 starters on his All-America team, and three more Bulldogs on his second team. But the unquestioned star was **Ted Coy**, the strong, wiry fullback, and a savage runner with a knack for breaking tackles. Even Harvard captain Lothrop Withington called the 1909 Yale team "both individually and collectively the most powerful college team I have ever had the good fortune to play against or see in action."

■ **Cubs Win! Cubs Win!** The only team to win more than one World Series in the 1900s was the Chicago Cubs. Frank Chance's fundamentally sound, pitching-rich Cubbies posted a 116-36 record in 1906 (still the best winning percentage, at .763, in major-league history), only to lose to the crosstown rival White Sox in the World Series. But in '07 and '08, the Cubs swept to NL titles and easy World Series wins over the Tigers, becoming the first team to win consecutive Fall Classics. The stopper of the redoubtable pitching staff was Hall of Famer Mordecai "Three Finger" Brown (he won 75 games over the three pennant-winning seasons), whose curveball Ty Cobb once described as "the most devastating pitch I ever faced."

■ **Jump Start.** When the century began, basketball was less than 10 years old. But it had already caught fire on college campuses, where it fulfilled Dr. James Naismith's vision of being a popular winter pastime. The first great college power was Joseph Raycroft's Chicago University squad of 1907-09. The Maroons, led by center John Schommer (who also played on the Chicago U. football team), accumulated a 55-4 mark over three seasons.

■ **Close But No Cigar.** From 1907 to 1909, Hughie Jennings built an offensive juggernaut in Detroit, where the Tigers led the AL in runs scored and batting average each season. Ty Cobb led the way, batting .350, .324 and .377, but each season, the Tigers lost in the World Series. After losing to the Cubs in '07 and '08, they took the Pirates to seven games in 1909. Babe Adams shut out the Tigers in the finale of that series, as Cobb (who batted .231) went 0 for 4.

	COLLEGE BASKETBALL	PRO BASKETBALL	HOCKEY	BASEBALL MLB		COLLEGE FOOTBALL	PRO FOOTBA
1900				Superbas (NL)		YALE Yale	
1901				Pirates (NL)	White Sox (AL)	Michigan	
1902				Pirates (NL)	Athletics (AL)	Michigan	
1903				Pilgrims		Princeton	
1904				Giants (NL)	Pilgrims (AL)	PENN Pennsylvania	
1905				Giants		Chicago	
1906				White Sox		Princeton	
1907				Cubs		YALE Yale	
1908				Cubs		PENN Pennsylvania	
1909				Pirates		YALE Yale	

NOTES: **Baseball:** American League began play in 1901. World Series began in 1903, but no Series was played in 1904, as New York Giant manager John McGraw declined Boston's challenge.
College football: Champions are mythical national champions for predated seasons prior to 1936, as chosen in 1941 by the Helms Foundation.

"There Weren't Any Rules"

At the beginning of the century, college football was still considered something of an Eastern phenomenon, the province of Harvard and Yale and a few other Ivy League schools. But then **Fielding Harris Yost** came to Michigan and changed the way the game was played, and perceived.

The enthusiastic, verbose and hyperbolic West Virginian maintained a hint of the Alleghenies in his accent throughout his adult life. Imploring his "Meeshegan" boys to "Hurry up! Hurry up!" he formed a squad that dominated the prepassing era of the 1900s. From 1901, when he began at Michigan, through 1905, his squad won 55, tied one, and lost one (to Amos Alonzo Stagg's Chicago Maroons, by 2-0, in '05), outscoring opponents 2,821 to 42. Though the forward pass would change the balance of power when it was legalized in 1906, Yost continued to excel in Ann Arbor, coaching 13 undefeated teams during his 25 years at the school.

When he took over at Michigan he placed a call to Willie Heston, a 185-pound halfback who'd played for him in a previous stop at San Jose Normal School in California. Though Heston had by then graduated, and was teaching school, he hopped a train to Michigan, where he scored 93 touchdowns in four seasons for the Wolverines. "As to rules, we didn't violate any in those days," Yost later said. "There weren't any rules."

His "Point A Minute" 1901 squad outscored the opposition 550-0 (beating Buffalo University by 128), and traveled to Pasadena for the first Rose Bowl game, played January 1, 1902. In front of a crowd of 8,000, the Wolverines stomped Stanford, 49-0. It would be another 14 years before the Tournament of Roses committee dared stage another bowl game. Yost's early Wolverine teams never relented, with quarterback Boss Weeks calling the next play while his teammates were getting up from the previous one, often snapping the ball while opposing players were still returning to their positions or catching their breath.

Heston recalled later, "Each player knew that if he met Yost on the campus or on the sidewalk, he would be stopped, and that Yost would proceed to instruct him how to block or how to charge. Quite often students would form a ring around them to watch the proceedings."

Yost's pep talks were stem-winders, and even outside of the locker room, he was legendary for his impassioned filibusters. Someone once asked Ring Lardner if he'd ever talked to Yost. "No," Lardner said, "my father taught me never to interrupt." But for all his bluster, Yost was respected by his players and admired by his peers.

"There are three things that make a winning football team," he once said. "Spirit, manpower and coaching. If the boys love Michigan, they've got the spirit, you see. If they'll turn out, that takes care of the manpower. I'll take care of the coaching."

COACHING WISDOM

"Students are not fools. The faculty that winks at crooked work by a coach or student manager can save its breath in preaching ideals in the classroom."

—Amos Alonzo Stagg, who coached the University of Chicago football team from 1892 to 1932, before the school dropped the sport due to "overemphasis"

"We traveled four in a berth and when it came to meal tips, the manager would put down a silver dollar for the whole team."

—Connie Mack, of the Philadelphia A's, on turn-of-century life in the majors

The Father of the AL

In founding the American League in 1901, **Byron "Ban" Johnson** did more than set the stage for the modern game of baseball. He helped to civilize the sport, refining its rules and its customs, pushing it toward unprecedented financial stability and widespread acceptance.

Beefy, humorless, and physically imposing, Johnson had no baseball experience beyond being the starting catcher in his school days at Marietta College. But in 1893, he took a leave of absence from his job as a reporter for the *Cincinnati Commercial-Gazette* to run a failing minor league organization called the Western League. In 1901, Johnson renamed the league the American League and pronounced it a competing major league (placing franchises in three cities where the NL had just disbanded teams), determined to compete for both fans and players with the established NL. "If we had waited for the National League to do something for us," he said in 1901, "we would have remained a minor league forever."

Paying higher salaries than the NL's ceiling of $2,400 per player, he raided more than 100 NL players for the AL's first season, and put competing franchises in four major league cities. (In each case, by its second season, the AL team outdrew its more established NL counterpart.) By the end of the 1902 season, the respected *Spalding Guide* was reporting that "the American League has more star players, and can furnish a better article of baseball than the National League."

Johnson's vision of "clean ball" was one that preached respect for umpires, banned alcohol sales, discouraged rowdiness in the stands, and fostered the idea of baseball as a family spectacle. In 1903, the NL called for peace talks, and the two leagues agreed to a truce. That fall, the American League's Boston Pilgrims beat the National League's Pittsburgh Pirates in the first World Series. Johnson served as president of the AL through 1927. "The making or amassing of money was not part of Ban Johnson's life," said Branch Rickey. "He lived for the American League and the game of baseball."

TOP OF THE NEWS: The Wright Brothers fly, Admiral Peary claims the North Pole and Ford introduces the Model T. There are new worlds to conquer in sports as well, as the American League and National League fight for supremacy (then make peace), college football fights to stay alive, and the countries involved in the modern Olympics fight over where and when the Games will be held.

Reading List

While newspapers are generally slow to recognize the appeal of sports to their readers, the most popular sports publication in the land is *The National Police Gazette*.

On the bookshelves, juvenile fiction embraces baseball. Jack Lorimer's *Champions* is the story of a high school baseball team whose captain is scrupulously honest (he corrects an umpire who calls him safe). Zane Grey publishes *The Short-Stop* and Albertus True Dudley writes *Making the Nine*.

But sports fans are also reading **The Sears, Roebuck Catalog** for all the latest modern equipment, especially in baseball, where everything from caps to gloves to bases to balls could be ordered.

Movies

Thomas Edison shoots a film called *How the Office Boy Saw the Ball Game* in 1906, the story of a boy who schemes to get out of work to see a baseball game, only to wind up in the seat next to his boss.

Politics

Hosting the second modern Olympiad in founder Baron de Coubertain's home city of Paris in 1900, the French balk at a schedule that calls for the finals in most events to be held on Bastille Day. The events are held a day later, on Sunday, but a half dozen U.S. competitors bow out because they don't want to compete on the Sabbath.

In 1902, the Pennsylvania Supreme Court rules in favor of the Phillies in the Nap Lajoie case, stating that he could not play for any other team in the state of Pennsylvania. But the AL, where Lajoie had signed with the Philadelphia A's, circumvents the decision. Connie Mack simply sells Lajoie's contract to Cleveland, and he plays all games except those in Philadelphia.

During the 1905 season, President Teddy Roosevelt warns that college football will be outlawed if safety measures aren't taken to curb the fatalities. Summoning representatives from Harvard, Yale and Princeton to the White House, he says, "The game of football must be made over or go." The result is the January 12, 1906 meeting—attended by Walter Camp of Yale, Captain Palmer Pierce of Army and William Reid of Harvard, among others—that creates the Football Conference Committee.

The first meeting of the committee creates a neutral zone at the line of scrimmage, requires a minimum of six men on the offensive line (thus outlawing the flying wedges that would start several yards behind the line), legalizes the forward pass and lengthens the yards required for a first down from five yards to 10. There are still 33 deaths in the 1909 season, after which the committee meets again to outlaw flying tackles and to require seven men on the line of scrimmage. The rules reduce the most vicious of the mass pile-ups at the line of scrimmage, allowing the game to open up and preserving its reputation in the public eye.

Sounds

"Take Me Out to the Ballgame," baseball's unofficial anthem, is written in 1908, with lyrics by Jack Norworth and music by Albert Van Tilzer. An instant hit in sheet music stores and on the vaudeville circuit, it doesn't make baseball fans out of the composers. Ebbets Field would honor Norworth with a special day in 1942; it was the first time he'd ever been to a ballpark.

Irving Berlin's first published song is titled "Dorando," about the 1908 Olympic marathon, and Italian Dorando Pietri's collapse on the final lap. Two classic fight songs—Navy's "Anchors Aweigh" and Georgia Tech's "Ramblin' Wreck"—also are composed in this decade. Then there's John B. Thomas' baseball ditty "The Princeton Dutchman": "Dat Princeton man he trows such balls/ Dat Yalesmen cannot see/ Dat Yalesman ven he hits dat ball/ He hits it not at all."

Playing Games

Anyone who thinks trash talking is a recent phenomenon needs only see the 1909 game Baseballitis. "Bonehead can't hit," says the shortstop on the cover. Each card includes similar repartee. On a two-bagger, the catcher grumbles, "First time he ever done it." While the hitter, safe at second, crows, "How's dat fer de cream?" Almost all the baseball games of

stripes. The 1905 New York Giants sport all-black uniforms, with a large NY on the chest, for the World Series.

Impressions of the '00s

From ESPN's Mike Tirico:

As a new century dawned, there was no hint that the sports world would become overcrowded. There was no professional basketball or football to populate the landscape. The absence of mass media helped teams make more of an impact than stars. This was college football's golden era. The great names in academics were the gold standard in athletics. Yale, Harvard, Princeton and Penn were among football's elite. Then there was the unique dominance of Michigan. Fifty-

the decade use cards to trigger the action, including such titles as Game of Batter Up and Fan Craze, which includes a deck of 54 cards with portraits of National Leaguers, and game actions on each card. (An American League deck is

"I would rather see our youth playing football with the danger of an occasional broken collarbone than to see them dedicated to croquet."
—Father John Cavanaugh, president of Notre Dame

released in 1906, three years later.)

There are several golf games, with the best of the decade being Substitute Golf, whose elaborate pieces include greens, traps and water hazards, used to assemble a course for players in a large parlor, using furniture as obstacles that shape the layout. Each player has a small metal mechanical golfer who swings a ball when the player pulls a handle.

Fashion

Black is very hot this decade. The Baltimore Orioles wear black uniforms with a big "O" on the breast, reminiscent of the old National League Orioles. The socks have orange and black horizontal

six games, a half decade's worth of games without a loss, highlighted by the 1901 team that was undefeated, untied, unscored upon. Their place in history was secured by the first-ever bowl victory, a 49-0 shutout of Stanford in **the inaugural Rose Bowl game**, held January 1, 1902, in Pasadena. This was also a time to start tradition. The first invite from the National baseball league to its American counterpart, a series to determine best in the world. Sure, the negatives were starting to germinate as well (there was great controversy over who would host the second Olympics in 1900), but this was a time when it seemed sports emphasized its place as entertainment in society instead of being a big business.

Debuts and Exits

1900 **The Davis Cup**, with a 3-0 U.S. win over Great Britain in Brookline, Massachusetts.

The five-sided home plate, in the National League only.

EXIT **Live pigeon shooting** dropped from Olympic schedule after a Belgian marksman kills 21 birds at the Paris Games.

EXIT **The Cleveland Spiders** among four National League teams voted out of existence.

1901 **The American League** as a major league, with an 8-2 Chicago victory over Cleveland.

The ballpark hot dog, first sold at the old Polo Grounds by Harry M. Stevens.

The National Bowling Championships, held in Chicago, for $1,592 in prizes.

1902 **The Rose Bowl in Pasadena**, the first college football bowl game, as Michigan beats Stanford, 49-0, on New Year's Day.

The spitball, whose eccentric behavior is discovered by minor league pitcher Frank Corridon.

The split skirt, for women's horse riding, introduced by Mrs. Adolph Ladenburg, at Saratoga, New York.

The St. Louis Browns, with a 5-2 win over Cleveland.

The first professional hockey team in the U.S., formed in Houghton, Michigan.

1903 **The World Series**, as the Boston Pilgrims beat the Pittsburgh Pirates, 5 games to 3.

Harvard Stadium, the first all-concrete sports stadium in America.

EXIT **Sole leather**, "or other hard or unyielding substances," in head protectors, ruled illegal in college football.

1904 **The National Ski Association.**

1905 **The Intercollegiate Athletic Association of the United States**, the forerunner of the National Collegiate Athletic Association, with 62 charter members.

1906 **The legal forward pass**, in college football.

1908 **Tarpaulins during rain delays**, introduced by the Pirates.

1909 **The three-point field goal**, in college football.

Shibe Park in Philadelphia, the first concrete and steel baseball park.

First official horseshoe-pitching contest in the U.S., held in Bronson, Kansas.

Full-time baseball coaches, when the New York Giants hire Arlie "The Freshest Man on Earth" Latham.

THE 1910s

Though baseball was the unquestioned national pastime, a new game was catching on, more representative of the rough-hewn realities of modern America. Football had branched out from the Ivy League campuses, into coal-mining towns and the growing cities of the industrial belt. There was nothing so organized as a national football league yet, but the game did have an early icon. He was a ruddy-faced, lantern-jawed Native-American hero who played baseball, ran track & field, dominated football and was, for his era, quite simply the world's greatest athlete.

JIM THORPE By Nicholas Lemann

The Natural

WAS JIM THORPE REAL? Manifestly he was—children of his are still alive—but he seems more a mythic figure, a 20th-century Paul Bunyan or Pecos Bill, than an actual one. The main reason for this is the sheer scope of his athletic accomplishment, which goes far past the limit of what is imaginable today. A Sac and Fox Indian raised in a tiny settlement in Indian Territory, Thorpe became a national sports figure as a college football star. To say this doesn't quite get it across, though. He dominated college football probably more than any one player ever has, playing offense, defense and special teams, and regularly scoring most of his team's points in a game. He scored more points in a season than anyone. And at the same time, he was probably the best, most dominant college athlete in track and field. He accomplished all this while playing for a peculiar, remote vocational training school for Indians that was more an anti-poverty program than a real college.

At the height of his college sports career, Thorpe went to Stockholm as a member of the U.S. team in the 1912 Olympics, and there he registered what may be the single most astonishing sports feat of all time: He won, by enormous margins, both the decathlon and the pentathlon. That's 15 separate events, ranging from sprints to middle-distance running to the javelin (he had never seen a javelin until a few weeks earlier) and the shot put. He finished first in nine of them.

During the 1910s, Thorpe played major-league baseball—not outstandingly, but in the majors—mostly for one of the leading teams, the New York Giants. And he was pivotal in the early years of professional football as organizer, promoter,

coach, and star player. If you're prepared to believe all the stories, he was also an extraordinarily gifted amateur at virtually every competitive physical activity ever devised, from marksmanship to cattle-roping to basketball to billiards to fishing.

Another reason Jim Thorpe seems mythic is that his life story has been played over and over as a tragic moral parable. If there were an American Bible he would be presented in it for our cautionary instruction. Thorpe is the natural man, the ur-Redskin. Thorpe himself, and various of his wives and children, not to mention generations of sportswriters, liked to present him as embodying a variety of supposedly innate Indian traits, such as swiftness of foot, innocence, wanderlust, and toughness. Warrior, scout, noble descendant of chiefs, he turned the playing fields of America into his personal wide-open range.

AND THEN CAME THE INEVITABLE FALL. Thorpe's triumphant year was 1912. In 1913, a newspaper in Worcester, Massachusetts, reported that before competing in the Olympics, which were then strictly limited to amateurs, he had spent two summers playing minor-league baseball, for minor-league money, in North Carolina. A great scandal ensued, in which he was barred from college sports and future Olympics, made to return his gold medals and his lavish Olympic trophies, and had his name expunged from the official Olympic records. His distant runners-up were retrospectively declared the winners of the decathlon and pentathlon.

The punishment seemed harsh at the time, and now it seems insanely so. Thorpe had made a few meager bucks playing in the minors. Plenty of other amateur athletes did the same thing but escaped punishment because they used assumed names. The scandal, in this version of the Thorpe myth, broke his magnificent, free, conquering spirit, and he spent the rest of his life in a spiral of disappointment: three marriages, innumerable jobs and homes, drinking problems, money problems, legal problems. For being guileless, for being an Indian who got above his station, Thorpe was singled out for humiliation. It wasn't until seven decades later—three decades after his death—that the recalcitrant International Olympic Committee gave in and returned his medals.

Even if you don't take this version of an undeniably sad story completely at face value, Thorpe's life still has the quality of a fable. His greatest years as an athlete were the years just before the rise of the national media culture. He was photographed, though less than you'd think, and very occasionally filmed. There was no commercial broadcast industry to record his prime—the first radio station wasn't chartered until 1920, and television was many years off in the future. There were no national news or picture magazines. The news, like the country, was overwhelmingly local. To the extent there was national news, it came over the fledgling Associated Press (incorporated in 1900) or through syndicates. Entertainment, a category that of course includes sports, was local too. Theaters in the big cities showed traveling vaudeville acts, not movies; the first feature-length silent film wasn't made until 1911. Pre-movie newsreels, of the kind that made the athletes of the 1920s famous, didn't exist.

So the public's information about Thorpe's exploits came from ragtime-era sports reporters, a group with a flair for the dramatic and poetic, and from old-fashioned word of mouth. Over the years his story was embellished by Hollywood

(*Jim Thorpe: All-American*, starring Burt Lancaster, 1951), by a series of inspirational biographies aimed at young boys, and by Thorpe himself, who tried to make a living for years by barnstorming the country telling a dramatic version of his story to lecture audiences. Therefore his life has come down to us as a pastiche of burnished, dreamy, too-pat anecdotes that may or may not be literally true:

Thorpe—born Wa-tho-huck, or Bright Path, in a one-room cabin in 1887—is a direct descendant of Black Hawk, the fearsome Sac and Fox warrior chief who died in 1832 leading his Thunder Clan in the last Indian war east of the Mississippi, a bloody but futile rebellion against federal troops to preserve ownership of ancestral land in downstate Illinois.

At the age of eight, Thorpe kills a big buck deer with a single rifle shot.

All through boyhood Thorpe battles with his father, Hiram, an enormous, ox-strong, ornery bootlegger, polygamist, and brawler. Hiram enrolls Jim in a nearby school. Jim runs away. Hiram loads him into a wagon and deposits him at the school's front door. Jim escapes by the back door and gets home before his father does.

Hiram Thorpe tells Jim he's going to send him to a school that is so far away he can't run home—the Haskell Institute, an Indian boarding school 300 miles away. There the leading football player, sensing a hunger for greatness in Jim, takes a shine to the scrawny lad and gives him a raggedy football made of leather straps sewn together and stuffed with rags. Nonetheless, Jim, as usual, chafes under the

World's Greatest.
Putting the shot in the 1912 Stockholm Olympics decathlon competition.

discipline of school. He escapes and rides a freight train all the way home. He enrolls in the local public school for a while and then runs away again, this time to Texas, where he works as a cowboy and returns home, at the age of 14, driving his own team of horses.

Personal tragedies befall Thorpe in more than his share, which inlays a deep streak of loneliness and melancholy on his soul. His twin brother dies when he is 10, his mother when he is 14, his father when he is 16, his first-born son when he is 30.

In 1903, Hiram Thorpe writes the U.S. Indian agent in charge of the Sac and Fox tribe suggesting that Jim be sent to the Carlisle Indian Industrial School in Pennsylvania "so he cannot run a way—he is 14 years old [actually, 16] and I Cannot do any thing with him…he is getting worse every day—and I want him to go and make something of him Self for he cannot do it hear—"

At Carlisle, where Indians are trained in the manual trades and sent out in summers to live with and work for farmers in the surrounding area, Thorpe is put into the program for apprentice tailors. His work assignments are all disastrously unsuccessful; he runs away from one, is apprehended by the school security force, and serves a spell in the Carlisle guardhouse.

ONE FATEFUL EVENING SOON AFTER THIS, in the spring of 1907, Thorpe, dressed in overalls and work boots, is wandering across the Carlisle campus with a group of friends from the tailors program. They pass the field where the varsity track team is practicing the high jump. Thorpe shyly asks if he can have a try at clearing the bar, which is set at five foot nine. The guys on the track team, snickering, say, Sure kid, try it. Whiz, over he goes. The next morning, Thorpe is summoned to the office of Pop Warner, Carlisle's human-bulldog track and football coach. "Boy, you've just broken the school record!" Warner exclaims.

So Thorpe is an overnight track star, the best by far that Carlisle has ever seen. But that isn't enough for him: he wants to play football too. He pesters Warner to give him a tryout; Warner, fearing an injury, refuses; Thorpe keeps pestering.

Finally, in the fall of 1907, Warner loses his temper and tells Thorpe that if he wants to play football so badly, he can give the team some tackling practice. He tosses Thorpe the ball—the first real football he has ever held. Thorpe runs the full length of the practice field, through the entire Carlisle varsity team, effortlessly scattering the bodies of all the men who try to stop him. "Nobody is going to tackle Jim!" he announces.

Now Thorpe is a two-sport star. In the spring of 1908 he begins collecting gold medals at track meets. In his first play as a varsity football player, he runs 70 yards for a touchdown. During the 1908 season Carlisle racks up a 10–2–1 record, and he is named a third-team All-American halfback. In the spring of 1909, for a track meet with nearby Lafayette College, the Carlisle delegation arrives in the form of the team manager and Thorpe, who enters every event, competes as the entire Carlisle team, and wins, collecting six gold medals and one bronze.

Then Thorpe goes down to North Carolina for his minor-league baseball sojourn. Fearing that his involvement in professional sports will disappoint Pop Warner, he leaves Carlisle entirely. His baseball league goes out of business, and he drifts back home to Oklahoma.

The Stockholm Double.
Handsome, unschooled and unruffled, Thorpe stands on the steps outside the dorms in the athletes' village. At right, Thorpe long jumping in the decathalon competition. He beat his next closest competitor by nearly 700 points. He won the final event, the 1,500 meters, by more than 50 yards.

In the summer of 1911, on the main street of Andarko, Oklahoma, Thorpe bumps into a friend from Carlisle who persuades him to go back there and finish his education. Or, alternatively, he receives a letter from Pop Warner promising him a tryout for the 1912 United States Olympic team if he returns. Either way, Thorpe is back at Carlisle for the start of the 1911–12 school year. "Where have you been?" Warner asks him. "Playing ball," says the laconic Thorpe.

In the 1911 football season, Carlisle goes 11–1 and Thorpe is a first-team All-American. The highlight of the season is an upset victory over Harvard, the best team in the country. Thorpe, whose legs are heavily bandaged from an injury, is supposed to spend the game on the bench. When Carlisle falls behind he can no longer just watch: He takes the field, bandages and all, and scores 13 of Carlisle's points in their 18–15 win.

Harvard's coach, the wonderfully named Percy Haughton, who so underrated Thorpe and Carlisle that he didn't even attend the game, afterward declares Thorpe "the theoretical superplayer in flesh and blood."

The following summer Thorpe sails for the Olympics in Stockholm. Always reluctant to practice and so naturally gifted that he doesn't have to, he spends the voyage napping in a hammock rather than working out with the team.

At the closing ceremony, King Gustav V of Sweden says to Thorpe, "Sir, you are the greatest athlete in the world!" Thorpe replies, "Thanks, King."

In addition to his two gold medals, Thorpe receives bejeweled trophies and gifts from the crowned heads of Europe worth $50,000; the congratulations of President William Howard Taft; official celebrations in Carlisle, Philadelphia, and Boston; and a ticker-tape parade in New York City.

In the 1912 season Thorpe scores 25 touchdowns and 203 points. Twice in the season he runs downfield swiftly enough to catch (or, in the more restrained version, recover) his own booming punts. In the Army game he scores 22 of Carlisle's 27 points, including a 90-yard touchdown run from a fake punt. Future president Dwight Eisenhower, a member of the Army team, is so severely hurt in his fruitless attempts to tackle Thorpe that he never plays football again. Carlisle goes 12–1 and Thorpe is a first-team All-American again.

In January 1913, a sports reporter happens upon a team picture of the 1910 Winston-Salem, North Carolina, minor-league baseball team, with Thorpe in it. The story breaks. The Amateur Athletic Union, which was in charge of selecting the American team for the Olympics, demands an explanation. Thorpe, incapable of dishonesty, writes a letter owning up: "I never realized until now what a big mistake I made by keeping a secret about my ball playing and I am sorry I did so. I hope I will be partly excused by the fact that I was simply an Indian schoolboy and did not know all about such things." The AAU, merciless, arranges for everything he has to be stripped away from him, including the loot he had brought back from Europe.

Thorpe signs a contract to play baseball with the New York Giants. He has a desultory career that ends in 1919, when Giants manager, John McGraw, calls Thorpe a "dumb Indian" and Thorpe blows his stack.

MEANWHILE, IN 1915, THORPE SIGNS ON with the Canton Bulldogs, an early professional football team, and takes up a life of baseball in the spring and summer and football in the fall. The Bulldogs immediately become champions, and are popular at the box office. In one game for Canton, Thorpe kicks a 90-yard punt. In another he kicks a 75-yard field goal. In still another, Knute Rockne, former player and future coach for Notre Dame, then star of Canton's archrival, the Massillon Tigers, tackles Thorpe behind the line of scrimmage. On the next play, Thorpe extracts his revenge, running right over Rockne on the way to a 60-yard touchdown. Then he saunters back to where the dazed, bloody Rockne is lying on the ground, and says, "Good boy, Rock. You let old Jim run for the people." In 1920, Thorpe is named president of the newly organized American Professional Football Association, headquartered in Canton.

When the 1920s, the golden age of sport, arrive, it is too late for Thorpe: He is in his mid-thirties and his powers have faded. He organizes and manages an all-Indian pro football team as a promotional vehicle for a dog kennel. He plays a few seasons of minor-league baseball. His wife leaves him. By 1930, his career as a professional athlete is over.

Thorpe moves to California. He remarries. He sells the film rights to his life story to Metro-Goldwyn-Mayer for $1,500.

He referees dance marathons. He serves as master of ceremonies for a vaude-

ville-meets-sports cross-country race. He plays bit parts in movies, usually as an Indian in full regalia.

In 1932, Los Angeles is host to the Olympics. America's greatest Olympic athlete is discovered to be living there and working as a ditchdigger for a dollar a day, unable to afford tickets. Very briefly the country takes him up again. He views the games from the presidential box, seated next to Herbert Hoover's long-forgotten vice president, Charles Curtis, who has Indian blood.

Thorpe's second wife leaves him. Harry Bennett, the thuggish head of security for Henry Ford, hires him to be a guard at the world's largest factory, the Ford River Rouge plant in Dearborn, Michigan. He has a heart attack. He moves to Oklahoma. He moves to Los Angeles. He is arrested for drunk driving and lectured by the judge about setting a bad example for America's youth.

He remarries again. He gets a job as a bouncer at a sports bar in downtown L.A.

Unsurpassed. On the field at Carlisle (above left), he made the team an instant national power. "No college player I ever saw had the natural aptitude for football possessed by Jim Thorpe," said Pop Warner. His kicking game was superb, and he was a fearsome ballcarrier. Dwight Eisenhower, who played against Thorpe while at Army, called him "the greatest I've ever seen."

He goes on the lecture circuit, recounting his life story while dressed in buckskins and a headdress. He headlines an all-Indian traveling song-and-dance troupe. He moves to the town of Pittman, Nevada, and opens a bar. He has another heart attack. He gets a job with the Chicago Park District teaching slum kids the healing power of sports. He moves back to Los Angeles.

In 1953, in his home in a trailer park in the town of Lomita, California, he dies of a third heart attack.

Thorpe's widow, unable to persuade the state of Oklahoma to erect a suitably grand tomb for him and unable to pay for one herself, strikes a deal with a promoter in the coal-mining town of Mauch Chunk, Pennsylvania. If the town will change its name to Jim Thorpe, she will agree to transport Thorpe's body there for burial. In the hope of setting off a tourist boom, the town votes in the change and Thorpe is buried on a hilltop at the edge of town, where a blue-collar neighborhood peters out into forest.

No tourism results from Thorpe's being buried in Jim Thorpe, Pennsylvania. Periodically someone in the town mounts a campaign to change the name back to Mauch Chunk. So far two name-change referenda have lost in close votes. Plans to erect memorials to Thorpe in Oklahoma and Carlisle have never worked out.

A man who lost to Thorpe in both the pentathlon and the decathlon at the 1912 Olympics, Avery Brundage, goes on to become the head of the United States Olympic Committee, and then the International Olympic Committee, for decades. From these positions, he stands firmly in the way of Thorpe's medals being returned. Finally Brundage dies, the AAU and the USOC restore Thorpe's amateur status, and, in 1982, the IOC puts Thorpe's name back in its official records and then issues new gold medals to one of his daughters in 1983.

Meeting His Match.
Baseball humbled Thorpe, though not as severely as it would Michael Jordan generations later. He played in more than 100 major-league games only once in his six-year career, mostly as a utility outfielder for John McGraw's Giants, and finished with a .252 career average and seven home runs.

NOT ALL THAT MUCH OF THE THORPE STORY is demonstrably untrue. (Okay, he wasn't a direct descendant of Black Hawk, and he didn't beat the entire Lafayette College track team single-handed.) Most of it consists of an actual life transmogrified into parable for the edification of children—a venerable American tradition, into which the lives of Washington and Lincoln have also been fitted. Thorpe is probably one of the last examples, because the advent of a media society has killed off oral legend keeping.

To the extent that there is a real version of the story, it involves a peculiar intertwining of two strands in American life: government Indian policy after the conquest of the West, and the bumpy early days of big-time sports.

Jim Thorpe was born into an unnecessarily extreme dispute among whites about what would be the best future for Indians now that they could no longer live in the traditional way because their lands had been taken. One camp believed in preserving the tribal cultures on reservations, the other in remaking the Indians into standard-issue Americans through radical assimilation. The founder of the Carlisle Indian Industrial School, a career army officer named James Henry Pratt, was the leader of the assimilationist camp.

Pratt thought of himself as the Indian's best friend (his biography is titled *The Red Man's Moses*), and though his attitudes today make the world's fattest target, it would be anachronistic to deny him a measure of respect. At a time when most

white people regarded Indians as subhuman savages who ought to be either killed or incarcerated, Pratt chose to devote his life to "improving" them. As a young officer and Indian fighter on the frontier, he was assigned to take a group of 74 Indian prisoners of war to a fort in St. Augustine, Florida, and guard them there. Instead of operating a maximum-security prison, he taught the Indians to read and write and let them guard themselves—something previously considered impossible. Then, in 1879, he persuaded the army to turn an abandoned barracks in Carlisle, not far from Gettysburg, over to him for conversion to a school.

CARLISLE WAS RUN ON THE MODEL of the Hampton Institute in Virginia, where former slaves were taught the trades, and it was also similar in spirit to the settlement houses for impoverished immigrants that were springing up in big cities at the time. Pratt's aim was the total, immediate annihilation of every trace of Indian culture: A student who arrived at Carlisle would have his hair shorn into an American style and his tribal name replaced with an American one. He would be issued American work clothes and made to practice Christianity. He would be closely supervised at every moment to make sure he conformed to American middle-class mores concerning sex, personal habits, timekeeping, eating, drinking, and work. The intensely religious Pratt's dream for his students, who were made to call him "school Father," was that they would one day blend into white society.

Thorpe, though raised completely within the assimilationist camp (Haskell, his earlier school, was run on the Carlisle model; one of his grandfathers was white), makes a good example of its failure to take. At the age of fifty he went to Washington as part of a group petitioning for the institution of tribal self-government for the tiny remnant of the Sac and Fox nation—just the opposite of Pratt's vision. He was obviously not comfortable in either the Indian or the white world. His spells in and around the tribal culture in Oklahoma, with its severely limited opportunities, were both quite regular and invariably brief. But in mainstream America he was received as an Indian, and held on to an Indian identity himself (in a painfully thin version featuring dress and lingo derived from Hollywood movies) for all of his life. Here he is writing, in 1929, from Las Vegas, in the neat penmanship that was drilled into him at Haskell and Carlisle, to his friend Chief Long Lance, a celebrity Indian of the day from whom he had borrowed money:

The Jack received and sure was a help. This is sure one tuff country to make ends meet, the family is with me and things have turned out OK. I made a little money working in a base ball picture, then sent for the Injuns....I dropped down here looking for some thing to do, but things are not ready as the plans for the Boelder Dam, have not been passed on, from Washington....[H]ave been running the country over trying to locate a coaching position. Looks good at Loyola Univ, a Catholic college in Los Angeles, shall here from it real soon, but can't as you know touch firewater—might be a good thing for me. Would rather land a job where I could have a little fuss....

Your red Injun friend, Jim Thorpe.

By the time of Thorpe's athletic heyday, Carlisle was an institution at the edge of collapse. Pratt had been forced out in 1904 because of an especially bitter public attack he had made on the reservationists at the federal Bureau of Indian

The Elder Statesman. Though Thorpe had passed his prime by the early days of the National Football League, he was still a terrific draw. Above, he shouts encouragement to his fellow Rock Island Independents in 1925.

Affairs. The head of the school from 1908 on, Moses Friedman, let things slip badly. Out of a combination of conviction and fear of awakening incipient anti-Indian sentiment in the town of Carlisle, Pratt had maintained a strict guardhouse atmosphere at the school. Friedman did not, and the result was that students regularly ran away or were arrested for drinking or committing petty crimes in town. Dozens of the girls became pregnant and were sent home. All this amounted to blood scented by the school's many bureaucratic enemies in Washington, and they began circling in the water.

The fame and success of Carlisle's sports teams served as a kind of inoculation against scandal. Pop Warner, who had left to coach at Cornell, was lured back by the offer of an enormous salary ($4,000 a year) and free housing. What makes the Thorpe minor-league baseball controversy of 1913 especially ridiculous is that the Carlisle football team on which he had played for years was essentially professional. The players lived and ate separately from the other students and were excused from the regular classes and training. Carlisle played no home games because it had no stadium; the team spent every fall barnstorming the country, sometimes playing more than once a week, ranging so widely that returning to Carlisle between games was impossible. They were a little like the Harlem Globetrotters without the jokes, an ethnic traveling show with one foot in modern football and the other in 19th-century wild west carnivals. Carlisle's cut of the box-office receipts from the football games went into a substantial slush fund, from which various school expenses were covered—and the athletes were paid. Carmelita Ryan, author of a 1962 Ph.D. thesis on the school, discovered that in 1907 and 1908 Thorpe was paid $500 out of the fund, far more than he made in 1909 and 1910 playing professional baseball.

THE THORPE OF THE GREAT ACHIEVEMENTS OF 1912 was hardly a schoolboy athlete. He was 25 years old, he was not really a student (he never graduated from Carlisle), he had consistently been a paid professional for five years, and by today's bar-set-low standards he was already an alcoholic. In pictures his face looks hard and tough, without a hint of innocence. Chances are that his confessional letter to the AAU (along with the accompanying "Where have you been?" "Playing ball" story) was concocted by Pop Warner and Moses Friedman to get themselves off the hook at a time when Carlisle was in trouble and a vogue for "amateurism" was being imposed on the rough-and-tumble sports scene. It's probably best to think of Thorpe not as a superhuman naif-of-the-plains, but as a guy born into impossible circumstances who was working hard at a job he happened to be genius-level good at.

In 1914 a congressional subcommittee conducted an investigation of Carlisle. Pop Warner was asked to leave. In 1918 the Bureau of Indian Affairs closed down the school. Today the old Carlisle barracks is home to the Army War College, a prestigious advanced training program for fast-rising colonels, some of whom live in the same buildings where the Indian students did.

What you'd want is for the meltdown of Carlisle and the bad business with the Olympic medals to have faded instantly into the background as Thorpe entered a glorious career in professional sports. But in 1913, there were hardly any professional sports in the modern sense.

Family Man. Thorpe with his sons Phil and Billy in 1931. His physical versatility was such that he bowled at a 200 average, and once won a ballroom-dance contest at Carlisle.

The sports world was very sharply divided into high and low classes. Golf, tennis, and track and field were for the emerging moneyed but genteel capitalist class (Thorpe's was the era when the first country clubs were built). Professional baseball and boxing (which was illegal in most of the country through the 1910s) were for the unrespectable blue-collar and immigrant rabble. The Olympics, which were new and unsteady on their feet—Thorpe competed in the fifth modern games, but the first three were only sparsely attended—were preoccupied with amateurism partly as a way of branding themselves as part of the high-class portion of the sports world. College football was another sport over which the forces of high-class propriety were vigorously trying to establish their control. In 1905, a year when there were 18 player fatalities during the college football season, President Theodore Roosevelt, proponent of the strenuous life though he was, threatened to outlaw the sport unless the colleges could settle it down. It took the establishment of governing conferences and associations, followed by a series of rules and eligibility changes, to make college football relatively safe and at least plausibly the domain of student-athletes.

WHEN THORPE LEFT CARLISLE, only one professional sport, baseball, was really a going concern. Even baseball was prone to regular episodes of violence, sexual scandal, and gambling—Thorpe's was the decade of the Black Sox scandal, after all. The hiring of Thorpe himself by the New York Giants demonstrates that even John McGraw, the greatest manager of the day, was not above a bit of naked publicity-stuntery. Still, in the 1910s baseball settled into a groove and established firm rules, a big audience, a workable publicity apparatus, and national stars like Ty Cobb, Walter Johnson, Honus Wagner and Christy Mathewson. Pro football, on the other hand, was in a condition analogous to that of pro softball today: It was a regional sport, played mostly in the big towns and small cities of industrial Pennsylvania and Ohio. Canton and Massillon were the big time. It attracted audiences the size of high school, rather than college, football's. Thorpe's arrival took the game to a whole new level—the level at which 5,000 people might turn out to watch a game. Loosely organized and prone to novelty teams and displays of trickery, pro football overlapped with a great Mark Twain netherland made up of semi-pro sports, ethnic minstrel shows, vaudeville acts, circuses, and traveling entertainments featuring amazing displays of physical prowess. Taken together, these constitute the primal goo from which the sleek, rich modern sports state evolved.

Jim Thorpe was a figure of this primitive sports era. He's usually presented as a man who was born too late—who should have been free to roam an uncomplicated open range. But this would have required him to come along back in the mid-1700s, at the very latest; the Sac and Fox had already been expelled from their upper Mississippi Valley Eden a good half century before Thorpe was born. It would be closer to the mark to say that he was born too early. His story demonstrates that being a superstar requires two things, achievement and a media-business apparatus. Possessing just the first, in incredible measure, he was consigned, because the second didn't exist yet, to a rough marginal life that today would be unthinkable for an athlete one tenth as good as he was.

Primitive Man.
With the Canton Bulldogs in 1920: "It would be closer to the mark to say that he was born too early."

TY COBB
Wild Courage

Driven by inner demons and an obsession to excel, Ty Cobb ran and hit his way into baseball immortality. But the diamond brilliance of the "Georgia Peach" was counterbalanced with an infamous personality which left his legacy a bittersweet one. Hall of Famer Sam Crawford summed up the character issue perfectly: "He was a difficult teammate and a dangerous opponent, but no one was better with a bat."

Possessing a violent temper and dark attitude, Cobb attacked umpires, teammates and even fans, once jumping into the stands to assault a handicapped heckler. But mostly Cobb attacked baseballs, punishing them persistently and severely. He won a dozen batting titles, including nine in a row from 1907-15, while hitting .320 or better for 22 consecutive seasons and hitting .400 three times. His .367 career average remains the unscaled Mt. Everest of baseball records.

A legitimate genius with a baseball bat, using a split grip to control it with surgical precision, Cobb was capable of placing the ball anywhere he desired. His exploits were so uniformly electrifying that he was able to challenge even Babe Ruth for the sport's center stage. Cobb, in fact, outpolled Ruth, Honus Wagner, Walter Johnson and Christy Mathewson to lead the initial induction class into the Baseball Hall of Fame in Cooperstown in 1936.

Always dangerous from the batter's box, he was positively deadly on the basepaths. Cobb was the original game disrupter as he danced between bases, taunting the opposition and forcing errors. Cleveland manager Lee Fohl, after witnessing Cobb running wild against his team, proclaimed "he stole everything but our uniforms" in exasperated admiration. Cobb stole home 54 times.

When he retired in 1928, he left behind career records in almost every statistical category, including most games played, most stolen bases, most RBIs and—his favorite—most runs scored. He also retired as the AL all-time leader in singles, triples and homers. Cobb's recognized career hits mark of 4,191 ultimately fell a half century later to the tenacious Pete Rose, a player whose highest average for a single season was lower than Cobb's career average.

Cobb was feared as much as he was admired by his peers, and he was more than a little pleased with the situation. Few could deny his dynamic ability to energize and dominate a game. Even baseball icon Connie Mack, a fierce adversary for years, grudgingly admitted the timeless fascination with Cobb's "wild courage" and baseball expertise. "You couldn't take your eyes off him for an

COBB:
NO ONE WAS
BETTER
WITH A BAT

JOHNSON:
"RAW SPEED,
BLINDING SPEED,
TOO MUCH SPEED"

instant because you never knew what he'd do next, but you knew it would be something exciting." —*Michael Point*

WALTER JOHNSON
Train in the Distance

Long before the "Ryan Express" began its run to the Hall of Fame, the "Big Train" was blowing batters off the tracks, setting a strikeout standard that endured for more than 50 years. No pitcher won as many games in the 20th Century, and few pitched in more difficult situations.

Johnson's 417 victories, highlighted by a dozen 20-win seasons, were almost solely the result of personal excellence. He joined the Washington Senators in 1907 as a 19-year-old Kansas farmboy fresh from a semi-pro stint in Idaho, and spent his entire 21–year career with the team, learning firsthand the sad truth of the woeful baseball adage, "Washington: first in war, first in peace and last in the American League."

In his rookie year, the franchise lost 102 games but Johnson rose above Washington's futility, accounting for nearly 40 percent of the team's wins in both 1910 and 1911. Improving on a 33-win performance in 1912, Johnson turned in a dream season in 1913, going 36–7 while leading the AL in every pitching category, finishing with a 1.13 ERA.

Batters knew exactly what to expect from Johnson: In Ty Cobb's words, "just speed, raw speed, blinding speed, too much speed." Johnson's fastball was delivered with a smooth, sidearm motion facilitated by his unusually long arms. The sweeping, almost underhanded delivery was patterned on the natural motion of skipping a stone. It was easy on the arm, yet hard for the batters to pick up.

A single run was frequently all Johnson needed, as 38 of his wins, including his 1920 no-hitter, came in 1–0 decisions. But the sad-sack Senators often couldn't manage even that; Johnson suffered 68 shutout losses, including 27 defeats by 1–0 scores.

Johnson became baseball's all-time shutout leader almost out of necessity, once reeling off 55⅔ consecutive scoreless innings, still the AL record. He also exhibited golden glove work, compiling six errorless seasons and helped to preserve many of his typically tight victories with his batting, which included 549 career hits.

Eighteen years into his career as a Senator, Johnson finally reached the World Series. He made the most of the overdue opportunity with a dramatic extra-inning victory in the seventh game of the 1924 Series, securing the only world championship in Washington franchise history. After a managing stint, Johnson retired in 1935, the year before he segued smoothly into the Hall of Fame as one of the "fabled five" charter inductees.

—*Michael Point*

ROGERS HORNSBY
Baseball Is My Life

It took being the best right-handed hitter in baseball history to get noticed while playing in the legendary shadows of Ty Cobb and Babe Ruth, but Rogers Hornsby, dubbed "the most exemplary batsman the game has known" by Branch Rickey, was more than up to the task.

No right-handed hitter can match Hornsby's .358 career batting average and no 20th-century batter of any sort matched his extraordinary 1924 season batting average of .424. He is the only NL batter to win two triple crowns, adding the rare statistical trophies to his MVP awards, as he also became the first NL player to be named the league's best two times.

Hornsby hit over .300 for 19 seasons but in the five-year span of 1921–25 he exceeded even his own superlative standards. His run of six consecutive batting titles had started in 1920, and in 1921, he hit a lofty .397. But Hornsby then soared above .400 three of the next four years in one of the most remarkable hitting streaks in baseball history.

Such future greatness was well disguised in 1915 when Hornsby tried out for the Cardinals as a 135-pound, choke-hitting shortstop. But after being dispatched back to the Texas League, Hornsby beefed up and changed his batting stance. By the next spring he had moved his feet to the back of the batter's box and his hands to the end of the bat. Striding aggressively toward the pitch with a powerful, level stroke that rocketed line drives in every direction, Hornsby had transformed himself into the "savage batter" who would terrorize NL pitchers for years to come.

Described as "hard to approach, difficult to understand" by Hall of Fame teammate Travis Jackson, Hornsby was a silent loner who didn't drink, smoke or read anything but box scores and *The Daily Racing Form*. He was blunt at best and rude as a rule but his gruff demeanor was more a matter of complete absorption than true meanness of spirit. Hornsby, who confessed to sportswriters that "baseball is my life and is the only thing I know and can talk about," simply wasn't interested in much away from the diamond.

Hornsby's heroics came with the extra burden of serving as a player–manager for much of his career. He took the Cardinals to their first world championship in 1926. A competent manager, he was also tactless and belligerent toward ownership and was repeatedly fired, despite some on-field success.

Hornsby's life was built around being in the batter's box. He was never happy on the bench, although he spent the remainder of his life involved with baseball as a manager and instructor. His 1942 induction into the Hall of Fame finally put the aloof and accomplished Hornsby where he belonged, in the company of his legendary peers.

—*Michael Point*

HORNSBY: "HARD TO APPROACH, DIFFICULT TO UNDERSTAND"

MAN O' WAR: "A BREATHING, HIGH-HEADED, FIERY HORSE"

MAN O' WAR
Big Red

At a time when America had just won the War to End All Wars, when more people lived on farms than in cities, when the nation's sports heroes were mythic, larger-than-life figures, the biggest hero of them all wasn't even a human. Instead, it was the fearsome, indomitable chestnut colt Man o' War, who captured the country's imagination in 1919 and 1920, leaving an indelible mark on horse racing.

The big-legged horse with the amazing stride (estimated at 28 feet by some experts) was born in Lexington, Kentucky, in 1917, the foal of Fair Play by Mahuba, in the stable of Major August Belmont. Beset with war losses, and despite some reservations (he sensed the colt was special), he sold Man o' War at an auction in Saratoga, for $5,000 to Pennsylvania horseman Samuel D. Riddle.

Riddle groomed him wisely, and when the horse they called Big Red made his racing debut as a two-year-old in 1919, he won nine of 10 races and quickly established himself among the finest horses in the land. His lone setback came at the Sanford Stakes August 13, 1919, when a botched start left Man o' War and two other horses in the gate, several lengths behind the blazing Golden Broom. Though he would yield by a neck in the end—appropriately, to a horse called Upset—Man o' War ran such a great race that day that Fred Van Ness, in *The New York Times*, noted, "Though defeated, Man o' War was not discredited." ("Upset" instantly joined the sporting lexicon, signifying an underdog defeating a heavy favorite.) After that day, Man o' War never lost again, never really came close to losing. His dominance was so awesome that he went off at 1–100 during one match race, and beat another horse by 100 lengths.

As a three-year-old, he took both the Preakness and the Belmont in 1920, then won his last race in October of that year, easily besting the highly regarded Sir Barton in a 1¼-mile match race in Ontario. He then was retired to stud, and spent the balance of his days at Faraway Farm in Lexington.

In 1950, when a nationwide panel of sportswriters voted on the best horse of the first half of the century, Man o' War won going away, taking 305 out of 388 votes. Two of his progeny—his son War Admiral and his grandson Seabiscuit—also finished among the top seven.

Summing up Big Red's significance after his passing in 1947, Joe Palmer wrote, "The old days now at last were dead, the last link snapped. The American Turf had lost, and perhaps would never have again, a single living symbol, a breathing, high-headed, fiery horse which meant, 'Racing!' to every man of racing, and to every wandering tourist from Portland or San Diego or Athens, Georgia."

People's Champion: Ouimet's great upset helped bring golf to the masses.

GOLF

The First "Open Coma"

When the 1913 U.S. Open began at The Country Club in Brookline, Massachusetts, it shaped up as a coronation for the two reigning golfers of the age, the British professionals Harry Vardon and Ted Ray. But by the time the fourth round arrived on Friday, they found themselves locked in a tense battle with an obscure American amateur who'd previously spent most of his time on the Brookline course as a caddy.

Francis Ouimet was 20 years old, a gardener's son, who'd grown up across the street from The Country Club, and spent much of his teenage years caddying for 28 cents a round. He'd often sneak onto the The Country Club course before play began at five in the morning, but he did most of his golfing at a nearby public course, Franklin Park. At the Open, he was accompanied by his caddy, 10-year-old Eddie Lowery, who played hooky to carry his clubs.

Ouimet tied for the lead with Vardon and Ray after three rounds, but then fell back in the fourth round. Coming out of nowhere, Ouimet birdied two of the last six holes—chipping for birdie from off the green at the 13th, then nailing a 12-foot side-hill birdie putt on the 17th—to force a playoff with Vardon and Ray the next day.

With his caddy repeating the lines of instruction that Ouimet taught him—"Keep your eye on the ball," "Take your time, you've got all day"—Ouimet played as though he had nothing to lose. "It was a wonderful mood to get into," he said. "I was numb."

He was, in the minds of many, in the first "Open Coma," that temporary state of brilliance that has gripped obscure unknowns in the National Open, and lifted them to the role of giant-killers. Just as the journeyman Jack Fleck would do in the '55 Open, Ouimet took on a legend (two in fact) in a playoff, and emerged victorious. In the 18-hole playoff, Ouimet shot a steady round of 72, while Vardon and Ray stumbled to 77 and 78. He didn't let down his guard until stroking the final, clinching putt. "For the first time I thought about the championship," he said. "I couldn't get my breath. The green began heaving beneath me. I couldn't even see the hole."

BASEBALL

1912 World Series

■ The Boston Red Sox hadn't won a pennant since 1904, when Giants skipper John McGraw declined to face them in what would have been the second World Series. So when the Bosox got back to the Fall Classic in '12, it was fitting that McGraw's Giants would be their opponents. Boston advanced behind Smokey Joe Wood, who'd gone 34-5 with a 1.91 ERA during the regular season. The Giants had the redoubtable Christy Mathewson and Rube Marquard. Boston jumped out to a 3-games-to-1 lead, but the Giants rallied with two easy wins. In the finale, Wood relieved Hugh Bedient in the eighth inning of a tie game, but gave up the go-ahead run in the top of the 10th. Mathewson came back to finish his complete game, but Fred Snodgrass' dropped fly ball in center and a misplay of Tris Speaker's easy pop foul—which dropped between Mathewson, catcher Chief Meyers, and the cursed Fred Merkle—gave the Red Sox a second and third chance. Speaker singled to tie the game, then Larry Gardner hit a long sacrifice fly to win it, the first of four Red Sox world titles in the '10s.

AUTO RACING

1911 Indianapolis 500

■ The inaugural Indianapolis 500 automobile race, at the brick-lined 2½-mile track of the Indianapolis Motor Speedway, was won by Ray Harroun, a 29-year-old engineer who designed engines for the Marmon Automobile Company in Indianapolis. As the only one of the 40 drivers in a single-seat automobile (he was convinced that on-board mechanics weren't worth the extra weight), Harroun had to weather pre-race protests from other drivers. When some charged he was a safety hazard, since without a mechanic he couldn't see cars coming from behind, Harroun improvised by bolting a small mirror to the front of his cockpit—and automobiling had its first rearview mirror. Harroun, spelled by relief driver Cy Patschke in the middle of the race, took advantage of his competitor's numerous pit stops to win by nearly two minutes, completing the 200 laps in 6 hours, 42 minutes, 8 seconds, an average speed of 74.6 miles per hour. Within a year, *The New York Times* described the crowd in attendance at The Brickyard as the "largest number to witness any sports event in the U.S."

BOXING

Johnson vs. Willard, 1915

■ Five years after Jack Johnson vanquished "Great White Hope" Jim Jeffries, he finally lost his title to a raw-boned Kansan named Jess Willard, who stood 6-foot-6, weighed 230 pounds and was four years younger than the 37-year-old champion. Under a blazing Havana sun, Johnson dominated the first 20 rounds, but seemed to tire in the 103-degree heat. The two men settled into listless sparring, until Willard connected with a swift shot to Johnson's chest in the 25th round. A round later, he laid Johnson out after four punches, the last a jab to the chin, for the KO.

COLLEGE FOOTBALL

1913 Army-Notre Dame

■ The future of football arrived on November 1, 1913, when Notre Dame traveled to West Point for its first game against Army, and brought a style of play that had never been seen in Eastern football. "The Westerners flashed the most sensational football that has been seen in the East this year," wrote *The New York Times*, "baffling the Cadets with a style of open play and a perfectly developed forward pass which carried the victors down the field 30 yards at a clip." The main Irish culprits were diminutive quarterback Gus Dorais and his favorite target, end and team captain Knute Rockne. Notre Dame took a 14-13 halftime lead, and the game hung in the balance in the third quarter when a goal-line stand by the Irish was highlighted by Dorais' end zone interception of a Vernon Prichard pass. In the fourth quarter, Notre Dame dominated, mixing the run and the pass, storming for 21 points. Dorais finished with a then-unheard-of 243 yards passing. The game was a watershed in the sport, leading to a reconsideration of the pass as an integral weapon in a team's offensive arsenal. "The press and the football public hailed this new game," wrote Rockne later, "and Notre Dame received credit as the originator of a style of play that we simply systematized."

Great Performances

■ At the 1912 Summer Olympic Games in Stockholm, American Jim Thorpe won the gold medal in both the decathlon and the pentathlon, only to have the medals stripped in 1913 by the IOC because he'd taken money to play minor league baseball … In 1914, Boston's "Miracle Braves," after sitting in last place well into mid-July, won the National League pennant by 10½ games, then swept the mighty Philadelphia A's (world champions three of the previous four seasons) in four straight. Brave aces Dick Rudolph and Bill James combined for all four wins, giving up one earned run in 29 innings.

Beantown Reigns

On April 20, 1912, Boston's new Fenway Park opened—with a monstrous left–field wall that for the first few years would be festooned with advertisements. The Red Sox of 1912, led by Tris Speaker's bat and the arm of Smokey Joe Wood, won the first of four world championships in the decade, this one made all the sweeter since it came at the expense of the New York Giants and John McGraw, who'd refused to play the Bosox the last time they had won the AL, in 1904. Though Boston dipped in 1913, they began a five-year string in 1914 in which they finished second, first, first, second, and first in the AL, winning all three Series they entered. Boston's young phenom **Babe Ruth** was the spark in the 1916 Series, going the distance to win the 14-inning Game 2 marathon. He broke Christy Mathewson's record for consecutive scoreless innings in the 1918 Series. The decade ended on a cursed note when, after the 1919 season, cash-strapped team owner Harry Frazee sold Ruth's contract to the New York Yankees.

■ **Harvard's Yard.** Percy Haughton was a second-team All-America as a player for Harvard in 1898. When he returned to coach his old school 10 years later, the Crimson had lost to Yale

six seasons in a row, without scoring. But that ended immediately, and by 1910, Harvard was a national champion again. Haughton found strength in numbers, often trotting out three different elevens before a game to intimidate the opposition. In 1911, Tack Hardwick—the man Walter Camp would later call "the most valuable player in the history of Harvard football"—came to Cambridge, where he'd excel as a halfback, tackler and kicker. Led by Hardwick, splendid open-field runner Eddie Mahan and talented kicker Charlie Brickley, Haughton's troops reeled off a 33-game win streak, from 1911 to 1915. They'd win four national championships during the decade.

■ **Close But No Cigar.** It was a maddening decade for John McGraw and his New York Giants. They won four National League flags but lost in all four World Series during the '10s. After the Polo Grounds was rebuilt in 1911, following a fire, the Giants won the first of three straight pennants. In '11 and '13 they lost to Connie Mack's Philadelphia A's, while in '12 they fell in the classic to the Red Sox, decided in the 10th inning of the final game. The Giants dropped to the basement in '15, but were back in the Fall Classic in 1917, only to lose to the Chicago White Sox. They would close out the decade with a pair of second-place finishes, but McGraw's troops would prove that persistence could pay, earning their glory in the next decade.

	COLLEGE BASKETBALL	PRO BASKETBALL	HOCKEY NHL	BASEBALL MLB	COLLEGE FOOTBALL	PRO FOOTB
1910				Athletics	H Harvard	
1911				Athletics	P Princeton	
1912				Red Sox	H Harvard	
1913				Athletics	H Harvard	
1914				B Braves	A Army	
1915				Red Sox	C Cornell	
1916				Red Sox	Pitt Pittsburgh	
1917				White Sox	GT Georgia Tech	
1918				T Toronto Arenas	Red Sox	Pitt Pittsburgh
1919		Canadiens	Seattle Metropolitans	Reds	H Harvard	

NOTE: **College football:** Champions are mythical national champions for predated seasons prior to 1936, as chosen in 1941 by the Helms Foundation.
Hockey: Stanley Cup champion determined in playoff between NHL and PCHA champions. 1919 Stanley Cup finals canceled due to influenza epidemic, with Seattle and Montreal tied 2-2-1.

Little Napoleon

"There has only been one manager," said the great Connie Mack, "and his name is **John McGraw**."

The pugnacious, imperious leader—"Little Napoleon" as he was called by some—forever changed the notion of what a manager did during his 30-year reign as the skipper of the New York Giants. Though he hit over .300 nine seasons in a row with the Baltimore Orioles, it was on the bench of the Giants—fashioning a 2,583-1,790 record from 1902–1932—that he became a legend.

"McGraw certainly did more to establish the profession of managing than anyone else in history," wrote baseball historian Bill James. McGraw led the inevitable move toward relief pitchers (when the statistic was figured retroactively, it was determined that McGraw's team led the NL in saves 17 times), provided clearly defined roles for his bench players, and was the first manager to hire a coach. And he excelled, winning three World Series and 10 National League pennants, eight of them from 1911–1924. The son of a Massachusetts Civil War veteran, McGraw argued often with his father about playing baseball as a youth, ultimately leaving home over the issue. McGraw had grown up with a shrewd understanding of the game and its rules, and he made a habit out of goading and abusing umpires, as well as his own players. Rogers Hornsby claimed McGraw would fine players for speaking with members of the opposition. Freddie Lindstrom recalled that the cardinal sin on the Giants club was "to begin a sentence to McGraw with the words, 'I thought…' 'You thought?' he would yell. 'With what?'"

Despite his prickly nature, he proved to be an excellent, compassionate teacher. Though Fred Merkle's famed error might have cost McGraw and the Giants the 1908 pennant, McGraw never blamed the young first baseman for it, and in fact gave him a raise prior to the 1909 season. Ultimately, Little Napoleon was respected as a canny, businesslike leader who took the game as seriously as anyone. "I suppose it was an important part of McGraw's great capacity for leadership," wrote Heywood Broun, "that he would take kids out of the coal mines and out of the wheat fields and make them walk and talk and chatter and play ball with the look of eagles."

COACHING WISDOM

"What is it? A prolate spheroid, an elongated sphere, one in which the outer leathern casing is drawn tightly over a somewhat smaller rubber tubing. Better to have died as a small boy than to fumble this football."

— John Heisman,
Georgia Tech football coach

"Often an All-American is made by a long run, a weak defense and a poet in the press box."

—Bob Zuppke,
Illinois football coach

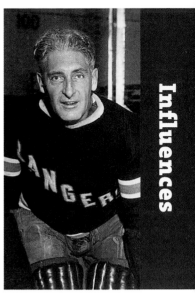

Hockey's First Family

With a loan from their lumber magnate father, **Frank and Lester Patrick** built Canada's first artificial ice rinks, in Vancouver and Victoria, and founded, in 1911, the Pacific Coast Hockey Association. It was in the PCHA, where both served as players, coaches, general managers and owners, that they drew the blueprints for the modern game of hockey. The league eventually was absorbed into the NHL, but its many innovations weren't forgotten. The Patricks introduced blue lines, numbered jerseys, the penalty shot, on-the-fly line substitutions, adding assists to scoring records, the two-referee system, and the concept of the modern playoffs (in which non-champions could still qualify for the postseason), which were inaugurated in the PCHA in 1918.

In short, in the words of Arthur Mann, "practically every forward step taken by professional hockey between 1911 and 1925 can be traced to the keen mind of Frank Patrick and the practical knowledge of Lester, who tried out every rule first to prove its soundness. Between the two, they just about made the game what it was before it hit the big cities below the border."

Lester excelled as a player as well. He lasted a year at McGill University before leaving to play hockey full-time. Playing in 1902 for a local team in Brandon, Manitoba, he was a revolutionary defenseman—among the first to suggest positioning defenders abreast (rather than one in front of the other). He was among the first to visualize the possibilities of a defenseman doing more than defending the attack; he brought the puck into the opponent's zone and scored a goal for Brandon in 1903.

In 1926, the Patricks sold three teams' worth of players from the Western Hockey League (the PCHA's antecedent) to the expanding NHL, at a price of $377,000, then started over again in the NHL. Lester coached the New York Rangers (leading them to a title in their second year of existence) and Frank would coach the Bruins. Over the next few years, as their influence in the league increased, many of their PCHA innovations became part of the NHL rulebook, some against the protestations of hidebound elements in the league. "I believe in keeping the game wide open," said Lester Patrick, when he arrived in New York. "Our followers are entitled to action, not for a few brief moments, but for three full 20-minute periods of a game. The open style of play calls for better stickhandling and speedier skating. What better system could the coaches and managers adopt to preserve and further popularize the fastest game in the world?"

TOP OF THE NEWS: The world of sports in this decade is torn both from the outside, by a Great War, and from within, by a series of ignominious and mysterious circumstances. The world's greatest athlete is stripped of his gold medals. It ends with the White Sox perpetrating the blackest moment in baseball's history. In between, the heavyweight champion loses his title in a knockout, then later claims he threw the fight.

Movies

In the film version of *Take Me Out to the Ballgame*, a baseball fan becomes so ecstatic about his team's win, he leaves the stadium without his wife. The players themselves are becoming celebrities: The Cubs' Frank Chance stars in a romantic drama called *Baseball's Peerless Leader* in 1913.

During the Giants-Athletics World Series of 1913, the Loew's Theaters chain stages evening showings in all 19 of their New York theaters of the silent, unedited film shot at the Series game earlier in the day. As James Mote explains in *Everything Baseball*, "After each 200-foot reel of baseball action was filmed, the reel was rushed from the Polo Grounds to a developing room to be processed in time for showing at seven o'clock that evening—or a mere three hours after the last out had been made. By the time the early reels were being shown in the theaters, the supply of later reels were arriving from the developing room."

Politics and War

The Federal government issues a work-or-fight order to Major League Baseball in July 1918, making players eligible for the draft and forcing the abbreviation of the season, which ends September 2. More than 200 major leaguers fight in the war, and three are killed in action. The great pitcher Christy Mathewson is exposed to poison gas during a drill and dies seven years later, in 1925.

Radio

Marconi's wireless helps save 705 passengers from the Titanic, including Dick Williams and Karl Behr. Williams, who stood in below-freezing water up to his shins for six hours—the doctors advised amputation—would go on to beat Behr in the finals of the 1914 U.S. Tennis Championships at Newport, Rhode Island.

Reading List

Virginia Woolf said of Ring Lardner that his "interest in games has solved one of the most difficult problems of the American writer; it has given him a clue, a center, a meeting place for the divers[e] activities of people whom a vast continent isolates, whom no tradition controls. Games give him what society gives his English brothers." Lardner spends much of the decade covering the society of baseball as a sportswriter in South Bend and Chicago (he would be deeply disillusioned by the Black Sox scandal). In the off-seasons, he writes intelligent, empathetic fiction, based on his experiences with ballplayers. Part of the series originally called *A Busher's Letters Home*, Lardner's short stoy "Alibi Ike" is published in the *Saturday Evening Post* in 1915. That prompts the following year's *You Know Me, Al*, generally regarded as the first adult novel about baseball.

The decade also features another wave of youth fiction, including Christy Mathewson's *Pitcher Pollack*, ghost written by John Wheeler, and Zane Grey's *The Red-Headed Outfield and Other Baseball Stories*.

The Sporting News, the St. Louis newspaper that is the oldest American sports weekly, celebrates its 25th anniversary. TSN began publishing in 1886 and quickly found success as a weekly national newspaper devoted solely to baseball, based largely on the correspondence of beat writers around the country, and the compilation of every one of a season's box scores.

Playing Games

Baseball still dominates, with titles like **World Series Parlor Baseball** promising "all the thrills of real baseball right in your own home. No knowledge of baseball necessary." But other games are trying to replicate the realism and the strategy

Stats

$10,000
Prize money for Ray Harroun, winner of the first Indianapolis 500, in 1911

Points scored by Georgia Tech in the most lopsided football game in college history, a shutout against Cumberland College, in 1916

100
Points scored by Leo Schlick in a St. Viator-Lane College football game in same season; Schlick scored 12 touchdowns and kicked 28 of St. Viator's 29 extra points in the 205-0 rout

51
The number of minutes it took to play the quickest major-league baseball game, a 6-1 Giants win over the Phillies in 1919

7
The number of times Jack Dempsey put Jess Willard on the canvas in the first round of their 1919 bout in which Dempsey took the heavyweight title

18⅓
Innings pitched in relief by George Zabel in a 1915 game for the Cubs; Zabel enters with two outs in first inning, then completes the 19-inning, 4-3 Cubs win over the Dodgers

41
Pounds of pennies donated by Chicago children to help finance the 1916 American Olympic effort

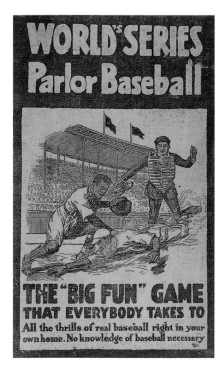

WORLD'S SERIES Parlor Baseball

THE "BIG FUN" GAME THAT EVERYBODY TAKES TO

All the thrills of real baseball right in your own home. No knowledge of baseball necessary

of the game. World Series Baseball Game, from 1916, includes a board with spinners for fielding, hitting and pitching. Play Ball, a couple of years later, features nine spinners for different game situations.

Sounds

By the end of the decade, praises are being sung to Babe Ruth. "Batterin' Babe," words by Jack O'Brien, music

> *"The pressure never lets up. Doesn't matter what you did yesterday. That's history. It's tomorrow that counts. So you worry all the time. It never ends. Baseball is a worrying thing."*
> **—American League pitcher Stan Coveleski**

by Billy Timmins, is typical of the approach: "He hears the call and then the ball is sailin' in the sky—/ A mile away it kills a cow—Wow—" Three songs called "Baseball" are published during the decade, including one that is included in the Broadway musical *Hello, Alexander.*

Fashion

The Giants introduce baseball's first interlocking NY, while a year later, in 1912, the Yankees don pinstripes for the

first time. But it's not an instant victory for understated good taste. In 1916, the Giants wear wide checks and the Dodgers sport a checkerboard uniform design. Principles of design in football uniforms remain rudimentary. But up in the stands, coonskin coats are about to become very popular, as two recently graduated seniors at the University of Illinois organize and then host the first homecoming, October 14, 1910.

Impressions of the '10s

From ESPN's Karl Ravech:

The decade from 1910 to 1919 brought unprecedented growth to baseball, new ballparks in places like Boston (Fenway Park) and Brooklyn (Ebbets Field). There was the formation and ultimate dissolution of the Federal League. As a result of that effort, players began to realize their own value and formed the Fraternity of Professional Base Ball Players. The guys between the lines wanted a greater share of the money being made by the owners.

Ultimately, money provided the grand old game with its first and most enduring black eye: the 1919 World Series. The Chicago White Sox, considered the best team in baseball, had their clubhouse infiltrated by gamblers. Some players were offered money to affect the outcome of the Series. Chicago lost to Cincinnati five games to three.

In the beginning, there were denials. Owners dismissed the notion that such poison could find its way into baseball. Then came the confessions.

Baseball, which never lacked for colorful characters, had always maintained a purity. Now the shine had worn off. A game that needed no fixing turned out to have the ability to be fixed. The game had lost its innocence. It's a cloud that not only baseball, but sports, has never been able to crawl out from under.

1910 **Presidential first pitches**, when William Howard Taft inaugurates an opening-day tradition in Washington.

The All-Professional Stanley Cup.

EXIT **South Side Park in Chicago**, the original home of the White Sox.

The original Comiskey Park in Chicago, with a 2-0 White Sox loss to the Browns.

Most Valuable Player awards in the major leagues, with Frank "Wildfire" Schulte of the Cubs and Ty Cobb of the Tigers taking the honors.

1911 **The Professional Golfers Association tour.**

The Indianapolis 500.

Six-man hockey, replacing the seven-man game.

The two-shot foul in college basketball.

1912 **The six-point touchdown**, with a rule increasing the number from five.

The 100-yard field with 10-yard end zones, standardized in college football.

Fenway Park, with an 11-inning, 7-6 win by the Red Sox over the New York Yankees.

Navin Field (later Briggs Stadium, later Tiger Stadium) with an 11-inning, 6-5, win by the Tigers over Cleveland.

The double-wing formation, introduced by Pop Warner.

1913 **Spring training outside the U.S.**, when the Yankees go to Bermuda.

Ebbets Field, with an exhibition between the Dodgers and Yankees, in which Casey Stengel hits the first home run.

EXIT **Mixed bouts**, fights between black and white boxers, banned by the New York State Athletic Commission.

1914 **The Federal League.**

Wrigley Field, under its first name, Weeghman Park, where the Federal League Chicago Whales played.

1915 **EXIT** **The Federal League.**

1916 **Fans allowed to keep balls** hit in the stands, an innovation of Cubs owner Charles Weeghman.

Uniform numbers in baseball, first worn by the Cleveland Indians on the sleeves of their uniforms.

1917 **The forkball**, introduced by Dave Keefe of the Philadelphia Athletics.

The National Hockey League.

THE 1920s

Fresh from a victory in the Great War, America celebrated its newfound power with a reckless intemperance, and embraced a different breed of sporting heroes, who were celebrated in print and newsreels. Radio broadcasts crackled into the nation's parlors, and sports pages were dominated by mythmakers, making legends of Jones, Tilden and Grange. But in this Golden Age of sports, the nation was held spellbound by the most oversized hero of any age, the man they called The Babe. "There was never anybody close," said his teammate, Joe Dugan. "He was a god."

Living Large

AS THE YEAR 1919 DREW TO A CLOSE the youthful Babe Ruth was sitting on top of the world. He was nearly 25, and at 19 he had still been incarcerated in the Baltimore reform school where he'd spent most of his boyhood. But now he'd been a big-league star for five years. He'd been the best left-handed pitcher in baseball. He'd won 18 games for the Boston Red Sox in 1915, his first full season in the majors, 23 the next year, 24 the year after that. He'd pitched a 14-inning complete game in the 1916 World Series, the longest World Series game ever played, and won it 2–1. He'd won two more World Series games in 1918 and broke Christy Mathewson's Series record for successive scoreless innings pitched.

He had also displayed astonishing ability as a batter. In 1918 he was Boston's cleanup hitter as he both pitched and played the outfield while lifting the Red Sox to their third American League pennant in four years and to their victory in the World Series (the last the Red Sox ever won). After that season Ruth demanded that his salary be doubled, really more than doubled, from $7,000 to $15,000. A war of words followed with the Boston owner, the debt-ridden theatrical producer Harry Frazee, and Ruth had to settle for $10,000 on a three-year contract, still an impressive deal for so young a man at a time when you could buy a comfortable six-room house for $3,000.

Ruth more than earned his salary in 1919. Primarily an outfielder now, he still pitched 133 innings for the Red Sox, filled in at first base and hit home runs as they had never been hit before. By mid-August he had broken the old American League record of 16, and by the end of the season he had an unprecedented 29. The frequency of his home runs awed people. (When Ty Cobb hit .383 in 1919 to lead the American League in batting, he had only one homer all season long.) Ruth led the majors in runs scored, runs batted in, extra-base hits, total bases and slugging average as well as in home runs. He was the player of the year, as he had been in 1918. He told Frazee he wanted his $10,000 contract renegotiated and this time he insisted that it be doubled, to $20,000. Frazee, still mired in debt, said he'd think about it, and Ruth left to spend the off-season in sunny California. He earned money appear-

PREVIOUS PAGES
Headlines. The Babe's cap, with his name on the headband, from the collection of Ruth devotee and onetime Yankee David Wells.

King of the Golden Age. The classic headshot of Ruth, photographed by Charles Conlon, in 1927.

ing in movie shorts and exhibition games, and chased women when he wasn't playing golf. He was having a ball as he waited for the New Year. The 1920s—the Roaring Twenties, the Golden Age of Sport, his time—were about to begin.

Ah, the 1920s, the most outlandish decade of the century, when everything was ballyhooed as the biggest, the best, the most extraordinary—and much of it was. The Twenties began really on November 7, 1918, four days before the end of the first World War, when a rumor spread through the country that peace had been declared. People tumbled cheering into the streets, offices emptied, bands played, strangers hugged and kissed. The news that it was a false report ended the celebration but not the emotion. Four days later when peace really did come—an armistice that began at 11 A.M. on November 11—the party started all over again. This time it lasted for 11 years, until the stock market crash in October 1929 put an end to the era of uproarious madness.

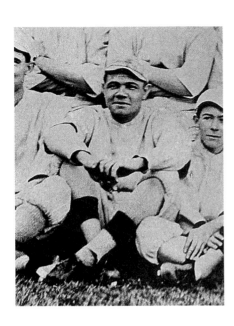

THE GOLDEN AGE OF SPORT that Ruth dominated started a few months after the war, in 1919, when Babe's home runs and the euphoria of peace had baseball fans pouring into major-league parks, with some teams doubling, tripling, even quadrupling attendance from a year earlier. In July a tough young fighter from the mountain states named Jack Dempsey won the heavyweight boxing championship by routing the 6-feet-6-inch, 245-pound Jess Willard, who had won the title from Jack Johnson four years earlier. Dempsey was five inches shorter than Willard and 58 pounds lighter, but he had knocked out 34 opponents in the previous three years, and he *looked* like a fighter: dark-visaged, rough, intense.

The war had engendered in Americans a need for heroes and a desire to be part of the action, however vicariously. When Dempsey destroyed Willard in three rounds, the reaction around the country was exhilarating. Dempsey had been derided during the war for avoiding military service, but the one-sided victory put him well on the way to becoming a national hero. It was a reflection of his newly acquired stature as well as of the racist attitudes of the times that he received little criticism when he announced that he was drawing the color line and would not meet black opponents in the ring. Cynics said this was not so much racial prejudice on Dempsey's part as it was an easy way for him to avoid risking his title against Harry Wills and Sam Langford, two black fighters who were the best heavyweights in the world other than Dempsey—and maybe including Dempsey. Because of their difficulties getting fights with good white boxers, Wills and Langford spent much of the 1920s fighting each other.

Baseball, boxing, and horse racing were the headline sports at the time (college football's biggest days were still ahead), and soon after Dempsey's victory Man o' War galloped to the center of the stage. The two-year-old colt won six straight races, then lost one and became famous. In that race, which was badly handled, Man o' War was left standing at the start, and was hopelessly behind with no chance to win before he could get into stride. His jockey sent him after the other horses anyway and, astonishingly, Man o' War caught and passed all but one of them. He nearly beat that one, too, but was half a length behind at the finish. The colt that beat him was named Upset, which added a piquant touch to the story. When the two met again Man o' War won easily, won twice more that year and in 1920, as a three-year-old, won all eleven of his races before being retired to stud. By that time he had tran-

Team Player. Ruth, in the 1916 team picture of the Red Sox, the year he led the AL in starts (41), shutouts (nine) and ERA (1.75), and held opposing hitters to a .201 average.

Stopper. In those years with the Red Sox, he was becoming the best lefthander in baseball, and an imposing World Series performer. He pitched a 14-inning complete game in the 1916 World Series, winning 2-1. "Pitching just felt like the most natural thing in the world," he once said. "Striking out batters was easy."

scended racing. Everyone knew Man o' War. He had won 20 of his 21 races, and the one defeat was a fluke. For the next 50 years, until Secretariat came along, Man o' War was the standard that other horses were measured against.

Bobby Jones was another new star. Only 17 in 1919, he caught the nation's eye when he reached the finals of the U.S. amateur golf championship. In 1920, at 18, he played in the U.S. Open for the first time and finished a strong eighth, only four strokes behind the winner. He was fifth in 1921, and after that finished first or second in the Open eight times in nine years before he retired from competitive golf at the age of 28. Even though he was an amateur throughout his career Jones overshadowed such dominant professionals as Walter Hagen and Gene Sarazen. His sweep of the four major championships in 1930, his last year of competition, was the perfect postscript to the Golden Age of Sport.

Ruth, Dempsey, Man o' War, Jones and Big Bill Tilden, who moved to the top of the tennis world in 1920. Tilden won both the U.S. and Wimbledon singles—becoming the first American man to win at Wimbledon—and excited the patriotic fervor still rampant in postwar America by leading the U.S. to a 5–0 sweep of defending champion Australia in Davis Cup play, at that time the most important tennis competition in the world. Tilden repeated his U.S.–Wimbledon sweep in 1921, went on to win the U.S. singles title six years in a row and powered America to seven straight triumphs in the Davis Cup. Even for people who never saw a tennis match Tilden was a national icon. (His homosexuality, which would have made him anathema at the time, did not become public knowledge until many years later.)

MEANTIME, THERE WAS RUTH ENJOYING HIMSELF in California, while in the wintry East, Frazee worked out what to do. Frazee knew the owners of the New York Yankees, Colonel Jacob Ruppert and Colonel Tillinghast Huston, whom he approached with a business proposition. At that time the Yankees weren't much. In the 17 years of their existence they had never won a pennant, and they had finished better than fourth only three times. But their wealthy new owners were trying to improve the team, and Frazee knew they'd be interested in what he had to propose. Would they like to buy Babe Ruth?

They would indeed. Ruppert and Huston paid Frazee $100,000 for Ruth, double the previous high for a ballplayer, and gave the Red Sox owner a $300,000 mortgage loan on Fenway Park, the Boston team's home field. The only snag was Ruth's salary demands. Before the deal was finalized the Yankees sent manager Miller Huggins all the way to California (by train; no air travel then) to talk to Ruth. The Babe was playing golf in Griffith Park in Los Angeles when Huggins caught up to him. Verbal sparring followed. Huggins said the Yankees couldn't pay what Ruth was demanding. Ruth said they'd better, or he'd quit. He could make as much money barnstorming the provinces. When the argument was settled, Ruth had what he wanted. The Yankees agreed to increase his salary to $20,000 a year, the highest a player had ever received to that point, and to give him a $1,000 bonus for signing. On January 5, 1920, the Yankees made the stunning announcement: Babe Ruth, the home-run king, was coming to New York! Eleven days later Prohibition went into effect, and the Twenties moved into high gear.

Ruth captivated New York, put his indelible imprint on it. He lapped up the city,

The Bambino's Bambina.
Ruth, holding his daughter Dorothy, outside the Yankee dugout.

partying hard and belting home runs nearly twice as often as he had in 1919. In 1920 he hit his 30th in July, his 40th in August, and finished the season with 54. In 1921 he was even better, turning in the most dominating season any batter has ever had. He hit 59 homers, 35 more than his closest challenger. His slugging average of .846 was 240 points higher than the second man, his 457 total bases almost a hundred higher. He drove in 171 runs and scored 177, far more than his closest rivals. With all this slugging, he still batted .378, third in the league and only 11 behind Ty Cobb. The Yankees won the American League pennant, their first ever, and repeated in 1922 and 1923.

It seemed unbelievable. Everybody was talking about Babe Ruth. His reach extended far beyond the everyday baseball fan to people who had only the most marginal interest in the game, or even in American sports. Italian-American immigrants in New York, caught in the excitement of the almost daily home run, would ask if the Yankees' baby, the *bambino*, had hit one that day. Nickname-happy sportswriters picked up "Bambino" and blithely bestowed on Ruth the title of the visiting Akhoond, or Sultan, of Swat, a section of India now part of Pakistan. "Babe," the "Bambino," the "Sultan of Swat"—the nicknames added to the sense of kinship Americans had for Ruth. Everyone felt close to the gregarious Babe, who waved to the crowd and grinned and chatted, signed autographs and was always in the public eye. He lived with a flair. When the talented but colorless Roger Maris was on his way to breaking Ruth's home run record in 1961, a veteran baseball man named Jimmy Dykes said, "Maris is a fine ballplayer, but I can't imagine him driving down Broadway in a low-slung convertible wearing a coonskin coat."

People who had never been to a big-league game jammed into ballparks to see Ruth, to bask in his aura, to watch him hit home runs. The Yankees' attendance in 1920 soared to 1,289,000, the first time a big-league team had drawn a million fans in one season; it was 40 percent above the old major-league record. Attendance went up in every big-league city except Boston (no more Babe) and Detroit, which was beset by labor unrest. Ruth was a big reason, but it was more than just the Babe's presence. It was the general upsurge in slugging that he triggered. A 2–1 game is esthetically pleasing but 9–8 games are more fun. Batting averages soared, runs came in clusters, home runs flew out of ballparks. When Ruth hit 29 in 1919, only five other players had hit as many as 10; but in 1920, when he hit 54, 15 others had 10 or more, and two surpassed the American League record the Babe had broken a year earlier. In 1921 five players other than Ruth hit more than 20, and in 1922 two hit more than 30 and one hit 42. The dam had burst. "I swing big," Ruth said, and soon everyone was swinging big, aiming at the fences, going for the downs, *whacking* the ball. Whether the ball was juiced up is still debatable, but officials helped by banning trick pitches (the spitter, the shine ball, the emery ball) and by insisting that during a game clean baseballs replaced dirty, discolored ones that were harder to see and therefore harder to hit.

Ruth had changed baseball, and people, old fans and new, liked what he created. The upsurge in interest was vitally important because, just before the end of the

Going Yard.
The classic swing, in a 1930 exhibition game at League Park in San Antonio.

1920 season, the shocking news broke that eight Chicago White Sox players had been accused of throwing the 1919 World Series to the Cincinnati Reds. A jury refused to find them guilty in 1921, but the newly appointed commissioner of baseball, Judge Kenesaw M. Landis, banned the eight players for life and they went down in baseball lore as the Black Sox.

How badly was baseball hurt by the scandal of the Black Sox? Attendance fell sharply in 1921—down nine percent in the American League, mostly in Chicago and Ruthless Boston, and six percent in the National League, mostly in disillusioned Cincinnati. But it went up in 1922, even though Ruth fell from grace that season. The Babe had a new five-year contract at a dizzying $52,000 a year, but he incurred the wrath of commissioner Landis by defying a rule about off-season barnstorming. He was suspended for six weeks at the beginning of the season, fought with fans and umpires and teammates after his return, was suspended four more times before the season was over, and lost the home-run title. It was a sour year for Ruth, but not for the attendance he had stimulated. His Yankees won the pennant again, and attendance generally went up and stayed up, for the most part, for the rest of the Twenties.

AMERICA WAS IN A PARTYING MOOD, enchanted by many lively things in and out of sport. The old, established football schools were challenged by the rise of Notre Dame under its colorful, baldheaded coach, Knute Rockne. Rockne's undefeated, untied 1924 team had a superb backfield that the revered sportswriter Grantland Rice indelibly labeled the Four Horsemen, after a Rudolph Valentino movie called *The Four Horsemen of the Apocalypse* (War, Famine, Pestilence and Death). Lyric sportswriting was characteristic of the era and added to the fun.

Prohibition's ban on alcohol was in full swing, but so were speakeasies, where you could get an illicit drink (Ruth knew many) and hip flasks, and lurid stories of bootleggers and rum runners and gangsters. Scandal, always fascinating, erupted in Washington where officials in President Warren G. Harding's administration were accused, tried and found guilty of financial corruption. Fads swept the country. The crossword puzzle arrived. A game called Mah-Jongg, brought back from China by an oil-company executive, became extraordinarily popular. Contract bridge superseded auction bridge and lasted after Mah-Jongg faded. A New Jersey minister and his paramour, his church's choir leader, were found shot to death on an abandoned farm, and the minister's wife was accused of the double murder. Her sensational trial and eventual acquittal—known as the Hall-Mills case—attracted national attention that rivaled that of O. J. Simpson 70 years later. There were other fascinating murders. There was the Scopes "monkey" trial in Tennessee. There were juicy sex scandals in Hollywood in this final decade of silent movies. There was the new phenomenon of radio broadcasting, nonexistent when Ruth was sold to the Yankees but exploding into prominence soon after. Championship fights and World Series games were broadcast for the first time, arousing even more interest in sports. Radio sets sold like hot dogs, and radio stocks doubled, tripled, quadrupled in value. The stock market was rising like a hot-air balloon.

Jack Dempsey was still in sharp focus. He knocked out two challengers in 1920, and in the summer of 1921, after a firestorm of ballyhoo that attracted 91,000 people to the fight in Jersey City, he knocked out Georges Carpentier of France. Dempsey was

The Sultan. The mighty swing was the stuff of myth. "He hits a ball harder and further than any man I ever saw," said Bill Dickey.

idle for two years after that, but in September 1923, in one of the most memorable bouts in boxing history, he knocked out a powerful Argentinean named Luis Angel Firpo in the second round, after being punched out of the ring by Firpo in the first round, a moment immortalized by the American painter George Bellows. Dempsey didn't fight again for another three years, until September 1926, when he lost his heavyweight title to Gene Tunney, but the war with Firpo made him a boxing immortal.

And Ruth bounced back in 1923 and 1924, winning the home-run race in both years. In 1924 he hit .378 to win the batting championship, too, outdistancing future Hall of Famers Tris Speaker, Harry Heilmann and Cobb by more than 30 points. Off the field Ruth was having a great time. He epitomized the slam-bang Twenties, an era crystallized in the image of the typical college football fan of the day: an enthusiastic alumnus in a Ruthian coonskin coat waving a college pennant while sharing sips of applejack from a hip flask with his date. Always defiant of authority, Ruth was at home in a society that embraced such boisterous, carefree attitudes. Women abandoned long hair for the boyish "bob," lifted their ankle-length skirts until hemlines were at the knee, applied lipstick and makeup that only "painted women" had used before. They wore flesh-colored stockings instead of sober gray or black, smoked cigarettes and danced the daring "shimmy" and the wild "Charleston." Young people in general were less deferential to their elders, listened to the loud new music called jazz, took "joyrides" in automobiles and became known as "flaming youth." They read with glee a novel about themselves called *This Side of Paradise*, published in 1920 by the 24-year-old F. Scott Fitzgerald. Ruth and Fitzgerald never met, but Babe reveled in the world Fitzgerald wrote about. He, like the new women, loved jazz (he and Bix Beiderbecke, the jazz cornetist, drank together on occasion), and even carried a wind-up Victrola (an early record player) on road trips. And he was a joyrider of dubious distinction, once overturning his touring car on a road south of Philadelphia and frequently being nabbed by motorcycle cops for speeding in New York City.

BUT IT CAUGHT UP TO RUTH IN 1925. He was breaking up with his first wife and carousing and drinking so much that he collapsed in spring training and had to undergo surgery for an abdominal ulcer. He was out of the lineup until June, played poorly after his return, defied his manager, was suspended, and was fined the then astounding amount of $5,000 (many major leaguers earned less for a full season). Fred Lieb, a New York sportswriter, wrote, "It is doubtful that Ruth again will be the superstar he was from 1919 through 1924. Next year Ruth will be 32, and at 32 the Babe will be older than Eddie Collins, Walter Johnson and Ty Cobb at that age. Babe has lived a much more strenuous life."

However, Ruth reformed again, this time for good. He still had fun, but it was tempered with a somewhat more sober wisdom. When Red Grange, the football star, was introduced to Babe after Grange turned professional at the end of the 1925 college season, Ruth gave the younger man some advice. "Kid," he said, "don't ever forget two things I'm going to tell you. One, don't believe everything that's written about you. Two, don't pick up too many checks."

During Ruth's 1925 debacle the Yankees fell to seventh place, but in 1926 the rejuvenated slugger hit 46 home runs and led the New Yorkers to the American League

Going Down Swinging.
Gehrig holds his ears while Ruth, as usual, makes an unholy racket.

championship for the fourth time in six years. A year later, now making $70,000, the home run king was challenged by his young teammate Lou Gehrig, who matched Ruth homer for homer from April through August before the Babe pulled away with a burst of 17 homers in September. He finished with a record 60, a peak reached only once (by Maris) in the next 70 years before Mark McGwire and Sammy Sosa broke new ground in 1998. With Ruth and Gehrig leading the way, the Yankees won 110 games in 1927, took the pennant by 19 games, swept the World Series in four straight, and were acclaimed the greatest baseball team ever.

Everyone seemed to be the greatest in the 1920s. The great Yankees won again in 1928 as Ruth hit 54 home runs, and they swept the Series for a second straight year. There was Johnny Weissmuller, a big, handsome fellow from Illinois, who turned competitive swimming into a glamorous sport. At 100 yards (and 100 meters) Weissmuller was supreme, the best in the world from 1922 to 1928. He lowered the world record for 100 yards five times, and his ultimate best, 51 seconds flat, remained unbroken for 16 years. Weissmuller won Olympic gold medals in 1924 and 1928, and was so unreservedly admired that he became a movie actor and starred in *Tarzan of the Apes* opposite Mia Farrow's mother, Maureen O'Sullivan.

Another swimmer, a sturdy young American freestyle star named Gertrude Ederle, who had won U.S. championships at 220 and 440 yards, put on a skin-tight bathing suit, smeared her body with grease to protect herself from the cold and swam across the English Channel. That created a sensation, because while five men in the previous 50 years had swum the Channel, Ederle was the first woman. Better than that, she swam the Channel two hours faster than any of the men had. Only 19, she was suddenly famous, and when she returned home to New York City she was given a ticker-tape parade up Broadway.

Helen Wills challenged France's Suzanne Lenglen, the longtime Wimbledon champion, for the unofficial title of Queen of Tennis. She lost a showdown with Lenglen but succeeded to the throne when the Frenchwoman turned professional in 1926, and after that Wills dominated the women's game. When the imperious Lenglen was signed by Charles C. ("Cash and Carry") Pyle, the promoter who guided Red Grange into professional football (he helped Grange make a small fortune), she insisted on being paid $50,000 up front. It was a gamble for Pyle but he paid her, and her tour of the United States was such a smashing success that Pyle made a bundle and gave Lenglen a $25,000 bonus.

There was Tommy Hitchcock, a socialite polo player. Polo was a posh sport, played and watched by a relative handful of people, but the common herd became fascinated by it in the 1920s when the United States, led by Hitchcock, defeated Great Britain in three highly publicized international matches. Scott Fitzgerald is said to have modeled the character of Tom Buchanan in his 1926 novel, *The Great Gatsby*, on Hitchcock. Paavo Nurmi, the superb Finnish distance runner who won nine Olympic gold medals during the 1920s, toured America in 1926, running in indoor track meets and beating everyone, and almost lost his amateur standing because of charges that he had been paid appearance money under the table, a common practice with amateur athletes in that cheerfully hypocritical age.

Home Life.
Ruth with his first wife Helen, whom he married in 1914.

Through all this, Ruth was riding high. Reformed or not, he still had a wonderful time. He continued to frequent his favorite speakeasies and do business with the neighborhood bootlegger. He played golf with Al Smith, the Democratic candidate for president in 1928, and caused a furor when he refused at first to pose for a picture with Herbert Hoover, the Republican candidate. He partied with Douglas Fairbanks and Mary Pickford, the most glamorous movie couple of the Twenties. He fell in love with a beautiful young widow named Claire Hodgson, a model and sometime chorus girl, and married her before the decade was out. The adjective "Ruthian," meaning outsize, heroic, grand, entered the language. The 1920s belonged to the Babe.

D EMPSEY LOST HIS HEAVYWEIGHT TITLE IN 1926, fought Tunney again a year later and lost again, but reinvigorated the loyalty of his fans by throwing a ferocious punch in the seventh that sent Tunney sprawling to the canvas for the famous Long Count knockdown. Fourteen seconds elapsed before Tunney rose to his feet, but then the champion held Dempsey off, continued to outbox him, and won the decision. There was little doubt that in their two bouts Tunney was the superior fighter, but the Long Count fiasco left many with the feeling that Dempsey had been robbed, that he had really knocked Tunney out, that he was still the champion. He was the hero, and while he was soon finished as a fighter, he remained a hero for the rest of his life. To much of the country, Jack Dempsey was always the champ.

Still, Dempsey's departure from the heights signaled a change in the Twenties. Tunney may have been an admirable fighter, but he was a bland champion who gave up the title a year later and retired from the ring. The aging Tilden ran into a quartet of French players (Rene Lacoste, Henri Cochet, Jean Borotra and Jacques Brugnon) who won everything in tennis in the latter years of the decade. The youthful Jones was looking toward retirement. Even though Charles Augustus Lindbergh delighted the country and the world by flying solo across the Atlantic in 1927, things generally weren't quite as much fun. The thrill of defying Prohibition was turning to a guilty uneasiness as crude mobsters like Al Capone turned rum-running and bootlegging into a dirty, killing business. Short skirts and hip flasks were beginning to look cheap. The scandals and murders were leaving a bad taste. A campaign to save Sacco and Vanzetti, immigrant anarchists who had been convicted of murder, failed and the two were executed. The stock market was still booming, but how long could it keep going up? The ineffective Hoover replaced the ineffective Calvin Coolidge in the White House. The charming but crooked Jimmy Walker was mayor of New York.

Yet the fabulous decade still had Babe Ruth. Although the Yankees dropped to second place in 1929, Ruth hit 46 homers to lead the major leagues for the tenth time. He hit more than half of his career home runs after 1925. He was still the king, still the most popular player, still the highest-salaried player, in the game. He'd been sitting on top of the world when the decade began, and he was up there when it ended, lord of all he surveyed. More than any other athlete, more than any other American, he personified the 1920s—loud, brassy, extroverted, troubled, overachieving, electric, unforgettable.

He hit his final homer of the Golden Age late in September 1929. Then his season ended, his glorious decade done. Eighteen days later the stock market blew.

The King and His Farewell.
Ruth's number was retired
June 13, 1948 at Yankee Stadium.
He died two months later.

LOU GEHRIG
Pride of the Yankees

The streak, inevitably, overshadowed the man. It remained mystical, elusive—that imposing number of 2,130 consecutive games played—a testament to the man's resilience but not a window to his remarkable character and talent. As brilliant a career as he had, it is Lou Gehrig's lot to be overshadowed, first by his teammate, then by the classic franchise for which he played, then by his own remarkable consistency and finally by the stoic heroism he displayed facing a disease that now bears his name.

"Let's face it, I'm not a headline guy," said Gehrig in the early Thirties, after he'd become established in the public mind as the quiet, well-muscled, even-tempered complement to the traveling circus that was Babe Ruth. "I always know that as long as I'm following the Babe to the plate, I could have gone up there and stood on my head. No one would have noticed the difference. When the Babe was through swinging, whether he hit one or fanned, nobody paid any attention to the next hitter."

So despite being one of the finest players of his era, hitting at least .300 his first 12 full seasons in the majors, driving in more than 100 runs 13 years in a row, hitting 23 career grand slams (a record that still stands), Gehrig was forever a supporting act. Even his greatest moments were invariably eclipsed: When he hit two crucial homers in Game 3 of the '32 World Series, few noticed—that was the day Ruth hit his "called shot" to center field. Earlier that season, Gehrig became the first player of the century to hit four homers in a game. But the next morning's papers led with the news that John McGraw had resigned as manager of the Giants.

The pitchers knew him well, understood the danger he presented with his strong, square stance at the plate and his clutch instinct for bringing in runners. While Ruth was hitting tape-measure moon shots, Gehrig became known for frighteningly hard line drives that moved like rifle shots across the outfield.

He upheld that level of consistency while playing in every Yankee game from June 1, 1925, through April 30, 1939, a string of 2,130 consecutive games that made a legend out of Gehrig and trivia answers out of Wally Pipp (whom Gehrig replaced in 1925) and Babe Dahlgren (who replaced Gehrig in 1939). When he pulled himself out of the lineup on May 2, he was still in the dark about the debilitating disease—later diagnosed as amyotrophic lateral sclerosis, a hardening of the spinal cord—that would kill him two years later.

The bad news came later that month, and when the

GEHRIG:
"THE LUCKIEST MAN ON THE FACE OF THE EARTH"

JONES:
"GOLF SEEMED TO HAVE BEEN INVENTED JUST FOR HIM"

Yankees held a special day for Gehrig on July 4, 1939, they created the sport's single most sentimental moment. Between games of a doubleheader, his teammates from the 1927 Yankees, including Ruth, came out to greet him. A few moments later, choking back tears, Gehrig pronounced himself "the luckiest man on the face of the Earth." It turned out to be baseball's first old-timers' day, beginning a tradition of the sport honoring its past heroes.

And when a healthy Cal Ripken Jr. finally approached and then broke the record 56 years later, Gehrig's life and feat were examined in a fresh light. Out of the shadows finally, "The Iron Man" could be appreciated for what he was: One of the greatest players of any generation.

BOBBY JONES
"In its proper place"

Nearly 70 years after his retirement, Bobby Jones is still the leader in the clubhouse, his greatest accomplishment remaining unmatched.

A lawyer by profession, Jones spent his entire career as an amateur, entering only six or seven tournaments annually. Yet in 1930, he won all four major championships, a sweep never completed before or since. Those four titles—the British Amateur, British Open, U.S. Open and U.S. Amateur—made up golf's original Grand Slam. Golf historian Charles Price wrote, "Golf seemed to have been invented just for him to come along and show us how well it could be played."

Wearing a white shirt and necktie, swinging hickory-shafted clubs, with a cigarette often hanging from his lips, Jones won 13 of the 21 major championships he entered between 1923 and 1930, finishing first or second in the U.S. Open eight out of nine years, dating back to 1922. In the process, he influenced middle-class Americans to take this country-club sport seriously. Then, following the Slam, he retired at age 28, walking away from the pressure and "leaving golf in its proper place, a means of obtaining recreation and enjoyment."

Though he was a stocky 5 feet, 7½ inches and 165 pounds, Jones had a graceful, self-taught swing that did not require much practice to maintain, yet made him one of the longest drivers of his era. On the greens with Calamity Jane, his trusty blade putter, Jones was a wizard under pressure. In 1929, having blown a six-shot lead during the final six holes of the U.S. Open, he made a wicked 14-foot side-hill putt on the 72nd hole to salvage a tie for first place with Al Espinosa, whom he then defeated by 23 strokes in a 36-hole playoff.

He later enabled others to enjoy the game, helping design the Augusta National Golf Club in Augusta, Georgia, and founding the Masters tournament, held there since 1934. He was first diagnosed with a spinal disorder in the late Forties, and died in 1971. Though Jones was never accused of racism, the tournament he created, at the course he designed, was considered the last bastion of the lily-white golf establishment. Lee Elder finally became the first black man to compete at Augusta, in 1975, having qualified by winning a PGA Tour event, the 1974 Monsanto Open.

Ultimately, Jones was golf's most celebrated gentleman, known for his courtesy, wit and charm. Today the United States Golf Association's sportsmanship award is given in his honor, but he did not come to that status easily. At the 1921 British Open, a 19-year-old Jones tore up his third-round scorecard and walked off the course at the 11th hole, disgusted with his 46 shots on the front nine. Around the same time, he injured a spectator with a thrown club. Later, after his transformation, Jones was often commended for assessing himself penalty strokes. He rejected the flattery. "You might as well praise a man for not robbing a bank," he said.

—*Mark Rosner*

HAROLD "RED" GRANGE
The Galloping Ghost

In the 1920s, when college football was one of the two major sports on the American landscape, Harold "Red" Grange dominated it like no one before, or perhaps since.

Changing direction with a fluid grace previously unseen on a football field and leaving numerous defenders grasping vainly at the orange number 77 on the back of his blue Illinois jersey, Grange had a glorious college career, highlighted by what might have been the greatest day in college football history. By 1925, he was so famous that he helped pave the way for emergence of pro football as a major spectator sport.

On October 18, 1924, the junior Grange led Illinois into the year-old Memorial Stadium, formally dedicated that day. The matchup, between undefeated powers Illinois and Michigan, held special significance since the rivals hadn't played since 1922, and both had gone undefeated in 1923. Grange returned the opening kickoff 95 yards, then scored on 67-, 56- and 44-yard runs from scrimmage—all in the first 12 minutes of the game. At that point, coach Bob Zuppke rested him, but Grange would return in the second half, running for a fifth touchdown and passing for a sixth one, during a day in which he accounted for 402 yards total offense. Reminiscing about Grange's winding, S-patterned broken-field runs, Zuppke wrote later, "Red had that indefinable something that the hunted wild animal has—uncanny timing and the big brown eyes of a royal buck."

As Grange's national renown grew, Grantland Rice conjured up a vision of the Illinois back as the "Galloping Ghost," and for the next couple of years, he was perhaps the biggest star in American sports, a newsreel fixture who captured the national imagination and appeared on the

GRANGE: "THAT INDEFINABLE SOMETHING THAT THE WILD ANIMAL HAS"

DEMPSEY: "THE GYMS WERE FULL OF FIGHTERS BOBBING AND WEAVING LIKE DEMPSEY"

cover of *Time* magazine ("Eel-hipped runnagade").

A day after his final varsity game in 1925, Grange and his agent, Champaign theater owner Charles C. "Cash & Carry" Pyle signed a deal with George Halas and the Chicago Bears. Near the end of that season with the Bears, Grange and the team went on a grueling East Coast tour, playing eight games in 12 days. That, and subsequent exhibitions, drew greater crowds than ever before for pro football (65,000 at the Polo Grounds, 75,000 at the Los Angeles Coliseum), making Grange a rich man. Measuring his galvanizing impact on the world of sport, Damon Runyon got it just about right when he wrote that Red Grange "is three or four men and a horse rolled into one. He is Jack Dempsey, Babe Ruth, Al Jolson, Paavo Nurmi and Man o' War."

In 1926, Pyle formed a league around Grange; the first American Football League (his team drew well, but the league folded quickly). A year later, Grange returned to the NFL as part of the New York Yankees, where a knee injury reduced him, in his words, to an "ordinary runner." But the final irony was sweet: He returned to the Bears in 1929 and became a defensive standout. His solo, game-saving, chest-high tackle of halfback Dale Burnett at the end of the 1933 NFL Championship Game was described by both Halas and Giants coach Steve Owen as the best defensive play they'd ever seen.

JACK DEMPSEY
The Gentleman Pugilist

Rising out of Colorado mining camp brawls and hobo jungles into the rough-and-tumble prizefighting world of the 1920s, Jack Dempsey became a superstar of the Jazz Age. The scowling heavyweight held the title from 1919 to 1926, participated in boxing's first million-dollar gate and transformed its dominant style. In the 1930s, remembered trainer Eddie Futch, "the gyms were full of fighters bobbing and weaving like Dempsey." The 6-foot-1-inch, 185-pounder retired with a 60-6-8 record, and a 1950 AP poll named him the greatest fighter of the half century.

Lean, square-jawed and ruggedly handsome, the 24-year-old devastated the hulking defending champion, Jess Willard, who couldn't answer the bell for the fourth round, on July 4, 1919. Two years and two title defenses later, Dempsey—exonerated, but still thought of as a war "slacker" for avoiding the draft due to family obligations—fought "Gorgeous" Georges Carpentier, a French war hero. The four-round knockout netted a record $1.8-million gate before more than 80,000, including John D. Rockefeller, Henry Ford, Al Jolson and George M. Cohan.

On September 14, 1923, the champion defeated Argentinian Luis Firpo in a bout described by Red Smith as among the "most wildly exciting" title fights ever. Dempsey knocked Firpo down seven times in the first, but went down twice himself—most memorably through the ropes and onto the press tables. Painter George Bellows immortalized the moment on a well-known canvas. The challenger lasted less than a minute of the second round.

Dempsey's 10-round loss to Gene Tunney on September 23, 1926—the first transfer of the heavyweight title by decision—actually heightened his wild popularity. But it was the rematch loss a year later in Chicago's Soldier Field, known as the Battle of the Long Count, that cemented his reputation as one of the greats. In the seventh, Dempsey knocked the savvy title holder down with his signature: a vicious left hook. But he did not go immediately to a neutral corner as Illinois rules specified. Referee Dave Barry turned his back to the dazed, supine Tunney, pointing Dempsey toward the far corner. Ringside observers estimate that Tunney was on the canvas five seconds before the referee started the count. Tunney rose at the count of nine to win a 10-round decision, and maintained later that he could have gotten up earlier. Dempsey always courteously believed him. "Dempsey was jobbed," said his trainer, Leo P. Flynn, after the fight. "Dempsey will fight him again, and knock him out again, just the way he knocked him out tonight." But there was never a rematch. Dempsey flirted with comebacks, but he never fought competitively.

Legendary trainer Ray Arcel described Dempsey as "a rough and ready guy, a tiger in the ring." Others called him a cobra. Grantland Rice declared him "the finest gentleman" he'd met during 50 years of sportswriting. Certainly Dempsey embodied many of the qualities of sport's Golden Age.

Though nicknamed the "Manassa Mauler," he performed on Broadway and visited Calvin Coolidge in the White House. He waded ashore at Okinawa with the Coast Guard in World War II, and later opened an eponymous Manhattan restaurant, where he posed for innumerable photographs with any asker—smiling, though almost always with his guard up.

—David Zivan

BILL TILDEN
The Beauty of the Game

The best tennis player of the first half of the century was also the most temperamental, a high-strung iconoclast whose sensibilities were rooted in the vanity of the theater. Possessed of a high carriage, imposingly broad shoulders, and a lean, strapping frame, Bill Tilden was at once more powerful and more graceful than his opponents. His flat first serve was the most feared of his generation, and his kicking second serve, "the American twist," was just as lethal. But it was in the physical chess match of the rally that the 6-foot-2-inch Tilden really showed his superiority, with a delicate touch, a masterly control of spin, and a brilliant sense of strategic perspective. "In any match between the

TILDEN: "THE PLAYER OWES AS MUCH TO THE GALLERY AS THE ACTOR OWES THE AUDIENCE"

perfect baseline player and the perfect net rusher," he once said, "I would take the baseliner every time." The implication was understood: He was the perfect baseline player.

The son of a Germantown, Pennsylvania, textile executive, Tilden was an upper-crust athlete who bloomed late, but his dominance came suddenly and lasted for much of the 1920s. After his weak backhand was exposed by rival "Little Bill" Johnston in the 1919 National finals, Tilden spent the winter practicing on a friend's indoor clay court in Newport, Rhode Island, emerging with a fierce topspin backhand that was unsurpassed. And in 1920, at age 27, he began a remarkable streak of six straight U.S. championships, and a leading role in the record seven straight American victories in Davis Cup play. He won back-to-back Wimbledons twice, in 1920-21 and 1929-30.

Though the expression is used frequently in sports, it's rare at the championship level that an athlete can actually "toy" with an opponent; yet Tilden regularly played devious cat-and-mouse games with his overmatched foils. At the 1920 Wimbledon final against Australia's Gerald Patterson, Tilden lost the first set 6–2, and then winked at the actress Peggy Wood, his guest sitting in the friends' box, before proceeding to thrash Patterson over the next three sets. (He had done the same thing against Patterson earlier that year in Davis Cup play, dropping the first set 7-5, before reeling off three straights sets to win the match.) "The player owes as much to the gallery as the actor owes the audience," he once said.

He went pro in 1930 and made a fortune, which he spent just as quickly, traveling the world, lounging with movie stars, living the high life. For all the good times, his later adult years were marked by the unkeepable secret of his homosexuality (he was imprisoned twice for soliciting minors) and a profound loneliness. Since his college days, he'd been without a family, finding occasional solace in a series of alliances that were forbidden at the time. So he died a broken man, both penniless and discredited, his portrait removed from the very walls of the Germantown Cricket Club where he learned the game.

But nothing could obscure Big Bill's true legacy, as the aristocrat who brought the elitist game to the masses. Franklin P. Adams wrote that Tilden "was more of an artist than nine-tenths of the artists I know. It is the beauty of the game that Tilden loves; it is the chase always, rather than the quarry."

Down Not Out: Dempsey came off the floor—almost literally—to KO Firpo.

BOXING

Four Minutes of Fury

The most furious heavyweight title fight of the century occurred September 14, 1923, in front of a sold-out crowd of 90,000 at the Polo Grounds. It was a battle between revered champion Jack Dempsey ("The Manassa Mauler") and Argentine challenger Luis Firpo ("The Wild Bull of the Pampas"), and in the four minutes of action, both men lived up to their nicknames.

Writing in *The New York Times*, Elmer Davis noted that, "From the first instant, the fight had been a fight, a fierce exchange of wallops unbroken by any strategic maneuvers." The bruising Dempsey, giving up a 24-pound weight advantage, slipped coming out of his corner, and was knocked down five seconds into the fight. But he recovered quickly and began pounding the Argentine relentlessly. He knocked Firpo down seven times in the first round, neglecting the pre-fight instructions to return to a neutral corner after a knockdown. As soon as Firpo regained his feet, Dempsey would pour in again. Late in the first round, after Firpo got up from the seventh knockdown, he anticipated Dempsey's rush and caught him on the point of the chin with a freight-train right, which lifted Dempsey off his feet and sent him tumbling back through the ropes, onto the press row and the first row of spectator seats. Sportswriters broke Dempsey's fall, and helped him back into the ring at the count of nine. But as the bell rang to end the round, the champion looked hurt, and in trouble.

"I was badly dazed," he'd recall later. "I was seeing double. When the bell rang, I went out and hit every Firpo I saw." He returned to knock Firpo out in the second, in his fifth and final successful title defense.

Dempsey later called it the "toughest fight I ever had—that giant was a real bull." Though the "long count" fight in Dempsey's rematch with Gene Tunney is better known, Dempsey-Firpo was held in higher regard by observers who saw both. Davis described it as "about the greatest fight in the history of pugilism." In a 1950 Associated Press poll, the Dempsey-Firpo fight was voted the most dramatic sports event of the first half century.

BASEBALL

1926 World Series Cardinals vs. Yankees

■ The retooled Yankees had bounced back from a dismal 1925, and won the American League in a rout. With Babe Ruth leading the attack, the Bronx Bombers took a 3-2 Series lead over player-manager Rogers Hornsby's Cardinals. But the Cards won Game 6, as Grover Cleveland Alexander, by now 39 years old, won his second game of the Series, a 10-2 complete-game drubbing of the Yankees. (Alexander had been waived by the Cubs earlier in the season after clashing with manager Joe McCarthy, who in the Thirties would move to New York and help perpetuate the Yankee dynasty.)

A day later, with the Cardinals clinging to a 3-2 lead in the seventh inning of Game 7, Hornsby called again on Alexander (who, some teammates insisted, was hung over from a long night of carousing). Rookie Tony Lazzeri was up with two outs and the bases loaded when Alexander was summoned. "Alex, we're in a tough spot," Hornsby told the pitcher when he arrived at the mound. "There's no place to put Lazzeri." "I'll be damned if you're not right," said Alexander. "I reckon I better strike him out." Which he did (though not before Lazzeri poked a 1–1 pitch just foul down the left–field line). Alexander stayed in the rest of the game. With two outs in the ninth, he walked Babe Ruth—who'd already homered four times in the Series. When Ruth tried a surprise steal of second, NL MVP Bob O'Farrell gunned him down. The Cardinals had won their first world championship.

COLLEGE FOOTBALL

1922 Princeton-Chicago

■ Chicago dominated this battle of undefeated intersectional rivals through the first three quarters, in front of a sold-out home crowd of 32,000 at Stagg Field. With the Maroons leading 18-7 early in the fourth quarter, Princeton's Howdy Gray returned a fumble recovery 40 yards to bring the Tigers within 18-14. With five minutes left, they went up 21-18 on a fourth-down plunge by Henry Crum at the Chicago goal line. But Chicago wasn't finished, and drove to first-and-goal at the Princeton six with two minutes remaining. Three carries by John Thomas, who'd already scored three touchdowns, brought Chicago to the Princeton one. But he was stopped on fourth down by Harland "Pink" Baker, who because of a blown assignment was left unblocked. "There was so much yelling and screaming going on, and Chicago's linemen didn't shift properly," recalled Princeton lineman Don Griffin. The Tigers went on to their first unbeaten season since 1903.

HOCKEY

1928 Stanley Cup Finals

■ The Patricks were already the most famous family in hockey in 1926 when they joined the NHL, with Lester taking over as coach of the New York Rangers. In only his second season in the NHL, Patrick had brought the team into the NHL finals, against the Montreal Maroons, who took a 1-0 series lead. In the second game, Ranger goalie Lorne Chabot was hit in the face with a puck and knocked unconscious. NHL teams dressed fewer players in those days, and because Maroons coach Eddie Gerard wouldn't let Patrick send for either of his backups in the stands, the Rangers had to take someone from their bench. There were no volunteers and Lester Patrick soon realized that he—though 44 years old, seven years out of the pros, with only a whiff of experience as a goalkeeper—would have to take over. The Maroons peppered the goal with shots, trying to rattle the desperation substitute, but the Rangers played fanatically, and took a 1-0 lead early in the third period. Though Nels Stewart tied the game for the Maroons with six minutes left, Patrick held on from there, finishing with 18 saves, as the Rangers won 2-1 in overtime. After the winning goal, they rushed to Patrick and carried him from the ice, and went on to win the series (with Joe Miller—quickly signed from the New York Americans—in goal). "The boys saved me," said Patrick after the Game 2 surprise. But his appreciative players knew the truth was just the opposite.

Great Performances

■ Nothing tops Red Grange's four touchdowns in the first 12 minutes against Michigan in 1924... But at the Olympics in Paris earlier that year, American swimmer Johnny Weissmuller—19 years old, 6-foot-3, and movie–star handsome—won the 100- and 400-meter freestyle, anchored the gold-medal winning 4X200-meter relay team and even played on the U.S. water polo team, which took the bronze. By 1927, Weissmuller held world records at every distance from 100 to 800 meters. He won two more Olympic gold medals in 1928... In 1927, the New York Giants won their first NFL title, outscoring the opposition 197–20 while going 11–1–1.

Hometown Heroes

The decade was a bittersweet one for the most dominant franchise in the National Hockey League. **The Ottawa Senators**—a team truly representative of its city, with a roster heavily populated by local players—won four Stanley Cup titles during the Twenties. But the franchise ended the decade on the verge of financial collapse, unable to adapt to the changes that were sweeping the game.

A charter member of the NHL, the Senators were owned by local sports editor Tommy Gorman of the *Ottawa Citizen*. The first three Stanley Cups, in 1920, '21 and '23, came with brilliant right-winger Jack Darragh (who died in 1924 from acute peritonitis) leading the charge, and legendary goalie Clint Benedict between the posts. Known as "the praying goaltender," because he spent so much time on his knees, Benedict led the NHL in goals against average for five straight seasons. Despite the loss of Darragh, and the eventual decline of Benedict, a low-scoring but experienced Ottawa team rallied for one more title, in 1927, beating the Boston Bruins in the finals.

But by the end of the decade, the onset of the Depression and the weakening of local ties through expansion began to wear on the franchise. The beginning of the end came when the cash-poor Senators sold the contract of future Hall of Famer King Clancy to Toronto in 1930. A year later, they asked for a one-year leave of absence from the league, then returned in 1932 and posted the NHL's worst record for two seasons. The franchise was transferred to St. Louis in 1934, where it survived for one dismal season before disbanding. As hockey historian Douglas Hunter wrote, "When the NHL left the Senators behind, it also left behind the last vestiges of the authentic community-based professional team. New champions would be built from a grab bag of players who hailed from any old place."

■ **Top Dogs.** The Twenties were a time of chaos in professional football. The American Professional Football Association, formed at the Jordan and Hupmobile auto showroom in Canton, Ohio, in 1920, survived in a crude form before renaming itself the National Football League in June 1922. The Canton Bulldogs, sparked by player-coach Guy Chamberlin, dominated the NFL in 1922 and 1923, going 21-0-3 over that span. But the Bulldogs drew poorly in Canton. Prior to the 1924 season, the Cleveland Tigers purchased the Canton franchise and rendered it inactive, adding the Bulldogs' best players to the Cleveland team which, renamed the Cleveland Bulldogs, won the NFL title in '24, going 7-1-1.

	COLLEGE BASKETBALL	PRO BASKETBALL	HOCKEY NHL	BASEBALL MLB	COLLEGE FOOTBALL	PRO FOOTBALL NFL
1920			Senators	Indians	California	Akron Pros
1921			Senators	Giants	Cornell	Chicago Stal
1922			Toronto St. Pats	Giants	Cornell	Canton Bulld
1923			Senators	Yankees	Illinois	Canton Bulld
1924			Canadiens	Senators	Notre Dame	Cleveland Bull
1925			Victoria Cougars (WCHL)	Pirates	Alabama	Chicago Card
1926			Montreal Maroons	Cardinals	Alabama	Frankford Yellow
1927			Senators	Yankees	Illinois	Giants
1928			Rangers	Yankees	Georgia Tech	Providence Stea
1929			Bruins	Athletics	Notre Dame	Packers

NOTES **Hockey:** At the start of the decade, the Stanley Cup champion was determined in playoff between champions of the National Hockey League and Pacific Coast Hockey Association. The Western Canada Hockey League champion made it a three-way challenge in 1923 and '24, after which the PCHA disbanded. The WCHL changed its name to the Western Hockey League in 1925 before disbanding in 1926. **College football:** Champions are mythical national champions for predated seasons prior to 1936, in 1941 by the Helms Foundation. **Pro Football:** American Professional Football Association changed its name to National Football League prior to 1922 season. Team with best record at end of season named champion by NFL.

Rock

For most of the century, football coaches have been expected to act a certain way because, simply, that was the way **Knute Rockne** acted. He wasn't the most innovative strategist, and didn't win the most national titles, but Rockne might be the most influential football coach ever.

In his 13 years as head coach at Notre Dame (1918-1930), his teams went 105-12-5 as he shaped the most glamorous program in the sport. Along the way, he turned the position of football coach into an American archetype. "Rock sold football to the man on the trolley… the baker, the butcher, the pipe-fitter who never went to college," said Harry Mehre, who played for Rockne before pursuing a coaching career himself. "He made it an American mania. He took it out of the thousand-dollar class and made it a million-dollar business."

It was still the former when Rockne was promoted from assistant coach and chemistry department aide to football head coach in 1918. His first salary was $8,500 and for the first six years, he also served as the Irish trainer. The Irish went 3-2-1 that first season, but the next year, Rockne took advantage of the lifting of postwar travel restrictions, and began scheduling more intersectional rivals, adding national powers such as Georgia Tech (1922) and Southern Cal (1926) to the schedule. And in 1923, Notre Dame began playing intersectional games in New York City, tapping into the extensive "subway alumni" of Irish Catholic sports fans. On the field, Rockne's innovations ranged from subtle (taking local water on road trips) to broad (his refinements of Stagg's backfield shift eventually led to a Football Rules Committee change in 1927, requiring backs to stop for a full second before the snap).

Westbrook Pegler wrote that Rockne, at 5 feet, 8 inches and 170 pounds, looked like a "preliminary fighter who becomes doortender in a bar. His nose is a bit smashed and his skull is more nude than otherwise. And when he talks, it is like a battered old oil can giving champagne."

Those talks were intoxicating. His famous exhortation to "win one for the Gipper" at halftime of the 1928 Notre Dame–Army game was only the best known of his stem-winders, but Rockne understood that emotion was forever a part of football. "A team in an ordinary frame of mind will do only ordinary things," he said. "In the proper emotional state, a team will do extraordinary things."

For all his rhetorical fame, Rockne wasn't a cheap sentimentalist. Prior to the 1930 Army game, in freezing rain and snow at Soldier Field in Chicago, Rockne sat in the locker room during the 15 minutes before the team took the field, not saying a word, allowing the tension to build up. When an official came to inform him it was time, Rockne stood up, said, "Come on, boys," and that was it. Notre Dame scored in the last four minutes to win, 7-6, en route to its second straight unbeaten season.

Though Rockne died in a plane crash a year later, his impact was felt for the balance of the century. His winning percentage of .881 is still the best in history. In 1969, when he was named the greatest coach in the first 100 years of college football by a poll of writers, coaches and players, 89 of his former players had themselves gone on to coach.

Influences

The Judge

Judge **Kenesaw Mountain Landis** preferred to be called Commissioner, though the terms used in the press—"czar" by many writers, "dictator" by *The New York Times*—were more accurate. The white-haired, dead-earnest Landis ruled baseball with absolute power, and it's more than a coincidence that in the 24-year period, from 1921-44, baseball exploded in popularity and prestige, while dragging its feet on player movement and integration.

Until 1921, the sport was ruled by a three-man National Commission, consisting of the AL and NL presidents, and the owner of the Cincinnati Reds. Landis was brought in by the owners at a time when the sport was suffering, both in the public eye (from the outraged fallout after the Black Sox scandal, when eight members of the Chicago White Sox took money to throw the 1919 World Series) and internally (where resentment of autocratic AL president Ban Johnson persisted).

When the owners offered Landis the job, he took it only on the condition that he would have absolute power and a free hand to implement his decisions. That effectively killed the National Commission, and gave the new commissioner broad discretionary powers to rule in "the best interests of the game."

He dispensed summary judgment on the eight players, even after they were acquitted in a Cook County court. "Regardless of the verdict of juries," wrote Landis, "no player that throws a ball game, no player that entertains proposals or promises to throw a game, no player that sits in a conference with a bunch of crooked players and gamblers where the ways and means of throwing games are discussed, and does not promptly tell his club about it, will ever again play professional baseball."

Landis was less a visionary, in the words of historian John Thorn, than an autocrat. While he helped rid baseball of its taint of scandal, he refused to integrate the majors, all the while denying that he was doing so. When Bill Veeck Jr. informed Landis of his plans to buy the Phillies in 1942 and sign black players, his bid was ignored. The club was turned over to the NL and later sold for a sum only half of Veeck's offering price.

But when faced with the Black Sox scandal, Landis did the right thing. In so doing, he freed the sport to take its place as the unquestioned national pastime. Of baseball in the Twenties, the Yankees' Tommy Henrich once said, "Landis cleaned it up, and Babe Ruth glorified it."

TOP OF THE NEWS: The Roaring Twenties see turbulent world events abroad, but the birth of mass culture at home. Movies begin talking, radios begin connecting the country, the first television picture flickers on a screen. And sports begin to exert a persistent presence in daily American life, not just at the ballpark and in the paper, but on the radio, in the bookstore and toy store—even in movie theaters.

Movies

In the 1925 comedy **The Freshman**, a geeky, bashful college student—the butt of jokes around his campus—gets a chance to become a star on the football team. Harold Lloyd starred in the rousing crowd pleaser, much imitated in the years to come.

The Battling Orioles, released in 1924, finds a group of members from the 1874 Baltimore Orioles (which finished last in the National Association and didn't finish out the schedule) trying to develop the son of a deceased teammate into a major leaguer. In *Life's Greatest Game*, a son who is presumed dead winds up pitching for a team managed by his father. Wallace Beery stars in a version of *Casey at the Bat*, in which the climactic strikeout comes by way of a doctored baseball.

Fashion

It's a big decade for emblems. The Athletics bust out blue elephants on their uniforms in '21, partly because John McGraw had referred to them as "white elephants" 20 years earlier. Two years later, the two birds land on the Cardinals bat logo. And in 1928, Chief Wahoo—still several decades from being a litmus test for political correctness—shows up on the Cleveland home jerseys. Also in the '20s, the Detroit Tigers first use their classic Old English script D.

Football uniforms are more colorful (when they're washed, which isn't frequently, especially on road trips). The Duluth Eskimos take the field wearing the best warm-up jackets ever, three-quarter-length white mackinaws with an igloo logo on the back.

Politics

In 1922, the Supreme Court hands down its landmark ruling in favor of organized baseball. In a suit brought by the Federal League Baltimore Terrapins, the court ruled that the sport is not "commerce" and therefore not subject to anti-trust laws.

Sounds

In 1926, Irving Berlin writes the music for "Along Came Ruth," with lyrics by Christy Walsh (the Babe's ghost writer), Addy Britt and Harry Link.

Playing Games

The Roaring Twenties is full of tabletop games that evoke the spirit of the age. There's Saratoga Horse Racing Game ("A Big Money Game of Chance"), Fore Country Club Golf, a boxing game called Tip-Top that uses two spinning tops, in a miniature ring, to represent the Dempsey-Willard heavyweight title fight. There's also a deluxe football box called The Yale-Harvard Game that

includes a large felt field and an iron-cast football player who kicks a wooden ball through metal goal posts.

Big Six: Christy Mathewson Indoor Baseball Game promises "All the Thrills of the Diamond" and includes a complex spinner with gradations on one end that yield nearly 300 different play results. It also includes starting lineups from each major-league club. Home Base Ball receives a testimonial from John McGraw, while Big League: The Perfect Indoor Base Ball Game, is endorsed by Honus Wagner, Connie Mack and Ty Cobb. Which doesn't stop Cobb, two years later, from coming out with his own game, called Ty Cobb's Own Game of Baseball. A dice roll sends a batted ball to various squares on a 30 X 30 grid laid over a baseball field.

Reading List

On October 18, 1924, after Notre Dame defeats Army, 13-7, *New York Herald-Tribune* sportswriter Grantland Rice sits down at his typewriter, and

$1
Amount paid for the Duluth NFL franchise in 1925, by Ole Haugsrud and Dewey Scanlon

5' 1"
The height of Soapy Shapiro, a blocking back for the Staten Island Stapletons in 1929, who was the shortest player in NFL history

26
The number of innings pitched by both Boston's Joe Oeschger and Brooklyn's Leon Cadore in major league baseball's longest game, a 1-1 tie in 1920

.424
The batting average compiled by St. Louis second baseman Rogers Hornsby in 1924. It's the highest of the century, but he still finished second, to Brooklyn right-hander Dazzy Vance, in the MVP balloting

119,912
Number of people who watched Notre Dame beat USC, 13-12, at Soldier Field in Chicago on November 16, 1929, the largest crowd at a football game in North America

$5,000
Amount Red Grange received to sign an endorsement deal with a shoe company in 1925

$10,000
Amount Grange received to sign an endorsement deal with a doll manufacturer the same year

OLD GOLD CIGARETTES

Smoother and Better

Presenting....
BABE RUTH
in the Blindfold cigarette test

"OLD GOLD'S mildness and smoothness marked it 'right off the bat' as the best"
Babe Ruth

Not a cough in a carload.

bangs out the most famous lines in the history of sports journalism: "Outlined against a blue-gray October sky, the Four Horsemen rode again. In dramatic lore they are known as Famine, Pestilence, Destruction and Death. These are only aliases. Their real names are Stuhldreher, Miller, Crowley and Layden. They formed the crest of the South Bend cyclone before which another fighting Army football team was swept over the precipice of the Polo Grounds yesterday afternoon as 55,000

> *"The Washington Senators and the New York Giants must have played a doubleheader this afternoon: the game I saw and the game Graham McNamee announced."*
> —Ring Lardner, upon listening to a World Series broadcast in 1924

spectators peered down on the bewildering panorama spread on the green plain below." After Notre Dame publicity man George Strickler poses the four players—Harry Stuhldreher, Don Miller, Jim Crowley and Elmer Layden—on horses, the picture is picked up by wire services, and the era of mythmaking sports journalism is in full swing. It's a good year for Rice: On the same day as the Four Horsemen are christened, Illinois' Red Grange runs roughshod over Michigan. Grange's nickname is already waiting; Rice has been referring to him as "The Galloping Ghost."

The decade features the first issue of **The Ring** magazine, "the bible of boxing," and Ernest Lanigan's *Baseball Cyclopedia*, an early effort at a definitive baseball encyclopedia.

Impressions of the '20s

From ESPN's Linda Cohn:
Growing up in New York Ciy in the early 1900s, Gertrude "Trudy" Ederle didn't learn to dog-paddle until she was nine. Ten years later, on August 6, 1926, the 14 hours, 31 minutes she took to cross the English Channel broke all previous records by more than two hours, making her the first

woman, and the first American, to cross the channel.

More inspirational than her physical accomplishment, however, was her drive and determination to reach her goal despite the adversity of swimming in a storm that dragged her 14 miles off course, and prompted her trainer twice to suggest she give it up for another day.

But with support from her father and sister, and telegrams from her mother, she persevered and beat the odds. Speaking on dry land, she said, "When I was being swept off course to the North Sea, someone shouted, 'Trudy, give up?' ... I thought to myself, I'll keep going until I collapse or get there. I got there."

1920 The Negro National Baseball League.

College football on the radio, with WTAW of College Station carrying a Texas 7-3 win over Texas A&M.

The American Professional Football Association, later to become the National Football League.

Dog races with mechanical rabbits.

EXIT **The spitball** and other trick pitches ruled illegal in major league baseball.

The office of the baseball commissioner, with the election of Judge Kenesaw Mountain Landis, who takes office in 1921.

1921 **Baseball on radio**, with Harold Arlin doing the play-by-play on KDKA in Pittsburgh of a Pirates' 8-5 win over the Phillies.

The Green Bay Packers join the NFL.

NCAA track & field championships, held at the University of Chicago.

Paddle tennis, formed in the church gymnasium of the Judson Memorial Church in New York City.

Boxing on radio, a "no decision" between bantamweights Packey O'Gatty and Frankie Burns from Jersey City.

1922 **Basketball clinics**, by Chuck Taylor.

1923 **Yankee Stadium**, with the Yankees beating the Red Sox, 4-1.

1924 **The Winter Olympic Games**, originally called International Winter Sports Week, in Chamonix, France.

Forest Hills as the home of the U.S. Tennis Association National Championship.

The Boston Bruins join the National Hockey League.

The Hart Memorial Trophy, for the NHL's Most Valuable Player, with the selection of Ottawa's Frank Nighbor.

1925 **The New York Giants** join the NFL.

1926 **College graduation** as a criterion for eligibility in the NFL.

New York Rangers, **Chicago Black Hawks** and **Detroit Cougars** (later the Red Wings) join the NHL.

1927 **The Harlem Globetrotters**, with a game in Hinckley, Illinois.

1929 **Out-of-town training camps in football**, as the Chicago Cardinals train in Coldwater, Michigan.

Legal forward passing in all three zones in hockey in the NHL, though passes are not permitted across either blue line.

THE 1930s

Sports proved resilient during a brutal decade that began with the leveling effect of the Depression and ended with the nation reluctantly eyeing another great war. Though millions of Americans were out of work, they still followed the games as an escape. Sports also served as a way in for outcasts and immigrants. At the 1932 Olympics, America recognized its first great female athlete. A few years later, the country embraced a black heavyweight champion. The fight for true equality wouldn't come for decades, but in the '30s, the trailblazers made their mark.

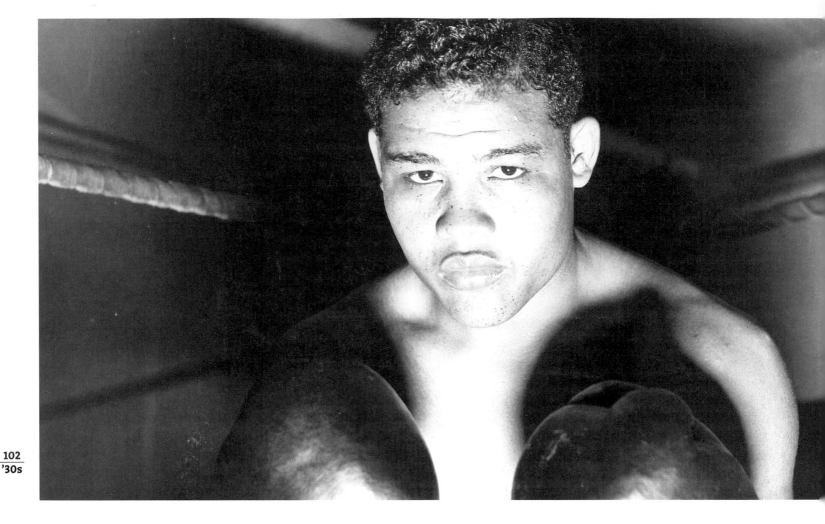

JOE LOUIS & BABE DIDRIKSON By Wilfrid Sheed

The Bomber and . . .

THE 1930s WERE SNEAKY. Nothing much seemed to be happening, but everything was on the brink of happening. At first glance, the nation seemed much too busy looking for work to try anything new, and besides, it still had kind of a hangover from the excitement of the decade before. Radio, talking pictures, mass-produced phonograph records—who had time for anything more?

Yet in the wings, TV was already in full rehearsal, getting ready to change everything all over again; and similar convulsions were in the works everywhere, in everything from transportation to bathing suits. In 1940, as in 1930, Americans still trundled slowly across the continent by train, or wobbled precariously over the Rockies in planes that seemed to crash at least once a month, invariably taking a celebrity down with them. By then, though, jet engines were on the drawing board, along with radar and penicillin and pressure cookers and God knows what all. And, as the famous Futurama exhibit at the 1939 World's Fair would demonstrate, whatever wasn't being

PREVIOUS PAGES
The Long Journey. Trail-blazing shoes—Louis' boxing shoes and Didrikson's track and field spikes.

the Babe

planned was being dreamed about in that dreamiest, most deceptive of decades.

Other things people were dreaming about back then included full civil rights, truly emancipated women and getting the smoke out of Pittsburgh. Yet progress seemed stalled on all fronts, and after 10 years blacks still moved to the back of the bus, women had the kitchen completely to themselves, and Pittsburgh was worse than ever. Also, men's sports were segregated and women's sports were genteel, sweat-free and underpopulated, and no official action was contemplated "at the present time."

So in place of formal change, or open revolution, we got freelancers like Joe Louis and Babe Didrikson, who, simply by making things better for themselves, made a better world for everyone else as well, and showed other athletes how to push still further. There was no common cause or sweeping vision about this. Joe worked his side of the street and Babe worked hers, and it's only now that we can see them both as essential '30s characters working unconsciously on different corners of the same project—the Future—which, to the eyes of the Hungover Decade, had to be better than *this*.

Famous Firsts. In the '30s, Louis and Didrikson were The First Gentleman of Sports and The First Lady in Sports. "Joe worked his side of the street and Babe worked hers."

Joe Louis was unofficially expected to be the First Gentleman of Sports: his nation's Number One Good Example at home, and virtually a branch of the diplomatic service abroad.

In fact, he was expected to behave just like Joe Louis, who may actually have been the only champ ever to come anywhere near these specifications, not just by staying out of jail and remembering to smile occasionally (Joe never remembered to smile) but by actually accomplishing something hard to put in a simple sentence but absolutely essential to the style and flavor of sports in America ever since.

Technically speaking, Joe did not quite have to integrate boxing. There had already been several black champions in the lighter divisions, which didn't count so much, and one heavyweight champion, too. But the latter, the incorrigible Jack Johnson, had been such a defiantly bad example that he had in effect resegregated the Crown, obliging Joe Louis to start over again from the beginning, as the "anti-Johnson," the perfect gentleman. And it was actually this cleaned-up, intentionally idealized image of the Black Athlete that would wind up being Joe Louis's great legacy, not just to boxing but to American sport in general, and to America itself.

ATER ON, LOUIS WISHED THAT HE'D DONE MORE, and he said that he envied Jackie Robinson's "fire" in pushing integration the rest of the way. But as usual, Joe was being too modest. At his particular moment in history, there was absolutely no way he could have done what Robinson did—until, that is, someone like Joe Louis had come first and cleared the way. When Joseph Louis Barrow first showed up in the national spotlight in the early 1930s, the most (and only) famous black movie star was still Stepn Fetchit, a minstrel-show "darky" of the old school, and around the same year Louis was winning the heavyweight title, Benny Goodman was creating an uproar in a northern city (Chicago) by bringing a black musician onstage to play with his white ones.

If Joe Louis had tried being even one tenth as uppity as Robinson, he would surely have gone the way of Harry Wills, the great black heavyweight who could never buy a title fight with Jack Dempsey, or of the legendary Sam Langford, the "Boston Tarbaby," who couldn't even buy one with Jack Johnson, a fellow Negro. If one black fighter was a tough sell, two was akin to an icebox in Antarctica—until Joe Louis had cleared the way.

Long before that, however, sports had been the weak link, or loose brick, in the wall of bigotry. Spectators like to see the Best, and athletes like to play against the Best, too, and between them they'll usually find a way. Thus, even in that most segregated era, white ballplayers regularly got together the minute their season was over to play ball with their black counterparts. Names like Satchel Paige and Josh Gibson entered white consciousness in the curious split way that blacks so often did. On one level, they were not as good as "our" heroes—not as smart or mentally tough—but on another, dreamier one, they were giants, legends, supermen. Paige could throw a ball harder than normal mortals, Gibson could hit farther, and Cool Papa Bell could outrun electricity itself. I'd heard all of these myths as a child in the early 1940s, before I'd even heard of Jackie Robinson, and had absorbed them, along with Batman and Captain Marvel, as quasi–realities.

In short, segregation had made black Americans both larger and smaller than life. Joe Louis would have to steer between both images, as a polite, slow-speaking field-

Boundary Jumping. Didrikson getting airborne in the long jump—then still known as the broad jump—during her spectacular, headline-making performance at the 1932 AAU national championships, where she won six gold medals and broke four world records.

hand by day and a Dark Destroyer by night, who preyed upon white folk and beat them senseless, one after the other. Later, Muhammad Ali would petulantly call Joe Louis an Uncle Tom without ever realizing how much this particular "Uncle" had done for him. Because, long before Ali came along, Joe Louis had sold that icebox in Antarctica, and by somehow persuading the white public to like and even identify with at least one black athlete, he had opened the way for successors like Ali to make fortunes fighting, in effect, nothing but other black fighters. It was the sale they had said couldn't be made.

It is worth underlining that up until the end of World War II, all of Joe Louis's challengers were white. This was the image he had to sell first: that of a black man methodically stalking and beating up white boys the way white sheriffs had immemorially beaten up black ones. Against the orderly, understated sports background of the 1930s, the picture still can startle. There was nothing deferential about Joe's style. He pounced impatiently from his stool each round with just one thing on his mind and in his face: to corner his victim, cut off all hope immediately, and beat the living daylights out of him. Uncle Tom was never like this. People who compared Louis to a jungle cat were not just being racist; no fighter has ever come closer to the single-mindedness and unity of eye and body of a cat than Joe Louis. And heaven help the opponent who blinked. Joe's reflexes were so fast that he would later say, "I knew I was through when I could *see* my openings," and his fists danced in instant attendance, moving the few inches it takes to knock a man out as fast and as hard as a fist can move.

It was the great Vengeance Dream come true. Malcolm X would say that every black child dreamed it along with Joe, and wanted to be Joe one day. Meanwhile, every white kid just had to get used to it. "He never could have beat Jack Dempsey" was a formula that helped a little. But the fight films on the newsreels every month were awfully convincing, and Louis had to be very polite indeed between fights to make the nightmare acceptable.

THE DEPRESSION WAS ALSO THE HEYDAY of the far-out success story. Readers couldn't get enough of movie stars being discovered at soda fountains or working on oil rigs, because it heightened the sense of possibility for everyone. And no celebrity ever came from farther out than Joe Louis, the eighth child of an Alabama sharecropper who'd been placed in a mental home and thus become a nonperson before Joe was born. And his mother, Lilly, had lengthened the odds still more by taking up with a man who had five more children to add to the pool, making the total household an easy one to get lost in, or to lose one's voice in (Joe's trademark silences may have come from trying, and failing, to get a word in edgewise).

Yet Louis always talked of his childhood as a blissful one, spent shinnying up trees and splashing around in swimming holes. So it must have seemed, anyway, from the vantage point of industrial Detroit, where the family moved when Joe was 12. Although the Depression hadn't quite arrived, it was always hard times for families like the Barrows, and even young Joe had to work in a Ford factory for a while. It speaks wonders for Lilly Barrow's optimism and dreamy determination that, out of God knows what family income, she managed to scrape up enough extra to pay for violin lessons for Joe. And this little bit of sweat money would make all the difference, turning the family fortunes around in no time and making a famous artist out

On the Way Up. Emerging as a title contender, Louis decks Primo Carnera in the sixth round of their 1935 fight at Yankee Stadium. He fought 14 times that year.

of Joe as well—because he wisely spent most of it on trips to the gym, where he studied the manly art of self-defense as hard as any violinist. "Don't jab at the target, jab through it"—every word Joe ever uttered about boxing bespoke a craftsman in love with his work and its secrets.

FIRST AND LAST, THE CRITICS WOULD ALWAYS CALL HIM a puncher, not a boxer, as if one had to choose, because the punching was so spectacular and mind numbing. Joe had been endowed with that gift of the gods, a knockout punch that needs no buildup or context, but can do a whole night's work in a single gorgeous moment. From his first amateur fight on, the game was to guess when the lightning would strike. First round? Second round? Which one has Mr. Louis decided on?

Such a gift draws attention fast—and not just from his mother, who saw through the shortened stage name of "Joe Louis" soon enough, but also from the sharpies of the netherworld, led, fortunately, by a brilliant Detroit numbers-game operator named John Roxborough, who would proceed, if not precisely to create the Joe Louis of legend, at least to nudge him powerfully in that direction.

Like most every other black manager in America, Roxborough's abiding dream was to produce his very own Jack Johnson, but without the mistakes. What gave him an edge was that he also knew that boxing wasn't the half of it, and along with the hooks and jabs, Roxborough imparted some "Nice Nellie" precepts worthy of Professor Higgins himself: Joe must never be seen to gloat over a fallen opponent, never be photographed with a white woman or entering a nightclub by himself, must wear a poker face at all times, etc. These were rules that might add up to "Uncle Tom" to later generations, but not to this particular one.

In the 1930s, "class" was still an abstract ideal, open to anyone, from Amy Vanderbilt to Joe DiMaggio, who had the grace and grit to claim it. This was not just the decade of the "Common Man," but also of "every man a king," and every American was free to regard himself as an aristocrat-in-waiting, until proved otherwise.

Nor did *class* just mean "white man's class." Back then Harlem was a style center unto itself, with its own high standards of elegance and "rightness" in clothing, manners, and even wisecracks. The jazz musicians themselves wore jackets and ties on their nightly trips to the stratosphere, and today's rappers, with their ballooning shirts and baggy pants (and no musicianship!) would have been laughed off the stage.

At any rate, no one at the time ever accused Joe of acting white or being anyone but himself, and whatever small concessions he may have made were more than canceled by the one he didn't make. Perhaps because boxing smacks so much of the carnival and the freak show, it has always been the easiest sport to integrate—up to a point. Everyone wants Apollo Creed to be the best in the world, and to win all his fights, except for tonight's. He has to lose to Rocky, the white man, in the final reel, or the deal is off. This was Jack Johnson's one unforgivable sin, and according to Roxborough, the same apple was offered to Joe by a New York promoter with the words "We can't have Negroes winning all the fights around here."

But Louis's dream did not include throwing fights, and, luckily, fans didn't seem to mind watching him win all his fights anyway, because he did it so elegantly. Roxborough's rules of etiquette had unwittingly proved to be box-office magic, because they added an air of mystery to a normally straightforward pastime. ("What

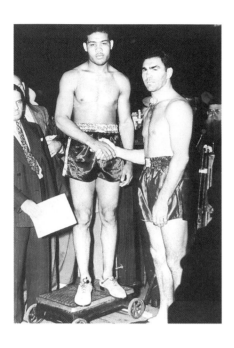

"More Than a Boxing Match."
Above, Max Schmeling and Louis shake hands before their much-anticipated rematch in June 1938.
At right, Louis—a national hero at last—greets admirers after the fight, having knocked out Schmeling in the first round.

does he want?" and "What is he thinking?" are questions that probably wouldn't be asked again until Muhammad Ali came along.) And one last tip, from his trainer, Jack Blackburn, had completed an irresistible sales package. Since blacks don't win many fights by decision, said Blackburn, "let your fists be the referee."

Louis's unabashed head-hunting, combined with the deadpan and the no-gloat principle, made his performances incomparably dramatic, and with a little help from the shrewd New York promoter Joe Jacobs, Louis soon met the only qualification you absolutely need for success in this peculiar profession: He filled the seats with customers, like a regular champion.

So Roxborough's job was over, and the rest was up to Joe, and to fate. Breaking through the bigotry wall all by himself would certainly have been a sufficient achievement, but it might also have led nowhere. As long as Louis didn't bring in a lot of other blacks with him, he could safely be cordoned off as an isolated phenomenon, a genius in a million, and a testament to the land of opportunity to boot. Only in America!

The hard part has always been to get the second minority family onto the block, and in this Louis would receive indispensable help from the perfect white villain. Adolf Hitler had already done American blacks an enormous favor by walking out on the great track star Jesse Owens at the Berlin Olympics of 1936. For one brief moment, a descendant of slaves had become a representative American, and a great one. And by defining himself as a bigot, Hitler had implicitly defined us, too, as the exact opposite. So maybe we should look into that someday soon.

At first, Der Fuhrer was not about to make the same mistake with Joe Louis. Maybe he had seen some fight films, and had even felt a primal twinge of fear himself. (One opponent was so scared of Louis that he refused to leave his corner at first, and even people who only saw the fight on film sympathized completely.) Adolf knew better than to bet his ideology against such a force, at least for a while.

But then Joe went and lost one, and it was the perfect one to lose. A German journeyman named Max Schmeling had spotted a chink in Joe's defenses and proceeded to knock Louis out in 12 rounds. And Der Fuhrer got his hopes up and became a boxing expert overnight, as he would later become a military genius; and just like that, Joe Louis's place in history was assured forever.

Adolf Hitler's racist claptrap would provide just the hoopla the return match needed to became a major world political event, and by fight time half the planet and all of a jam-packed Yankee Stadium was baying for poor Max's blood, including Joe Louis himself. There was no way Joe could have lost this fight anyway—he never made the same mistake twice—but getting him mad was probably unwise. "I hates that Schmeling," he was quoted as saying (they became good friends later), and the two minutes or so it would take him to prove it have probably since been shown as often as any piece of sports film from the first half of the century.

More to the point, it seems they were heard on radio by every black American alive at the time, and it is well within the bounds of sports hyperbole to guess that the American civil rights movement may have been born that very night in at least some hearts. Certainly the sports department of the movement was. For maybe the first time ever, blacks and whites had rooted with all their hearts for the same guy, and once the team principle has entered a sport, if only for a moment, a mighty new force goes to work immediately—namely, the need to win at any cost. For instance, no sooner had one Southern Conference college used its first black athlete, then all of them were doing it, and as they used to say, "There went the neighborhood," and the one next to it, until there wasn't a segregated sport left standing in America.

SOCIOLOGICALLY AS WELL AS PUGILISTICALLY SPEAKING, the great Schmeling massacre was an impossible act to follow. But once again Hitler came through, and World War II would throw Joe Louis one more fat pitch, which he would proceed to hit almost as hard and definitively as he hit Max Schmeling.

"There's nothing wrong with America that Hitler can cure," he said artfully. (Incidentally, Louis seldom bothered to talk unless he had something immortal to say: "He can run but he can't hide," "Nobody got hurt but the customers." Joe's ratio of familiar quotations to total words spoken must hold their own kind of record.) Obviously, there was still plenty wrong with America, but not enough to keep Louis from volunteering for the army and fighting exhibitions all across the map for Uncle Sam, cheerfully giving away his talent during what should have been his best years.

When the war was through, so was Joe, as a fighter anyhow. He had entered the service on a tide of boxing triumph, which included maybe the second most-watched sports film of all time, his epic comeback knockout of Billy Conn. But in 1946, these two would fight again, and it would be history repeated as farce, a chilling demonstration of what a few years off can do to heavyweight legs and reflexes, and with them, the will to win itself.

Fortunately, Conn had lost even more than Louis, and indeed the champ still had enough left to polish off any "Great White Hopes" that could still be found now that the Depression was over. But his great achievement by then was that he'd already reduced the phrase to a joke, by beating up so many of them: "Bums of the month," they'd wound up being called, which is a spectacular demotion from either greatness or hopefulness.

Now that he'd cleared the decks for black challengers, though, Louis lost to the first one he faced, Jersey Joe Walcott, in every respect but the score, then did lose to Ezzard Charles. Not long after, he was finally knocked out—and out of boxing—by a real white hope named Rocky Marciano, an irony that neatly ends the era.

After that, Joe Louis's only outstanding opponent was the IRS, and he never had a chance. The revenuers were still taxing the nation at wartime levels, and their approach to their victims was equally warlike. Joe got no credit for talent depletion or for his general services to the nation, but was hounded like a pickpocket, or like Al Capone himself. Yet he never seriously soured on the country that was doing this to him. "We are on God's side," he'd said (immortally as usual) during the war. It remained an article of faith with him and was the chief cause of his famous quarrel with Muhammad Ali. On other fronts, Joe was reasonably hip if not militant about racial injustice, and gave money to all the cutting-edge organizations. So his Ali problem wasn't just a case of a fuddy-dud snarling at a whippersnapper, but of a devout integrationist who detested the Black Muslim doctrine of re-segregation that Ali espoused. Louis actually liked white people and had worked wonderfully well with them, and he believed in a Rainbow Coalition long before Jesse Jackson coined

A Step Ahead.
Didrikson (at far right) said she came to the Olympics "to beat everything in sight, and that's just what I'm going to do." Then she won the 80-meter hurdles and the javelin.

the phrase, a position that seemed reactionary in the 1960s but not so bad now.

Yet Louis did wind up in Ali's corner, literally, for a few fights, and Muhammad finally had the grace to say, "When Joe's in the room, I am not The Greatest." (Ali probably was, at least as a fighter.) Luckily, the question of "who's best" can never be answered for absolute sure, otherwise a lot of sports bars would have to close immediately, but as more and more black heavyweights marched through the door that Louis had opened, their bodies seemed to get progressively bigger and faster, and Ali's seemed a great leap forward even from these.

On paper, anyway, Ali runs Louis off his feet every time, so long as Ali doesn't blink. And in real life, Ali's body was built to last longer than Joe's, too, but this would prove a mixed blessing. Although Ali's unique return to the top of his game after a three–year layoff during the Vietnam War would have been quite beyond such earlier models as Louis and Dempsey, he paid a steep price for it.

Chink in the Armor. Louis seemed indestructible during his first 17 title defenses, until overmatched Pittsburgh fighter Billy Conn, at right, nearly took the title from him in June 1941.

JOE LOUIS' LAST YEARS WOULD CERTAINLY HAVE THEIR SAD SIDE, but he never became anything that might reasonably be mistaken for punchdrunk. In fact, Louis seems to have weathered a temporary mental breakdown in the 1970s, perhaps reminiscent of his father's, and a bout with cocaine addiction—which you could still acquire by accident back then—with considerable mental stamina. Even in the demeaning roles to which his finances would drive him, such as refereeing wrestling matches and greeting customers in Las Vegas, Joe never seemed precisely pathetic, but more like just what he was, a distinguished man paying off his debts with dignity and without complaint.

In one sense, the public actually gave Louis too much credit by assuming that all his troubles were caused by the IRS or by crooked management, and not seeing his own extravagant hand in any of them. In fact, Joe's generosity had always risen automatically above the level of his income. Whatever he didn't give away he squandered in the kind of terrible investments that seem to magnetically attract rich athletes. All the money that was left over from these activities Joe spent anyway, on the High Life. In the long, buttoned-up period before the 1960s, nothing of this kind was officially reported but everything was rumored. In the same way that we knew about Jack Kennedy's girlfriends, we knew that Joe liked to swing a bit, if only to make up for all that public perfection. Since the truth itself used to arrive in the form of a rumor, we just had to guess our way according to taste.

Louis ran through four marriages to three wives, but this was no big deal. While Hollywood was monitoring the nation's morals so scrupulously on film, it was also accustoming the citizenry to the casual non-event divorce, and Joe's record seemed about average for a celebrity. But was it really possible that he also had affairs with Sonja Henie and Lana Turner? Such liaisons would seem pretty hard to hide, but the press could, by unspoken agreement, hide just about anything from the public in the pre-1960s.

The reporters themselves knew, however, and liked to let you know that they knew, so their attitude to their subjects may now provide the best clue available as to how it all added up. If, for instance, they told the world that Joe Louis and Joe DiMaggio were "class guys," it meant that their sins were more than canceled by certain other qualities: most notably, of course, a willingness to talk to reporters, even in defeat, but including something else intangible, some superior essence, that connoisseurs prided themselves on recognizing immediately and infallibly, be they writers or

rivals. When Rocky Marciano, in victory, wept over Joe Louis's prostrate form, he was saluting that very same quality. Joe Louis was The Champ forever, as FDR was The President, not just because of his tenure but because he embodied the term. John Roxborough's rules of etiquette wouldn't have worked with just anybody. They required a natural gentleman to implement them, and this Joe Louis would remain, in all manner of circumstances, till the day he died. Which, by good chance, was just what history ordered for that particular time and place.

I F HISTORY ALSO ORDERED UP BABE DIDRIKSON, it obviously had something very different in mind. Superficially, if not at heart, the Babe was the mirror opposite of Joe Louis. Foul-mouthed by the standards of the time, and boastful by any standards, Didrikson openly reveled in victory and simmered in defeat. In equal parts bumptious and preposterously talented, she hit the genteel world of women's sports like a Texas cyclone, banging open doors and blowing over conventions that had stood for centuries, but haven't stood since.

Convention number one was that women weren't as competitive as men. But Mildred "Babe" Didrikson was made of competition. From all accounts, she was the kind of kid who wants to race you to wherever you're going and back, who later couldn't even take up sewing without hunting up a sewing bee and winning second prize for a dress she most expertly made herself.

Not surprisingly, the Babe (who was reputedly named for the distance she could hit baseballs) soon ran out of little girls to play with and had to make do with boys: undoubtedly much of her later abrasiveness traces directly to that. These were not the kinds of nice little boys you'd normally want your daughter to play with, but blue-collar ragamuffins from hardscrabble Texas, who probably taught her every dirty trick she would ever need, including the strategic use of boasting, to rile and rattle opponents, and to draw crowds as well. Everyone wants to whip a braggart and everyone else wants to see a braggart whipped, and maybe some day they might even pay good money for this.

Which brings us to convention number two: that it was extremely unladylike to play games for money. But in Beaumont, Texas, this made no sense at all. Hardly a soul from that part of the world was far enough above the poverty line to cherish, or even comprehend, the Amateur Ideal. Babe's competitiveness and a poor kid's yen for the Good Life were joined at the hip. After you've become the best at something, you naturally try to become the richest, too—the richest in her large Norwegian family, and in Texas, and in the world.

The collision course was set, like an obstacle race with a brick wall at the end of it. Even while the Depression was beginning to crush the life out of towns like Beaumont, all the few national sports events for ladies remained resolutely amateur, as if real ladies always had enough money. But fortunately, before Babe came to the wall, she discovered basketball, which was just passing through a twilight zone between pro and amateur in the Southwest. By taking a nominal job at the Employers Casualty Company of Dallas, Didrikson was able to become a star basketball player and live the life of Riley on the side, while keeping her amateur status spotless.

Both the down- and the upside of this was the fact that she soon became a hardened and unmistakable professional, whose gift for self-promotion rivaled that of such contemporary hot dogs as Slapsie Maxie Rosenbloom in boxing, and her fellow Southwesterner Dizzy Dean in baseball. Dizzy, who was actually known to laugh

Jill of All Trades.
Didrikson made herself a world-class golfer through practice, but she was naturally gifted at several other sports. She had a 170 bowling average, and reportedly could punt a football 75 yards.

at hitters while he was striking them out, coined a phrase that spoke for the whole region. "If you can do it, it ain't bragging." To which Babe might have added: "And if they can't prove you didn't do it, you did it." By her late teens, myths had begun gathering around her. She never denied any of them, and may even have launched a few herself. If people wanted to believe that she once scored 100 points in a basketball game, great. Maybe they'd pay to see her do it again—and maybe her opponents would be awed enough to let her.

Thus the Babe pumped herself up into that most saleable commodity: a legend, complete with a retinue of debunkers who only made it more interesting. Could she or couldn't she? Step right up. Consequently it is often hard to gauge Didrikson's early achievements, except in events that kept reliable records and attracted accurate reporting. Sticking to these, one finds that she was indeed a fine basketball player, frequently outscoring whole teams of opponents, and that at track and field, she was actually as good as she said she was. On one unforgettable day, she entered the AAU national competition as the sole representative of Employers Casualty and walloped all the other teams put together by winning five events outright, and tying for first in a sixth.

S UCH TALENT ALONE MIGHT STILL NOT HAVE quite cut it at the country club, but the possessor of it was deemed, as Jesse Owens would be, more than good enough to represent her country in the Los Angeles Olympics of 1932, where for the first and last time in her life, Didrikson, aged 21, would experience unqualified admiration and ungrudging respect. Entered in just three events this time, she set world's records in two of them, and only missed another gold medal in the high jump on a technicality.

The high jump is a persnickety sport which has to be done just right, and Babe seldom did anything just right. Her record-setting javelin throw, for instance, was an improvised affair unlike anything even she had ever done before, and her style in the 80-meter hurdles was equally homemade, the product of jumping over assorted hedges and fences when young. As a natural athlete glorying in her gift, Didrikson always found the kernel of fun in a game; the one thing she could never bring herself to do was simply run in a straight line, without jumping or throwing anything.

For the next 15 minutes or so (in celebrity time) Didrikson's life must have seemed like one long victory lap. Her myths were now in worldwide circulation, and so for a moment were her words, including her telling remark at the start of the games. Was she nervous? someone asked. "Oh, no," she said, "I was just playing against girls." And she advised other women to sharpen their skills and their nerves by practicing against males, too.

And then she hit the wall. An Olympiad is like a small war, and talent may get you promoted in wartime. But peace is more complicated, and no sooner had American girls gone back to playing against each other instead of foreigners than Babe was shown her place.

It seems that even before the applause had died down, some bureaucrat at the AAU had found an automobile ad with a picture of Babe in it. And even though Didrikson had not in fact authorized the ad, no inquiry was felt necessary. She was out, and that was that. And when she tried to take up tennis instead, she found herself out of that, too, before she could even determine if she was any good at it.

Suddenly the national interest that she had represented so splendidly at Los Angeles cut the other way. America couldn't have someone like that playing for it at Wimbledon—at least not while great ladies like Helen Wills and Helen Jacobs and Alice Marble were still around.

Which left golf, but at first this sport was equally resistant, and even more blatant about it. After winning the West Texas Open in 1935, Didrikson found herself out on the sidewalk again with no explanation given at all this time—perhaps because it was so obvious, perhaps because it was so embarrassing. The problem with Babe was not her gender but her class. Quite apart from her own crudeness, Didrikson had attracted all the wrong sorts of people to the club, fans who stomped and whistled and hadn't the faintest idea how to behave in church. And the ladies of Texas were not going to stand for it.

THERE WAS NO APPEAL AGAINST THIS, and no other organized women's sport to turn to. So, as her Olympic glory began to fade with the speed of public memory, she seemed to transmogrify into the equivalent of a high-class circus act, making top dollar, for instance, as a ceremonial pitcher for the House of David baseball team—"eight bearded men and a girl"—and pitching the occasional inning of big-league exhibition games.

The irony of this was that, as Michael Jordan would also learn one day, baseball doesn't yield to sheer athleticism as other sports do, and for once Babe wasn't that hot at something. But who cared? By now her ambition had apparently been pared back to sending more and more money home, in which cause she would offer, like George Plimpton, to play anybody at anything: boxing with Babe Ruth, billiards, Ping-Pong, name it. In fact, she even put together a vaudeville routine, featuring a harmonica, which she played to an energetic draw, and lots of good ol' gal chatter, as she became more Texan with each passing day.

The one thing that saved her from disappearing forever into her own cartoon was the sobering sport of golf, which she had been playing quietly for years, though she always preferred onlookers to think she'd just taken it up the day before. Unlike many great natural athletes who feel they don't get enough credit for hard work, Didrikson didn't want any credit for it at all. Everything came easily to her was the story line, and to this day some people still believe that her very first drive went 250 yards, and that she later would hit one 400 yards—using a putter, no doubt.

Once again, Michael Jordan could set them straight. Babe had to work as hard as anyone to master this sport, and the great Gene Sarazen, with whom she played some exhibitions, claimed that she actually worked almost as hard as Ben Hogan himself, studying his (Sarazen's) every move and then practicing it herself until her hands bled.

Fortunately, the golf establishment allowed second chances. And since it hadn't given any reason for throwing her out, it didn't need to give any to take her back in 1943. But it's reasonable to surmise that the leveling effects of wartime had penetrated even golf by then. And maybe the money and attention Babe would undoubtedly bring in had begun to look a little better, too. With so many male athletes otherwise engaged, women in sports suddenly found themselves facing a window of opportunity like unto a barn door. And didn't golf have a duty to entertain the public? Wartime morale-building covered a multitude of amusements, and even the strippers undressed in red, white, and blue.

G.I. Joe. Louis, by now a sergeant in the U.S. Army, arrives in London, November 4, 1944. Within a year after the war, he was back in the ring (winning a rematch with Conn), and, at right, outpoints Jersey Joe Walcott in 1947.

Perhaps it also helped that the Babe had eased their minds on another, more delicate front. A third convention about women athletes, unspoken but universally accepted, decreed that the best of them couldn't be "real women." And although Didrikson confounded this by sewing up a storm and dressing in pretty clothes, and although she certainly was no muscle-bound hunk but a graceful and miraculously well-coordinated young lady, her femininity remained a hard sell. "She is a beautiful woman," wrote one sportswriter with the casual cruelty of the day, "from the neck down." Paul Gallico put it even more bluntly: "She would not or could not compete with women at their own best game—man-snatching."

But then in 1938, she went and got married, and stayed married. To be sure, George Zaharias was a funny kind of choice for a romantic partner: a portly ex-wrestler who'd worked under the title of "The Weeping Greek from Cripple Creek" and would eventually eat his way up to the 400-pound class. Nevertheless, he was a husband, and a real one.

Babe's obvious and reciprocal physical affection for George made it clear that he was no beard, or front man, for a you-know-what. In fact, Didrikson's attitude to sex seemed completely "normal," and the young women who would gradually join her on the golf tour even found her a bit of a matchmaker, full of advice about which men looked like good bets and which didn't, based presumably on at least some experience.

HOW MUCH the "new breed" actually listened is another question. In a somewhat thin-lipped assessment written years later by a rival named Betty Hicks, the Babe comes across as a stale joke, with her endless self-promotion and mechanical boasting. In short, in just a few years Babe Didrikson had gone out of style, at least temporarily. By the 1940s the replacement of live entertainment by movies and radio had begun to favor cooler entertainers in every field: DiMaggio and Bing Crosby were "in," Babe Ruth and Al Jolson were quaint, and for the moment, Babe's stylized eccentricity seemed as dead as vaudeville.

"But," Hicks pauses to exclaim, "we owed her so much!"—starting, by chance, with their very own existence in the sport. Babe had indeed brought money and attention to women's golf—enough to revolutionize the game. However old hat her personality might seem to her rivals, it was brand new to golf, and it worked like thunder. "I just loosen up my girdle and let her rip" was the Babe's idea of an inside tip. The crowd roared, and her colleagues stifled their groans and cashed their checks.

In fact, the checks themselves were pretty much Didrikson's doing as well, because before she came along there simply wasn't enough money to split. But those crowds that came to hear Babe's wisecracks stayed to admire her game until at last there was a public, a clientele, that could be counted on to turn up next time as well as the times after. Suddenly, the Babe's career had a point and a purpose, and she lifted her game to meet it as great champions do. At what seemed like just the right moment after the war, with a different kind of future in the balance, Didrikson entered that transcendent, walking-on-water phase known as "the zone," and reeled off 17 tournament victories in a row. With the proceeds of these and other exploits, the Babe and a few friends felt emboldened to launch their very own Ladies Professional

Domestic Bliss.
Above, Didrikson with her husband, George Zaharias, returns to America on the *Queen Elizabeth* in 1947.
At right, newlyweds Louis and Marva Trotter, in Harlem in 1935.

Golf Association in 1948. The currently flourishing LPGA, with its worldwide hookups, is undoubtedly Babe Didrikson's most solid legacy. But every woman athlete probably owes her a little something just for opening things up and licensing them to be themselves, whatever that might be.

Yet the Babe was no feminist. The one thing that the tour made almost comically clear was that she couldn't tolerate losing to other women. Gene Sarazen was one thing, Louise Suggs was something else. Women were her subjects, dammit, she had always beaten them. Every defeat was an insurrection that had to be put down fiercely, and anyone who beat her twice was a personal enemy to be raged at and humiliated.

Like other early trail-blazing females—from Mae West to Amelia Earhart—Didrikson was basically a solo turn, not a team player. And when the real team players began to roll up, the territory soon became too small for the old gunfighter. As the competition improved, there was no way Babe could still dominate it the old way. Was she a legend or wasn't she?

Babe Didrikson's early death was not quite as tragic as most such deaths. Her unexpected assault by colon cancer at the age of 41 actually enabled her to win the Ben Hogan Comeback of the Year Award in 1953, as she bounced back from a colostomy to play two more years of top-level golf, before fading at last and dying bravely in 1956.

There was really no role for the Babe to play in life other than hero. She died at the height of her powers, but with no obvious place to go, and her death called for the absolute maximum of worldwide grief and praise. It's hard to imagine what a longer life could have added to that. But Babe Didrikson would probably have thought of something.

Such an improvised career has its limitations as a role model. The Babe's swaggering style was, like Muhammad Ali's, partly the joyous expression of a unique talent. The message was "be yourself—don't even think of trying to be like me!"

But if Didrikson had no linear descendants, she had plenty of sisters, real and imaginary, from Annie Oakley, the sharpshootress, and "Texas" Guinan, the sassy nightclub madam ("Hello, sucker")—both of whom were celebrated in 1940s shows—to the mythical pistol-packin' Mama, and Rosie the Riveter of World War II. She wasn't a new kind of woman, but an old kind in a new setting.

Joe Louis, people used to say, didn't knock down doors, he walked through them quietly. But from where the Babe sat, knocking down the door and making a noise was half the fun. And the noise carried. One of the secret weapons of men's sports is the "Hot Stove League," the conversation that never stops but keeps all the games alive between seasons. And nothing feeds the stove better than a big, juicy character like Babe Ruth or Yogi Berra or Babe Didrikson. As Yogi (allegedly) said, "I never said half the things I said." But strictly speaking, he didn't have to say any of them. His job was to provide the image, the archetype. The stories would take care of themselves.

If Babe Didrikson's legacy had to be boiled down to two sentences, they might be: 1) Like Joe Louis, she changed the atmosphere in the room, and 2) She finally got women's sports into the conversation. And they've been in and out of it ever since.

JESSE OWENS
That Golden Moment

In explaining his upright, square-shouldered running style—in which his feet seemed to barely touch the ground—Jesse Owens said he ran as if the track were a hot stove and he was doing his best not to get burned. Owens became a legend by standing up to the heat, and never more spectacularly than in Lane One at the Olympic Stadium in Berlin on August 3, 1936. On that day he wasn't just competing against the world's best sprinters, he was racing an ideology. Up in the chancellor's box, Adolf Hitler was poised for the assertion of Aryan supremacy at the expense of the United States and its "African auxiliaries," as he called Owens and the other black runners.

With the defeat of Joe Louis at the hands of German heavyweight Max Schmeling not yet seven weeks old, Owens won the 100-meter dash with a late surge in 10.3 seconds. The next day, with help from an unlikely source—Luz Long, designated by Hitler himself as the Aryan superman—Owens won the long jump, walking off arm-in-arm with Long after the winning leap. He added gold in the 200 and ran the lead leg on the winning 4x100-meter relay. His four track & field gold medals in a single Olympics would be unequaled until Carl Lewis did it in the same events in 1984.

Unlike Lewis, who came to the Los Angeles Games already a millionaire, Owens returned home with no future in track, the result of a vindictive AAU ruling that stripped him of his amateur status for refusing to stay in Europe for an exhibition tour. And despite his sensational college career (at the Big 10 Championships in 1935, he broke three world records and tied a fourth in 45 minutes), his four gold medals and his role in destroying the Aryan myth, he was unable to destroy the prejudice that awaited him at home. He did not win the Sullivan Award in 1936—a white decathlete did—nor was he allowed in the front door to the Waldorf-Astoria, even for a reception in his honor. "I wasn't invited up to shake hands with Hitler—but I wasn't invited to the White House to shake hands with the president, either," Owens said, though typically devoid of malice.

Owens lacked the political gravity of Muhammad Ali or Jackie Robinson. Instead, he was content to live his life within the system. Working on behalf of the USOC, he helped avert a wholesale walkout of black athletes in Mexico City after John Carlos and Tommie Smith were suspended for their black-gloved protest salute. For his efforts he was called "Uncle Tom" by some blacks and whites. "We all know what's wrong with this world," Owens said. "You

OWENS:
"HE BELIEVED
IF YOU DO GOOD,
GOOD WILL
HAPPEN TO YOU"

BAUGH:
"CALM POISE,
NONCHALANCE
UNDER FIRE"

know it. I know it. I can't change it with wild words."

Retirement was rarely easy for Owens, who was twice hit with income tax evasion charges and once filed for bankruptcy. He claimed the gold medals kept him alive. "Time has stood still for me," he said. "That golden moment dies hard."

With television raising the profile of the Olympics in the 1960s and '70s, Owens was in demand as a motivational speaker. The humble man who was forced to race against horses and dogs after losing his amateur status was able to enjoy a comfortable existence in the last years of his life before the pack-a-day smoker died of lung cancer in March 1980.

"He was impossible to have dinner with," said Bud Greenspan, who produced the acclaimed documentary series *The Olympiad*. "People would line up for his autograph and he would sign every one with the greatest care. It would take hours. He believed that if you do good, good will happen to you, and nothing ever diminished the belief."
—*Mark Wangrin*

SAMMY BAUGH
Opening Up the Game

In the backyard of his home in a town called Sweetwater, under the big sky of countless West Texas afternoons and evenings, the teenage Sammy Baugh mapped out the future of football. Suspending an old tire by a rope from a tall tree branch, the resourceful young Baugh would start it swinging back and forth, then drop back 10, 15 or 20 yards, and practice throwing a football through it for hours on end. He couldn't have known it at the time, but he was changing forever the way football would be played.

When the three-sport high school star (the "Slingin' Sammy" nickname came from baseball) took a scholarship offer from Texas Christian University, he became the ideal catalyst for coach Dutch Meyer's revolutionary "Aerial Circus," a precursor to the controlled passing games of the modern era. "For calm poise, for nonchalance under fire, no college passer has equaled the fabulous Baugh," said grid legend Pudge Heffelfinger. Operating as a tailback out of the old single-wing, Baugh won 29 games at TCU from 1934–36, playing heroically in the 20–14 "Game of the First Half of the Century" loss to SMU in 1935. He was named All-America the next year, passing more often—and from more exotic positions and angles—than anyone in the game before him.

Grantland Rice thought the lanky, raw-boned, 6-foot-3-inch, 180-pounder looked "too reedy" to succeed in the pros, but Baugh quickly proved all doubters wrong. He signed with Washington a week before the 1937 season after a brilliant negotiating ploy in which he announced he was shunning pro football to coach the TCU freshmen. He electrified the league his first season, leading the NFL in passing and quickly becoming the league's most feared punter (he still holds the single-season punting average record, 50.4 yards). His crowning moment came on frozen Wrigley Field in the 1937 NFL title game, when he threw for 354 yards, including touchdown passes of 55, 78 and 33 yards in a second–half comeback, as the Redskins beat the Bears, 28–21. Though he was the toast of Washington, the man owner George Preston Marshall called "*the* franchise," Baugh remained a Texan through and through. "I thought it was beautiful," he said of Washington, "but I didn't stay there a damn day longer than I had to. I'd head back to Sweetwater as soon as I got out of the uniform."

Baugh was simply a better passer than anyone of his era (his single-season record for completion percentage, 70.1, stood until 1982). But it wasn't just the frequency and success of Baugh's passing, it was the manner. He is believed to be the first quarterback consistently able to throw passes to receivers before they made the cuts in their routes, so that both the ball and the receiver arrived at the same place at the same time.

His versatility also was legendary: In 1943, Baugh led the league in passing, punting and interceptions. And after successfully converting to a T-formation quarterback in 1944, he excelled for nine more seasons before retiring in 1952. In 1994, he was one of four quarterbacks named to the NFL's 75th Anniversary team.

In interviews that year, Baugh made it clear he'd love a shot at the modern game. "There wasn't one rule that made you want to pass," he said of the old days. "I saw good offensive players cut because they couldn't play defense. The league finally figured people liked a scoring game and they opened it up."

JOSH GIBSON
The Black Babe Ruth

The Negro League Baseball Museum in Kansas City says Josh Gibson hit 972 home runs in his 18-year-career, while Gibson's plaque in the Hall of Fame in Cooperstown estimates the number was "almost 800." Anyone who saw him play will agree that the precise figure doesn't matter much. Gibson was a colossus hidden in the shadows. "When I broke in with the Baltimore Elite Giants in 1937, there were already a thousand legends about him," said Roy Campanella. "Once you saw him play, you knew all of them were true." From the other side of the color line and the other side of the plate, the right-handed Gibson was often called the "black Babe Ruth." But that, in a way, misses the point, because Ruth had his moment in the American spotlight. Gibson never did.

The son of a Pittsburgh mine worker who brought his family north from Georgia during the black migration of the 1920s, Gibson was a teenager studying to be an electrician when his baseball talents were first discovered. He

GIBSON: "A THOUSAND LEGENDS... ALL OF THEM WERE TRUE"

HUTSON: "NOBODY ELSE IN THE LEAGUE COULD TOUCH HIM"

began and ended his career with the Homestead Grays, but it was on the Pittsburgh Crawfords of the mid-1930s that he became a legend, as the clean-up hitter of one of the great teams ever assembled. For a time, the squad included five future Hall of Famers: Satchel Paige, Cool Papa Bell, Judy Johnson, Oscar Charleston and Gibson. The 6-foot-1-inch, 210–pound Gibson had a cannon for an arm and a menacing demeanor at the plate—a vision of coiled power and economy of motion. "There was no effort at all," recalled Judy Johnson. "You see these guys now get up there in the box, and they dig and scratch around before they're ready. Gibson would just walk up there, and he would always turn his left sleeve up, and then just before he swung, he'd lift that left foot up." The quick bat provided a staggering mixture of power and average. Over four consecutive seasons, Gibson hit .464, .384, .440 and .457 in league play.

In the late Thirties and early Forties, there were hints that Gibson would be the first black to play in the majors. In exhibitions against major leaguers, he proved himself among the best in the game. "He hits the ball a mile," said Walter Johnson. "Throws like a rifle. Bill Dickey isn't as good a catcher." Bill Veeck said that Gibson was "at the minimum, two Yogi Berras." Both the Pittsburgh Pirates and Washington Senators put out feelers, but neither made an offer.

Gibson's life was marked by tragedy. In 1930, his 17-year-old wife died giving birth to their twins. Forever longing for the shot to break the color line, he had numerous bouts with serious depression in his later years. Reports out of Mexico had him drinking beer in the dugout between innings and experimenting with heroin. His twilight years were spent shuttling between ballparks and sanitariums, as he succumbed to alcohol- and drug-induced headaches and nervous breakdowns. When he died of a stroke, at age 35 in January 1947, he was eulogized as one of blackball's greatest stars.

Just three months after his death, Jackie Robinson broke the color barrier.

DON HUTSON
The Alabama Antelope

On the first play of his pro career, Don Hutson ran straight down the field, caught Arnie Herber's rainbow pass, and eluded an overmatched Beattie Feathers for an 83-yard touchdown reception, the crucial play in the Green Bay Packers' 7–0 win over the Chicago Bears. It was 1935, the "Alabama Antelope" had arrived, and the NFL would never be the same.

Though at the end of the century many were arguing that Jerry Rice was the best receiver in pro football history, there could be no question that Don Hutson remained the most *dominating* receiver ever. Before he retired for good in 1945, he obliterated the NFL's receiving records as completely as Babe Ruth had rewritten baseball's home-run marks, doubling many of the single-season and career-receiving marks that were standing when he came into the league. In the process, he did as much to reinvent the passing game as Washington quarterback Sammy Baugh. "He was *the* greatest receiver," said Baugh. "There wasn't any doubt about it; nobody else in the league could touch him. You couldn't turn him loose on one man. He could hurt you pretty quick."

Hutson arrived at the perfect time—in 1934, the NFL had reduced the circumference of the football by an inch to make it easier to throw. In 11 seasons, Hutson led the league in receiving and touchdowns eight times each, led in receiving yardage seven times and was the leading overall scorer five times (he also was an accomplished place-kicker). As the NFL MVP in 1941 and 1942, he lapped the field in receptions, catching 58 and 74 passes when no one else in the league could muster as many as 30. Against Detroit in 1945, Hutson caught four touchdown passes and kicked five extra points, accounting for 29 points in a single quarter, another of his NFL records that still stands.

Hutson revolutionized the game despite being a marked man in an era when defenders had much more latitude to obstruct receivers. Wearing eye black to cut down the glare of the sun, the 6-foot-1-inch, 185-pound Hutson was deceptively strong, able to shake off the unlimited contact then allowed before the ball was in the air. But his main asset was his sprinter's speed (he once ran a 100-yard dash in 9.7 seconds). "He was so difficult to defend against," said Bears halfback Luke Johnsos, "because half the time he didn't know himself where he was going."

While Hutson could improvise with the best, he is generally regarded as the first receiver to run a specific, defined route—probably a down-and-out pattern—and the first to devise a repertoire of misdirection and fakes that threw defenders off the trail. Hutson was such an intimidating presence that Bears coach George Halas once said, "I just concede him two touchdowns a game and hope we can score more."

His coach, Curly Lambeau, remembered this vision of Hutson in action: "He would glide downfield, leaning forward as if to steady himself close to the ground. Then, as suddenly as you gulp or blink an eye, he'd feint one way and go the other, reach up like a dancer, gracefully squeeze the ball and leave the scene of the accident."

DON BUDGE
The California Comet

The story goes that Don Budge was near the end of his 1935 Wimbledon semifinal loss to Baron Gottfried von Cramm when Queen Mary and her party entered the royal box. Of German nobility, von Cramm had learned the

BUDGE:
A PRODUCT OF
THE PUBLIC COURTS
OF CALIFORNIA,
AND THE FIRST EVER
TO WIN THE
GRAND SLAM

game with the likes of King Gustav of Sweden, and he bowed from the baseline. The lanky 20-year-old American—so a British newspaper reported—sent a cheerful, freckle-faced smile in the queen's direction and waved.

It never happened—if anything, Budge said later, he had paused to wipe his brow with his shirt sleeve at about the time Her Majesty arrived—but certainly the myth demonstrates the demeanor and style which made the 6-foot-1-inch redhead a beloved figure of the long-pants era. A product of the public courts of California, he was by 1938 the dominant player in the world, and became the first ever to win the Grand Slam.

Possessing quickness and a powerful serve—his nickname was "The California Comet"—he rose to success with a stroke tennis writer Allison Danzig once called "probably the most potent backhand the world has ever seen."

The New York Times declared that Budge's July 20, 1937 Davis Cup interzone victory against von Cramm would be "forever memorable in every land where lawn tennis is played." Indeed, Hitler had phoned the German player just before the lengthy match and was tuned in by radio. The local crowd, Budge recalled, "was so quiet I'm sure they could hear us breathing." The United States had not won the tournament since 1926, and Budge's win sent the Americans into the final against England, where they recaptured the Cup.

But 1938 was his banner year, perhaps the greatest season in tennis up to that time—indeed, the term Grand Slam had not even been coined when Budge won the championships in Australia, France, Great Britain and the United States. The year began with an indication of his dominance, as he destroyed Australian champion John Bromwich 6–4, 6–2, 6–1.

During the French championship, the worthiest clay court opponent in the world—von Cramm—was in a Nazi jail on trumped-up charges, and Budge, along with other greats, like Joe DiMaggio, had sent an open letter of protest to the Germans. But von Cramm remained imprisoned, and Budge won the final handily in under an hour. By the time he soundly defeated Englishman Bunny Austin in the Wimbledon final—also taking the doubles and mixed doubles titles—his dominance was unquestioned. He helped the U.S. defend its Davis Cup title that summer, and repeated his Wimbledon feats at Forest Hills in September, defeating longtime doubles partner Gene Mako in the singles final.

Budge was sometimes accused of inconsistent attention, giving up sets in which he held a commanding lead. Once, in 1936, he attributed a discernible sluggishness to an overindulgence in malted milks the night before. But he coupled these shortcomings with an almost invincible ability to bear down when the effort was most required. American great Bill Tilden said he considered Budge "the finest player 365 days a year who ever lived."

—*David Zivan*

SATCHEL PAIGE
Don't Look Back

For much of the Thirties and Forties, Satchel Paige was the standard-bearer for all that was good and loose and exciting about Negro League baseball, a bottomless reservoir of myth and motion and mystical powers. Though he would not break the major leagues' color barrier, his consistent excellence against big leaguers—while pitching on the barnstorming circuit—offered incontrovertible proof that the best black players were as good, if not better, than white major leaguers. Dizzy Dean, outpitched by Paige, 1–0, in an extra-inning barnstormer in 1934, said Paige was the best pitcher he'd ever seen. "My fastball looks like a change of pace alongside that little pistol bullet old Satchel shoots up to the plate." Joe DiMaggio flatly called him "the best I've ever faced—and the fastest."

Born in Mobile, Alabama, Paige earned his nickname carrying bags at a local train depot. His pitching prowess was first discovered at an Alabama reform school, and by age 18 he was pitching for the Birmingham Black Barons, the first of dozens of teams for whom he'd play. Though exact numbers are elusive because of the informal nature of barnstorming, *The New York Times* estimated that he pitched in some 2,500 games during his career, threw 55 no-hitters, once started 29 games in a single month and might well have won 104 of the 105 games he started in 1934 while on the legendary Pittsburgh Crawfords.

What major leaguers saw when facing Paige was indelible, an awesome mixture of speed and location that was unprecedented. He called that ace fastball his "small ball." "It starts out like a baseball, and when it gets to the plate, it looks like a marble," said Hack Wilson. Paige responded, "You must be talkin' about my *slow* ball. My *fast* ball looks like a fish egg." Casey Stengel said of Paige, "He threw the ball as far from the bat and as close to the plate as possible."

Behind the jovial manner, there was always a hint of sad, rootless wanderlust to Paige. He fought his own civil rights battles in the barnstorming days, refusing to pitch in towns where he and his teammates couldn't find lodging or a decent meal. His contract squabbles with Negro League owners sent him to Santo Domingo to play for Dominican Republic dictator Rafael Trujillo's team in 1937, and to the Mexican League in 1938, where his incredible right arm finally failed him. He returned to the States in the fall of 1938, seemingly a spent pitcher. But his arm miraculously recovered, and Paige would be the marquee player for the Kansas City Monarchs for the next decade, leading them to two Negro League World Series.

Deeply hurt when Jackie Robinson was chosen over him to break the major leagues' color barrier, Paige showed up a year later, in 1948, signed by Cleveland Indians owner Bill Veeck. At the age of 42—*at least*—he was both the old-

PAIGE:
"EVERYBODY
KNOWS
OL' SATCH
WAS BORN"

ARMSTRONG:
HE CAN SURE
WEAR YOU DOWN

est rookie in major-league history and a living legend. He drew over 200,000 fans to his first three starts, and posted a 6–1 record down the stretch to help the Indians win the pennant and, ultimately, the World Series. His age continued to be a matter of dispute and humor. Asked whether he had a birth certificate, Paige scoffed, and replied, "Aw, everybody knows Ol' Satch was born."

But it would be wrong to classify Paige as some kind of clown prince. The Baseball Hall of Fame was reluctant to recognize the Negro League stars, and when a separate wing of the Hall was announced for Negro League players in 1971, Paige rejected the half-honor, preferring to wait for his due—induction as a full member. "I was just as good as the white boys," he said. "I ain't going in the back door of the Hall of Fame." Full recognition came later that year. It was a moment that resonated for Paige and for every Negro Leaguer.

HENRY ARMSTRONG
Homicide Henry

He knew only one direction: forward. And only one gear speed: "high," wrote *Boxing Illustrated.* And from October 1937 until August 1938, Henry Armstrong put on an accelerated exhibition of title fights like boxing had never seen and likely never will again. Typically weighing in around 130, Armstrong and his handlers sought to bring him out of the towering shadow of heavyweight Joe Louis and into the pugilistic limelight. The way to do this, they reasoned, was to fight for, and win, three different titles at once.

He had come a long way for a shot. Born Henry Jackson in rural Mississippi on December 12, 1912, Armstrong grew up in St. Louis, graduating high school in 1929 as the class poet laureate. He then held an assortment of odd jobs including dishwashing, which he feared would ruin his hands, and trained in the local YMCA. There, in 1931, he met promoter Harry Armstrong, who brought the young talent to California. Taking his manager's name, the former Henry Jackson spent a few years beating up on amateurs in and around Los Angeles, but got his break when singer Al Jolson and his wife, Ruby Keeler, saw him fight. They bought out his contract for an unscrupulous trainer pal, Eddie Mead, who took the young fighter to New York in 1937, where the title quest began.

Armstrong, his "incongruously muscular torso mounted on thin, almost weightless legs," as writer Barney Nagler put it, had 22 knockout wins that year before his October 29 featherweight title bout in Madison Square Garden against Petey Sarron, a skilled, courageous Alabamian. Some thought Armstrong would be weakened by dropping to 124, and indeed Sarron countered Armstrong's buzz-saw attack effectively for the first two rounds, then taking the third on a low blow by Armstrong. But Armstrong's looping right in the sixth, capping off several rounds of punishment, dropped Sarron to his knees, where he remained.

"Homicide" Henry then won 14 more tune-ups over the next seven months, earning a May 31, 1938 shot at Barney Ross' welterweight belt. The Chicago-based Ross was admittedly past his prime, but was also one of the toughest boxers of the decade, and entered the ring the favorite at 147 pounds to Armstrong's 133. Although Armstrong is remembered for his "windmill" style—which often cost him rounds for errant blows—against Ross he showed a different style, staying inside to neutralize the champion's superior reach. On the unseasonably cold evening, outdoors in the Madison Square Garden Bowl, Ross survived all 15 rounds, but it was over long before. "I can't say he's a hard one-punch hitter," said Ross, who retired after the bout, "but he certainly can wear you down."

On August 17, Armstrong returned to the Garden, where lightweight champ Lou Ambers proved the fiercest defender of the three. While Armstrong led on the cards throughout the bout, his mouth was cut so badly that the referee threatened to stop the contest in the 10th. "The ring is full of blood," he told Armstrong in his corner at one point. "It's your blood." Armstrong continued without a mouthpiece, swallowing the blood and pressing his attack. Despite giving up three rounds to fouls, he took his third title on a close 15-round decision, and "finished the bout on wabbly legs [sic]," according to James P. Dawson in *The New York Times.* Ambers agreed with Ross that Armstrong did not pack an especially powerful punch, but noted that he "sure hustles you."

In 1940, Armstrong barely missed the middleweight crown as well, in a controversial draw with Ceferino Garcia. By then he had developed a taste for the boozy high life which would leave him penniless at retirement in the mid-1940s. But a fighter who finishes at 151–21–9 is not without inner resources. His legendary drive, which enabled him to maintain a furious pace throughout a fight, also dragged him out of the gutter and into the Baptist ministry. In 1956, he wrote *Gloves, Glory, and God,* an autobiography, and he worked with underprivileged youth in Los Angeles until his death in 1988.   —*David Zivan*

SAM SNEAD
The Swing

Across generations, golfers might disagree about who was the greatest player ever, but from Grantland Rice to Lee Trevino, they've agreed on one thing: No one ever swung a club better than Sam Snead. "I think Sam Snead had the best golf swing of anyone I have ever had the pleasure of playing with," said Trevino. "It was an absolutely flawless swing."

There have been other great ones, but none of them produced a record 81 PGA victories, like Snead. He won seven major titles—the Masters and PGA Championship three

SNEAD: "AN ABSOLUTELY FLAWLESS SWING"

times each and the British Open once.

Snead's career spanned four decades; then he spent two more decades on the seniors tour. He played with an intimidating combination of power and grace. A multi-sport athlete in high school, the 5-foot-11-inch, 175-pound Snead had a natural, fluid swing. While some top players favored the arms or legs in their swings, Snead made good use of both.

"For pure animal grace, the sight of Sam Snead murdering a tee shot; Babe Ruth swinging from the heels; and, yes, Jack Dempsey raining savage destruction on a foe—these remain for me the acme of tigerish reflexes in human form," Grantland Rice once wrote.

Snead was successful despite putting problems that became so severe he reverted to straddling the ball and addressing it sidesaddle. But then, the genesis of Snead's career was unconventional, too. Raised on a farm in Ashwood, Virginia, Snead learned golf as a caddy, starting at age 10 on a course at the Homestead Hotel, where his father, Harry, worked on the boilers. Snead said he developed his accurate eye hunting squirrels as a young boy. He played in bare feet when he was young, and startled Masters officials by competing shoeless for a few holes at Augusta National on a dare from a friend. Initially labeled the hillbilly from backwoods Virginia, Snead earned the more dignified name "Slammin' Sammy" as he competed with Ben Hogan for major titles.

Fans loved Snead's country charm, and he was responsible for increasing the interest in golf during the 1930s. But for all his successes, Snead's career is also largely defined by the ones that got away. He finished second four times at the U.S. Open, the only major he never won. In 1947, he missed a 2 ½ footer to lose on the final hole of a playoff.

Eight years earlier, Snead would have won the Open by making a par 5 on the final hole at the Philadelphia CC. Unable to see the leader board from the 18th tee and thinking he needed a birdie to beat Byron Nelson, he drove into the rough, hit into two bunkers, and finished with a triple-bogey 8, tumbling into fifth place. Years later, he said, "I don't think I felt any lower, ever, than I did that day."

Snead survived his disappointments to stare down other challenges. At the 1942 PGA in Atlantic City, Snead played in front of a gallery that included servicemen from Fort Dix who were rooting for his opponent, Jim Turnesa, a corporal in the U.S. Army. Snead was heckled by the gallery, and twice during the first half of the 36-hole final, someone kicked Turnesa's drives out of the rough. When tournament officials nearly stopped the match, Snead said, "These bums don't scare me. I'm going to win it." And he did.

—*Mark Rosner*

Opening Act: Hewitt laterals to Karr to win the '33 NFL championship.

PRO FOOTBALL

The First (and Maybe Still the Best)

Beyond its historic significance, the first ever NFL championship game would stand as one of the great title shootouts in history, featuring six lead changes, some historic razzle-dazzle and a memorable finish. The NFL was split into two divisions for the 1933 season, paving the way for the first official title game. On December 17, the Eastern Division champion New York Giants visited the Western titleist Chicago Bears, in front of a large Wrigley Field crowd of 25,000 on a foggy, unseasonably warm day in Chicago. The league had been opened up in '33, with relaxed passing rules and the institution of hashmarks, both of which led to a new round of offensive inventiveness.

In the first quarter, the Giants' Mel Hein gained 15 yards on a rare center sneak (technically a pass, because an odd line alignment made Hein an eligible receiver). The Giants went ahead, 21–16, in the fourth quarter when Ken Strong, bottled up on a reverse to the left, lateraled back to Harry Newman, who scrambled right before noticing that Strong had drifted into the end zone. He threw a pass across the field, which Strong caught before falling out of the end zone and into the first-base dugout. But late in the fourth quarter, after driving to the Giants' 33, the Bears' Bronko Nagurski faked a drive into the line before throwing a jump pass to end Bill Hewitt, who had broken free on a crossing pattern. An instant before being tackled, Hewitt lateraled to right end Bill Karr, who carried the final 19 yards on the play, giving Chicago a 23–21 lead.

The game wasn't settled until the last play, when Red Grange made a game-saving, chest-high, open-field tackle of Giant halfback Dale Burnett, preventing him from lateraling to the trailing Hein.

TENNIS

1937 Davis Cup

■ Increasing war tensions only added pressure to what would become the most famous Davis Cup match in history, the 1937 semifinal between the United States and Germany, held on Wimbledon's neutral grass courts. The fifth and deciding match was an epic struggle between the gifted, powerful American Don Budge and Baron Gottfried von Cramm, the regal, blond-haired German. After von Cramm, playing what he would later describe as "absolutely

the finest match I have ever played in life," took the first two sets, Budge changed strategy and, lashing out more consistently with his killer backhand, won the next two sets. In the final set, von Cramm jumped to a 4-1 lead, before Budge rallied again, forcing the issue at the net. In the 14th game, von Cramm heroically staved off five match points before Budge won with a sprawling cross-court winner, to win the set, 8-6. Bill Tilden, coaching the German side, would later call it the greatest tennis match ever played.

COLLEGE FOOTBALL

1935 SMU-TCU

■ By the time 10-0 SMU took the field against 10-0 TCU in Fort Worth, the fans in the Southwest Conference were calling it the "Game of the First Half of the Century." With a Rose Bowl berth and a national championship on the line, SMU jumped in front 14-0 behind All-American halfback Bobby Wilson. But then TCU's Slingin' Sammy Baugh started the Horned Frogs rally, with a lengthy drive in the second quarter and a game-tying touchdown pass in the fourth. SMU drove to the TCU 36 on the ensuing drive; then Wilson caught a long bomb—on fourth-and-seven—to win, 20-14.

BASEBALL

1934 World Series

■ After scrambling back from seven games out of first place on September 5 to pass the New York Giants for the NL pennant, the Cardinals dirt-churning, hard-sliding Gas House Gang (perhaps the original trash talkers) faced the powerful Detroit Tigers in the 1934 World Series. The Tigers went up three games to two and headed back to Detroit to wrap up the Series. But Paul and Dizzy Dean, who had combined for 49 pitching wins during the regular season, gave up just three runs and 13 hits over the final two games. In the finale, the Cardinals scored seven runs in the third, then added two more in the sixth, punctuated by Joe Medwick's hard slide into Marv Owen at third base—which prompted a near riot of bottles, fruit, and vegetables when Medwick returned to left field in the bottom of the inning. (Commissioner Kenesaw Mountain Landis ordered Medwick pulled for his own protection.) The final was 11-0, and the Cardinals had their second title in four years.

HOCKEY

1935 Stanley Cup

■ The first all-Canadian final in nearly a decade featured one of the great goaltending performances in history, as Montreal Maroons' Alex Connell, who'd carried the team through two rounds of playoffs, proved the difference. At Maple Leaf Gardens for Games 1 and 2, Connell was at his acrobatic best

again, as the Maroons shocked regular-season champion Toronto, 3-2 and 3-1, then sewed up the series back in Montreal.

Great Performances

■ The Grand Slams in golf (Bobby Jones in 1930) and tennis (Don Budge in 1938) broke new ground, and clarified the concept of "The Majors" to fans in both sports.

The Great Unknown

■ Did Babe Ruth really "call" that vaunted home run against the Cubs in the 1932 World Series? Yes, though he never pointed to center field prior to his crucial shot, which broke a 4-4 tie in the third game of the Series, and paved the way for the Yankees' sweep. The controversy over Babe pointing misses the point, as Robert W. Creamer wrote in his acclaimed biography, *Babe:* "It's an argument over nothing, and the fact that Ruth did not point to center field before his home run does not diminish in the least what he did. He did challenge the Cubs before 50,000 people, did indicate he was going to hit a home run and did hit a home run. What more could you ask?"

The Truly Bizarre

■ In 1932, the league decided to hold a playoff game instead of a vote to determine the NFL champion (previous titles went to teams with the best winning percentage or, in the event of a tie, was decided by a vote of league owners). But a steady blizzard in Chicago forced the game indoors, so the Chicago Bears and Portsmouth Spartans battled it out on the dirt floor of Chicago Stadium, just a day after a traveling circus left town. To accommodate the surroundings, the game was played on an 80-yard field (the ball was placed back 20 yards every time a team moved beyond midfield), goal posts were moved to the goal lines and hashmarks were added, so that plays would always be snapped near the center of the field. The Bears scored in the fourth quarter on a Bronko Nagurski pass to Red Grange, then added a late safety en route to a 9-0 win. In so doing, they became the answer to a brutal bar-bet trivia question–what was the first NFL title won indoors?

Shadow Champions

Two of the best baseball teams of the '30s never reached the World Series. The 1932-34 **Pittsburgh Crawfords**, Gus Greenlee's high-profile, high-salaried (relatively) power of the Negro National League, were an itinerant monolith. "The Crawfords played everywhere, in every ballpark," recalled one veteran. "And we won. Won like we invented the game." The team sported the two greatest players in Negro League history—pitcher Satchel Paige and catcher Josh Gibson—as well as three other future Hall of Famers: manager–first baseman Oscar Charleston, third base mainstay Judy Johnson and legendary centerfielder James "Cool Papa" Bell. Greenlee would inaugurate the signature event of the Negro Leagues—the famed East-West All-Star Game— and also build the first stadium designed solely for a black team, the $60,000 Greenlee Stadium. On Independence Day, 1934, Paige struck out 17 in no-hitting the crosstown rival Homestead Grays.

At the beginning of the '30s, Cum Posey's Grays were the dominant Negro League team. In 1931, the Grays posted a barnstorming record of 136-10, while Josh Gibson hit 75 home runs (he'd later jump to the Crawfords and Greenlee, along with several teammates, for more money in

CRAWFORDS of 1932
3-18-32

'32). The ace of the Homestead staff was future Hall of Famer Smokey Joe Williams, who pitched effectively well into his 40s. Those Negro League champions never had a chance to compete for a full season against their white counterparts, but on the off-season barnstorming circuit, they would prove their mettle. One review of the black-white barnstorming games showed the blacks winning 309 of 438 games.

■ **Gopher Run.** The saying around the University of Minnesota football team was that there were as many anecdotes about head coach Bernie Bierman as there were Gopher losses. Which is to say, not many: From 1932 through 1941, Bierman's Gophers dominated midwestern football, going 63-12-5 and winning five national championships. Those Thirties-era Gophers were a reflection of their coach, stern and businesslike—they walked on the field, so as not to expend energy, and rarely relied on emotion to win games. Yet Bierman's players were no automatons. Locked in a scoreless tie late against Nebraska in 1936, Gopher Bud Wilkinson fielded a punt on his own 28 and ran toward the middle of the field, drawing all the defenders toward him. At the instant he was about to be overrun by Husker tacklers, Wilkinson heaved a lateral to Andy Uram at the 25, and Uram ran 75 yards through a slew of scrambling Nebraska defenders for the winning touchdown.

	COLLEGE BASKETBALL	PRO BASKETBALL	HOCKEY NHL	BASEBALL MLB	COLLEGE FOOTBALL	PRO FOOTBALL NFL
1930			Canadiens	Athletics	Notre Dame	Packers
1931			Canadiens	Cardinals	Southern Cal	Packers
1932			Maple Leafs	Yankees	Southern Cal	Bears
1933			Rangers	Giants	Michigan	Bears
1934			Black Hawks	Cardinals	Minnesota	Giants
1935			Montreal Maroons	Tigers	Minnesota	Lions
1936			Red Wings	Yankees	Minnesota	Packers
1937			Red Wings	Yankees	Pittsburgh	Redskins
1938	Temple (NIT)		Black Hawks	Yankees	TCU	Giants
1939	Oregon (NCAA)	LIU-Brooklyn (NIT)	Bruins	Yankees	Texas A&M	Packers

NOTES **College basketball**: The first NIT, and then the NCAA tournament, instituted a year later, settled the first true champions in college basketball. **College football**: Champions are mythical national champions, as chosen for predated seasons through 1935 by the Helms Foundation in 1941; as voted by sportswriters in Associated Press poll from 1936. **Pro Football**: Team with best record at end of season named champion by NFL th 1932, when tie for first place forced playoff game. League instituted a season-ending championship game for the 1933 season.

The Yankee Skipper

Joe **McCarthy** took over the Chicago Cubs in 1926. And midway through his first season as a big-league manager, he put future Hall of Famer Grover Alexander on waivers. The proud, pugnacious pitcher wound up with the Cardinals, and went on to become the hero of that season's World Series. But McCarthy had proved his point—he stamped himself as his own man, and by doing so began one of the most successful managerial careers in baseball history.

In his 24 seasons as a big league manager, McCarthy never had a losing team. And with the New York Yankees he won eight pennants and seven World Series, including four world titles from 1936-39, compiling a winning percentage of .615 in 3,487 games. He was a master tactician without being a dictator. He respected different personalities and once said that "a manager who cannot get along with a .400 hitter ought to have his head examined." Even players who didn't get along with him respected him as a leader. "I hate his guts," said Yankee Joe Page. "But there never was a better manager."

Though temperamental and intense, McCarthy was self-controlled. "I never challenged an umpire except on rules," he once said. "I never went to the mound to take out a pitcher, and I never roamed the dugout. I was there, seated in the middle, the command post." Under McCarthy's command, the game was altered. He was the first manager to divide his pitching staff into starters and relievers. And he is believed to be the first manager to enforce a dress code on the road. He even told his players to shave at home or the hotel. "This is your job," he said. "Shave before you come to work."

While he was blessed with great talent in New York, McCarthy had an impact wherever he went: the Cubs improved by 14 games his first season in Chicago; the Yankees by 8½ his first year in New York, and the Red Sox by 12½ his first season in Boston.

McCarthy's teams were hustling, confident, and fundamentally sound squads that played for big innings and rarely beat themselves. "He had a tenacious memory, never forgot any little thing that an opposing player might do," wrote baseball historian Bill James, who called him the greatest manager in baseball history. "He was well organized. Unlike McGraw, who tried to handle every detail of his team's routine ... McCarthy hired good coaches and relied upon them."

While McCarthy's no-nonsense attitude won him some enemies along the way—he tangled with Rogers Hornsby while managing the Cubs, and with Babe Ruth while with the Yankees—he remained a vigilant, utterly professional manager who constantly put his team in a position to win games.

"So I eat, drink and sleep baseball 24 hours a day," he once said. "What's wrong with that? The idea of this game is to win, and keep winning."

COACHING WISDOM

"I'm not worried about the game. No business in the world has ever made more money with poorer management. It can survive anything."

—New York Giants manager Bill Terry, analyzing the long–term financial prospects of major league baseball

"Fight them until hell freezes over, and then fight them on the ice."

—TCU football coach Dutch Meyer

The Elusive Ideal

The single most important force in promoting the modern Olympic ideal in America, **Avery Brundage** believed that the Olympics should be above politics. Yet he spent much of his career locked in political infighting, defending both the wisdom and purity of that belief.

A high school track & field star raised in Chicago, Brundage went to the University of Illinois, and later came in sixth in the pentathlon and failed to finish in the decathlon at the 1912 Olympics (the year Jim Thorpe won the gold in both events).

His name would become synonymous with the American Olympic movement. He served as head of the Amateur Athletic Association for seven years, the president of the U.S. Olympic Committee for 24 years and, in 1952, began a 20-year reign as president of the International Olympic Committee. His last major decision was that the 1972 Munich Olympic Games should go on, after a day of mourning for the 11 Israelis slain by Palestinian terrorists.

As far back as the 1964 Tokyo Games, Brundage recognized that "[t]he biggest problem today is that the Olympic Games have become so important that political people want to take control of them. Our only salvation is to keep free from politics."

In this last goal, he was a failure.

When some Americans wanted to boycott the 1936 Olympics in Berlin, in protest of the Third Reich's treatment of Jews, Brundage didn't merely argue against the boycott, he charged that those who supported it were communists, in the thrall of "Jewish propaganda." He often seemed an apologist for Hitler's regime. Decades later, his actions still seemed contradictory. Writer Brad Herzog has noted that, for many American athletes of the Sixties, the last straw was when Brundage removed the shot of Tommie Smith and John Carlos' "black power" salute from the official '68 Olympic highlight film. He'd urged the banishment of the two from Mexico City after their medal ceremony, but 32 years earlier, he'd never complained about the Nazi salutes that predominated the '36 Olympics.

For all that, it was Brundage who fought fiercely for the notion that the Olympics were important for what they represented—a chance for nations to put down their political differences and compete for a fortnight on a purely athletic playing field. Neither his contributions nor shortcomings can be overlooked, so he stands at the end of the century as a flawed visionary. To his credit, he understood that the Olympics were fundamentally different, and that if they were handled as just another business, it would be easy for its caretakers to lose sight of their larger worth. "When I'm gone," he said, "there's nobody rich enough, thick-skinned enough and smart enough to take my place, and the Games will be in tremendous trouble."

TOP OF THE NEWS: As the free world moves closer to another world war, the great sports events of the decade—Jesse Owens' four gold medals at the Munich Olympics, Joe Louis' battles with Max Schmeling—become part of a larger morality play pitting Democracy against Facism. The effects of the Depression are felt throughout the sports world—attendance in Major League Baseball is off 12 percent from the '20s and salaries dip as well—but spectator sports have become a vital part of the national culture. Even in bread lines in Philadelphia and St. Louis, fans listen to the 1931 World Series.

Movies

Film critics and sports fans are arguing about Leni Riefenstahl's flawed 1936 classic *Olympia,* a riveting record of the 1936 Berlin Games. Riefenstahl is commissioned to film the Games by the Nazi Party, as "a song of praise to the ideals of National Socialism." Though the film includes some of the most memorable athletic sequences ever filmed, it also glorifies Nazism.

In the Marx Brothers' classic **Horse Feathers**, Groucho plays the new president of Huxley College (which hasn't won a football game since its founding in 1888), determined to do whatever it takes to put a winner on the field for the school's big battle with Darwin University. S. J. Perelman is among the screenwriters. Gridiron musicals are surprisingly popular: Bing Crosby sings in *College Humor;* Judy Garland makes her feature debut in *Pigskin Parade*. And college stars like Jay Berwanger, Bobby Wilson and Bill Shakespeare make cameos in the movies, in this case, the 1936 "gridiron drama" *The Big Game*.

There are a glut of fight pictures, each one seemingly more preposterous

than the next. In 1936's *Cain and Mabel* (the first boxing musical), Clark Gable plays a boxer forced into a trumped-up romance with a Broadway starlet (Marion Davies) whom he despises. In 1939's *Golden Boy*, William Holden has to choose between a career as a boxer or a violinist. They aren't all bad: Among the best is 1931's *The Champ*, starring Wallace Beery (who won an Oscar for his role), about a has-been prizefighter and his loving son, played by Jackie Cooper. There are real boxers in 1932's *The Prizefighter and the Lady*, in which future heavyweight champ Max Baer starred as a fighter who falls for gangster's moll Myrna Loy; Jack Dempsey also appeared. In 1937's *Kid Galahad,* Wayne Morris stars as a young fighter who loses his girlfriend, Bette Davis, to promoter Edward G. Robinson.

Fashion

It is the best of times, it is the worst of times. In 1936, the interlocking N and Y first appear on the front of the Yankees' home uniforms. In the National League, the Reds try a disastrous one-year experiment of wearing red pants and white jerseys for some games at home. The White Sox' two-year run of navy blue road uniforms (referred to by some opponents as "sailor suits") is discontinued in 1931. In football, stripes are all the rage—**in 1936 the Chicago Bears break out new uniforms,** as modeled by Bronko Nagurski. The new threads have 14

different stripes, blue and orange, on the shoulders and sleeves of their white jerseys; the socks are nothing but blue and orange horizontal stripes.

Politics

The members of the Texas State Legislature are so thrilled by TCU's 1938 national championship in college football that it votes the next year to issue purple and white license plates, in honor of the feat.

Playing Games

National Pastime, invented by Clifford A. Van Beek of Green Bay, Wisconsin, is the first tabletop baseball game to attempt to accurately replicate big-league performances with dice and individual player cards. Patented in 1923, the game is advertised in the early Thirties before succumbing during the Depression. A close imitation of the game, APBA Baseball, would find success in the 1950s and beyond.

Reading List

After more than a decade as sports editor and columnist of *The New York Daily News*, **Paul Gallico** "retires" from sportswriting in 1936 to write such best-selling novels as *The Poseidon Adventure* and *The Snow Goose*. But in 1937, Gallico publishes a memoir called *A Farewell to Sport*, which is commercially successful. George Plimpton, of *Paper Lion* fame, would later credit Gallico's book with inspiring his career in "participatory" journalism.

> *"I long ago come to the conclusion that all life is 6 to 5 against."*
> —Damon Runyon, *Money From Home*

Impressions of the '30s

From ESPN's Robin Roberts:

Pride, dignity, and grace immediately comes to mind when I think of this decade. Qualities embodied by **Jesse Owens**. He silenced Hitler in Berlin, and back home a nation rejoiced. My mother, a young teenager living in Akron, Ohio, remembers the pride that filled the black community because of Owens and Joe Louis. You always knew when Louis was fighting. The entire neighborhood would gather on the front porch of the only house on Lucy Street with a radio and cheer on their hero. The country was suffering through the Depression, and sports provided an escape. These were athletes the average fan could relate to. Their salaries were modest but their accomplishments grand.

Debuts and Exits

1930
Electronic scoreboards in football First erected at Michigan Stadium, above both end zones.

The Sullivan Award Given to the nation's outstanding amateur athlete; Bobby Jones is the first winner.

The ground-rule double.

1931
Legal gambling in Nevada.

1932
EXIT **Flying blocks, flying tackles** Outlawed by the NCAA.

1933
The two-fisted backhand in tennis Popularized by Australian men's star Vivian McGrath.

Baseball's All-Star Game, as Babe Ruth homers and is named MVP of the first "Midsummer Classic."

Hashmarks become mandatory on NFL fields; after debut in the '32 playoff game, played indoors at Chicago Stadium.

Horse racing's first tote board at Arlington Park in Chicago.

1934
The College All-Star Game Annual exhibition battle between NFL champs and rookies; Bears tie All-Stars, 0-0.

The Masters in Augusta, Georgia. Horton Smith wins with a four-round score of 284.

The penalty shot in the National Hockey League.

EXIT **The fatter football.** Another full inch is taken off the girth of the ball in the NFL.

EXIT **The fatter basketball.** The circumference is reduced from 32 to 30 inches, making the ball easier to dribble and shoot.

1935
The three-second rule in college basketball.

Night baseball in the major leagues, as Cincinnati beats visiting Philadelphia, 2-1, on May 24.

The Orange Bowl in Miami. Bucknell beats Miami, 26-0, on New Year's Day.

The Sugar Bowl in New Orleans. Tulane beats Temple, 20-14, on New Year's Day.

The board game Monopoly, in which the most landed-on space is Illinois Avenue.

The Heisman Trophy Given to the nation's outstanding college football player; Jay Berwanger is the first winner.

1936
The Associated Press' weekly college football poll, as Minnesota ends the season ranked No. 1 by the writers.

The NFL Draft Jay Berwanger is selected first, by Philadelphia, but never plays pro football.

1937
The Cotton Bowl in Dallas. Texas Christian beats Marquette, 16-6, on New Year's Day.

EXIT **Center jumps** after each score in college basketball.

1938
A 14-club limit for bags in tournament play, as mandated by the USGA.

The "Grand Slam" in tennis After Don Budge swept Wimbledon, Australian, French and U.S. titles.

Michigan's famous "winged" helmet design Painted by head coach Fritz Crisler.

1939
NCAA basketball tournament.

Baseball's Hall of Fame opens in Cooperstown, New York.

THE 1940S

"I honestly feel that it would be best for the country to keep baseball going," said FDR, in a letter to Kenesaw Mountain Landis. Even as America fought in World War II, spectator sports continued, serving as an oasis of normalcy amid a world in chaos. And when the nation emerged triumphant in 1945, the game seemed more

important than ever. In the final era of
baseball's unquestioned superiority, the game's
two shining lights were equal and opposite:
Boston's Splendid Splinter was surly and
preternaturally gifted; New York's Yankee
Clipper was dignified and graceful. The two
stars framed the sensibilities and great hopes
of the century's most tumultuous decade.

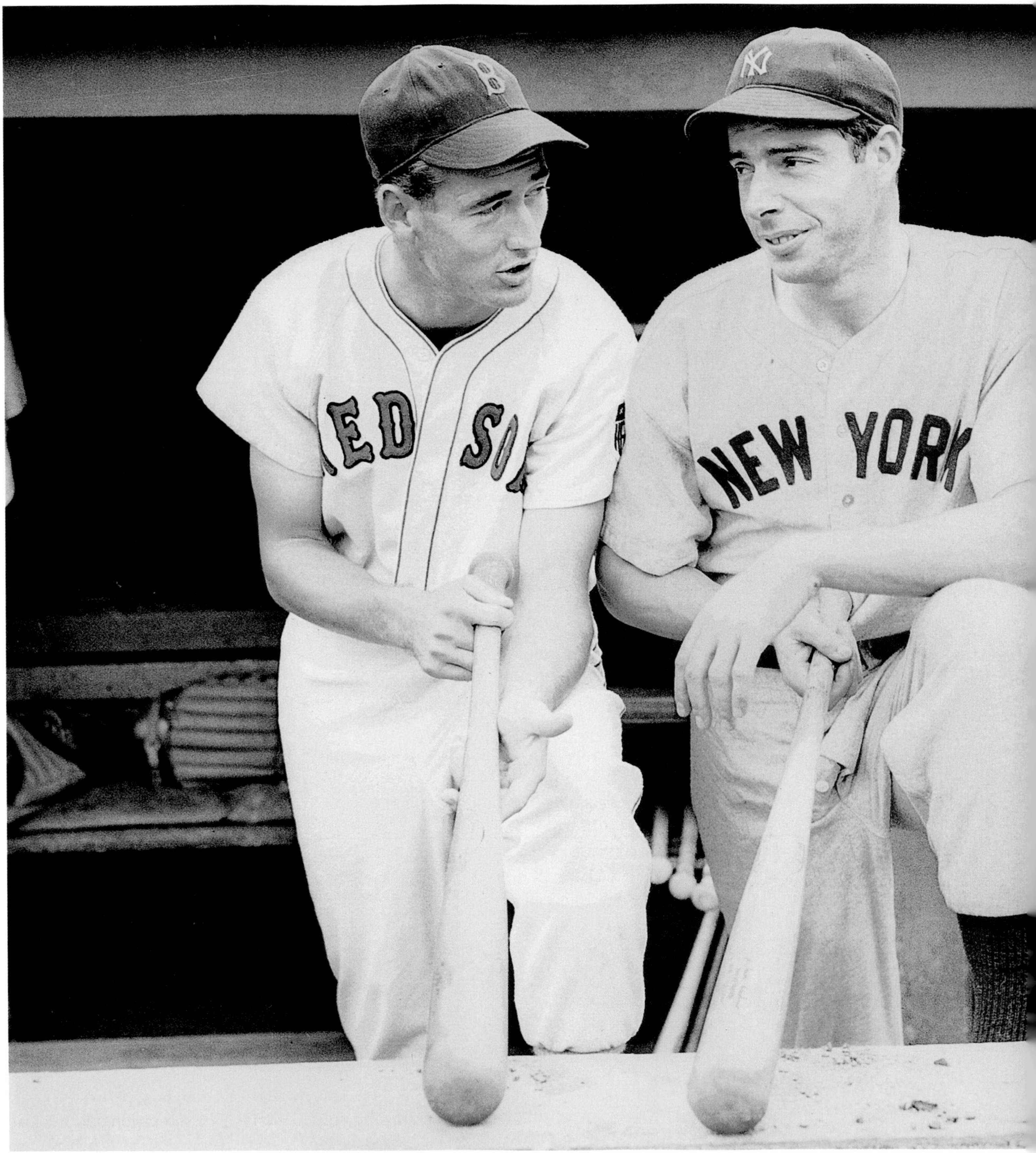
NEW YORK

The Stuff of Dreams

"GOD KNEW WHAT HE WAS DOING," says Kay Starr in a those-were-the-days video from *Reader's Digest.* "He let me sing at a perfect time." Not the Fifties, when she recorded schlocky pop hits like "Bonaparte's Retreat" and "The Rock and Roll Waltz," but the Forties, when she was interpreting jazzy standards with big swing bands. And Joe DiMaggio—*Willie Mays'* hero—and Ted Williams, who on those rare occasions when his stroke wasn't right would say, "I don't feel swishy up there," were taking long, beautiful swings for the Yankees, the Red Sox and America.

What with Steven Spielberg's *Saving Private Ryan,* Tom Brokaw's *The Greatest Generation* and young people retro-dancing to the jumpin' jive, the Forties seem to have become the decade of the late Nineties. So why not get misty about a time when the National Pastime was so grand and dreamlike that people must have known that nostalgia was just around the corner, and great hitters were driven by natural grace, sheer pride and two, three, four hundred dollars a game.

On the other hand, it was during the Forties that God saw fit for the Swing Era to end, for people to find robust unfiltered cigarettes salubrious, for African-Americans still to be excluded from most hotels and restaurants, for Hitler and Mussolini and Tojo to damn near take over the world, and for Williams and DiMaggio to miss three whole seasons in their primes. We can oversimplify the Twenties by "Ain't We Got Fun," the Thirties by Depression, the Fifties by Repression, the Sixties by Anti-repression, the Seventies by Disco Tacky, the Eighties by Greed, and the Nineties by Boomers Not Getting Any Younger, but the Forties swung in several ways. The first 23 months were still the New Deal struggling to gain ground against Hard Times; then until August of 1945 we had World War II, which brought Americans together (the ones it didn't kill, cripple, or sour) and brought on unprecedented prosperity (which drew Americans out into the suburbs); then came the Bomb, Cold War, labor unrest, racial clashes and Red scares, which pulled the Democrats into three parties, split the Allies with an Iron Curtain, and brought up the notion that subversion and nuclear fission might blow the world to smithereens.

PREVIOUS PAGES
Weapons of Mass Destruction.
The bats used during their banner seasons of 1941 by Joltin' Joe and the Splendid Splinter.

The Masters.
Williams and DiMaggio in the dugout at Fenway Park before a Yankees-Red Sox game in August 1942.

Baseball, throughout, held together. Professional football and basketball were small potatoes in the Forties, college sports were regional, and thanks to the war there were only four Wimbledons and one Olympic year. Golf had its Snead and Hogan; racing its Whirlaway and Citation (each won a Triple Crown with Eddie Arcaro up); boxing had Joe Louis, Sugar Ray Robinson, and Zale vs. Graziano; but baseball was the national pastime as it never had been before and never would be again. And yes, its stars included Rapid Robert Feller and Stan "the Man" Musial, great players both (and over in the Negro Leagues, Satchel Paige and Josh Gibson), but Joltin' Joe DiMaggio and Ted "The Splendid Splinter" Williams were The Men. God let them hit (and DiMaggio, run and field) at a perfect time. Pauline Kael has called the movie *Golddiggers of 1933* "pure Thirties." Williams and DiMaggio were pure Forties.

As pure as Betty Grable painted on a B-29?

Well, DiMaggio was a Bronx Bomber. And both he and Williams were, like Grable (and swing dancing, and jitter-bugging, too), leggy. Jane Russell in *The Outlaw* (1943) displayed (notoriously) cleavage, but she was exceptional. Forties babes had gams. A study showed, in fact, that the legs of American women were measurably longer than the previous generation's; at any rate, as push-up bras are to the Nineties, hose were to the Forties. During the war, when materials were so scarce that a man in possession of a pair of nylons was dealing from an unfair advantage, many a gal had to simulate stockings—drawing seams down the backs of her legs with eyebrow pencil. Knockouts' legs—and also their hair— were long and flowing, and they wore flowing clothes—tailored, yes, and with shoulder pads maybe, but the emphasis was on the long natural lines of dignified lissomeness, not the magnified ins and outs of hips and bust. Rita Hayworth in *Gilda* and Lauren Bacall in *To Have and Have Not* (the sinuous little wiggle she does at the end of the picture is twice as sexy as Sharon Stone's parted thighs) stretched out on Harry Truman's piano come to mind.

The model outfielder-slugger's build of the Fifties and Sixties would be compact, tensile-strong: Mays, Henry Aaron or (to take a beefier and perhaps therefore frailer example) Mickey Mantle. In comparison, Depression kids Williams and DiMaggio were largely arms and legs (and in Ted's case, neck). When Williams was a senior in high school he was 6 foot 3 inches, 145 pounds. The scout from the Tigers told Williams' mother, "I had a lot of good moves," as Williams recalls in *My Turn at Bat, The Story of My Life*, "but I was so scrawny a year of professional baseball would kill me. Literally kill me." Four years later, already a big-league star, he was still gangly, ran oddly. "It's certainly reasonable to assume that at 6 foot 4 inches, 175 pounds, a skinny bean, I looked more lackadaisical in the field than I was. A little guy with shorter limbs, making the same moves, is going to look like he's doing it quicker, like he's really hustling."

At bat, though, the Williams limbs flowed. The way he coiled and uncoiled with a bat in his hands has been compared to the helical, almost graspably magical swirl of a barber's pole. (They used to be common phenomena, those poles, striped like candy canes.)

DiMaggio's long legs—set so wide apart in his batting stance that he seemed hardly to stride at all—were more widely wieldy. He played centerfield, the rangiest outfield position, and he played it (let us not choose our words lightly) ineffably, where-

Diamond in the Rough. Williams wrote that when he was a 17-year-old in San Diego—and 6 feet 3 inches, 145 pounds—he was "so scrawny a year of professional baseball would kill me."

as Ted played left, the least demanding field, and he played it passably (sometimes taking off his glove between hitters to swing it like a bat, honing his swing without which life to him didn't mean a thing). Neither of them were base stealers (the Forties were not base-stealing times), but Joe covered ground with great unshowy dispatch from first to third, from second to home, his legs stretching like great scissors on the turns. Wrote Grantland Rice:

No greater effort than a breeze that blows / Across the field when some fly ball is struck.
A drifting phantom where the long smash goes, / That has no helping teammate known as luck.
No desperate stab—no wild one-handed catch, / Few ringing cheers that churn the summer air.
A shift—a turn—a movement none can match, / The ball drifts down—DiMaggio is there.

A swing—a slash—the ball is on its way, / But still no effort as the ball sails on.
The whipping ash still keeps the foe at bay, / A blur against the blue—and then the ball is gone.
Ty Cobb has ruled—and Ruth has sung his tune— / Tris Speaker was a melody in rime—
DiMaggio—you won't forget him soon— / Here is the master artist of our time.

SO "JOLTIN' JOE" and one of Williams' nicknames, "The Thumper," had the wrong ring, really: too clunky. "Whirlaway" would have fit either of them better.

In the Forties no one was built like Sammy Sosa, much less like Mark McGwire. The closest thing to "muscle candy" supplements was steak, and weight lifting was believed to make athletes muscle-bound (though Williams devised pulley devices with which he exercised just those muscles he believed to be important to his stroke). McGwire's and Sosa's swings—enormous upper-body strength whipping a light bat, *zip*, and the top hand released so as to pass maximal torque around bulging biceps, shoulders and pecs—are contemporary astonishments, like the transmission of an entire library's information to another continent in a nanosecond. McGwire and Sosa have responded with a sort of genius to the late–breaking slider (which only a few pitchers threw in the Forties), the split-fingered fastball (which didn't emerge until the latter Seventies), and the burgeoning homer-dollar-ratio imperative. And a beautiful thing the Nineties swing is in its way, but that top-hand release lends a briefly ecstatic, *ta-daaaah* element not in keeping with the contained flow of the Forties.

Williams was a great adjuster who used a lighter bat as he got older. The reason he complained publicly about not being able to hit the slider, he told his biographer Ed Linn, was that he liked hitting it and wanted to trick pitchers into giving it to him more often. Still, as diluted as Nineties pitching talent may be by the expansion from sixteen big-league teams in the Forties to however the hell many there are today, Joe and Ted might well not be able, in a Nineties season—against wave after wave of fresh relief pitchers throwing 90-mile-an-hour stuff that dips or bends at the last moment—to hit way over .300 and 30 to 40 home runs, and drive in 130 to 150 runs while striking out fewer than 50 times (which is what they did in the Forties), with that Forties swing of theirs.

But that Forties swing...

Do you have *Baseball, an Illustrated History*, the book spun off by the Ken Burns baseball video series? Look at page 269: DiMaggio at full follow-through extension. (You will have seen that picture, perhaps in the form of an imitative painting, if you are any baseball fan at all.) Now look at page 272: Williams dropping the bat at the

Damaged Goods. Many doubted whether DiMaggio could produce on a major-league level because of his slight frame and his injured left knee. "You've bought yourself a cripple," said Bill Terry, after the Yankees purchased his contract from the San Francisco Seals.

end of follow-through.

Whereas Nineties artificial-fiber uniforms are as skintight and flexible as can be, the unsleek Forties outfits of heavy, baggy wool helped make the men on the field—big, old, rawboned farmerish guys, most of them, but some of them thick-bellied and a few rather weedy or downright runty—look more like somebody who might conceivably be your uncle than Mark or Sammy. And yet, don't Joe and Ted (uncluttered by batting gloves, shin guards, sweatbands, or logos) look more like Greek sculpture, or like photographs of Nijinsky? DiMaggio had massive thighs, but they were all of a piece with his lankiness. How *could* he be quite so smooth? The mystery was preserved by the liquefaction of his clothes. In DiMaggio's case, in Yankee Stadium, they were pinstriped—formal, but with some billow, like classical robes or Old Glory.

All in the Family. Dom DiMaggio (above right) always took the easy way out—he said his brother was the best right-handed hitter he'd ever seen, and that his teammate Williams was the best left-handed hitter.

To the Woodshed. Williams at Yankee Stadium (right) during July 1941, the year he'd hit .406.

IF YOU WERE A KID IN THE FORTIES who lived in one of the ten cities that had a big-league team or two (or in the case of New York City, three), you could take public transportation to the park, buy a ticket for fifty cents or less, and see baseball stars in the flesh, in broad daylight (and in Cleveland you could watch a coach named Jackie Price driving a cart around in the outfield to catch batting-practice flies, and Max Patkin clowning goonily in the first-base coaching box during the game, if the score wasn't close, and you might find yourself sitting in the bleachers next to Bill Veeck, the flamboyant, down-to-earth showman-owner of the Indians). But if you were anybody who lived anywhere else, you had to be satisfied with glimpses in the newspapers or the newsreels, or you could listen to games on the radio and imagine. It was in the Forties that baseball began to be televised, but only occasionally. Ballplayers were a long way from becoming as accessible as kiddie cartoons. There was some night baseball in the Forties (DiMaggio said it cut two years off his career, because it was so hard to get loose for a day game after the odd one under the lights), but the standard medium was natural light. "Baseball was meant to be played in God's own sunshine," said Clark Griffith, owner of the Washington Senators. There were certainly no *indoor* stadia. You couldn't tune in at 11 P.M. to catch the evening's highlights upstaged by wiseacre commentators.

Although they both came from California, Ted and Joe did not hug each other, or take bows. You might see a news photo of them posing together smiling, but they never came off as bosom buddies to each other or their teammates, and certainly not to their fans. Each man was dour and distant in his way. DiMaggio's "reticence might only have been a product of his shyness," Robert W. Creamer has written, "but it came out like dignity. And class." Has any American public figure been spoken of as having class since Frank Sinatra? Today the term *dignified* is seldom applied to anyone except African-Americans and Hilary Clinton, but in the Forties, when men went to ballgames wearing hats, jackets and ties (whose lines hold up quite well against the *high* fashions of today), dignity was something everyone might aspire to, and Joe and Ted, in different ways (Ted made a point of almost never wearing a necktie), exemplified it. DiMaggio's most famous statement was, in answer to the question why he played so hard all the time, "There might be someone in the park who's never seen me play before." When Williams had a chance to sit out a double-header (teams often played two games for the price of one back then) and finish out the 1941 season batting a rounded-off .400, he rejected that notion out of hand, played both games, got six hits, including a tremendous home run in eight at bats, and finished at .406. "The

record's no good," he said, "unless it's made in all the games."

In many ways, the two of them counterbalanced: Joe, right-handed in a park favoring left-handed hitters; Ted vice versa. Joe from northern California (San Francisco, solid fishing family); Ted from southern (San Diego, father a heavy-drinking ex-horse soldier, mother a tambourine-banging Salvation Army girl embarrassingly well known around town, neither of them home very much). Joe, a night-clubber; Ted, an outdoorsman who got to bed early. Joe, the all-around player; Ted, the principled pull hitter who only occasionally deigned to adjust his swing so as to poke the ball to left (once with an inside-the-park homer to clinch the 1946 pennant) although fielders bunched on the right side against him. Joe almost immobile awaiting the pitch; Ted fidgety. Joe, admired for reaching out to do whatever subtle or dramatic thing it took to help his team win a game. (The talent-loaded Yankees won 10 pennants and 9 World Series in his 13 seasons.) Ted stubbornly reigning over his selective sphere of influence: biding his time between at-bats and then from pitch to pitch, taking a lot of bases on balls, holding out for the optimally drivable strike. (The pitching-poor Red Sox won one pennant and no World Series in his 17 full seasons.)

JOE WAS A BASICALLY INARTICULATE PERSON who handled the press very well by being severe. Ted was an impulsively outspoken person whose stature was somehow confirmed by the vehemence with which scribes tried to tear him down. In those days, the dominant sports-commentary medium was newspapers. Williams would come into the dugout before a game and say, "What's that smell? Oh, it's just writers." (He was careful, however, to say only good things to and about umpires and pitchers, whose input affected his hitting.) The most fun for a sportswriter in the fiercely competitive Boston market was sitting up in the pressbox (or even farther away—Williams's most gleeful critic, the witty and bibulous Dave Egan, seldom even came to the park), righteously portraying the city's greatest sports star as a bum. The height of sportswriting insiderdom in New York was to be a buddy of Joe's, who knew his thinking, suppressed the rough edges of his personality, and buffed up his utterances—to legendary, if often corny, effect. As their successors would do to the similarly contrasted basketball giants Bill Russell and Wilt Chamberlain, the typists of the Forties carved DiMaggio in stone and crucified Williams.

Each had his most historic year in 1941. From May 15 to July 16, DiMaggio never once failed to get at least one hit in a game—in 56 consecutive games. The next longest such streak, going back into the mists of history and on into the mists of the present, is 44 games. DiMaggio smoked heavily, developed ulcers, couldn't sleep, but he made the streak, like everything else he did on the field, look easy, considering how momentously it gripped the nation. He had held out for a modest raise (to $42,000) in the spring of 1940 and home crowds had booed him, but the 1941 streak established him as a wonder man. During the last 20 or so games, radio bulletins kept the nation abreast of each of his at-bats. (During Red Sox games, the Fenway Park scoreboard operator would relay each bulletin to Williams in left field so he could pass it on to Joe's brother Dominic, Boston's centerfielder.) The baseball world was less enthralled by Williams's .400 hitting, but in retrospect it is an achievement comparable to DiMag's streak: Ted was the first man to hit .400 for a season since 1930 and the last one to this date. He also won the '41 All-Star game for the American League with a towering, game-winning

The Streak. DiMaggio rides on his teammates' shoulders, July 2, 1941, after hitting in his 45th straight game, breaking Wee Willie Keeler's consecutive-game hit streak. At right, fifteen days later, he smiles after going hitless for the first time in 57 games.

home run—DiMaggio, from first base, scoring the winning run quietly and Williams laughing, clapping his hands, bounding gawkily around the bases with uncharacteristically open delight.

On December 7, 1941, Japan bombed Pearl Harbor, and America entered the war against the Axis powers. "Nothing is more certain," proclaimed Winston Churchill on the radio, "than that every trace of Hitler's footsteps, every stain of his infected and corroding fingers will be sponged and purged and if need be blasted from the surface of the earth. Lift up your hearts. All will come right. Out of the depths of sorrow and of sacrifice will be born again the glory of mankind." But even after America pitched in (with what was then the 18th largest army in the world), the Fascists had all but conquered Europe, and the forces of the Rising Sun had Asia in a stranglehold. German submarines were sinking tankers carrying American oil to eastern U.S. cities.

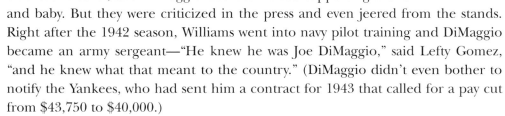

Hank Greenberg had entered the army during the 1941 season and finished his tour two days before Pearl Harbor. He re-upped, and served until the middle of the 1945 season. When Bob Feller enlisted in the navy two days after Pearl Harbor, the ceremony was broadcast live on the radio nationwide. Williams and DiMaggio both accepted deferments, Williams as the sole supporter of his divorced mother, and DiMaggio because he was supporting a wife and baby. But they were criticized in the press and even jeered from the stands. Right after the 1942 season, Williams went into navy pilot training and DiMaggio became an army sergeant—"He knew he was Joe DiMaggio," said Lefty Gomez, "and he knew what that meant to the country." (DiMaggio didn't even bother to notify the Yankees, who had sent him a contract for 1943 that called for a pay cut from $43,750 to $40,000.)

DiMAGGIO WAS 28 WHEN HE WENT IN; Williams, 25. Each gave up three seasons so potentially prime that the juices still flow in what-might-have-been memories today. Williams never saw any action in World War II (in Korea, in the Fifties, he flew thirty-nine combat missions, once bringing his jet in after it had been set ablaze by enemy fire), and DiMaggio's duties consisted mainly of playing ball on army teams, but they served their country for the duration. Meanwhile, baseball survived. President Roosevelt, thanks in part to some lobbying by the Senators' Clark Griffith, sent Baseball Commissioner Kenesaw Mountain Landis a letter saying that it would be best for the country's morale if regular play continued: "Baseball provides a recreation which does not last over two hours or two hours and a half, and which can be got for very little cost. And, incidentally, I hope that night games can be extended because it gives an opportunity to the day shift to see a game occasionally." The Westinghouse Electric Company reported that stadium lights would use up less power than fans would individually if they stayed home reading.

"Baseball marches on," wrote Dan Daniel in *The Sporting News*. "It marches on in martial tread, cognizant of its duties and its responsibilities, and the hazards which confront it on land, sea and in the air.... 'Frivolous,' snorts Hitler. 'Ridiculous,' gutturals Mussolini. 'Marvelous,' says the American."

Two Classic Swings. "Ted Williams is the best hitter I ever saw," said Mickey Mantle, "but DiMaggio was the most finished player. DiMag could hit, throw, field, and run the bases."

In tribute to the players who were going to war, J. G. Taylor Spink waxed even more eloquent in that publication:

> Look well at these heroes of our diamonds, let their pictures become indelible in your minds. For they go, nobody knows where, and nobody knows when once again you will see them in their habiliments of the diamond, scorching the infield, poised on the mound, tearing across the outer reaches, swinging the sticks of baseball valor....
>
> If your outfielder fans twice or thrice, don't strain your vocal cords into vociferous displeasure. He is supporting his aged parents, but the Army has sent its call to the colors. He goes—and he knows not where, nor whether he will once again gaze into that packed grandstand, whether he will peer into those shirt sleeved bleachers in 1943, 1944, or ever.

When the Cardinals came from way behind to overtake Brooklyn in the 1942 National League pennant race, Alpen Brau, a St. Louis beer company, ran a big newspaper ad in which Hitler was depicted cowering before a cardinal perched on a bat. "Listen to the little Red Bird, Adolf," said the ad, "it's telling you YOUR LEAD ISN'T BIG ENOUGH EITHER!"

It was the other St. Louis team, however, which became emblematic of wartime baseball. The Browns were the only major-league team that had never won a pennant. But by the end of 1943 the Yankees, for instance, were without most of the starting players on their 1942 championship team. In the course of the war years, there would be pitching appearances by a one-legged veteran and a sixteen-year-old. In 1945, the Senators would start three Cubans every day; they also had an Italian and a Venezuelan, and their five starting pitchers were all knuckleballers.

George McQuinn, the Browns' 35-year-old first baseman who had flunked several induction physicals, said, "We realized that DiMaggio and Williams and all the rest of the big stars were off in the service. We were as good as anybody." The Browns had a catcher, Frank Mancuso, who had injured his back so badly while trying to master parachuting that he'd already been discharged from the army and was unable to look straight up in the air for a pop-up. They had a pitcher, Sigmund "Jack" Jakucki, who drank heavily and had been out of organized ball for six years. In 1945 they would start a one-armed outfielder, Pete Gray. In 1944 they won the American League pennant. Baseball from 1942 through 1945 may be summed up by the title of William B. Mead's excellent account of wartime ball: *Even the Browns.*

Then the Germans surrendered. Asked what had turned the tide, British Field Marshal Montgomery said it was America's dogface foot soldiers, in trousers as baggy as those of Forties ballplayers. "I take my hat off to such men," said the generally far from effusive Montgomery. "I have tried to feel that I am also an American soldier myself." On September 2, 1945, Japan's emperor Hirohito (although many of his military leaders wanted to fight on to the last man, even after Hiroshima and Nagasaki) finally surrendered. "I got my papers at the Navy Pier," said Bob Feller, "walked out, they took a few pictures, I jumped on a plane, came back and pitched against Newhouser. Beat him four to two, struck out a dozen. What I liked most was the headline in the Cleveland paper: 'This Is What We've Been Waiting For.'"

Four more years of Forties baseball, with Williams and DiMaggio again in the fore. The nation's economy and birthrate boomed, and so did baseball attendance. In 1946, the Red Sox won the pennant and Williams was the American League's Most

Men in Uniform. Following the '42 season, Williams and DiMaggio went on active duty. Williams went into pilot training and DiMaggio became an army sergeant.

Valuable Player. In 1947 it was the Yankees and DiMaggio (although Williams won the Triple Crown, leading the league in batting, home runs and RBI). In 1949 the Yankees won the pennant—on the last day of the season, head to head against the second-place Red Sox—but Williams was the MVP again.

Baseball was changing, though. In 1947 Jackie Robinson became the first black player in the modern major leagues, and the action began to turn less lopey—became quicker, jiggier, more explosive. As befit the Atomic Age. Black players had been a novelty act; now they began to set standards. This would become more and more the case in music, too. The smartest indigenous music became bebop; the bounciest, rhythm and blues. When rock 'n' roll kicks in, where is your swing and sway? America would never be the same, and about time. Kay Starr was good, but while her prime may have been a gift from God, it was deep-structural discrimination that made her more blessed in the Forties than Billie Holiday. And Williams and DiMaggio more blessed—as Williams made a point of mentioning when he was inducted into the Hall of Fame—than Gibson and Paige.

In baseball, the stretches between bursts began to seem more like *longeurs*. TV made elements of the game more observable than ever, but the pasture-wide picture didn't fit the screen. The war had had a shaking and leveling effect that made workers, wives and businessmen less accepting of traditional parameters, less respectful of authority. There was a lot more money on the table, and people began to think more in terms of not leaving any there—even of going beyond what was there to what might be construed to be there. Pretty soon baseball would be feeling a need to market itself (light shows on the scoreboards!) in competition with faster forms of entertainment.

DiMaggio's last good year was 1950. In the first three games of the 1951 World Series he was swinging the bat so raggedly that the word pity actually cropped up in newspaper accounts. In the fourth game he hit a homer, and in the final game (the Yankees beating the Giants in six) he got a double in his last at-bat, but after the Series he said, "When baseball is no longer fun it's no longer a game. And so, I've played my last game of ball." He went on to marry Marilyn Monroe, unhappily; to serve as a dignified endorser of a coffee-making machine; and to appear on ceremonial occasions. In 1999, after surgery for lung cancer, he emerged from a coma to chew out his doctors for giving interviews about his condition. They desisted. Months later he died, a tough out.

Williams in the Fifties had a lot more hits left in him (in 1958 he hit .388 with 38 home runs, an on-base percentage of .516 and a slugging percentage of .731), but he was fighting in Korea for most of 1952 and 1953, never played as many as 150 games in a season after 1949, and said that he was never as good a hitter after injuring his elbow in 1950. He retired in 1960, after hitting a home run in his final at-bat and declining to tip his cap—"Gods do not answer letters," wrote John Updike. In the Eighties, when gods were merely celebrities and big bucks had replaced batting averages as baseball's prime statistical indicators, Williams' old teammate Birdie Tebbetts said Ted "is not a man for his age. The only place he'd be at home is the Alamo."

Nobody is more at home in baseball history, however, than the Williams and the DiMaggio of the Forties, a decade with legs.

Wedding Day. DiMaggio gives Marilyn Monroe a kiss January 14, 1954, the day they wed in San Francisco.

JACKIE ROBINSON
A New Kind of Hero

When Jackie Robinson crossed the white line and took the field on April 15, 1947, he wasn't just breaking major league baseball's color barrier by becoming the first black big-leaguer of the century. He was setting into motion the most sweeping social changes of the postwar era. "For the first time, we had a black man at the center of white consciousness to root for," wrote Roger Wilkins. "Before Jack came to the Dodgers, America really hadn't acknowledged—over any length of time—full black heroes."

That would all begin to change because of Robinson's talent and resolve.

Abandoned by his father at an early age, Robinson was raised by his mother, a maid in Pasadena, California. Finding an outlet in sports, he eventually became the first UCLA student to letter in four sports. After serving a tour of duty in the army, he spent most of the 1945 season with the Kansas City Monarchs as a reserve infielder.

The Dodgers signed Robinson after the '45 season and, in the words of basketball great Bill Russell, "they picked up 20 million fans instantly." Dodgers president Branch Rickey, the visionary who signed Robinson and prepared him for the gauntlet he would have to run in 1947, knew that the first black player would be subject to all manner of provocation, both emotional and physical. In Robinson, he saw a man with the sort of willpower to weather that barrage of opposition. "Above anything else, I hate to lose," said Robinson. And in 1947, losing meant losing his temper. Through that glorious rookie season, Robinson swallowed his anger and played through the vicious hazing to which he was subjected around the league. "I'm not concerned with your liking or disliking me," he said. "All I ask is that you respect me as a human being." He was named NL rookie of the year. Two years later he won the MVP award, batting .342 and driving in 124 runs. In his 10 seasons with the Dodgers, the team won six pennants, came excruciatingly close to winning two others (1950 and 1951), and finally brought a world championship home in 1955.

"Thinking about the things that happened," said Robinson's friend and teammate Pee Wee Reese, "I don't know any other ballplayer who could have done what he did. To be able to hit with everybody yelling at him. He had to block all that out. To do what he did has got to be the most tremendous thing I've ever seen in sports." Robinson brought to the game a sense of combative daring and an ability to distract pitchers to the point of frustration (he stole home 19 times in his career). Hall-of-Famer Duke Snider called Robinson "the greatest competitor I've ever seen; I've

ROBINSON:
"ALL I ASK IS THAT YOU RESPECT ME AS A HUMAN BEING"

HOGAN:
"HE'S FIGHTING FOR EVERY INCH, EVERY FOOT, EVERY YARD ON A GOLF COURSE"

seen him beat a team with his bat, his ball, his glove, his feet and, in a game in Chicago one time, with his mouth."

Robinson's entry cleared the way for other blacks, in baseball and beyond. "He meant everything to a black ballplayer," said the Yankees' Elston Howard. "I don't think the young players would go through what he did. He did it for all of us, for Willie Mays, Henry Aaron, Maury Wills, myself." Mays was among the many players who never forgot what he owed Robinson. "Every time I look at my pocketbook," he said, "I see Jackie Robinson."

So the past taught the future a valuable lesson. And at the end, as Robinson wrote in his autobiography, *I Never Had It Made*, the tables were balanced. "The way I figured it, I was even with baseball and baseball with me. The game had done much for me, and I had done much for it."

And, he might have added, much for the country as well.

BEN HOGAN
"Players Were Afraid"

It was called the Hogan Mystique. And it was responsible for Ben Hogan's towering presence in the golf world. With his trademark white cap pulled low over his steely gray eyes, the wiry Hogan attacked the course, and his opponents, with a stoic, controlled ferocity. By the time he retired, he'd cemented a reputation as one of the three or four best golfers in history, and almost certainly the most feared one.

"I can't explain it, because I'm not a psychologist," said Byron Nelson. "But players were genuinely afraid of Ben, afraid of playing with him. He wasn't ugly to them, but there was something about that cold stare of his."

"I thought I was a hard fighter," said Bobby Jones after a round with Hogan. "I thought Walter Hagen and Gene Sarazen both were. We're not in a class with this fellow Hogan. He's fighting for every inch, every foot, every yard on a golf course."

He'd been fighting courses since an early age, shaped by a turbulent childhood that rendered him both intense and often distant, even to his friends. Raised by his mother after his blacksmith father committed suicide when Ben was nine, Hogan grew up in Fort Worth, quitting his newspaper delivery job at age 12 to caddy at Glen Garden Country Club. Though he'd turn pro at 17 and join the tour two years later in 1931, it wasn't until 1940 that he finally won the first of his 63 tour events. He was 34, a veteran of the U.S. Army Air Corps, before he hit his stride, winning the PGA in 1946. That tournament began a streak in which Hogan won nine of his next 16 majors. From 1940 through 1960, he finished in the top 10 of every U.S. Open he entered, winning four of them (five, if you count the de facto U.S. Open of 1942, the Hale American National Open; Hogan always did). From 1941 through 1956, he finished in the top seven of every Masters he entered.

His greatest victory came after his gravest moment.

Seriously injured in a head-on automobile accident in 1949, Hogan struggled back to win the 1950 U.S. Open at Merion. Legs bandaged, straining under the grueling 36-hole format of the final two rounds, he struggled to a tie with Lloyd Mangrum and Tom Fazio, but returned the next day to shoot a brilliant 69 and win the playoff.

Though his tournament schedule was severely curtailed after the accident, Hogan continued to dominate the tournaments he did play. In 1953, he became the first—and still only—golfer to win three professional majors in a single year. He won the Masters with a then-record 274, took the U.S. Open at Oakmont, then won the British Open at Carnoustie, in the only year he competed in the event. (Only a scheduling conflict prevented him from taking a shot at the Grand Slam. British Open qualifying overlapped with the last two days of the PGA Championship.)

"From tee to green, there never was anyone to compare to Hogan," said Gene Sarazen. He'd gained that superiority through a fanatical devotion to practice—often doing so for eight hours a day or more. It made him a consummate tactician, able to drive powerfully and convert opportunities with any club in his bag. During his career, Hogan demonstrated the value of sheer persistence of effort, and the enduring virtue of the game itself. As he told one interviewer, "I know that I have had greater satisfaction than anyone who ever lived out of hitting golf shots."

OTTO GRAHAM
The Champion

The test of a quarterback is where his team finishes," said Paul Brown. "By that standard, Otto Graham was the best of all time." His record is unmatched: In 10 pro seasons, Graham led the Cleveland Browns to 10 championship games, winning seven of them.

With his shock of close-cropped black hair and the thick eyebrows that set off his dark eyes and sharply handsome features, he was a terrific athlete and a fearsome competitor who seemed to excel at everything: playing a year of pro basketball for the Rochester Royals (who won the league crown in the NBL, a forerunner to the NBA), even dominating the Browns' training-camp Ping-Pong table.

Graham had been a single-wing tailback in college at Northwestern, where he was an All-American in basketball. But Brown felt he'd be the perfect man to play quarterback in the new T-formation offense, which he planned to install for his Cleveland Browns, charter member of the All-American Football Conference, which began play in 1946. Brown signed Graham to a contract in 1945, while both men were still in the navy, and his young quarterback won the job in the third game of the 1946 season, leading the Browns to the first AAFC title.

There's no question that Brown's visionary system—full-time assistant coaches, thick, sophisticated playbooks, exten-

GRAHAM:
10 SEASONS,
10 TITLE GAMES

MUSIAL:
"THE CHARACTER,
THE SOUL, THE
ACCESSIBILITY"

sive scouting and a coherent training regimen—contributed to Graham's success. And the Browns of that era were deep in talent, with Marion Motley powering the running attack, and Dante Lavelli and Dub Jones among the dazzling collection of receivers. But "Automatic Otto" made the whole system run. As the operator of football's first truly modern offense (employing a straight T-formation, with plenty of motion and misdirection), he possessed the poise, athleticism and intellect that the job demanded. "I could throw a pass to a spot as well as anyone who ever lived," he told *Sports Illustrated*, "but that's a God-given talent. I could never stand back and flick the ball 60 yards downfield with my wrist like Dan Marino does." How eagerly Marino would love to trade his wrist for Graham's rings.

After winning four straight titles in the AAFC, the Browns (along with the Colts and 49ers) joined the National Football League in 1950. They opened that season by routing heavily favored two-time NFL defending champion Philadelphia. And they quickly proved themselves the class of the league, gaining the title in a thrilling 30–28 win over the Los Angeles Rams (all the sweeter to Cleveland football fans, since the Rams had bolted to L.A. from Cleveland in 1946).

Though Cleveland lost the title game the next three years, Graham finished as a winner, routing the Lions 56–10 in 1954, and then, after Brown lured him out of retirement, winning another title in 1955. He argued with his coach frequently, but respected him as well. They put together the NFL's first dynasty of the postwar era. And as a player, he never had to sit at home and watch a title game.

STAN MUSIAL
The Man

Stan the Man: There was as much reason as there was rhyme to the nickname given the quintessential Cardinal. No player has been as popular with baseball's best fans and few ever did as much to warrant and reward such loyalty as the gracious and ever obliging St. Louis superstar who retired with more than two dozen NL records to his credit.

His statue stands in front of Busch Stadium and it's a perfect tribute, since Musial was a monument to big league baseball. Hall of Fame broadcaster Harry Caray was convinced Musial easily outshone all others. "He was the greatest star—the character, the soul, the accessibility—nobody combined that with as much baseball greatness as Musial."

Musial turned down a basketball scholarship to Pitt in 1938 to sign a contract as a left-handed pitcher. He knocked around the low minors for a couple of years until an injured left shoulder ended his pitching days. Brought up to an injury-depleted St. Louis team in late 1941, Musial immediately proved he belonged, hitting .426 and turning in defensive gems. Two years later he was the league MVP.

Musial, who hit .310 or better in his first 16 full seasons, was the personification of consistent production throughout his career, finishing with 1,949 runs and 1,951 RBIs, but his decade run from 1948 to 1957 was a hot streak unmatched in its era. Winning five batting titles while posting a .340 batting average during the decade, he also averaged 31 home runs, 39 doubles and more than 110 runs and RBIs.

A slugger with the bat control of a contact hitter, Musial, never struck out as many as 50 times in a season. He was as dependable as he was productive, setting the NL consecutive games record and becoming the first in history to play 1,000 games at two positions.

His trademark corkscrew stance, which twisted his torso away from the pitcher, was unorthodox, but it was also a thing of kinetic beauty when Musial brought his perfectly motionless bat to sudden life. Musial was in the World Series his first four full years but never again, effectively robbing many of the first generation of television baseball fans of the opportunity to see him shine in championship play. In two dozen consecutive All-Star contests Musial used the mid-season classic as a national showcase, often providing its most dramatic moments; he still holds seven records in the Midsummer Classic.

Musial's excellence was so predictable and his appeal so pervasive that his nickname, as perfect a fit as any in sports, was given him by opposing fans. His teammates called him "Stash," but the fiercely partisan Brooklyn bleacher bums, who bemoaned his every plate appearance and its inevitable assault on the 297-foot right–field fence at Ebbets Field, greeted him with grudging admiration, sighing "Here comes The Man again."

In final affirmation Musial's only statistical peer during the period, Ted Williams, who offered compliments about as often as he bunted and was rarely willing to acknowledge even the outside possibility of comparison, flatly stated, "If there was a better hitter it was Stan Musial."

—*Michael Point*

SUGAR RAY ROBINSON
The Way He Moves

A visitor to George Gainford's New York gym mentioned a "sweet" fighter he had observed working out in the legendary trainer's stable.

"Sweet as sugar," Gainford replied. The nickname stuck, and was attached in front of another he'd acquired when he borrowed a friend's union card for an amateur tournament.

It had "a nice ring to it," Ray Robinson said later. "Sugar Walker Smith [his given name] wouldn't have been the same." And neither would boxing history, which probably coined the "pound for pound the best" phrase for the dominating champion. Virtually untouched in his first 40 bouts, Robinson's first defeat, a 10-round decision, came at the hands of Jake LaMotta, the only man to beat him between 1939 and 1951. Over a storied 175–19–6 career—with 109

ROBINSON:
"MONEY IS FOR
SPENDING. MONEY
IS FOR HAVING
A GOOD TIME"

RICHARD:
"I CAN ONLY
PLAY ONE WAY"

KOs—Robinson was stopped only once. Ten of his losses came after he had turned 40.

"Robinson could deliver a knockout blow going backward," wrote *The Ring*'s Bert Sugar. "His footwork was superior to any that had been seen up to that time. His hand speed and leverage were unmatchable." After winning Golden Gloves titles in 1939 and 1940, Robinson began a 24-year pro career in which he held the welterweight title from 1946–51, and the middleweight title five separate times between 1951 and 1960. He was widely admired for his versatile blend of power and grace when he defeated Tommy Bell in 1946 for the vacant welterweight title. He defended that belt five times before moving up for a 1951 middleweight title bout with LaMotta, in a fight later dubbed the St. Valentine's Day Massacre, and immortalized in the film *Raging Bull*.

Born May 3, 1921, in the same poor Detroit neighborhood in which Joe Louis was raised. Robinson's rise and fall in many ways forged the archetype of the black superstar. An internationally popular figure in the Forties and Fifties, Robinson once owned a Harlem nightclub (Sugar Ray's), a dry cleaner, a lingerie store, and a barber shop, and drove a flamingo pink Cadillac. He was accompanied on his European tours by his career-long trainer Gainford, several family members, a valet, a barber who doubled as his golf pro, and even a dwarf mascot. "Money is for spending," Robinson once remarked. "Money is for having a good time." He never regretted his sprees, but they eventually forced him to box long past his prime. In 1965, when Madison Square Garden honored the retired champion with a large special trophy, Robinson didn't own a piece of furniture sturdy enough to place it on. But by 1968 he was back in the public's adoring eye, singing on *The Tonight Show* and later making a guest appearance on *Mission: Impossible*.

His colorful career earned him many admirers. Muhammad Ali, who once asked Robinson to be an adviser, credited Sugar Ray's "matador" style as an inspiration. Jesse Jackson spoke at his funeral in 1989. And A.J. Liebling admired his diverse skills. "The thing about Robinson that gets you is the way he moves," he wrote, "even when shadowboxing." —*David Zivan*

MAURICE RICHARD
The Rocket

At a time when hockey was played with a brutal deliberateness—uncurved sticks and vicious checking, tightly conservative attacks and frequent fighting—the dark-eyed Montreal native Maurice "The Rocket" Richard burst into the NHL with a style as furious and original as any the game had ever seen.

The injury-prone Richard broke an ankle and a wrist during his three years of junior-league hockey, then broke his right ankle 16 games into his rookie season with the

Montreal Canadiens. With a passionate commitment to rehabilitation, he returned in the 1943–44 season to take his place on the Canadiens' famed "Punch Line," with Toe Blake at left wing, Elmer Lach at center and the left-handed Richard leading the charge on the right wing. In the 1944 playoffs, Richard scored 12 goals in nine games (including five in one game against the Maple Leafs) and his dominance became apparent. He was faster than any of his contemporaries, and an adept shooter. "The Rocket" struck fear in the hearts of goaltenders around the league with his sniper's skill at finding corners.

"What I remember most about the Rocket were his eyes," said goalie Glenn Hall. "When he came flying toward you with the puck on his stick, his eyes were all lit up and flaming like a pinball machine. It was terrifying." He was the first player to score 50 goals in a season, during the 50-game campaign of 1944-45. It was the only goal-a-game pace in NHL history until Wayne Gretzky surpassed the feat in 1981-82.

When the Canadiens were fighting for first place with the Detroit Red Wings in 1955, Richard wound up in a brutal brawl, jabbing a stick in the face of the Bruins' Hal Laycoe, and punching linesman Cliff Thompson during the melee. NHL president Clarence Campbell suspended Richard for the balance of the season and the playoffs, prompting an unprecedented outpouring of protests and death threats by outraged Richard fans at the NHL's offices in Montreal. When Campbell attended the next Canadien home game, he was pelted with fruit and epithets. After the first period, someone threw a tear-gas bomb near Campbell, sparking a riot that resulted in looting along St. Catherine Street, causing an estimated $100,000 worth of damage.

When he retired in 1960, Richard had a single regret: That he never recorded enough assists to win a scoring title, despite being the league's top goal scorer five times. But he won eight Stanley Cups, including five straight at the end of his career, and his 544 career goals, 50-goal season, and 82 playoff goals were all records at the time of his retirement. And his mark for most overtime goals in the playoffs (six) would stand into the next century.

Never one to let up, never one to mellow, the fiery Rocket burned until age diminished his talent. "I can only play one way," he said. "The hard way."

EDDIE ARCARO
Double Triple

He had a marvelous instinct for avoiding difficulty," remembered Patrick Lynch of the New York Racing Association. "You rarely saw him reaching for a hole or snatching a horse up." Those abilities—coupled with a "gutsy, no-fear riding style," as the *Jockey News* put it—led Eddie Arcaro to victory in five Kentucky Derbies, six Belmont Stakes and six Preakness Stakes. "Nobody had his sense of the way the race was being run," remembered vet-

ARCARO: "NOBODY HAD HIS SENSE OF THE WAY THE RACE WAS BEING RUN"

CITATION: IN 1948, HE WON 19 OF 20 RACES, AND THE TRIPLE CROWN

eran trainer Jimmy Jones. Arcaro won the Triple Crown twice (in 1941 with Whirlaway and in 1948 with Citation) and narrowly missed it a third time, taking a close second in the Derby with Nashua in 1955. During his 30-year career, he raced 24,092 times and had 4,779 wins. Other jocks surpassed his $30 million earnings for his stables, but, as one historian wrote, "During his prime he received the best of America's top horses." His mounts led the stakes earnings list in 1940, 1941, 1946, 1948 and 1950–55. *Sports Illustrated* once called him "the most famous man to ride a horse since Paul Revere."

Winning five out of 21 Derby attempts (only Bill Shoemaker, with 26, had more Derby mounts), and six of 15 Preakness appearances, Arcaro's nickname was "The Master," and not simply because of his success. He was breathtakingly quiet in the saddle, and set the standard for the practice of switching the whip from side to side. His style was widely emulated. "When I was growing up in Puerto Rico," recalled Angel Cordero Jr., "my father would give me movies and pictures and tell me that if I wanted to be a jockey I had to learn to ride like Eddie Arcaro."

Born in Cincinnati in 1916, George Edward Arcaro's career became synonymous with some of the greatest thoroughbreds of all time. In 1948 he guided Citation to Horse of the Year honors and one of the easiest Triple Crowns ever. Arcaro's 1952 victory on Hill Gail was the first Derby to be televised coast to coast, and when he won the Preakness in 1957 on Bold Ruler, Vice President Nixon presented him with the Woodlawn Vase trophy.

The 45-year-old jock retired in 1962, and was founder and president of the Jockeys Guild, the first organization to provide health insurance and other benefits for jocks. When he died in 1997, *The New York Times* noted that his "casual elegance did not always hide his intensity." "You can't ride only on Saturday," Arcaro said once. "You have to want to win every race, not just the big ones." —*David Zivan*

CITATION
"A Privilege to Ride"

Three-year-old Citation, a bay colt, took second place in the Chesapeake Trial at Havre de Grace, Maryland, on April 12, 1948. His regular jock, Albert Snider, had disappeared on a winter fishing trip in the Florida Keys and Eddie Arcaro was the replacement. Despite the runner-up finish, it was the beginning of one of racing's most productive partnerships. He thereafter piloted Citation to 14 of his record string of 16 consecutive victories including the Kentucky Derby by 3½ lengths, the Preakness by 5½ and the Belmont Stakes by eight. Few horses have had a year like Citation's 1948, and no other thoroughbred would capture the Triple Crown until the great Secretariat in 1973.

Citation's origins might have promised large-scale glory. Calumet Farm patriarch Warren Wright, whose deathbed wish was that Citation become the first horse to earn $1 million, purchased Citation's dam, Hydroplane II, from England's Lord Derby in the spring of 1941. He had the mare transported to the United States by way of the Pacific, which took considerably longer but was preferable to potential attack by German U-boats. Sired at Kentucky's storied Calumet Farms by Bull Lea and trained by the legendary Ben Jones and his son, Jimmy, Citation was voted outstanding two-year-old colt in 1947, having won eight of nine races and earning $155,680.

But 1948, when he won 19 of 20 races and earned $709,470, would be his immortal year, the down payment on a career total of $1,085,760. The Derby win would be the colt's archetypal effort: speed complemented by full-race stamina and a will to win. After spotting stablemate Coaltown six lengths in the opening half mile, he simply ran him down. "Arcaro whacked Citation at the eighth pole," wrote James Roach in *The New York Times*, "just for insurance." The crowd, cooled by $1.25 juleps (souvenir glass included), was entertained but not surprised.

Citation entered the Preakness a 1–10 favorite and led wire to wire. He finished, *The Times* wrote, "a bit damp around the withers, but otherwise showing little sign of having taken some exercise." Stumbling a little at the start of the Belmont Stakes, the 1–5 favorite was challenged to a sprint by 28–1 longshot Faraway. But Faraway faded to last, and Citation won going away.

In his last race of 1948, Citation developed an osselet, or "hot spot" on his left foreankle, and did not compete as a four-year-old, often a thoroughbred's best year. But striving to fulfill Wright's 1950 wish, Calumet Farms raced Citation at five and six. He won only two of nine races in 1950, finishing second in the rest. As a six-year-old, in 1951, he won the $100,000 Hollywood Gold Cup to bring his career winnings over $1 million, and retired with 32 victories, 10 second-place finishes and two third-places in 45 starts. After the Preakness in 1948, Arcaro summed up the feelings of all the jocks who had ridden the colt. "It is a crime to take the money for riding such a horse," he said. "It is a privilege."

—*David Zivan*

BOB MATHIAS
Youth Is Served

At the 1948 California state high school track and field meet, an overly excited public address announcer told the crowd that the lanky hurdler/discus thrower with the size 13 feet standing before him on the awards platform was "America's greatest hope in the decathlon."

Bold talk, considering that 17-year-old Bob Mathias had never competed in a decathlon, and in fact had no experience in four of its 10 events. Even bolder when it involved a somewhat reluctant athlete who had only three months to master those events before the Olympic competition began

MATHIAS: "THEY DON'T GIVE POINTS FOR WORRYING"

at London's Wembley Stadium.

His coach, Virgil Jackson, wasn't even sure what the 10 events were when he first got the notion of having Mathias try the decathlon, but he knew this second son of a Tulare, California, physician was a very special athlete. "Work hard at it and I'll bet you make the Olympic team—in 1952," he told Mathias.

Three months later, the precocious Mathias stood atop the victory platform, the youngest male Olympic track and field gold medalist ever. Asked by a reporter what he would do to celebrate, Mathias said, "Start shaving, I guess."

He may have been young, but few decathletes were ever so naturally gifted. By age 11 he could high-jump five feet and long-jump 15 feet, and even a bout with acute anemia, followed in rapid succession by chicken pox, measles and whooping cough, did not slow him down. Finishing first 40 times during his high school career, Mathias was a quick study. He won the first decathlon he ever entered—he never did lose one—with the highest point total by an American in seven years. During his childhood illness, his mother, Lillian, taught him to relax by imagining the tension leaving his body, part by part, and never was that more helpful than in London at the '48 Games. Heavy rains muddied the track, and the athletes were required to finish the high jump with so little light that a white handkerchief was tied to the bar so they could see it. Mathias, huddling under a blanket between events and even dozing off when time permitted, conserved energy through the grueling two-day event. "They don't give points for worrying," he was fond of saying.

Following the Olympics, Mathias headed to prep school and then to Stanford, where he led the Indians to the 1952 Rose Bowl. After the London Games, he had told a reporter he wouldn't defend his title in Helsinki in 1952—"Not for a million dollars"—but the promise of making Olympic history proved irresistible. He false-started in the 100 meters and pinched a nerve in his left hip in the second event, the long jump. But he gritted it out, breaking his own world record by 62 points and winning by 912 points, the largest margin in Olympic history. After finishing the 1,500, the first two-time Olympic decathlon champion limped to his brother Jimmy sitting in the stands and said, "I wanted you to be the first to hear of my retirement." He was 21.

Mathias returned to Stanford, graduating in 1953, and after a stint in the Marine Corps and in Hollywood, he ran for Congress. Elected to four terms as a U.S. Representative, he later pushed for passage of the Amateur Sports Act of 1978, a bill of rights for athletes, and he was an outspoken opponent of the 1980 Olympic boycott. After leaving Congress, Mathias spearheaded the creation of the U.S. Olympic training center in Colorado Springs, which he supported passionately.

"We shall never know how many truly superior athletes in this country missed their opportunity for Olympic greatness," Mathias mused, "because they did not have the wherewithal to make the most of their God-given, natural athletic talents."

—*Mark Wangrin*

A True Fall Classic: Robinson crosses the plate in his first Series.

BASEBALL

The Fabulous Finale of '47

A few days before the 1947 World Series, Jackie Robinson found out he'd won the Rookie of the Year award. Then the man who'd been at the white-hot center of perhaps the most pressurized season ever joined his Dodger teammates for the World Series. In a finish befitting the remarkable year that went before, the Dodgers tangled with the New York Yankees in one of the most dramatic Series ever.

The Yankees were up two games to one when New York journeyman Floyd "Bill" Bevens got the start in Game 4. Though he walked eight and gave up a run (on two walks, a sacrifice and a groundout) over the first eight innings, he went into the bottom of the ninth with a no-hitter and a 2-1 lead. His no-hitter was still intact with two out and two on in the ninth, when pinch-hitter Cookie Lavagetto stroked a double off the right–field wall, winning the game for the Dodgers, and evening the Series.

The Yankees won Game 5, and went for the clincher in a wild Game 6, which lasted longer (3 hours, 18 minutes) and used more players (38) than any previous Series game. Brooklyn went up 4-0, fell behind 5-4, then scored four more times to take an 8-5 lead in the top of the sixth. In the bottom of that inning, with two runners on, Joe DiMaggio blasted a line drive toward the bullpen in left-center. But Dodger utility outfielder Al Gionfriddo made a stunning catch near the fence, robbing DiMaggio of a possible homer, and maintaining the Dodgers' lead.

Compared to those arresting moments, Game 7 was anticlimactic, as the Yankees stormed back from a 2-0 deficit, took a 5-2 lead, and turned it over to reliever Joe Page, who gave up just one hit in the last five innings. Red Barber, the Brooklyn announcer who'd shared the microphone with Mel Allen on the first televised World Series, remembered congratulating the dejected Dodgers in the losers' locker room, and feeling as though they'd accomplished something of incalculable significance: "They'd lost the World Series but they'd won their biggest assignment—they'd accepted Jackie Robinson."

HOCKEY

1942 Stanley Cup Finals

■ The Detroit Red Wings had a dismal 1941-42 regular season, finishing fifth in the seven-team NHL, before upsetting Montreal and Boston in the playoffs. In the finals against Toronto (which had knocked off the regular-season champion New York Rangers earlier in the playoffs), the Red Wings stormed to a three games to nothing lead in the best-of-seven series. That's when Toronto's Bill Taylor said, "Don't worry about us, we'll beat them four straight." The Red Wings led 3-2 in the third period of the fourth game, before goals by Syl Apps and Nick Metz rallied the Leafs to a 4-3 win. Toronto goalie Turk Broda then shut Detroit down in Games 5 and 6 to force the series to a seventh and final game. And in Maple Leaf Gardens, the Leafs rallied from a 1-0 deficit, with three goals in the final period, becoming the only team this century to win a championship after trailing three games to none in the final series.

COLLEGE FOOTBALL

1946 Army–Notre Dame

■ The two dominant national powers in the first year of postwar football met at Yankee Stadium in November, Army ranked No. 1 and Notre Dame ranked No. 2, averaging a total of 65 points per game between them. But the clash of the titans became a defensive stalemate, ending in a 0-0 tie. It was hardly a dull game—the top-ranked Cadets crossed midfield 10 times, the Irish did so four times. Army quarterback Arnold Tucker had three interceptions on defense. And in the Cadets' biggest stand, they stopped Bill Gompers on a fourth-and-two from the Army four. For his part, Notre Dame's Johnny Lujack, stifled in the air, saved the game on defense with a diving tackle at the ankles of Army's Doc Blanchard, who had broken into open field at the Irish 37. The tie broke the Cadets' 25-game winning streak, but Army was still ranked No. 1 after the game. Three weeks later, Army barely beat Navy, 21-18, and that slip cost the Cadets the mythical national championship, as the Associated Press voted Notre Dame No. 1 in its final poll of the 1946 season.

BOXING

1941 Joe Louis–Billy Conn

■ It looked like another routine "bum of the month" for Joe Louis, whose 18th title defense came against the 25-year-old Pittsburgh challenger Billy Conn, who was giving up a 25-pound weight advantage to the champ. Conn surprised Louis in the early rounds, proving more mobile than Louis had expected. Conn was ahead on points when he began pummeling the champ in the 12th. Three rounds from the title, ahead on points, Conn made the mistake of going for the knockout. In the 13th, he traded flat-footed blows with Louis and got hurt. The champ closed the fight with a vicious right hook that sent the valiant challenger spinning to the canvas. "I guess I got too much Irish in me," said a chastened Conn after the fight. "I lost my head. You can't trade punches with that man. I had him on the hook and I let him get away. I was okay, though, wasn't I?"

HORSE RACING

1948 Kentucky Derby

■ The Run for the Roses featured the long-awaited showdown between the blazing-fast, front-running Coaltown, and the much heralded colt Citation, Calumet Farm's stable mates. Pre-race speculation centered on whether Coaltown could keep the pace over the Derby's mile-and-a-quarter track, made soft and muddy by morning showers. But by the third turn, Coaltown was out in front by six lengths, and the big question was whether Citation could ever get close enough to make his challenger's stamina an issue. But Citation's jockey Eddie Arcaro drove his mount hard around the final turn and caught Coaltown on the home stretch, pulling away for a 3½-length win. The great race was a sign of great things: It was Arcaro's fourth Derby win and the beginning of a Triple Crown for Citation, making Arcaro the only jockey ever to ride two Triple Crown winners.

Great Performances

■ Perhaps the most stunning championship blowout in professional sports history occurred December 8, 1940, when the Washington Redskins faced the Chicago Bears in the NFL Championship game. Sammy Baugh led the hosts, who had the highest scoring offense in the NFL, and had defeated the Bears, 7-3, just three weeks earlier. But on this day the T-formation that the Bears had been tinkering with for years finally came to full fruition (T-formation innovator Clark Shaughnessy, on break prior to Stanford's Rose Bowl appearance, had been called in to make refinements before the game). The Bears scored on Bill Osmanski's 68-yard run on the third play of the game, and humiliated the Redskins, 73-0. It was a watershed day for football. By the end of the decade, nearly every football team in the land—high school, college and pro—was running the T.

The Reign of the Black Knights

During the war years, Army football coach Earl "Red" Blaik had a distinct recruiting advantage: He could offer active servicemen with previous collegiate experience three more years of athletic eligibility. Many of those second-chance veterans played on Blaik's awesome Cadets of '44 and '45, which won all 18 of its games and two national championships, while averaging more than 50 points a game, outscoring opponents 916-81.

The Army team was so deep that in 1944 its marquee backs, **Felix "Doc" Blanchard** and **Glenn Davis**—"Mr. Inside and Mr. Outside," who would win the Heisman in '45 and '46—played on the second team. That season Army routed defending national champion Notre Dame 59-0, and won its closest game, against second-ranked Navy, 23-7. There was less depth on the '45 team, when "Touchdown Twins" Blanchard and Davis rose to the first team, but Army was still unbeatable, routing Notre Dame, 48-0, and defeating arch-rival Navy (again ranked No. 2 in the country), 32-13.

■ **New Leafs.** With five Stanley Cups in the decade, the Toronto Maple Leafs were hockey's reigning power of the

Forties, and few powers have been more balanced (Toronto placed just two players on the All-NHL first team during those five seasons). General manager Conn Smythe retooled his team with a new coach (Hap Day) and a new captain (splendid center Syl Apps) in the early Forties, while hanging on to redoubtable goaltender Turk Broda. The Leafs turned it around in '42, coming from three games down to the Red Wings to win their first title in 10 years. By the end of the decade, Toronto became the first team in NHL history to win three straight Cups.

■ **Aggies Rule.** At Oklahoma A&M, later Oklahoma State, revered coach Henry Iba had created a sensation with shot-blocking seven-foot center Bob Kurland. The NCAA had ruled Kurland's goaltending defense—swatting away balls heading down for the basket—was illegal prior to the 1944-45 season. So the Aggies adapted, and beat defending champion Utah in the first round on the way to winning the '45 tournament (where the rest of the country saw one of the first dunks, which Kurland called his "duffer shot"). The next season, with five returning lettermen joined by five former players back from the war, A&M sported a juggernaut. Kurland led the nation in scoring, and added 72 points in his three tournament games. The Aggies beat North Carolina, 43-40, in the final, and became the first school to win back-to-back NCAA titles.

	COLLEGE BASKETBALL	PRO BASKETBALL NBA	HOCKEY NHL	BASEBALL MLB	COLLEGE FOOTBALL	PRO FOOTBALL NFL
1940	Indiana		Rangers	Reds	Minnesota	Bears
1941	Wisconsin		Bruins	Yankees	Minnesota	Bears
1942	Stanford		Maple Leafs	Cardinals	Ohio State	Redskins
1943	Wyoming		Red Wings	Yankees	Notre Dame	Bears
1944	Utah		Canadiens	Cardinals	Army	Packers
1945	Oklahoma A&M		Maple Leafs	Tigers	Army	Cleveland R.
1946	Oklahoma A&M		Canadiens	Cardinals	Notre Dame	Bears
1947	Holy Cross	Warriors	Maple Leafs	Yankees	Notre Dame	Cardinals
1948	Kentucky	Bullets	Maple Leafs	Indians	Michigan	Eagles
1949	Kentucky	Lakers	Maple Leafs	Yankees	Notre Dame	Eagles

NOTES **Pro Basketball:** In its first three seasons, the league that became the National Basketball Association was known as the Basketball Association of America. After a merger with the National Basketball League after the 1948- the new league became the NBA. **College football:** Champions are mythical national champions as voted by sportswriters in the Associated Press poll.

Coaches

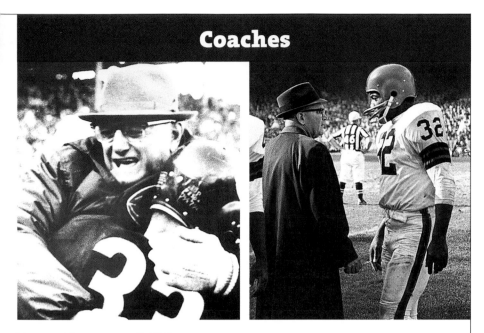

Papa Bear and PB

In 1940, **George Halas** (left)—in his second tour of duty as the head coach of the Chicago Bears—coached his team to the 73-0 obliteration of the Washington Redskins. In 1949, **Paul Brown** (right, in later years with Jim Brown)—coaching a team named after him—won his fourth straight All-America Football Conference championship, just two days after the franchise was accepted into the NFL. Halas and Brown were two giants of the coaching profession, and both were in their prime in the Forties.

Halas, the wily, cantankerous "Papa Bear" who played for, coached, and owned the Chicago Bears, walked the sidelines for 40 seasons in Chicago, with only six losing campaigns. The Bears dominated the Forties, winning four NFL titles.

He had been a three-sport letterman at Illinois, but football became his livelihood. Halas was in Ralph Hay's Hupmobile showroom at one of the meetings in 1920, when the forerunner of the NFL was formed. By 1922, he'd taken control of the Decatur Staleys, moved the team to Chicago, renamed them the Bears, and began shaping the game. But Halas' greatest teams were his "Monsters of the Midway" of the early '40s, featuring crack T-formation quarterback Sid Luckman, and four future Hall of Famers on his front line. Under Papa Bear's emotional leadership, the Bears were notoriously cranky hosts—cutting off hot water to visiting locker rooms and phone communications from the press box to the visiting bench. "Football is a game of emotions," he said. "For me, that is the heart of its appeal."

Brown was cerebral, the first coach to shuttle in plays through linemen, to use playbooks, facemasks and a full-time set of assistant coaches. His success came through uncommon innovation and unshakable leadership. There were still some doubters of Brown when Cleveland arrived in the NFL in 1950, after having won all four AAFC titles. But Cleveland won the title its first year in the league, and advanced to the title game in each of its first six seasons in the NFL. Brown demanded complete dedication from his charges. "You are a member of the Cleveland Browns," he would tell them. "You are the New York Yankees of football. You will conduct yourself in a proper manner. I expect you to watch your language, your dress, your deportment." His teams were often perceived as bloodless and efficient. In truth, they were a reflection of his clear-minded dedication to the craft of football. "He brought a system into pro football," said Sid Gillman. "He's an organizational genius. I always felt that before Paul Brown, coaches just rolled the ball out on the practice field."

COACHING WISDOM

"Those who say players spend too much time on football when they should be studying should remember that a student who lets the game come between himself and an education wouldn't study anyway."

—Howard Jones,
Southern Cal football coach

"If you don't win, you're going to get fired. If you do win, you've only put off the day you're going to be fired."

— Leo Durocher,
Brooklyn Dodgers manager

The Mahatma

In the 1920s, as general manager of the St. Louis Cardinals, **Branch Rickey** created the modern farm system in baseball. In the late 1950s, as the head of the renegade Continental League, he prompted the widespread expansion which nearly doubled the size of the majors over the next 40 years. But while these and countless of his other contributions changed baseball, it was what Rickey did in the Forties that revolutionized it.

Raised in a strict Methodist home in Ohio, Rickey was a man of devout principles. He promised his mother he'd never go to a ballpark on Sunday and lived up to his word, to the detriment of his playing and managing careers in the major leagues. Despite this, Rickey created the Sunday doubleheader, as well as the Ladies' Day promotion, batting cages and sliding pits, and the modern Knot Hole Gang promotion in St. Louis, by which youngsters got free admission to games. Verbose and articulate, headstrong and thoughtful, the crafty Rickey was known in baseball circles as "the Mahatma," an inscrutable thinker who always seemed a few steps ahead of the competition. "To say that Branch Rickey has the finest mind ever brought to the game of baseball is to damn with the faintest of praise, like describing Isaac Stern as a fiddler," wrote Red Smith.

As GM of the Cardinals, and later the Brooklyn Dodgers, Rickey had long wanted to open the major leagues to black players. When Commissioner Kenesaw Mountain Landis—a de facto segregationist—passed away in 1944, Rickey saw his opportunity. Over the next three years, he set the stage for breaking the color barrier. And though 15 of the 16 major league owners voted against allowing blacks to play, the new commissioner, A. B. "Happy" Chandler, overruled the majority and supported Rickey and the Dodgers.

It was Rickey's understanding of the reaction that a black player would get—and his foresight to ask Jackie Robinson to rise above it, rather than fighting back—that paved the way for the success he found when he joined the Brooklyn Dodgers in 1947. Despite death threats, player revolts, fan ugliness, and an atmosphere of oppressive tension, Robinson persevered, thereby changing baseball, changing sports, and changing the country in the process.

Much has been made of the fact that Rickey had other reasons for integrating baseball—for starters, it helped the Dodgers get a leg up on their opposition. But other owners had the same opportunities, and didn't take the steps. Rickey had to be taken at his word when he said, "I couldn't face my God much longer knowing that His black creatures are held separate and distinct from His white creatures in the game that has given me all I own."

Robinson pointedly expressed his admiration for Rickey and his work: "I really believe that in breaking down the color barrier in baseball, our 'national game,' he did more for the Negroes than any white man since Abraham Lincoln."

TOP OF THE NEWS: As the country comes together for the war effort, professional sports is shaken up, and the college game is dominated by the service academies. Afterward, there's more time and money for everything. New professional football and basketball leagues form in 1946. And then a year later Jackie Robinson takes the field with the Dodgers, and the modern age of American sports begins.

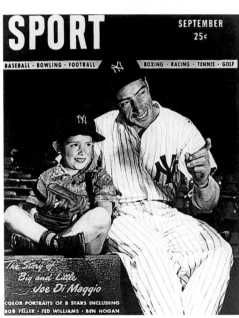

Reading List

The first issue of **Sport** magazine is published in 1946, with Joe DiMaggio and his son on the cover. The magazine is a hit with young adults, many of whom start tearing out Ozzie Sweet's idyllic full-color player portraits and putting them on their bedroom walls. Two years later, Dell starts publishing a slick, oversize monthly called *Sports Illustrated*, edited by the famed Stanley Woodward, and including some of the best sportswriters of the day. But this incarnation of *Sports Illustrated* goes under within six months.

Two publishing traditions begin in the Forties, with the first editions of *The Sporting News Official Baseball Guides* (a series inherited from the Spalding Company) and the first annual volume of the *Ring Record Book and Boxing Encyclopedia*.

One of 1941's most creative works of fiction makes *The New York Times*, though not its bestsellers list. A Wall Street broker named Morris Newburger creates a fictional school, called Plainfield Teachers College, and, posing as school PR man Jerry Croyden, regu-

larly calls in the scores of its lopsided wins and the exploits of a Chinese sophomore halfback named John Chung. The *Times* and other papers dutifully follow the story, noting Chung's strength comes from eating rice between quarters. Croyden/Newburger issues a press release on November 13, saying Chung and his teammates flunked midterm exams. Four days later, *Time* magazine prints a story revealing the hoax.

Sounds

Lots of baseball songs again. "Joltin' Joe DiMaggio," recorded by Bob Chester and His Orchestra with vocal by Bob Haymes, includes the lyric, "He started baseball's famous streak/ That got us all aglow/ He's just a man and not a freak/ Joltin' Joe DiMaggio." In the same year comes George M. Cohan's "Connie Mack Is the Grand Old Name," an ode to the Philadelphia legend: "Since the great William Penn/ Who's the best loved of men?/ Connie Mack, Connie Mack/ Connie Mack." Players themselves start getting into the act as well. In 1949, Ralph Branca, Carl Furillo and Erv Palica record "The Brooklyn Dodgers Jump," by Joseph A. Ricciardello.

Playing Games

Former major leaguer Ethan Allen designs a new tabletop baseball game called All-Star Baseball, which marks the biggest breakthrough in decades, and leads to more accurate simulations that will come out in the future through such strategy games as APBA Baseball and Strat-O-Matic. Rather than using a series of spinners for different situations, Allen conceives of giving each player a different disk, so that a player who hits more homers in real life will do the same in the

game. Other games will come and go, but All-Star Baseball will become the most successful baseball board game ever, manufactured continuously by the Cadaco Company for more than 50 years.

Fashion

The helmet becomes mandatory in the NFL in 1943, and five years later, Rams halfback Fred Gehrke paints a pair of **ramhorns** on the standard dark blue Rams helmet. The look of the game is changed forever. Within 10 years, the Colts are sporting their distinctive horseshoe logo, and by the early '60s, virtually every team in pro football—save the resolutely old school Browns—have helmet logos.

Movies

In 1940, Redskins star passer (and off-season cattle rancher) Sammy Baugh heads to Hollywood to star in a 12-episode Western serial called *King of the Texas Rangers*. Despite his fame, Baugh rarely ventures out at night, and passes up all the celebrity parties. "It didn't make sense to be showboating all over Hollywood," he says, "and spending a lot of money for a steak when I could take that money back to Texas and buy a whole cow."

HE TAUGHT HIS TEAMS THE WAY TO WIN...AND AMERICA THE WAY TO LIVE!

Few men lived so fully! Few pictures have captured so much! The simple things he loved! The quiet greatness of the man himself! Here is an All-American thriller for All-Americans!

KNUTE ROCKNE ALL AMERICAN

with **PAT O'BRIEN**
GALE PAGE · RONALD REAGAN
DONALD CRISP

Directed by LLOYD BACON
A Warner Bros.–First National Picture
Presented by WARNER BROS.

In 1940, Pat O'Brien stars as the irrepressible Irish coach in **Knute Rockne, All-American**, with the crucial role of his star player, George Gipp, played by a young Ronald Reagan.

Two years later comes the release of *The Pride of the Yankees*, with Gary Cooper playing the part of Lou Gehrig, in one of the sports world's first three-hankie biopics.

> *"Sport was the main occupation for all of us, and continued to be mine for a long time. That is where I had my only lesson in ethics."*
> —Albert Camus

Impressions of the '40s

From ESPN's Rich Eisen:

There was no such thing as sports gridlock back in the 1940s. Heck, there may have been no such thing as grid-lock. There was no flourishing NFL, let alone an NFL Europe. Hardly an NBA or an NHL of which to speak. We had baseball. The National Pastime. But it would be foolish to suppose these were simpler times. In 1943, at the prime age of 25, Ted Williams left the game for three seasons—to serve in the military during World War II. Perhaps Hank Aaron would have broken Teddy Ballgame's home-run record instead of the Babe's. And, of course, there would have been no Aaron had there been no **Jackie Robinson**. The face of sport, let alone baseball, changed forever after 1947, a transformation that only he could have ushered in with the necessary grace and style. This decade's achievements will resonate deep into our future sports centuries.

Debuts and Exits

1941 **EXIT** **Football players without helmets,** after the retirement of Dick Plasman of the Giants.

1942 **EXIT** **Regular-season overtime games in the NHL,** discontinued because of wartime restrictions.

1943 **Unlimited substitutions** in the NFL.

The All-American Girls Professional Baseball League.

1944 **The goaltending rule** in college basketball.

1945 **The Hockey Hall of Fame** opens in Toronto.

1946 **The Basketball Association of America,** forerunner to the NBA.

Expansion to the West Coast by a professional league, with the relocation of the Rams from Cleveland to Los Angeles.

Integration of pro football, for the first time since the Twenties, with the appearance of fullback Marion Motley and middle guard Bill Willis for the AAFC Cleveland Browns against the Seattle Seahawks.

First baseball team to travel entirely by air, when New York Yankees sign a contract with United Air Lines.

The All-American Football Conference.

1947 **EXIT** **The color barrier in major league baseball,** when Jackie Robinson takes the field for the Dodgers April 15

Baseball's Rookie of the Year award, with Jackie Robinson taking the honor.

The Little League World Series, held in Williamsport, Pennsylvania.

First annual NHL All-Star Game.

EXIT **Zone defenses** in pro basketball, outlawed by the BAA.

The World Series on television, as the match-up between the Yankees and Dodgers is shown in the New York City area.

The College World Series, with Cal beating Yale, 8-7, in the finals. Yale first baseman George Bush would go on to bigger things.

1948 **The mandatory eight count** after a knockdown in boxing.

EXIT **The Negro National League.**

1949 **EXIT** **The All-American Football Conference,** after the Baltimore Colts, Cleveland Browns and San Francisco 49ers are absorbed by the NFL.

The National Basketball Association, after the BAA merges with the National Basketball League.

A rule making warning tracks in the outfield mandatory, for all major league baseball stadiums for future seasons, after voted by owners in July.

THE 1950s

The postwar boom brought suburbs, superhighways, teenagers and rock 'n' roll, and also signaled big changes in sports. While baseball reigned supreme in the national consciousness, the country that emerged from World War II was increasingly drawn to the gladiators of the National Football League. The pro game was uniquely suited to the popular new medium of television. And a stoic, crew-cut quarterback—a symbolic field general for a nation at Cold War—proved to be the ideal reflection of the country's passions at play.

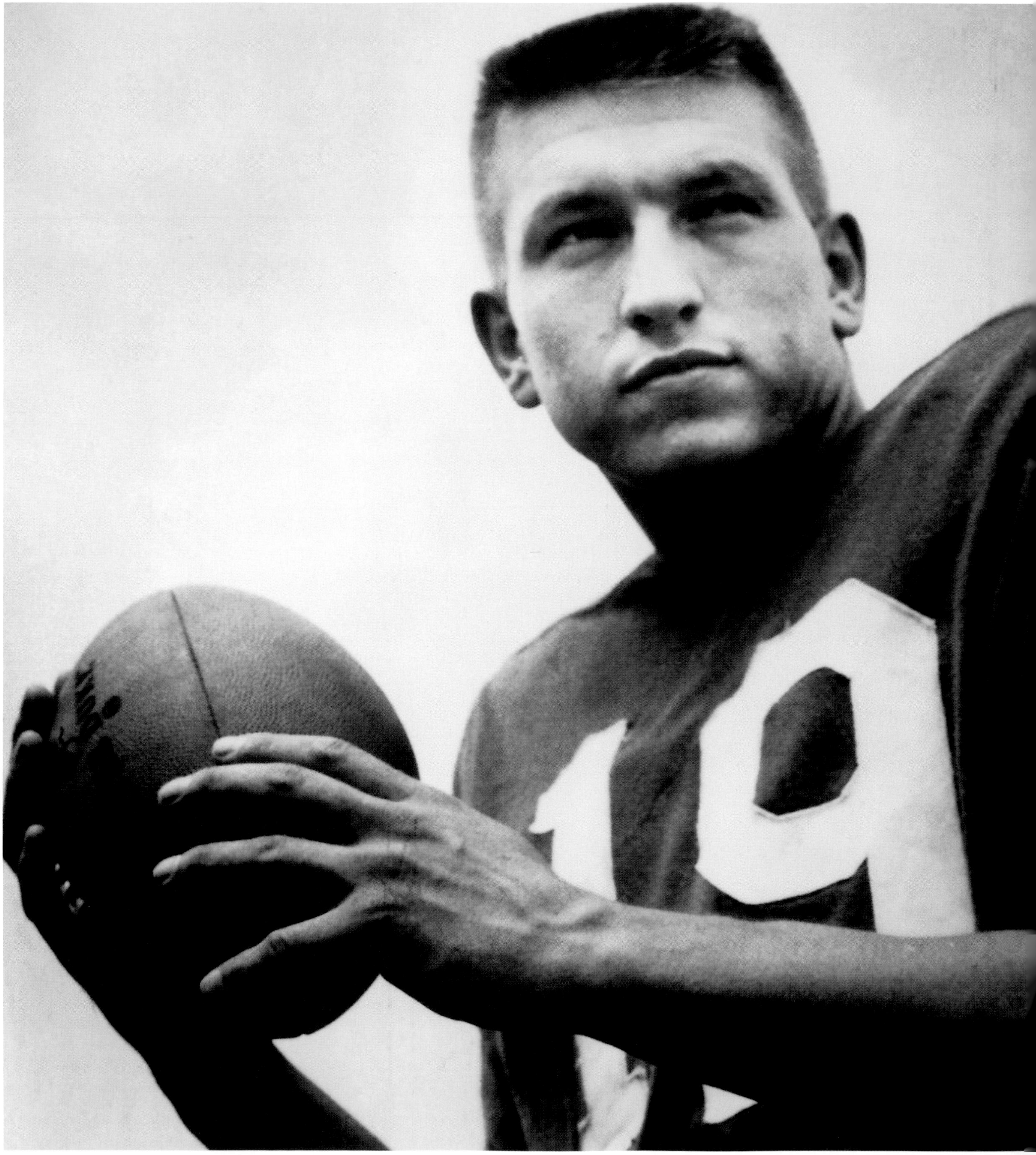

JOHNNY UNITAS By Dick Schaap

Sunday's Best

The Supreme Court ruling on Brown *v.* Board of Education, *which occurred in the middle of the decade [the 1950s], was the first important break between the older, more staid America that existed at the start of the era and the new, fast-paced tumultuous America that saw the decade's end. The second was Elvis Presley.*

—David Halberstam, *The Fifties*

The third was Johnny Unitas.
Which is overstating.
But not outrageously.

PREVIOUS PAGES
An Icon of the Era.
Unitas' high-tops were a perfect representation of his all-business style of leadership. A decade later, these were what Joe Namath—in his low-slung white cleats—was rebelling against.

Not the Prototype.
Crew-cut, square-shouldered, Unitas looked like a quarterback only after you saw him play.

A T THE START OF THE 1950s, no one outside of friends and family had heard of Elvis Presley, Dr. Martin Luther King Jr., or Johnny Unitas. By the end of the decade, each of these men who had been born into the Depression had played a major role in igniting a revolution—in American culture, in American society and in American sports. Rock 'n' roll, desegregation and the blitz had stormed the English language.

Clearly, the King's provocative moves and music and Dr. King's provocative movement were more radical developments, more significant historically, but just as surely, the revolution sparked by Unitas, his teammates on the 1958 Baltimore Colts, and their opponents on the New York Giants, dramatized, in Halberstam's words, the break "between the older, more staid America" of 1950 and "the new, fast-paced tumultuous America" of 1959.

Professional football came of age, began to challenge the supremacy of big-league baseball in the Fifties—on December 28, 1958, to be specific, the day the Colts and the Giants collided in Yankee Stadium for the National Football League championship; the day that Johnny Unitas lifted himself and his team to the top of his game; the day that the budding romance between football and television was, if not consecrated, at least consummated. That game, that day, a compelling drama orchestrated by Unitas and acted out before a vast and fascinated audience, has been called ever since "the greatest game ever played." It may also have been the most significant. It spawned America's obsession with pro football and nurtured America's obsession with television. It shaped the rest of the century.

Pro football, a game demanding passion as much as control, echoed the new music, and with its staccato bursts of fury, and integrated lineups (big Jim Parker protecting Unitas with Lenny Moore flanking him, a pair of gifted African-Americans), the sport reflected the new society. By then, Elvis was sizzling on the charts, and Dr. King was spearheading the Montgomery protests—each man a strong and unmistakable voice that contradicted the labeling of their contemporaries in the Fifties as "The Silent Generation."

Johnny Unitas, who spoke most eloquently with his arm, didn't spend a lot of his time dwelling on either of his fellow revolutionaries. His own taste in music ran more to Perry Como than to Presley; in footwear, more to high-top black cleats than to blue suede shoes; and integration was hardly an issue with him. Unitas had grown up in the South Hills section of Pittsburgh, a working-class neighborhood that was homogeneous only economically, his playmates a blur of nationalities and races. Even his college team in the early 1950s at the University of Louisville in the southern-border state of Kentucky was, somewhat surprisingly, integrated, and one of his black Louisville teammates, Lenny Lyles, was, by 1958, one of his Baltimore teammates.

With his crew-cut hair, blue-collar look, and blue-collar outlook, Unitas personified the "more staid" citizens who came of age in the Fifties, many of them first-generation Americans who were relieved to find themselves living in a prosperous country that was at peace, who were convinced they could and would improve themselves economically, who believed in the rightness of America and in the breadth of its possibilities, and in the existence and goodness of God. Unitas' father died when he was only five. His work ethic came from his mother, who was born in Lithuania and worked as a bookkeeper for the city of Pittsburgh. Johnny went to a parochial high school, St. Justin's, and dreamed, like so many other Catholic schoolboy football players, of attending the University of Notre Dame.

BUT FOR JOHNNY UNITAS, the fifties began with rejection. In the fall of 1950, he was a star quarterback in high school, but a skinny one, 6 feet tall and barely 145 pounds. He visited South Bend, Indiana, the home of Notre Dame, and for a week worked out for the backfield coach, a former Notre Dame player named Bernie Crimmins, who then sent him home. Crimmins told Unitas that he was too light to play with the big boys, too small for Notre Dame. Stereotyping was a national passion in America in the fifties, and Unitas did not measure up to the stereotypical Notre Dame quarterback. Right height, wrong weight. (An even sturdier stereotype in the Fifties and on into the Sixties, Seventies and Eighties was that African-Americans could not play quarterback, not in big-time college football and certainly not in the pros.)

(Crimmins, who had been a quarterback himself when he entered Notre Dame, eventually switched to guard and in 1941, his senior year, earned some All-America

Long Time Coming. Unitas was drafted in the NFL as a lightly-regarded, skinny quarterback out of Louisville—and quickly cut by the Pittsburgh Steelers.

mentions—as a 5-foot-11-inch, 185-pound guard. It's hard to imagine how a 185-pound guard could consider a 145-pound 17-year-old too small to play quarterback, but that was Crimmins's verdict. Ironically, a couple of years later, after Unitas had grown in physical stature and in skill, Crimmins, by then the head coach at Indiana University, tried to persuade Johnny U. to transfer from Louisville to I.U. This time Unitas rejected Crimmins, perhaps because he felt Crimmins was too short to be a head coach. Unitas chose to stay in Louisville, which was—further irony—Crimmins' hometown.)

Turned down by Notre Dame, Unitas turned south to the University of Louisville, then as now a school better known for its basketball program than its football. In 1950–51, in fact, before Unitas entered Louisville, the Cardinals, with a 19–7 record, were one of 16 teams to qualify for the NCAA basketball tournament; the 1950 Louisville football team lost twice as many games as it won.

Unitas enjoyed a remarkable growth spurt between high school and college—a "phantom" spurt. As a freshman at Louisville in 1951, he was listed in the football media guide at 175 pounds and 6 foot 3 inches, which might have impressed even Notre Dame, if it had been accurate. Unitas had a good freshman season, came off the bench to lead Louisville to four straight victories, earned the nickname "Mr. Sparkplug," and then grew shorter. As a sophomore, he was listed in the Louisville brochure at 185 pounds and 6 foot 1, the height that he maintained for the rest of his collegiate and professional career. (Coincidentally, the man who was then Notre Dame's most recent All-American quarterback, Bob Williams, was, at 180 pounds and 6 feet, 1 inch in 1949, slightly smaller than Unitas.) The media guide announced that Unitas, despite his diminished stature, was "already a legend here in Louisville." In his sophomore season, Unitas embellished the legend, leading Louisville to a 41–14 victory over Florida State, which was not quite the football power it became under Bobby Bowden in the Eighties and Nineties. Unitas completed 17 of 22 passes, three for touchdowns, against the Seminoles; in the first half, he completed 12 of 13.

AT LOUISVILLE, Unitas did considerably more than throw passes. He punted, returned kickoffs and punts, and played safety on defense. It was the dying days of the era of the two-way player, and the last of the breed among the pros, incidentally, was, like Unitas, a Pennsylvanian with an Eastern European background: Chuck Bednarik, who was a center and a linebacker, and a force, offensively and defensively, for the Philadelphia Eagles. Unitas was no Bednarik on defense, but he was a capable athlete, promising enough to be drafted in the ninth round in 1955 by his hometown NFL team, the Pittsburgh Steelers. The NFL draft was not exactly an infallible gauge of talent in the 1950s; the year after the Steelers took Unitas in the ninth round, the Green Bay Packers did not select Bart Starr until the 17th round. Both of these underrated quarterbacks thrived in the NFL and played into the 1970s, then won election to the Pro Football Hall of Fame.

The Steelers were not flawless judges of talent, either. With four quarterbacks to choose from in 1955, they cut Unitas in training camp and kept the other three, among them Ted Marchibroda, whose life and career often intersected Unitas's. In 1951, when Unitas took charge of the Louisville offense for the first time, he re-entered the game with the Cardinals losing, 19–0, to St. Bonaventure University (he

A New Home. The rich ethnic mix of Baltimore quickly took to the no-nonsense Unitas, a Pennsylvanian with eastern European ancestry.

had started the game), which was quarterbacked by his fellow Pennsylvanian Marchibroda. Unitas threw three touchdown passes and fell just a point short, 22–21, of catching up to the Bonnies. Marchibroda was a first-round draft choice of the Steelers in 1953, but spent only four undistinguished seasons playing in the NFL.

Yet, like Unitas, Marchibroda eventually became a significant part of football history, not in Pittsburgh but in Baltimore. Marchibroda went on to coach the Baltimore Colts, after Unitas left the team; the Indianapolis Colts, after the team left Baltimore; and the Baltimore Ravens, after that team left Cleveland.

By 1957, the Steelers were wise enough to make Purdue quarterback Len Dawson, a future Hall of Famer, their first draft choice, but they were not wise enough to play him. Dawson sat on the bench for three seasons, the last two while Bobby Layne, who was also bound for the Hall of Fame, guided the team. It is quite likely that if Pittsburgh had held on to Unitas, he, too, would have been no more than an understudy to Layne.

When the Steelers dropped Unitas and no other NFL team rushed to pick him up, he had little choice but to spend the 1955 season with the Bloomfield Rams, a semi-pro team in the Greater Pittsburgh League. He received $6 a game for playing for the Rams. The following season, in response to a phone call from the Baltimore Colts—who were undermanned at quarterback and most other positions—he went to training camp and made the team—as the third-string signal caller. Unitas received a raise from his Bloomfield salary, but not an enormous one. He was paid $7,000 for the 1956 season; at the time, no one in pro football was earning a six-figure salary, not even any member of the Cleveland Browns, who had played in six NFL championship games in a row. Pro football, in the mid-fifties, trailed big-league baseball drastically in pay scale as well as in popularity.

When the Colts backup quarterback, Gary Kerkorian, gave up football to attend law school, Unitas moved up to number two, and when the starter, George Shaw, suffered an injury in the fourth game of the 1956 season, Unitas stepped into the lineup. The Colts had no compelling reason to be optimistic about Unitas' future or their own. In 1956, as undistinguished as Unitas' personal history may have been, the Baltimore Colts' team history was markedly worse. In fact, if you wanted to select the weakest franchise in the post–World War II history of pro football, the Colts were certainly legitimate contenders. They came into existence in 1947, transplanted from Miami to represent Baltimore in the upstart All-America Football Conference, a league created to challenge the NFL. The Colts endured three losing seasons in the AAFC, ending their feeble run with a 1–11 season in 1949. The NFL then absorbed the AAFC and took in three of its cities—Cleveland, San Francisco, and Baltimore. The Colts had no trouble adjusting to the NFL; they finished a familiar 1–11 in 1950, their first NFL season, and then, wisely, dropped out of the league.

Baltimore harbored no team in 1951 or 1952, but in 1953 the Dallas Texans, after their first and only season in the NFL, were taken over by the league, then sold to Baltimore, where they became the Colts. Naturally, in their one season, the Texans had achieved a 1–11 record. Reincarnated as the Colts, the team improved dramatically, winning three of 12 games in 1953 and 1954, then five in 1955, which was Baltimore's seventh consecutive losing season, dating back to the AAFC.

The 1956 Colts, maintaining the tradition, lost three of their first four games, with Shaw as the starting quarterback. But after Unitas took over, the team split its

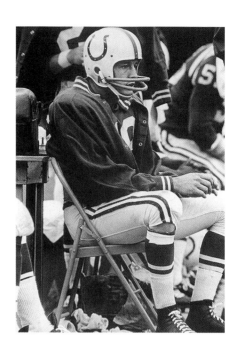

The Student.
Unitas was not just cool but preternaturally observant. He seemed to take everything in, both on the field and off.

remaining eight games, then did not suffer through another losing season for the next 15 years—not until 1972, when Unitas, at the age of 39, was in his 17th, and final, season with the Colts. By then, the Colts had won three NFL championships and a Super Bowl, a stunning reversal of their earlier fortune. Clearly, Unitas was the major reason for the improvement. In 1969, when the National Football League celebrated 50 years of existence, Unitas was named the starting quarterback on the NFL's all-time team.

N HIS ROOKIE SEASON, in 1956, Unitas started one of the most remarkable streaks in the history of professional sports—a streak that, while it has never been revered like Joe DiMaggio's 56-game hitting streak (football statistics have never had the glitter or impact of baseball stats) is every bit as impressive. Beginning in 1956 and extending into 1960, Unitas, the unheralded product of the University of Louisville and the Bloomfield Rams, threw at least one touchdown pass in 47 consecutive regular-season games, 49 games in a row if you count two championship games.

Not only is that record still standing going into the 21st century, no one has ever come close to it. The second-longest streak is 30 games, by Dan Marino during his NFL youth in the 1980s. When Pete Rose hit safely in 44 straight games in 1978, he came closer to matching DiMaggio's "unbreakable" record than anyone has come to matching Unitas's. In comparision, Brett Favre, who rivals Unitas among the greatest quarterbacks ever, has never gone through even one full season throwing a touchdown pass in each of his 16 games.

Unitas initiated another streak in 1957, his first full season, when he led the league in number of touchdown passes. He finished atop that category for four straight seasons, through 1960, another mark that has never been equaled.

In 1958, Unitas was only 25 years old, but he was already approaching the peak of his game, a peak he managed to sustain, when he was free from injuries, well into his thirties. He was in the midst of his two monumental touchdown streaks when he led the 1958 Colts to nine victories in their first 10 games; the ninth victory, 35–27 over San Francisco after trailing by 20 points at halftime, clinched the NFL's Western Conference championship, the first title in the Colts' history. (Geography has never been one of the strong suits of professional sports leagues: In 1958, the Baltimore Colts, based on the Atlantic coast, were in the NFL's Western Conference, the Chicago Cardinals in the Eastern. By the end of the century, things had not changed much: The Cardinals, transplanted to Arizona, were in the Eastern Division of the National Conference, and Carolina in the Western. Rand-McNally was obviously not the NFL's playbook.)

The Colts had very swiftly built a formidable team by 1958, with six future Hall of Famers in the starting lineup, and another, the head coach, Weeb Ewbank, on the sidelines. On defense, tackle Art Donovan and end Gino Marchetti were headed for the Hall; on offense, Unitas was joined, and abetted, by his favorite target, Raymond Berry; his favorite blocker, Jim Parker; and a young running back, Lenny Moore, who, in only his third season, had averaged more than seven yards per rushing

Film School.
Unitas preparing for the '58 title game with coach Weeb Ewbank and favorite target Raymond Berry.

attempt. Three other starters—fullback Alan Ameche, defensive tackle Gene "Big Daddy" Lipscomb, and defensive end Don Joyce—were named to the Pro Bowl.

Ewbank, Unitas said, "was the perfect coach for me because he'd always get the players' input." Even at 25, after only two full seasons in the league, Unitas had unusual confidence in his own mental and physical abilities. "My first year I was learning," Unitas said. "By the end of the second year, it was like a complete revelation, like a cloud had moved away. I'd get a feel for how to move defenses into coverages that I wanted. I'd keep a chart on every defensive back, his tendencies."

Unitas was one of the handful of quarterbacks in NFL history who redefined the position. Sid Luckman, the first pro to popularize the T–formation, was another. Joe Namath was, too, as was Joe Montana. Each brought something special to the game—rare ability, attitude, charisma, or a blend of the three. Unitas was totally in command of his team; he called the plays and set the tone. He had remarkable self-confidence, backed by equally remarkable ability. He excelled under pressure, saving his finest performances for the brightest spotlights. He was unbelievably tough, mentally and physically. "I often thought that sometimes he held the ball one count longer than he had to," Merlin Olsen, the Hall of Fame defensive tackle, once said, "just so he could take the hit and laugh in your face." Unitas himself said, "You don't arrive as a quarterback until you can tell the coach to go to hell."

Raymond Berry, who was Unitas's prime target on the field, summarized Johnny U.: "I can tell you about his uncanny instinct for calling the right play at the right time, his icy composure under fire, his fierce competitiveness, and his utter disregard for his own safety." Quarterbacks would kill for a far lesser compliment.

One for the Ages.
At bunting-bedecked Yankee Stadium (right), the Colts jumped quickly on the proud Giant defense, taking a 14–3 first-half lead. When it ended two hours later with the first overtime game in NFL history, Unitas—mobbed by Baltimore fans while leaving the field (above)—had become a living legend.

THE ONLY GAME THE 1958 COLTS LOST before they clinched the conference title was to the champions of the Eastern Conference, the New York Giants, who were in the early years of a surge that would take them to six NFL championship games in eight seasons. The Giants beat the Colts in midseason in New York, 24–21, but Unitas sat out that game, nursing cracked ribs. Seven weeks later, the two clubs met again in New York for the NFL championship. The Giants had qualified by winning a playoff for the Eastern title, defeating Paul Brown, Jim Brown, and the rest of the Cleveland Browns, 10–0. The Giants had their own imposing roster. Roosevelt Brown, Frank Gifford, Sam Huff, Andy Robustelli, Emlen Tunnell, and even a rookie wide receiver named Don Maynard would go to the Hall of Fame, along with two assistant coaches, Tom Landry and Vince Lombardi, and the owner of the team and his heir, Tim and Wellington Mara, making a total of 17 future Hall of Famers directly involved in the 1958 championship game. Besides, Gifford and his Giant teammate Pat Summerall would be two of the enduring broadcast voices of professional football from the Sixties to the end of the century.

With Unitas healthy, the Colts were originally favored by 3 points to beat the Giants for the championship; when big money poured in on the Colts, the spread grew to 3½ points. One bookmaker told *Newsweek* magazine that it was "the biggest action event" he had ever seen; he said at least $100 million had been wagered.

CBS Sports was set to televise the title game for the third time. Their first two broadcasts had provided less drama than any decent edition of *Playhouse 90*, the classic series that debuted on the air the same year the NFL championship did. In 1956,

the Giants beat the Chicago Bears by 40 points; the following year, the Detroit Lions beat the Cleveland Browns by 45. In 1958, the Colts and the Giants had a chance to appeal to a rapidly expanding audience. At the start of the 1950s, only nine million television sets were scattered across the country; by the end, 90 million sets saturated the U.S. Milton Berle, Sid Caesar, and Ed Sullivan grew into TV titans during the decade; Dick Clark's *American Bandstand* launched its marathon run.

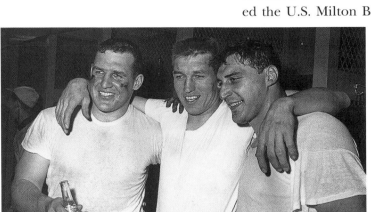

TWO INNOVATIONS of the 1950s had a direct impact on the 1958 championship game. The New Jersey Turnpike, one of the earliest turnpikes, made it possible for Colt fans to drive from Baltimore to New York in about three hours—20,000 Colt fans made the pilgrimage to Yankee Stadium by turnpike and train—and a magazine called *Sports Illustrated*, the first weekly sports magazine, in the fifth year of its existence, saved prime space for the late-breaking story of the NFL title game.

For more than a half, the 1958 NFL championship game bore little resemblance to a classic game, a game for the ages. With Alan Ameche running for one touchdown and Unitas passing to Raymond Berry for another, the Colts led 14–3 at the half. In the third quarter, marching toward a touchdown that would give them a commanding 21–3 lead (and give viewers across America an excuse to turn off their TV sets or switch channels), the Colts drove to a first down on the Giants' 3-yard line. But then the New York defense suddenly stiffened and stopped the Colts, a stand that inspired the Giants' offense to mount a counterattack. A pass from Charlie Conerly to Kyle Rote gained 62 yards, and when Rote fumbled as he was tackled, teammate Alex Webster picked up the loose ball and went another 24 yards, down to the Colts' one-yard line, setting up a touchdown that cut Baltimore's lead to a precarious 14–10.

Early in the fourth quarter, the Giants scored again, this time on a pass from Conerly to Frank Gifford, and the favored Colts found themselves trailing 17–14. The score was the same when the Colts got the ball on their own 14-yard line with only 1:56 left in regulation. Unitas went to work, combining perfectly with the most unlikely of wide receivers, Raymond Berry, who was playing with contact lenses, a bad back, and one leg shorter than the other. Berry was not very big, not very strong, and not very fast. All he was, was very good. On three consecutive plays in the last two minutes of regulation time, Berry caught passes from Unitas for a total of 62 yards, putting the Colts in position for Steve Myhra to kick a game-tying 20-yard field goal with seven seconds to play.

Then the NFL championship went into overtime, the first sudden-death overtime game in pro football history. It was a new concept that made the whole package more appealing to television. The Giants won the toss and chose to receive. Unable to threaten, they punted, and Baltimore took possession on its own 20-yard line. The Drive began: the 13-play drive that, in only his third pro season, defined Unitas' career and elevated his sport.

On first down, Unitas handed the ball to L. G. Dupre, who ran 11 yards for a first

Champagne Dreams.
Steve Myhra, with an orange soda, and Alan Ameche, with a beer, flank Unitas in the victorious Colt locker room after the overtime win over the Giants.

down. Then Unitas bid for the bomb, hoping to produce sudden death suddenly, but his long pass to Moore was deflected. After Dupre gained two yards, it was third and eight, and with Berry covered, Unitas turned and connected with Ameche, who barely got the first down at the Baltimore 41.

Dupre picked up another four yards, but then Unitas, unable to find an open receiver, was tackled for an eight-yard loss, and the Colts faced third and 14 on their own 37-yard line. Unitas looked first to Moore, then to Berry, cutting toward the sideline. Unitas threw and hit Berry for a 21-yard gain, first down on the Giants' 42, approaching field-goal range, approaching victory.

Unitas called another pass play, with Berry the primary target. But as the two teams lined up, Unitas noticed the Giants' middle linebacker, Sam Huff, shifting to help defend against Berry. Unitas changed the play, as he did so often during his career. "I call about 10 percent of the plays," coach Ewbank once said; Unitas called the rest. Now he switched to a trap play, handed the ball to Ameche, no longer shadowed by Huff, and Ameche drove 22 yards, to the 20, definitely within field-goal range; first down for the Colts.

On the ninth play of The Drive, Dupre was stopped for no gain. On the 10th, Unitas teamed up successfully with Berry for the 12th time in the game, gaining 12 yards to the eight-yard line, earning another first down, the Colts' 27th to the Giants' mere 10. Berry's 12 catches had gained 178 yards; Unitas had passed for 349, which was more yardage than the Giants gained all day, passing and running.

Grand Master. Well into his 30s, Unitas would go to two Super Bowls with the Colts, the first with the youthful Don Shula after the '68 season. Joe Namath was waiting.

On first down, on the 11th play, Ameche ran for a yard, to the 7. Everyone knew what was going to happen: One or two more plunges into the line, and then Myhra would kick a field goal, and the Colts would be champions. But on second down, instead of calling a running play, Unitas opted for a pass to Jim Mutscheller heading toward the right corner of the goal line.

It was one of the most memorable plays in NFL history, ranking with Joe Montana to Dwight Clark for the catch that produced the winning touchdown in the 1981 NFC championship game, and with Joe Namath to Don Maynard, a pass close to 70 yards in the air that lifted the New York Jets to the 1968 American Football League championship. (Coincidentally, Montana and Namath and Unitas all grew up in the Pittsburgh area, their Hall of Fame skills forged in western Pennsylvania's red-hot football crucible. Unitas and George Blanda were pioneers of that strong-armed tradition, maintained in the closing years of the 20th century by Dan Marino and Jim Kelly.)

Mutscheller caught the pass from Unitas and fell out of bounds at the 1-yard line.

"Weren't you taking a chance, risking an interception?" Unitas was asked afterward.

"When you know what you're doing," Unitas said, "you're not going to be intercepted."

On the next, almost anticlimactic, play, Ameche plunged into the end zone. The Baltimore Colts had a 23–17 victory and the first championship of their existence. Bert Bell, the commissioner of the NFL, called it "the greatest game I've ever seen"; *Sports Illustrated* entitled its story of the contest "The Best Football Game Ever Played" (somewhat schizophrenically, *SI*'s headline over the continuation of its coverage shifted superlatives and read "Greatest Game"); and even a decade later, when *Sport* magazine asked a panel of 100 coaches, players and authorities to pick football's greatest game, the 1958 championship received more than twice as many votes as the runner-up, the Green Bay Packers' Ice Bowl victory in 1967.

THE COLTS' VICTORY WAS, in some ways, as controversial as it was monumental. When the Colts got inside the 20-yard line during sudden death, gamblers who had bet on the Giants began rooting for Baltimore to go for a field goal. If the Colts had kicked a field goal and won by three points, then the people who had bet on the underdog Giants *plus* 3½ points would have won their wagers. By disdaining the field goal and going for the touchdown, Unitas and the Colts had, in gambling parlance, *covered*—won by more than the point spread—which meant that the people who had bet on the Colts were winners. There were rumors that Carroll Rosenbloom, the owner of the Colts, had placed a huge bet on the Colts *minus* 3½ points, and that, for thousands and thousands of reasons, no one was happier than he when Ameche scored. The accusation was never proved; Unitas occasionally cracked jokes about it. But when Unitas was serious, he defended the logic, wisdom and effectiveness of the plays he called. And no one could argue with the result.

The combination of heroics and controversy played out on national television did wonders for pro football, creating new interest and excitement from coast to coast. The sport soared as the 1950s came to an end. The Cleveland Browns had Jimmy Brown, the greatest runner in the history of football. In the communications center of the world, the New York Giants had Gifford, Rote, Huff, Robustelli, and Roosevelt Brown fueling a torrid run. And just before the decade ended, Vince Lombardi moved from the Giants to the Green Bay Packers and began building a dynasty that

The Best. In a poll conducted by the National Football League in 1969, Unitas was named the league's greatest player of its first 50 years.

would convert millions of Americans to Packer fans. And, of course, Baltimore had Unitas. He was the player of the year in 1959 and twice more in the Sixties.

Late in the Sixties, Unitas was named the greatest player in the first 50 years of the NFL.

Ironically, at the end of the 1968 season, Unitas played a role in a game that rivaled the 1958 championship game in impact: Super Bowl III, the Baltimore Colts against the New York Jets, the game that legitimized the upstart American Football League, the game in which Joe Namath guided the Jets, underdogs by 19 points, to a stunning victory over the Colts. The game belonged to Namath, heir to Unitas as king of the quarterbacks, but Johnny U., who had sat out most of the 1968 season with an aching elbow, did come off the bench to lead the Colts to their only touchdown. And two years later, when Unitas was 37, he teamed up with tight end John Mackey on a 75-yard touchdown pass that started the Colts on their way to their only Super Bowl championship. (More than a quarter of a century later, John Elway became the second quarterback to win his first Super Bowl at the age of 37.) Mackey, who is also in the Hall of Fame, was once asked what it was like to play with Johnny Unitas; they were teammates for nine seasons.

"It's like being in the huddle with God," Mackey said.

Which is overstating.

But not outrageously.

Near the End.
Relegated to the bench, Unitas trots off the field in Baltimore. "They tell you things change at 40," said Unitas. "But they don't tell you how much."

MICKEY MANTLE
Our Symbol

If the key to Babe Ruth's appeal was that he seemed to be a mythic, larger-than-life character, then it's just as true that the core of Mickey Mantle's charisma was an all-too-human, life-sized heroism. The three-time MVP, successor to Joe DiMaggio as the standard-bearer of Bronx Bomber supremacy and center-field glamour, Mantle was during his career the most feared slugger in the game. And perhaps the most loved.

The son of an Oklahoma mine worker who'd played semi-pro baseball, Mantle was named after Mickey Cochrane and groomed for the big leagues from an early age, learning to switch-hit by age five. He would arrive in the majors at 19 years old in 1951, a broad-shouldered, thick-necked country boy with an astounding combination of power and speed. Al Lopez said he had "more power than Babe Ruth," and Lou Boudreau was convinced Mantle hit the ball harder than Ted Williams. During his 18 seasons, he hit 536 home runs, led the Yankees to 12 pennants and seven world championships, and became the living embodiment of a distinctly American brand of soft-spoken heartland stoicism at work and hard-drinking, hell-bent abandon at play.

But even in his rookie season, the litany of crippling injuries began. Playing right field in the 1951 World Series, with instructions to help out the aging Joe DiMaggio in center, Mantle closed quickly on a Willie Mays fly ball. DiMaggio called him off at the last instant, and Mantle caught his spikes in a Yankee Stadium storm drain, tearing cartilage in his knee. The long series of baseball injuries exacerbated his deteriorating left leg, hurt earlier playing high school football. Later in his career, he'd endure shin splints, torn muscles, pinched nerves and a broken foot, suffered while scaling a chain-link outfield fence in Baltimore. By the early 1960s, Mantle looked like a football gladiator in the dressing room, heavily taping both legs before each game. "I figure I got all the breaks in spite of my legs," he once said. "Otherwise, I'd have been in the mines."

Baseball fans will forever argue whether Mays or Mantle was the better player. But the consensus seems to be that while Mays had the longer and more productive career, Mantle was the better player when both men were at their best. Bill James flatly calls him the "greatest player of the Fifties," and his four best seasons—the triple-crown year of 1956, plus '57, '61 and '62—were superior to Mays' best years.

All of which explains some of the outpouring of affection and grief that accompanied Mantle's death from liver cancer in 1995, at age 63, less than two years after he bravely confronted (and conquered) a lifetime of alcoholism. Even at

MANTLE:
"I FIGURE I GOT ALL THE BREAKS.... OTHERWISE, I'D HAVE BEEN IN THE MINES"

HOWE:
"HE WAS IN CONTROL OF THE WHOLE GAME," SAID GRETZKY

his most vulnerable, he remained a hero. Bob Costas, delivering the eulogy at Mantle's funeral, put it best: "He was our symbol of baseball at a time when the game meant something to us that perhaps it no longer does. Mickey Mantle had those dual qualities so seldom seen—exuding dynamism and excitement, but at the same time touching your heart, flawed, wounded. We knew there was something poignant about Mickey Mantle before we knew what poignant meant. We didn't just root for him, we felt for him."

GORDIE HOWE
Mr. Hockey

The seemingly indestructible son of the Saskatoon prairies, Gordie Howe, known as "Mr. Hockey" to one and all, was the dominant figure on the violent front lines of the hockey wars for decades, reaffirming with each passing year that, while the ice was graced by many superstars, it had seen only one true superman in the pre-Gretzky era. As Detroit Red Wings coach Jack Adams put it in the late Sixties, "There is Gordie Howe and there are other hockey players who are merely great."

A smooth and deceptively swift skater with long, gliding strides, Howe never looked rushed, and his confident composure unnerved goalies almost as much as his incredibly powerful wrist shots. Wayne Gretzky, whom Howe befriended as an 11-year-old and mentored in his early professional days, always admired the ease with which he worked his wonders. "He was in control of the whole game," said Gretzky. "He seemed to do everything so gracefully."

Howe was a rare combination of scorer and enforcer, meting out sly paybacks to all who challenged him. Referee Vern Buffey marveled at the discreet damage he did to his opponents. "You're working a game and you see a player down. You know that Howe did it, but how can you prove it?"

When he finally hung up his Red Wings jersey in 1971, Howe had led Detroit to four Stanley Cup victories, playing more games and scoring more points than anyone in NHL history. Retiring as a 21-time All-Star and six-time winner of the league's Most Valuable Player and leading scorer trophies, Howe had undeniably earned his rest and recuperation.

But after the Houston Aeros of the new WHA drafted his sons Mark and Marty, Howe reenlisted in the hockey wars as a venerable 45-year-old in 1973. It was body-checking business as usual as he led the Aeros to the league's championship and won the MVP award.

The saga continued in 1977, when the WHA New England Whalers outbid several NHL franchises for the Howes' services. It allowed Howe one last NHL season in 1979-80, when the Whalers were absorbed into the original league. Howe finally played his last professional hockey game at age 69 in the opener of the 1997 International Hockey League season, becoming the first, and undoubtedly last, to play in six decades.

Howe's 32-year career combined legendary longevity with record-setting productivity, and his influence extended beyond his years on the ice. Gretzky, who would ultimately break many of his records, had his boyhood admiration of Howe reinforced as an adult, stating simply, "He'll always be the greatest player who ever lived. And the classiest, too."

—*Michael Point*

BOB COUSY
The Master

His instrument of choice was a basketball, but Bob Cousy was no less than a virtuoso. Playing point guard for the Boston Celtics from 1950 to 1963, Cousy was an artist who defined his position with speed, quickness, deft passes and peerless peripheral vision.

The 6-foot-1-inch Hall-of-Fame point guard led the NBA in assists eight consecutive seasons and made the all-NBA first team 10 times. He once had 28 assists in a game, 12 in one quarter, an NBA-record 19 in a half. He averaged 18.5 points for his career, scoring frequently with running bank shots, using either hand. He revolutionized his position and the game with long behind-the-back passes and no-look passes from all angles, including to teammates trailing behind him on the fast break. Cousy led a fast break that was considered incomparable until Magic Johnson showed up in Los Angeles during the 1980s.

He became such an icon that when players at any level tried unsuccessfully to reproduce his moves they were asked, *Who do ya think ya are, Bob Cousy?* "I compare him to a master jazz musician holding a jam session in some nightclub at four A.M. in New York City," said former teammate Tom Heinsohn, who added that Cousy understood even while blowing solos, he was part of a larger band. "He would improvise based upon what he heard, what he saw, and everybody else would accompany what he did. Let me put it in perspective—if you think Magic Johnson could pass, if you think John Stockton can pass, multiply that by 10 and you have Bob Cousy."

Historians note that Cousy's first behind-the-back dribble occurred on January 11, 1949, when he was a junior at Holy Cross. Trapped along the right side, he went behind his back, cut to the left, and made a running left-handed hook shot to beat Loyola. "I hadn't thought about doing it," Cousy later recalled. "I just did it."

Though Cousy had become a legend in the Boston area during college, Celtics coach Red Auerbach was not impressed. Criticized by fans and media for not drafting Cousy, Auerbach responded, "We need a big man. Little men are a dime a dozen. I'm supposed to win, not go after local yokels." Cousy would end up with the Celtics before he ever played an NBA game, his name picked out of a hat by Boston after the team he was on, the Chicago Stags, folded. Auerbach eventually procured his big man, when 6-foot-9-

COUSY:
"THE GREATEST BACKCOURT MAN WHO EVER LIVED"

GIBSON:
SHAKING HANDS WITH THE QUEEN WAS A LONG WAY FROM SITTING IN THE COLORED SECTION OF THE BUS

inch Bill Russell joined the team in 1956. Cousy and Russell jump-started the Celtics dynasty that year, winning six NBA titles in seven years before Cousy retired in 1963. By that time, Auerbach's tune had changed. "What can you say when you know you're gonna lose the greatest backcourt man who ever lived?" said Red. "Nobody will ever take his place. There's only one Cousy."

—*Mark Rosner*

ALTHEA GIBSON
A Long Journey

The modern age of tennis began in the summer of 1950, when the esteemed former champion Alice Marble wrote a guest editorial in *American Lawn Tennis* magazine, scolding the leaders of tennis for enforcing a de facto color line. "If Althea Gibson represents a challenge to the present crop of players, then it's only fair that they meet this challenge on the courts," wrote Marble, and within two months, the USLTA capitulated and invited Gibson to the Nationals at Forest Hills. And like that, it was done. In tennis, the role of Jackie Robinson would be played by a woman.

Over the next decade, the lily-white racial walls in tennis began to crumble, brought down by the powerful strokes and swift movement of Gibson. And she truly came a long way: born on a cotton farm in South Carolina and raised in Harlem, where she'd first shown her aptitude for racket sports playing paddleball in a Police Athletic League program on 143rd Street in New York City.

In the early 1950s, Gibson's very presence blazed trails on both sides of the Atlantic, where, at both Forest Hills and Wimbledon, she became the first black woman to compete for a title. But by 1955 she was dropping in the American and world rankings, and considered retiring. It was in that year that she met Sidney Llewellyn, a part-time teaching pro who sparked a renaissance in her game, teaching her to maximize her height advantage (she stood 5-foot-10-inches) on her powerful first serve, and further streamline her elegant, powerful serve-and-volley game.

Instilling in Gibson many of the same motivational techniques of visualization and positive self-talk that would become standard for sports stars a generation later, Lewellyn helped her harness her talent and concentration, and she quickly rocketed back up the rankings. In 1956, she won 13 tournaments in a row, taking both the French and the Italian titles in singles, and the Wimbledon doubles, but falling in singles at Wimbledon and Forest Hills. In 1957, she enjoyed her greatest season, becoming the first black to win a singles title at Wimbledon and returning a week later to a ticker-tape parade through the streets of New York City. "Shaking hands with the queen of England was a long way from being forced to sit in the colored section of the bus going into downtown Wilmington, North Carolina," she wrote later in her autobiography. Two months later, Gibson won the U.S. Championships at Forest Hills, defeating

Louise Brough in straight sets in the final. By then she'd become one of the most popular players in tennis. She gave a gracious acceptance speech, which was greeted with "the longest demonstration of hand-clapping heard in the stadium in years," according to *The New York Times*.

Perhaps Gibson's greatest accomplishment was her ability to advance the notion that sports could be a laboratory for the best impulses of human nature, a way to bridge racial divides and teach a lesson to the culture as a whole. "I am just another tennis player, not a Negro tennis player," she said in 1956. "Of course, I am a Negro—everybody knows that—but you don't say somebody is a white tennis player, do you?"

RAFER JOHNSON
The Chosen One

Few athletes in the 20th century better embodied the Olympic ideal than Rafer Johnson, the factory worker's son who rose from poverty, injury and adversity to become the world's greatest athlete, winning the most dramatic decathlon competition in Olympic history.

As Johnson was rewriting the record book in his event, he was also expanding the possibilities of social integration. At a time when the black experience in America seemed defined by its social limitations, Johnson unfailingly lived as though those rules didn't apply. In the 1950s, he was the student body president of his junior high and his high school in predominantly white Kingsburg, California, and won the same office while attending UCLA. In 1958, during the heart of the Cold War, he went to Moscow, knocked off the Soviet world record holder Vassily Kuznyetsov in the decathlon—and was enthusiastically embraced by Soviet fans, who cheered him wildly, carrying him from the stadium on their shoulders.

Though his crowning glory came at the 1960 Summer Olympics in Rome, there was always a sense of sublime possibility in Johnson's life. He came to California from Texas at age five, his father lured by the social and economic opportunity in the San Joaquin Valley. At 16, Johnson watched two-time gold medalist Bob Mathias compete in Tulare, California, and decided the decathlon was for him. Though he was a four-sport star in high school, and played under John Wooden on the basketball team at UCLA, he dedicated himself to the decathlon and quickly became world class (setting a world record in only his fourth competition). An injury kept him from his best performance in the 1956 Olympics, at Melbourne, where he took the silver.

Four years later, after fighting off another injury from a car accident (which kept him out of training for 18 months), he qualified for the Olympic team again, and became the first black to carry the American flag at the opening ceremonies. The decathlon provided the richest drama of the 1960 Games, but the Soviet Kuznyetsov would be a footnote. Johnson's main competitor was one of his

JOHNSON: REWRITING THE RECORD BOOKS IN THE DECATHLON

MAYS: "I ALWAYS TRY TO DO SOMETHING NEW"

closest friends, the Taiwanese decathlete and fellow UCLA track man C. K. Yang, who had trained with Johnson.

The final event became the stuff of athletic legend as the two friends battled, with the gold medal in the balance. With a slender lead going into the final event, the 1,500 meters, Johnson had to finish within 10 seconds of Yang to win the gold. Four times around the Olympic track, with the crowd's roar building steadily, Johnson kept Yang in his sights, grimly staying in stride, answering every burst. Down the home stretch, both men were wobbly, but Johnson succeeded, trimming almost five seconds off his personal best and finishing 1.2 seconds behind Yang. And then the two exhausted friends leaned against each other for support. "All I could think of in that 1500 meters was, 'This is the last race I'll ever run in my life,'" said Johnson. "I wanted that one real bad. But I never want to go through that again, never."

But Johnson was hardly through. After nearly a quarter century of post-Olympic community service, he was chosen in 1984 to light the torch at the opening ceremonies of the Summer Games in Los Angeles. Still fit and sculpted at 48 years old, he remained a shining example of the Olympic spirit.

WILLIE MAYS
A Kind of Genius

Talullah Bankhead compared his genius to Shakespeare's. His beloved first major-league manager, Leo Durocher, called him "Joe Louis, Jascha Heifetz, Sammy Davis and Nashua rolled into one." They were reduced to outlandish superlatives because they'd never seen anything quite like Willie Mays before, never seen someone do so many things so well, or do routine things with such an uncommon flair.

There is no simple typecasting for Mays, because he was the modern game's original five-tool player, able to hit, run, field, throw (Joe DiMaggio said Mays had the game's strongest arm) and hit for power. With his cap flying as he circled the basepaths, his Giants jersey billowing out as he raced across the wide expanses of center field, Mays generated more excitement than anyone else playing the game in the Fifties, much of it far removed from home plate.

"I always try to do something new," he said. "I don't try to do what the other fellow does. People come to ball games to see fellows do something different."

He'd learned from growing up with baseball. The son of a Birmingham steelworker, Mays was playing competitively at age six, in semi-pro ball by 14, and at age 15 signed a contract with the Negro Leagues power, the Birmingham Black Barons (stipulating he could only take road trips in summer, so he could finish high school). The Yankees and Red Sox, dragging their heels on integration, both scouted Mays in Birmingham before passing on him, and they would pay dearly for their willful ignorance.

At 20, he was the spark for the Giants' improbable pennant comeback in 1951 and, after two years of army duty in 1952–53, returned in 1954 to lead them to the world championship. The Indians entered the Series heavily favored but were never the same after Mays' magnificent game-saving, over-the-shoulder basket catch of Vic Wertz's screaming liner, which preserved a tie in the eighth inning of Game 1, and lives on for generations to come as live televised sports' first magic moment.

Mays won his first of two MVP awards in 1954, and continued to play with consistent excellence for much of the next two decades, finishing his career with 660 homers. But despite his professionalism, he was often misunderstood and patronized. His enthusiasm was so infectious, and the cautious politeness developed from his Jim Crow upbringing so pronounced, he was subtly typecast by the media early in his career as a jovial simpleton. Some writers even mocked his trademark all-purpose greeting of "Say, Hey."

He weathered all the storms—divorce, financial difficulties, media backlash, racism—and emerged a stronger though quieter man who continued to play the game with an unbridled joy that finally waned in his last years. One night, in 1973, his final season, he came home after a game and began crying. "How can you explain that?" he asked. "It's like crying for your mother after she's gone. You cry because you love her. I cried, I guess, because I loved baseball and I knew I had to leave it."

ROCKY MARCIANO
The Rock

He never was a great fighter," recalled legendary trainer Lou Duva. "But he never got beat." Rocky Marciano was called too small, too light and too crude, but he proved, finally, too tough. After holding the heavyweight title from 1952 to 1956, he retired 49–0, with 43 knockouts, an astonishing record that continues to make him a contender in debates about history's greatest fighters.

Born Rocco Francis Marchegiano on September 1, 1923, in Brockton, Massachusetts, the stocky slugger excelled in several sports as a boy, even trying out as a catcher with the Cubs organization in 1947. But his early boxing exhibitions, remembered his trainer, Charley Goldman, were "so awkward we just stood there and laughed. He didn't stand right. He didn't throw a punch right. He didn't do anything right." By the early Fifties, however, Marciano had mastered his own crouching style, featuring a toe-to-toe attack and a devastating right he nicknamed "Susie-Q." Standing just under 5-foot-11-inches with a 68-inch reach (compared, for example, with Ali's 82 inches), his fighting weight averaged less than 185. Yet he won his first 16 pro bouts by knockout, and that early success made him promotable enough for an October 26, 1951, fight with 37-year-old Joe Louis, who had come out of retirement a year earlier. Marciano sent him back to retirement, by KO in the eighth.

MARCIANO: "HE JUST HAD MORE STAMINA THAN ANYONE ELSE"

SHOEMAKER: THE MOST STORIED CAREER IN HORSE RACING

The "Brockton Blockbuster" fought Jersey Joe Walcott for the heavyweight title on September 23, 1952, a bloody battle before more than 40,000 fans in Philadelphia's Municipal Stadium. The boxer Walcott knocked the brawler Marciano to the canvas with a left hook in the opening round—his first time down in 43 fights—prompting Marciano to ask, "Who did that?" when he returned to the corner. The action was furious thereafter, with Marciano continuing his customary, stubborn advance and Walcott picking him apart. Marciano was badly cut on the nose in the fifth, and by the fateful 13th round, the 38-year-old Walcott enjoyed a comfortable lead. Then, incautious for a moment, Walcott bounced off the ropes into a savage straight right, Rocky's "first really clean punch," as *New York Times* writer James P. Dawson described it. And that was all Marciano needed, as Walcott went down for the full count. A May 1953 rematch in Chicago ended in a first-round KO.

Marciano's only other time down came in his sixth and final title defense, the September 21, 1955, classic against superb stylist Archie Moore. A crafty boxer in the same mold as Walcott, Moore dodged a second-round Marciano lunge with a blazing counter right, drawing blood and sending the champion to his knees. Marciano rose at the count of two, looking more determined but no more cautious. In the sixth round, which *Sports Illustrated* writer Budd Schulberg called "a beautiful spectacle of pain and skill and endurance," Marciano's relentless punching turned the tide. Moore was counted out in the ninth after a barrage had him slumped in his own corner—a dramatic finish for Marciano's career. Under pressure from his wife and mother—and, at 32, having earned more than $4 million—Marciano retired the following April. He died in a small-plane crash in 1969, trying to squeeze in one more personal appearance before his 46th birthday the following day.

"He could hurt you, sure, but it was the quantity of his punches," remembered Moore 30 years after the loss. "He just had more stamina than anyone else in those days. He was like a bull with gloves." —*David Zivan*

BILL SHOEMAKER
Horse After Horse

Coming into the first turn of the 1986 Kentucky Derby, 54-year-old jockey Bill Shoemaker was dead last in heavy traffic. He had already won 8,536 races—more than any other jock at the time—but the Derby had eluded him since his 1965 victory on Lucky Debonair, and at that moment in the race, behind an unusually wide-open field of 16, few would have expected roses. Ferdinand, the most recent effort in the 30-year-plus collaboration between Shoemaker and trainer Charles Whittingham, had entered the gates a long shot at nearly 18–1, and had been jammed coming out.

But the veteran Shoemaker began picking off the field

one by one on the outside, moving into fifth by the top of the stretch, where he found the close pack of leaders. And suddenly, on that first Saturday in May, when a bit of daylight shone through on the inside, The Shoe dropped his colt toward the fence and went to the whip left-handed, moving irretrievably into the lead. He won going away. Five years later, in *Newsday*, Steve Jacobson would remember the ride as the "Willie Mays catch" of horse racing. Shoemaker's wife recalled that, three weeks before, he had watched another old-timer's unlikely victory—Jack Nicklaus's stunning win at Augusta—and declared it an omen.

By the time of that win, arguably the pinnacle of the most storied career in thoroughbred racing, the 4-foot-11-inch, 95-pound Shoe had been the winningest jockey of all time for 16 years, having reached victory 6,033 on September 7, 1970. A master of the "high crouch" style, where the jockey shifts his weight forward off the horse's middle, Shoemaker's trademark "soft hands" coaxed his horses to victory while others whipped away. After riding 40,350 mounts, he retired as the all-time winningest jockey, with 8,833 victories, among them five Belmont Stakes, four Derby winners and two Preakness Stakes.

The brilliant career was marred by at least one ignominious moment. The four Derby wins should have been five; on Gallant Man in 1957, Shoemaker stood up in the stirrups just before the end of the race, having mistaken a furlong post for the finish, and gave the win to Iron Liege. Although the loss was his main professional regret, the Fabens, Texas, native did not let the mistake dim his natural toughness. When Shoe was born, in 1931, weighing less than two pounds, the doctor said he wouldn't survive the night, and he was placed in a shoebox on the lid of a warm oven. He would grow up to box in the 85-pound class on his high school team.

Shoemaker's promising second career as a trainer was detoured by an April 1991 single-car accident in California which left him paralyzed from the neck down. Charged with drunk driving, Shoemaker's subsequent lawsuits against the hospital and the state sullied his longtime reputation. Just the year before, in 1990, Shoemaker had completed a global farewell tour, somewhat controversial because of the fees he charged the tracks to appear. But the crowds came out for a last look at the first jock to earn $100 million in prize money, the jockey who, as 1987 Derby winner Chris McCarron put it, could "get runs out of horse after horse after horse after horse."

—*David Zivan*

AL OERTER
"You Die for Them"

Al Oerter, by his own admission, was a chronic complainer. "Nothing is ever right," he sheepishly confessed to an interviewer in 1963, midway through one of the greatest runs in Olympic history.

OERTER: "WHEN YOU THROW AGAINST OERTER, YOU DON'T EXPECT TO WIN"

Truth is, Oerter must have liked it that way. Even though he entered four Olympics as an underdog—one as a near cripple—he left with four Olympic records and four gold medals in the discus.

"When you throw against Oerter, you don't expect to win," said Jay Silvester, favored to beat him in 1968. "You just hope."

Born in Astoria, New York, in 1936, Oerter was a skinny youth who figured he'd enter his father's contract plumbing firm after a stint in the military. He began throwing the discus as a lark, and through hard work he turned himself into an athlete, earning a track scholarship to Kansas.

Well-muscled but incredibly lithe—and one of the first athletes to value wheat bread over white and broiled meat over fried—Oerter upset Oregon rancher Fortune Gordien to win at Melbourne in 1956, and afterward made the bold statement that he planned to win five straight Olympic titles. Few figured he'd win even two, but then he outheaved countryman Rink Babka in Rome four years later.

Even fewer gave him a chance in Tokyo in 1964. Already bothered by a slipped disc in his neck, he tore rib cartilage a week before the competition. Numbed by ice and Novocain and wrapped in tape from sternum to navel, Oerter threw anyway, doubled over in pain after releasing each attempt. On his fifth try, the one he vowed would be his last, he threw 200 feet, 1 inch to pass Ludvik Danek of Czechoslovakia and win the gold.

"These are the Olympics," Oerter said. "You die for them."

The fourth medal came in Mexico City in 1968, when he bested Silvester with a career-best 212 feet, 6 inches, despite throwing with a torn thigh muscle in a heavy rain. Wrote Neil Amdur in *The New York Times*: "At four-year intervals, the world is treated to 29 days in February, a United States Presidential election and Al Oerter winning an Olympic gold medal."

After Mexico City, Oerter announced his retirement, concentrating on his career as a data communication engineer and raising two daughters. But he came back to finish fourth at the 1980 Olympic Trials at the age of 43, throwing the discus more than 33 feet farther than his first gold-medal winning toss 24 years earlier. He finished one spot away from qualifying for the Olympics for the fifth time.

He was still throwing into his 60s, speaking at shot put and discus camps, though he remained reluctant to criticize a thrower's technique. Oerter's success did not come from style or even his size (6-foot-4-inches, 260 pounds), just the overwhelming determination that Olympic rings belonged on a flag—and to him.

"I was never the best discus thrower at any of those Olympics," he said. "I was just the best prepared."

—*Mark Wangrin*

Opening Act: Alan Ameche's sudden-death touchdown.

PRO FOOTBALL
1958 NFL Championship Game

During the long afternoon of December 28, 1958, the House that Ruth Built became the launch pad for pro football's ascendance, and the classic title game between the NFL's marquee team of the late Fifties, the New York Giants, and Weeb Ewbank's upstart Baltimore Colts, led by Johnny Unitas, captivated the nation.

The Giants fell behind 14-3, but a goal-line stand in the third quarter swung the momentum, and early in the fourth quarter, Charlie Conerly hit Frank Gifford on a 15-yard touchdown pass to put the Giants up 17-14. That was still the score when the Colts got the ball at their own 14 with 1:56 left. Unitas expertly worked the clock and the Giants' defense, sending decoys to the sidelines, and throwing three crucial passes late in the drive to Raymond Berry. Steve Myhra, who'd had a kick blocked in the first quarter, kicked a 20-yard field goal with seven seconds left in regulation.

So the NFL had its first overtime game, and a new kind of excruciating suspense. With the first score winning the game and the title, every play, every ball exchange, was fraught with nerve-racking import. After holding the Giants on the first possession of overtime, the Colts got the ball on their own 20. Twice early in the drive, Unitas converted in clutch situations, with a pass to Alan Ameche on third-and-eight that barely gained a first down, and a scrambling 21-yard throw to Berry on third-and-14. Ameche's 22-yard run on a Unitas-audibled trap play brought the Colts into field goal range at the Giant 20. Later, a gutsy pass to Jim Mutscheller moved the ball to the one. Ameche plowed through the Giant defense to win the game 8 minutes and 15 seconds into overtime.

The verdict was quick and extreme: NFL commissioner Bert Bell called the game "the greatest I've ever seen," and *Sports Illustrated* called it "The Best Football Game Ever Played." Coming seven years after Bobby Thomson's "Shot Heard 'Round the World," the '58 game had a different feel—because it was seen live on network TV by some 40 million people. "The classics of the pre-television era have been perpetuated only in the minds of the spectators on hand and by the newspaper accounts," wrote Tex Maule. "This, for the first time, was a truly epic game which inflamed the imagination of a national audience."

BASEBALL
1951 National League Playoff

■ Game 3 of the Dodgers-Giants best-of-three playoff series determined the National League champions, after "The Miracle of Coogan's Bluff" brought the Giants back from 13½ games out of first place in mid-August. Brooklyn scored three runs in the top of the eighth, and took a 4-1 lead into the bottom of the ninth. With one out, one run in, and two men on, Dodgers manager Charlie Dressen made the fateful decision to pull Don Newcombe and insert Ralph Branca (jersey number: 13), to face Bobby Thomson. Thomson took the second pitch, up and in, and hit it into the left-field bleachers, prompting Russ Hodges' memorable call ("The Giants win the pennant! The Giants win the pennant!") and one of the century's best trivia questions: Who was on deck? Yes, it was a young Willie Mays.

TRACK AND FIELD
Mile Run, 1954 Commonwealth Games

■ Billed as the first duel of sub-4:00 milers, this August 6 race in Vancouver matched England's Roger Bannister, the first man to break the four-minute barrier, against Australian John Landy, who had broken Bannister's record just weeks earlier. The buildup, and a U.S. TV audience, guaranteed the race's prominence. But it remains memorable for those who saw it because of the finish. After leading for the entire race, Landy rounded the final turn on the home stretch in the lead, and looked back over his left shoulder to see how close Bannister was. At that instant the "Running Doctor" bolted past Landy's right shoulder to win in 3:58:8.

BOXING
1952 Marciano vs. Walcott

■ It was the first title shot for the undefeated Rocky Marciano, the hard-charging Italian-American bruiser from Brockton, Massachusetts. Though a 9–5 betting favorite, the challenger nearly didn't make it out of the first round. The veteran Jersey Joe Walcott clipped him with a smart left hook in the first round, dropping Marciano to his knees. From there, the taller, heavier and more experienced champion dominated the action through the first five rounds, but they butted heads in the sixth, leaving Walcott with a gash over his right eye. Walcott soldiered on, and after 12 rounds he led on all three fight cards. Marciano, who needed a knockout to win, was relentless, and in the 13th, he finally connected with a short, vicious right, which seemed to collapse Walcott instantly. Marciano was the new world champion, and he retained his title for 3½ years before retiring in 1956. At the end of the century, he was still the only heavyweight champion ever to finish his career undefeated.

COLLEGE BASKETBALL
1957 NCAA Championship Game

■ It was the game everyone wanted to see, pitting undefeated, top-ranked North Carolina, with Frank McGuire's "underground railroad" of New York City recruits, against Kansas and super sophomore Wilt "The Stilt" Chamberlain. Carolina had to survive a triple-overtime semifinal a night earlier against Michigan State to get to the title game. The Tar Heels collapsed on Chamberlain early, daring his teammates to hit from the outside, and took a 12-point lead halfway through the first half. But after moving to a man-to-man, Kansas closed the gap quickly, and Chamberlain took control in the second half. But Kansas couldn't put the Tar Heels away, and after Tommy Kearns hit a foul shot with 20 seconds left, the two teams were tied at the end of regulation. Chamberlain's late block preserved the tie at the end of the first overtime. A bench-clearing brawl nearly ensued after Chamberlain and Carolina's Pete Brennan tangled. Late in the third overtime, with Kansas up by one, Chamberlain rejected another shot, but North Carolina's Joe Quigg rebounded the ball and was fouled trying to shoot. With six seconds left, he hit both free throws, and North Carolina's perfect 32-0 season was complete. The game raised the stature of college basketball across the country, and solidified North Carolina's reputation as one of the meccas of the sport.

Great Performances

■ Just two seasons after compiling a 3-21 record for Baltimore, the Yankees' Don Larsen threw his perfect game in the crucial fifth game of the 1956 Dodgers-Yankees World Series. The final out was recorded on a called third strike (with Dale Mitchell looking), but the Perfecto wouldn't have been possible without the help of a great running catch in the fifth by Mickey Mantle.

Boom Years for the Sooners

From 1948 through 1950, **Bud Wilkinson**'s Oklahoma Sooners put together a 31-game winning streak. But those teams have been overshadowed by an even more impressive Sooner juggernaut, the back-to-back national champions of 1955 and '56, which helped the Sooners reel off a 47-game win streak in the mid-Fifties.

Wilkinson's Sooners were fast and fit, a team that sprinted into and out of huddles, constantly putting pressure on opposing defenses, and devising increasingly complex ways to get the ball to All-America halfback Tommy McDonald, who scored in every game of the '55 season. And the defense was as stifling as the offense was spectacular, allowing 5.5 points a game in '55, and 5.1 points per game in '56, when only four of its 10 opponents scored.

The 47-game streak, which began in 1953 and ended with a 7–0 upset loss at home to Notre Dame in 1957, revealed Wilkinson to be a master of consistency and preparation. It was his stated goal to spend four hours in preparation for every hour of practice. His players believed in him and his exacting methods, and came away with a confidence bordering on arrogance that made them all the more intimidating.

But it was Wilkinson's refinements of the split–T formation—giving runners an option of hitting any available hole on off-tackle and sweep plays—that made Oklahoma so hard to defense. "We thought we could even move the ball on a professional team," said OU fullback Billy Pricer. "That's how much confidence we had."

■ **Rocket's Men.** From 1951 to 1960, the Montreal Canadiens played in all 10 Stanley Cup finals, winning six, including an unprecedented five straight from 1956-60. Toe Blake's Canadiens were among the strongest NHL teams ever to take the ice, placing four men on the All-NHL first teams in both 1956 and 1959. Beside the explosive veteran right winger Maurice Richard, there was splendid young center Jean Beliveau (and, in 1957, the arrival of Richard's brother Henri, the "Pocket Rocket"), defensive stalwart Doug Harvey, and goalie Jacques Plante, who brought the first functional goaltender's mask into the game in 1959. The Canadiens of the Fifties were so explosive that they forced the league to change its rules in 1956, so that as soon as the team with the manpower advantage scored on a power play, the penalized player could return to the ice. Montreal's power play had been so potent that the Habs frequently scored two or three goals on one penalty, as the rules at the time required a penalized player to sit out the entire two minutes, regardless of scoring.

	COLLEGE BASKETBALL	PRO BASKETBALL NBA	HOCKEY NHL	BASEBALL MLB	COLLEGE FOOTBALL		PRO FOOTBALL NFL
1950	CCNY	Lakers	Red Wings	Yankees	Oklahoma		Browns
1951	Kentucky	Royals	Maple Leafs	Yankees	Tennessee		Rams
1952	Kansas	Lakers	Red Wings	Yankees	Michigan State		Lions
1953	Indiana	Lakers	Canadiens	Yankees	Maryland		Lions
1954	La Salle	Lakers	Red Wings	Giants	Ohio State (AP)	UCLA (UP)	Browns
1955	San Francisco	Nationals	Red Wings	Dodgers	Oklahoma		Browns
1956	San Francisco	Warriors	Canadiens	Yankees	Oklahoma		Giants
1957	North Carolina	Celtics	Canadiens	Braves	Auburn (AP)	Ohio State (UP)	Lions
1958	Kentucky	Hawks	Canadiens	Yankees	LSU		Colts
1959	California	Celtics	Canadiens	Dodgers	Syracuse		Colts

NOTES: **College football**: Champions are mythical consensus national champions as voted by sportswriters in the Associated Press, and, beginning in 1950, by coaches in the United Press (UP), which became the United Press International (UPI) poll in 1958.

The One and Only Casey

Managing is getting paid for home runs someone else hits," **Casey Stengel** once said. And few men ever had more success at it, or were more idiosyncratic about it, than Stengel. The beloved and bewildering skipper might simply be regarded as everyone's crazy uncle if it weren't for the fact that there seemed to be a method in so much of his madness. In 12 years managing the Yankees, Stengel's teams won 10 pennants and seven World Series. Stengel's Yankees won the World Series in each of his first five seasons (breaking the record of four straight titles, set by Joe McCarthy's Yanks in the Thirties).

Along the way, he defied baseball wisdom at almost every turn. It wasn't just that Stengel often went against "the book," it was that there frequently seemed to be no rhyme or reason to his actions. Al Lopez, a former protégé who managed against Stengel in the Fifties, once said, "I swear, I don't understand some of the things he does when he manages. I've tried to figure them out, but they just don't make sense."

Born Charles Dillon Stengel in Kansas City in 1890, he gave up dental school to pursue a full-time baseball career, and was an adequate major leaguer ("I had many years that I was not so successful as a ballplayer as it is a game of skill") before pursuing a managing career, which began with desultory results. He managed three years in Brooklyn and six years for the Boston Braves, never finishing in the first division, and topping .500 just once.

But after a stint in the Pacific Coast League, where Stengel's Oakland Oaks won 321 games in three seasons, he was summoned to replace Bucky Harris as manager of the Yankees in '49. With a veteran team led by Joe DiMaggio often expressing bewilderment over his moves, Stengel juggled lineups, rotations and strategies, and led the Yankees to an AL flag and a World Series title.

Stengel's reputation as a double-talking clown tends to obscure the changes he brought to strategy. He used platoons more than any manager of his era, used the hit-and-run extensively, and had one of the quickest hooks in baseball history, using his bullpen much more often than his peers. Writer Bill James observed that Stengel seemed keenly aware of the double play, and for an assortment of reasons (the way he used his batting order, his tendency to hit-and-run, his policy of having his middle infielders cheat toward second base in possible double-play situations), his Yankee teams consistently turned more double plays than they grounded into, even though they annually had many more baserunners than their opposition.

And then there were the moves that resisted classification; Connie Mack said he'd never seen another manager who juggled lineups so often, or played hunches so successfully. Biographer Robert W. Creamer wrote of Stengel, "In baseball he had the kind of understanding of a situation that is often described as intuitive— immediate comprehension of a problem and its solution without recourse to orderly, reasoned analysis—but that is probably just rapid-fire, computer-speed deduction derived from long experience."

That long experience became one of the treasures of the sport. When he retired, Stengel said, "I want to thank all my players for giving me the honor of being what I was."

The Architect

For much of the century, college athletics was a loose confederation of schools, conferences and regional athletic organizations, whose central governing body, the National Collegiate Athletic Association—governed in name only. That began to change in the Fifties as Walter Byers, hired in 1951 as the first executive director of the NCAA, opened up the organization's offices in Mission, Kansas, and began bringing the far-flung schools under the NCAA's umbrella. College sports would never be the same.

"[W]hen you look at the decision to make intercollegiate athletics an entertainment entity, salable not only to the press but to TV, that was **Walter Byers**," said Donna Lopiano, the head of the Women's Sports Foundation. "And when you look at this huge establishment that got turned upside down in terms of whether it was an educational thing or not—the tail wagging the dog—give the credit to Walter."

Byers transferred from Rice to Iowa in the early '40s, and left to enlist in the Army without getting a degree. He got a job as a journalist, working for the United Press in several cities, before being hired as the assistant to Big 10 commissioner Kenneth L. "Tug" Wilson. When Wilson, then secretary-treasurer of the NCAA, decided that the organization needed a full-time executive, the 29-year-old Byers got the job. In the Fifties and Sixties, Byers increased the organization's investigative power and put together a national television package that made college football more popular than ever before. Later, he turned the NCAA men's basketball championship into one of the biggest revenue-producers in all of American sports (the last contract, with CBS, brought in over a billion dollars to the NCAA).

"The NCAA prospered, in my opinion, because of three factors—enforcement, football on television, and the basketball tournament," said former Big 10 commissioner Wayne Duke. "And Walter was the architect of all three."

For all his vision regarding the basketball tournament and the appeal of football, Byers was curiously blind about the role of women in intercollegiate athletics. He argued and lobbied against the Title IX law, passed by Congress in 1972, that guaranteed gender equity in athletic programs, at one point suggesting that it could mean the "possible doom of intercollegiate sports."

But by the end of Byers's reign, in 1988, the NCAA was more powerful than ever, and seemed to encompass much that was good, and much that was bad, about big-time collegiate athletics.

TOP OF THE NEWS: In the Fifties, the world of sports finds its first truly national audience. The first modern jet takes to the air in 1954 (making nationwide leagues more feasible) and the first color television goes on the market—as does the first "TV Dinner." Within four years the Giants and Dodgers are headed to California.

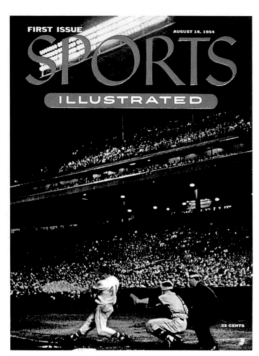

FIRST ISSUE — AUGUST 16, 1954 — SPORTS ILLUSTRATED — 25 CENTS

Politics

Speaking in front of a Senate subcommittee in 1958 on baseball's anti-trust exemption, Casey Stengel embarks on one of his most famous extended bits of Stengelese. "Well, I will tell you," Stengel begins in response to one question. "I got a little concern yesterday in the first three innings when I saw the three players I had gotten rid of, and I said when I lost nine what am I going to do, and when I had a couple of my players I thought so great of that did not do so good up to the inning I was more confused but I finally had to go and call on a young man in Baltimore that we don't own and the Yankees don't own him, and he is doing pretty good, and I would actually have to tell you that I think we are more the Greta Garbo type now from success." This went on for several minutes, all of it equally opaque. Senator Estes Kefauver called Mickey Mantle up to testify and asked him, "Mr. Mantle, do you have any observations—with reference to the applicability of the anti-trust laws to baseball?" At which point Mantle brought down the house by saying, "My views are just about the same as Casey's."

Reading List

Time Inc. publishes the first issue of its new weekly *Sports Illustrated*, dated August 16, 1954. The magazine would lose money for 10 years, but find success in the Sixties under the editorship of Frenchman Andre Laguerre, former press attaché to Charles de Gaulle. (During the Sixties, Laguerre will bring to national prominence such writers as Dan Jenkins, Frank Deford, Mark Kram, George Plimpton, Bud Shrake, Curry Kirkpatrick and Roy Blount, Jr.)

The first edition of Hy Turkin's and S.C. Thompson's *The Official Encyclopedia of Baseball* debuts in 1951.

A year later, Bernard Malamud's *The Natural* is published. Also in the decade: A.J. Liebling's *The Sweet Science*, a collection of magazine pieces on boxing, and two other acclaimed novels—Mark Harris' *Bang the Drum Slowly* and Walter Tevis' *The Hustler*.

Movies

The screen version of the Broadway musical *Damn Yankees* hits theaters in 1957. The tale of a faithful Washington Senators fan who sells his soul so the team can get one good hitter stars Tab Hunter as Joe Hardy, with Gwen Verdon and Ray Walston reprising their stage roles. Among the musical numbers is "Shoeless Joe from Hannibal, Mo."

Earlier in the decade, Burt Lancaster has the starring role in *Jim Thorpe—All American*, a biography of the life of the "world's greatest athlete." Directed by Michael Curtiz (*Casablanca*), it includes a memorable performance by Charles Bickford as Thorpe's college coach, Pop Warner.

Sounds

Rock 'n' roll hits the world, and Chuck Berry sings the praises of the "Brown-Eyed Handsome Man," inverting a century's worth of order in ball and strike counts in the process: "Two-three the count, and no one on/ He hit a high fly into the stands/ Roundin' third and a-headed for home/ It was a brown-eyed handsome man/ That won the game, it was a brown-eyed handsome man."

Television

On May 30, 1953, ABC debuts a Saturday afternoon *Game of the Week*, with Dizzy Dean and Buddy Blattner providing the play-by-play, as the Indians beat the White Sox, 7-2. Later that year, in the first NFL prime-time contest to be televised nationally, the DuMont Network shows the Pittsburgh Steelers beating the New York Giants, 24-14, on a Saturday night.

Playing Games

In the early '50s, J. Richard Seitz creates a spinoff of the old '30s game National Pastime called APBA Baseball. Besides giving each hitter a different card, Seitz' game provides ratings to fielders and pitchers. Later in the '50s, Strat-O-Matic develops a similar game, though its play is activated by drawing cards rather than rolling dice. The two games are an obsessive's dream, and all around the country—from the '50s until the dawn of the video/computer age—children of all ages replay lost seasons or create dream seasons with APBA or Strat-O-Matic games.

Football games are becoming more popular. The leader of the pack is Foto-Electric Football, which superimposes two sets of play cards (an offensive play and a defensive set)

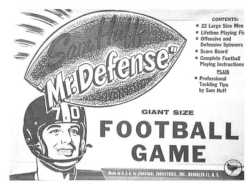

CONTENTS:
- 22 Large Size Men
- Lifetime Playing Fie
- Offensive and Defensive Spinners
- Score Board
- Complete Football Playing Instructions

PLUS
- Professional Tackling Tips by Sam Huff

onto a lit field. Sam Huff, the leader of the Giants' staunch defense, gets his own game, **Sam Huff's Mr. Defense** Giant Size Football Game. There's also Arm Chair Quarterback, Fooba Roo Football, Razzle Dazzle Football, the Varsity Football Game and, from the same company that manufactured All-Star Baseball, a game with spinners called All-America Football.

Radio

NFL innovator Paul Brown obtains a citizen's band transmitter and hooks a small receiver into the helmet of Cleveland quarterback George Ratterman so Brown can radio in plays during games. The Browns test the system during the 1957 exhibition season. Against the Chicago Bears, Ratterman can't pick up Brown's play calls, but he has no trouble hearing workers coordinating a halftime show honoring Armed Forces Day. The experiment finally is scrapped later in the exhibition season when Cleveland plays the Giants, who depend on former Brown Gene Filipski and their own radio receiver to intercept and decode the plays in a 21-9 Giants win. As usual, Brown is ahead of his time; the NFL installs a helmet radio system four decades later.

> *"Ninety feet between bases is the nearest to perfection that man has yet achieved."*
> —Red Smith

Impressions of the '50s

From ESPN's Bob Ley:

With his power, self-effacing manner, and perennial championships, **Mickey Mantle** perfectly embodied that time when anything seemed possible in America. At the middle of this American Century, he captured the imagination of baby boomers, who carry that image into the millennium. There was little doubt or dissent in the Fifties, as the Cold War cast life in simple and stark terms. Mantle's Yankees did the same for sport. Octobers were spent watching No. 7 patrol sacred ground. I was four years old in 1959, determined to hit left-handed. Because, as a switch-hitter, the Mick often did. Even though he sold his celebrity and his signature, when we later discovered that Mickey had human frailities, he was immediately forgiven and embraced. Hey, he's the Mick. No other recent death drove so many middle-aged men to tears. A mourner outside the memorial service spoke for millions: "I feel as if my childhood just ended."

Debuts and Exits

1950 **Black players in the NBA**, with the appearances of Earl Lloyd, Chuck Cooper and Nat "Sweetwater" Clifton.

The National Horse Racing Hall of Fame in Saratoga Springs, New York.

Racquetball, invented by Joe Sobeck in Greenwich, Connecticut.

1951 **The NBA All-Star Game.**

The ineligible-receiver rule in the NFL, prohibiting guards, tackles and centers from receiving a forward pass.

Coast-to-coast TV broadcasts, the first game of the Dodgers-Giants playoff.

Boxing on closed-circuit TV, with the broadcast of Joe Louis' knockout of Lee Sevold.

Coast-to-coast telecast of the NFL championship game, with DuMont broadcasting the Rams' 24-17 win over the Browns.

1952 **EXIT** **The single-wing formation**, abandoned by the Steelers, the last NFL team to switch to the T.

1953 **EXIT** **The Boston Braves**, who move to Milwaukee, becoming the first NL franchise in the century to move.

The International Tennis Hall of Fame in Newport, Rhode Island.

The Milwaukee Braves, with a 2-0 victory over the Reds.

1954 **The Baltimore Orioles** return to the American League when the St. Louis Browns franchise is transferred to Baltimore.

The 24-second clock in the NBA.

1955 **The Kansas City Athletics**, who move from Philadelphia.

Tennis balls with nylon and Dacron in their covers, which give truer bounces and longer life.

1956 **The NFL Players Association.**

EXIT **33 Hungarians** from the country's Olympic delegation, who defect to the U.S. during the Melbourne Olympic Games.

The Cy Young Award, with Don Newcombe taking honors as the majors' outstanding pitcher.

1957 **Baseball's Gold Glove awards.**

EXIT **The Brooklyn Dodgers** and **New York Giants**, who head to California, after the season.

1958 **Major league baseball on the West Coast**, with the San Francisco Giants beating the Los Angeles Dodgers, 8-0, in San Francisco's Seals Stadium.

The two-point option on points after touchdown, in college football.

1959 **The National Sportscasters and Sportswriters Hall of Fame** in Salisbury, North Carolina.

The American Football League, formed by Lamar Hunt.

EXIT **A Louisiana ban on interracial boxing matches**, declared unconstitutional by the U.S. Supreme Court.

THE 1960s

Caught in the quagmire of an unwinnable war abroad and an unfulfilled promise at home, the nation spent the decade in a schizophrenic spasm of pleasure and revulsion. For the first time, sports seemed out of step. Yet the fields of play still served as metaphorical battle-grounds for the proxy wars of the age. In Boston, where racism was palpable and intimidating, one man changed everything. Blessed with keen court sense, a maniacal laugh and the prickly pride of misunderstood genius, he was an exemplar of the first generation to insist that black was beautiful.

CELTICS 1966 WORLD CHAMPIONS
CELTICS 1965 WORLD CHAMPIONS
CELTICS 1964 WORLD CHAMPIONS
CELTICS 1963 WORLD CHAMPIONS
1
CELTICS 1962 WORLD CHAMPIONS
20

Nothing but a Man

I T WAS A JUMPY, CONFUSING TIME. On one hand you had people running around advocating "free love," and on the other, the landscape was littered with the most terrible acts of hate, these assassinations. Each day, it seemed, was spent at the barricades. Each day there was a new cause you expected to throw your body under a bus for. Each day, someone with an issue was demanding to know: Which side are you on?

And so you would think that nobody on these seething college campuses in the Sixties could find time for something as foolish, something as politically inconsequential, as basketball. But on Sunday afternoons, there were some of us who put aside changing the world for a few hours. We gathered in dorm lounges across America to watch the NBA, usually to watch Boston play Philadelphia. More specifically, to watch Bill Russell play Wilt Chamberlain.

Actually, to watch Russell beat Chamberlain.

Though I'm sure Russell didn't beat Chamberlain every Sunday. Just the Sundays I watched.

These were the days before cable television, before satellite dishes made it possible to see every game every night. There were only three networks then, and you could only rarely watch sports on TV. Where I was—in Binghamton, New York, a small city upstate, a few miles north of the Pennsylvania border—you could go a whole season and never see the Knicks on TV. Not like it is now, where you see your home team so often you know when the 11th man got a haircut.

In 1960, the NBA was a league with eight teams, mostly gathered in the Northeast, and none beyond the Mississippi River. By 1980, because of merger, expansion, or absorption, the NBA had more than doubled in size—as had the

PREVIOUS PAGES
Wearing of the Green.
The Celtics' Number 6—emblematic of defensive excellence and the possibilities of achievement and self-expression through team play—didn't just shape the NBA in the decade, it changed a city.

Defending the Throne.
"People say I owe the public this and I owe the public that," Russell said. "What I owe the public is the best performance I can give, period."

NFL and the NHL. This was a period of dynamic growth and expansion in American professional sports, the manifest destiny era. Baseball moved to Canada, for God's sakes, and football started eyeing Mexico.

But in the Sixties, the only time you could see the NBA was Sunday afternoons. And the main attraction was Russ and Wilt. Wilt was Goliath. He was 7 foot 1 inch, 290 pounds—huge, strong, and agile. Everybody was terrified of him. Chamberlain put up numbers that nobody, not even Michael Jordan, matched. The most points Jordan ever averaged for a season was 35. Chamberlain surpassed that average five times. One season he averaged an impossible 50.4. Chamberlain is the only man in the history of the NBA to average more than 24 rebounds a game, and he did that three times. One year, to silence critics who said he shot too much, Chamberlain led the NBA in assists. And by his own count, of course, Wilt led the world in scoring women.

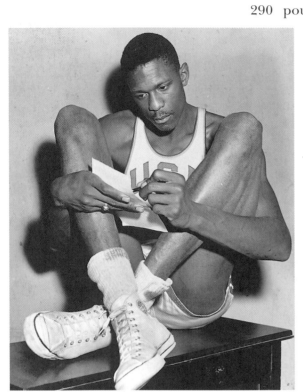

Top Don. At San Francisco, under coach Phil Woolpert, Russell—and future teammate K.C. Jones—led USF to consecutive NCAA titles.

RUSSELL, IN COMPARISON, WAS PUNY. He was 6 feet 9 inches and skinny; he weighed maybe 230 pounds. He had no offensive game to speak of; he never averaged as much as 19 points a game for a season. But defense and rebounding was Russell's side of the street. He blocked shots seemingly at will and always at opportune moments. He swept the boards with a grace and efficiency that stood in sharp contrast to Chamberlain's raw power. Russell played on springy legs, and won with guile and intellect.

Did I mention he won every time?

I have been a sportswriter for 30 years—long enough to know that it is unfair to reduce a team sport to a two-person rivalry. It's fine in tennis to talk about Evert vs. Navratilova, and in golf, to mythologize about Nicklaus vs. Palmer. But you can't cram basketball into that facile equation. There are too many other players on the court. It was never simply Russell vs. Chamberlain.

Yeah, sure.

And now that we are done with that disclaimer: From 1960 through 1969, Russell's team won nine championships; Chamberlain's, one.

If Wilt was larger than life, he was somehow smaller than Russell. Their rivalry appeared to be so one-sided that people tilted toward Russell almost to the point of absurdity. Wilt would get 44 points—there wouldn't be five players all season who'd score 44 points in one game—and people would write: "Russell held Chamberlain to 44."

I sat in a dorm lounge at Harpur College watching these games, thinking that Russell was the coolest cat on earth. The way he handled Chamberlain, it was like he was laughing at him. I watched Russell, wearing that jazzman's goatee—the first player ever to do so—standing slope-shouldered on the court like a saxophone player waiting his turn to blow, then suddenly soaring after the ball like a big black eagle, and I thought: This guy is so cool, he should play in sunglasses.

A couple of thousands of miles across the country, at the University of Missouri, my friend Jack sat in a dorm lounge watching the same games, thinking something murderously different. Jack was from Scranton, Pennsylvania. He loved all the

Philadelphia teams. He loved Hal Greer. He loved Paul Arizin before him. And of course he loved Chamberlain—and hated Russell, for those many Sundays when Russell crushed his hope.

It was during this time that the great sportswriter Jim Murray would write: "Bill Russell is like Wellington to Waterloo. Like Grant to Richmond. Like the Russians to Stalingrad. He is where the war ends." And my friend Jack watching these games where Boston played Philly, knew, sadly, that this was true.

"The picture I have is of a time-out," Jack recalls. "The 76ers are ahead by one point. The Celtics have the ball, and the camera is focused on their bench. Red Auerbach is explaining what he wants done, and Russell is just staring, focusing on something only he can see, locking it into his mind. And I'm watching this scene, and I'm saying, 'Uh-oh,' knowing that whatever Auerbach is saying, Russell will make it happen. And we are screwed."

Amazingly, in an era when NBA teams routinely scored 115 points a game, Russell made his mark without the ball in his hands. Maybe it's because Bill Russell invented

A Force in the Middle.
Russell blocks a shot by Iowa's Milt Scheuerman in the 1956 NCAA title game.

defense. No, that's wrong, because the way Bill Russell played defense has nothing to with the way, say, Pat Riley or Chuck Daly coach defense. Theirs is a defense that punishes the enemy until it gives up the ball; it's ugly, like war, even when it works. But Russell's signature moves—the controlled block or the lightning-quick rebound and outlet pass—were elegant transitions that instantly transformed defense to offense, often before the enemy realized what had happened.

In fact, nobody before or since has played defense the way Russell did. He didn't bend rims—he bent minds. Russell blocked shots at will, and blocked them not for show—not like the trash-talking egomaniacs of the Nineties who block shots to inflate themselves—but for psychological value. Russell used the blocked shot as a deterrent, to make you fearful of shooting anywhere within his range. He was always lurking, but you never knew when he was going to pounce. He might let you inside, once, twice, even three times, early in a game, encouraging you to believe he could be had, until, when the game was on the line, you went back one more time—and left with the ball in his hands and your heart on the floor. It was like playing Russian Roulette. The chamber with the bullet might be next.

"Russell would jump over you to block your man's shot," said John Thompson, the celebrated Georgetown coach who backed up Russell on the Celtics for a couple of years. "The word with kids now is 'Switch!' But I tell them the word on the Celtics was 'Russ!' You could hear that all over the floor. If your man beat you, all you could hear was people yelling 'Russ!'

"Russell redefined defense, he put the honor in defense. He's the guy who made people think there was something to it. Even Michael Jordan in all his greatness, what did he redefine?"

It made Bill Russell's game irresistible—except to Philly fans and L.A. fans. To the rest of us, though, Russell was Horatio at the bridge. He was the gatekeeper. He was the guy who emphatically said, "No! You can't score at this goal. This goal is my house." Yet there was something refined to his rejection, something superior and all the more maddening. It was almost as if you could hear him cackling as he tapped your shot to Couz or K.C.—as if he knew this was just a game.

N OT TO MAKE TOO MUCH OF RACE—but ever since the Civil War, it has been the most volatile flashpoint of our culture. Most of the world's wars have been fought over religion, but our struggles have always been about race. And like the schoolhouse, the ballot box, and the lunch counter, America's athletic fields were not always open to everybody.

Bill Russell came to the NBA in 1956, less than 10 years after the most significant event in American sports history, when Jackie Robinson integrated major league baseball. Although black athletes were playing in the NBA, the NFL, and baseball, there weren't that many yet. Some teams didn't have any. The Boston Red Sox, for example, were disgracefully slow in signing black players. So Russell was the first black athlete of any consequence in Boston, America's most racially charged big city.

It's intriguing to note that the great Celtics dynasty was fueled by Russell and Red

Clash of the Titans.
Russell vs. Chamberlain was the signature sports rivalry of the '60s. Above, Chamberlain hooks over Russell in the '64 NBA Finals …

Auerbach, a black and a Jew, two outsiders in clannish, Catholic Boston. You can only imagine how it must have delighted Auerbach, as combative a man as ever prowled a sideline, to build the greatest dynasty of that era, while the patrician-owned Red Sox remained mired in mediocrity despite Ted Williams, the greatest hitter in baseball. And to do it with a black man literally at the center of it all. Beating Boston with Russell must have been even better than beating Philly and L.A. You can picture Auerbach kneeling in a time-out, looking right into Russell's angry eyes and egging him on: "Let's show these Boston Brahmins what we're made of."

Russell was not like Joe Louis, who made whites happy by performing for them and by not agitating for social change. And Russell was not like Robinson, who courageously endured the virus of racism in silence as part of the pact he made with Branch Rickey to be the perfect pioneer and martyr if need be.

Russell represented a new type of black athlete: the educated, outspoken, defiant star seeking—no, expecting—respect just for who he was. In 1961, Russell boycotted an exhibition game in Lexington, Kentucky, when two of his teammates were refused service in a hotel coffee shop. In 1963, Russell was quoted saying, in

...in '66, the two nearly come to blows in the East finals. Referee John Vanak holds them apart, while Red Auerbach, behind Russell, prepares to intervene.

a *Sports Illustrated* story, "I don't consider anything I've done as contribution to society. I consider playing professional basketball the most shallow thing in the world." And, after being refused food service while on the highway: "Some [black] entertainers try to show whites that they are nice people. All of us are nice people, but this isn't a popularity contest. I don't care if the waitress likes me when I go into a restaurant. All I want is something to eat."

Russell's lineage could be found, not so much in Muhammad Ali—who stood on a separatist platform but craved the love of everybody—but in John Carlos and Tommie Smith, bowing their heads and raising their black-gloved fists on the medal stand at the 1968 Olympics: solemn, dignified, strong, unapproachable. The essence of Russell.

"Russell was the first man I ever heard call himself 'black,'" John Thompson remembered. "This was when it was an insult to call a man 'black,' when it was similar to calling a man a 'nigger.' Bill Russell called himself a black man. He was one of the first men I ever saw to truly acknowledge the fact that he was black, and to identify very strongly with his roots in Africa.

"Russell's manner was so strange and so different. He didn't preach at anyone. He didn't say anything unless he felt infringed upon. But if he felt there was an injustice going on, he'd open up his mouth and say so."

Needless to say, this played better with some whites than with others. Many older, conservative whites found him threatening and thought him ungrateful. Russell was never beloved in Boston—no black man ever has been. But Russell's manner was so calculatedly distant that he wouldn't have been beloved anywhere. It's impossible to believe we'd ever find Russell lighting the Olympic flame, as Ali did, as a sentimental stunt to launch a television spectacle. Russell led his whole life in such a way that nobody would even think to ask. In those days, to be cool was literally to be as stolid as ice—unmoved by what was happening around you, focused only on your goals, unreachable and omnipotent. And Russell was the essence of that kind of cool.

AND THAT COOL, DELIBERATE ATTITUDE gave him great appeal to young, educated whites, who were discovering black culture and rolling around in it, apparently hoping it would rub off on them. These were the halcyon days of the civil rights movement, after the historic *Brown* v. *Board of Education* decision and the emotional Birmingham bus boycott. From the mid Fifties through the late Sixties—the years corresponding to Russell's NBA career—black influence would be increasingly felt within the young, white baby boom culture that was so determined to build a better, more egalitarian country than the one they grew up in.

Elvis Presley sang music with a blatant sexual power stolen from black R&B entertainers. White kids couldn't get enough of it. Motown was formed and "crossover" was born; anything with a Motown label went to No. 1. The Beatles and Rolling Stones confessed their adoration for Chuck Berry and Little Richard. James Baldwin became one of white America's favorite authors; Dick Gregory became one of its favorite comedians. And Bill Russell, the NBA's Othello, became its favorite basketball player.

Mutual Respect.
Auerbach and Russell conferring on the bench. "Bill put a whole new sound in pro basketball," Auerbach said. "The sound of his footsteps."

Halting Start. At right, in Russell's first season as player-coach, 1966-67, the 76ers and Chamberlain finally broke through to win the title, getting off to a 46-4 start in the regular season. "They're playing the game we've played for the last nine years," said K.C. Jones. "In other words, team ball."

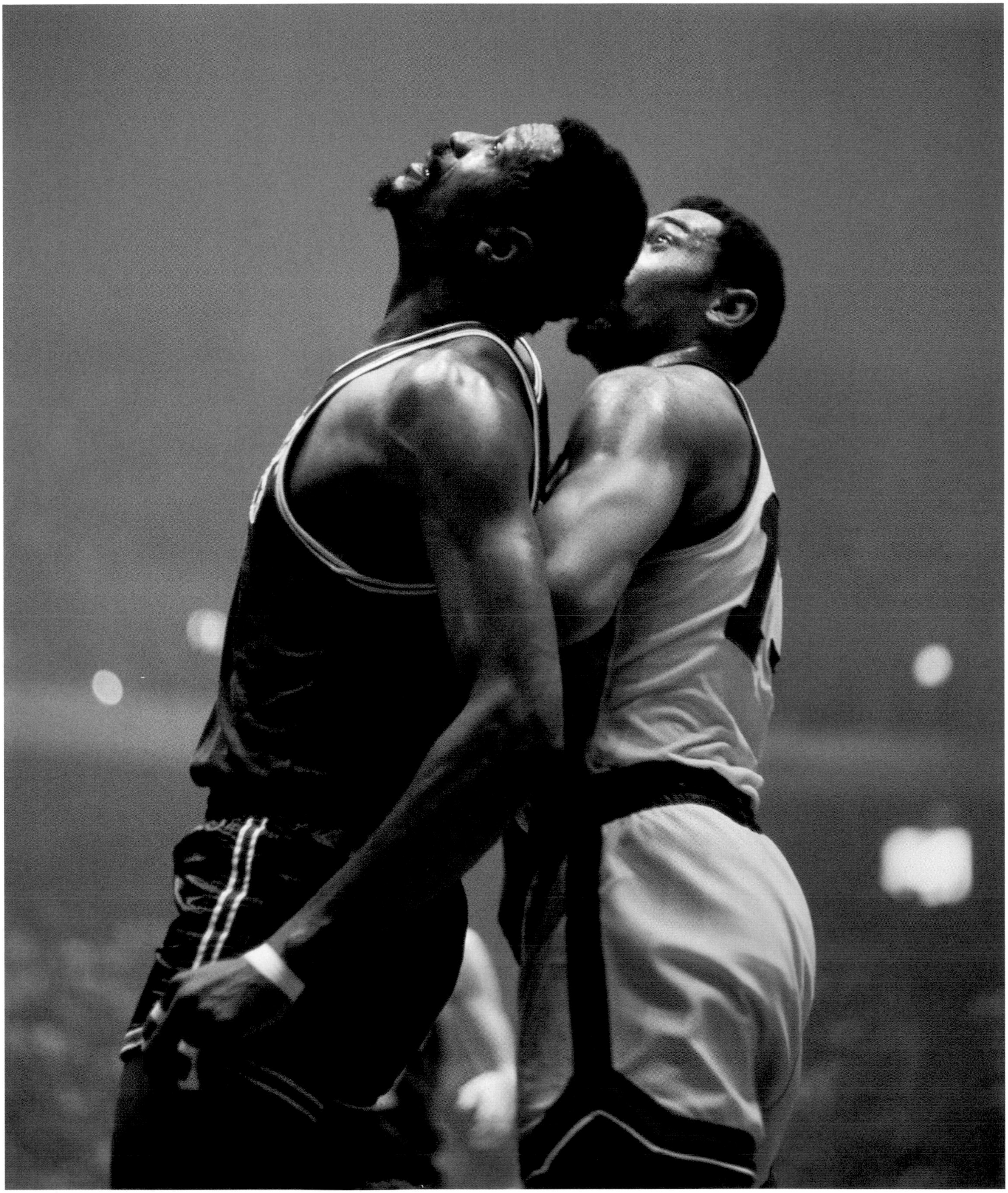

Young whites saw in Russell just what they were looking for: a black basketball player who was an antidote to all racial stereotypes. The game Russell played wasn't instinct and flash, it was intellect and guile. It wasn't basketball at all; in Russell's hands, it was chess. Russell wasn't a dumb jock, he was educated and articulate. He wasn't culturally unaware, he was socially conscious. He wasn't humble and grateful, he was proud and challenging. He was a black man succeeding on his own terms on a team where teamwork was the essence of success. Russell could function within the team and never sacrifice an ounce of originality. Plus, he was doing it in Boston, the roughest racial arena in the league. To many young whites, idolizing Russell became a means of personally redressing the core of racism in their parents' America.

R USSELL WAS EVEN MORE REVERED in the hippest white enclaves, because they fancied that he was one of them: an outsider and underdog who had to rely on his brains to succeed. How else could you explain Russell's David-like mastery over the Goliath, Chamberlain? Russell was so cool, so aloof; he was like Miles Davis, who was so hip he turned his back on his audiences when he played.

To blacks, Russell was mythic. His ability to win year after year allowed him to push the limits of what a black athlete could acceptably say. In a pantheon of defiant and dignified role models—Malcolm X, John Coltrane, Baldwin, Gregory—Russell belonged not just for what he did, but for how he did it. And rather than being punished for his stances, Russell was rewarded. He became the first black head coach in the NBA. How Auerbach must have loved doing that in Boston.

Of course, he paid a price for being Bill Russell. When you hold everyone at arm's length, you never feel anyone's embrace. He was always respected, but never really liked. His refusal to sign autographs angered his critics and confounded his friends. Thompson tells a story of driving with Russell to Maine for an exhibition, and seeing Russell befriend a small boy who attended the game. Thompson watched Russell laugh and joke with the boy, put his arm around him, shake his hand. Then, when Russell and Thompson headed for Russell's car, the woman who had brought the boy to the game asked Russell if he'd sign an autograph for him. And Russell, of course, refused.

This was the essence of Russell, of course: caring all for the substance of an experience and not at all for the surface. The rest of the world was left to see things his way—or not. Often it was not. And you wondered whether any of that disapproval penetrated through Russell's outer shell.

"The lady hadn't seen Russ be so caring with the boy," Thompson said. "All she knew was there was no autograph, and she got very annoyed with him. He didn't say a word. He just got in the car and drove off. I said, 'Russ, why wouldn't you sign the autograph for the kid?' And Russell said, 'It has no meaning, having an autograph.' Russell never ever gave me the impression that he cared about what people thought of him. But he had been so kind to this little boy, and the lady had been so huffy with him. I said, 'It must bother you. It must bother you.' And Russell drove on silently."

Thompson idolized Russell. To this day he keeps a pair of Russell's Celtic sneakers on his desk, and a framed picture with a personal inscription by Russell in his office.

Back to the Top.
Russell led the Celtics back to the top in '68, his second year at the helm, coming back from a 3-1 deficit to beat the 76ers in the Eastern Conference finals, then beating the Lakers in the Finals.

"I haven't figured him out yet, and I've stopped trying," Thompson says. "Russell always gave me the impression that he didn't want you to enter into his realm of thinking, his realm of space, his realm of anything, unless he invited you in. But if he accepted you into it, he was very kind. People don't know how generous he is."

What Thompson appreciated most about Russell was the secure feeling Russell provided him. Thompson is 6 feet 10 inches, and in those days weighed about 260 pounds. You wouldn't think a man that size would feel intimidated. But back then a black man in Boston walked on shaky ground.

"I always felt safe around Russell as a black person," Thompson recalls. "And I felt very much unsafe with him not around. Here's a guy who comes into the room and just looks like a warrior. He wouldn't be coming in with some polite 'It's nice to meet all of you.' He wasn't rude. But the way he carried himself was reassuring to me. He came closest to any man I ever met at living on his own terms."

Bill Russell played 13 seasons in the NBA and won 11 championships.

Do the math: Eleven rings. Ten fingers.

The only people close are Sam Jones (10) and Tommy Heinsohn, K.C. Jones and Satch Sanders (eight)—and they all played alongside Russell. Jordan has six. Magic Johnson has five. Larry Bird has three. Add Russell's two NCAA champi-

The Man. Russell was the first black head coach in a major American sports league in four decades, but his demeanor didn't change. "I can honestly say that I have never worked to be liked," he once said. "I have worked to be respected."

The Final Victory.
Russell and Bailey Howell celebrate after their seventh game win in the '69 Finals at The Forum in Los Angeles. His career ended with one last crucial win over Chamberlain.

onships, and his gold medal at the 1956 Olympics, and Russell is the greatest winner of all time.

"People can debate who was the greatest performer," says Thompson, "but the greatest winner defines itself."

I believe that some of Russell's more notorious stances—his refusal to sign autographs; his disdaining to accept induction into basketball's Hall of Fame; his frosty, almost contemptuous relationship with the media—may have somehow detracted from what he did. And Russell, as Thompson says, never felt it necessary to explain himself. But you can argue about what you thought of Russell, not about what he accomplished.

Put simply: Russell won. Like nobody ever.

Thompson saw it up close 35 years ago, and is amazed by it still.

"I never saw anybody more competitive than Russell was," Thompson says. "He did not like practice. I remember thinking when I first came to camp, thinking that he wasn't as good as I'd heard he was. He went through the whole camp in a jovial mood, laughing and chatting. So I looked at him, wondering. Then we opened the season in Boston against Detroit, and I was stunned at the change from what I'd seen in practice to what I was seeing in the game. His whole temperament changed. His facial expression changed. His game went to an entirely new level. The minute they threw the ball into the air, I would not have known this was the same man."

RUSSELL RAGED TO WIN. He burned to win. Despite that cool exterior, Russell burned so much that he threw up before games. His mastery of this rage—his ability to both control it and unleash it at the opportune time—defined the underlying intellect of his game. He never exposed fear, or doubt, or anger, or premature celebration. His demeanor was a constant, as much of a rock for his teammates as his presence under the basket. He could control the basketball game because he could control himself.

When Russell left the game, it was because he no longer raged. "If you are looking for a reason why I feel I have played enough," Russell wrote in *Sports Illustrated*, "I'll tell you this: There are professionals, and there are mercenaries in sports. The difference between them is that the professional is involved. I was never a mercenary. If I continue to play, I become a mercenary, because I am not involved anymore."

It was a bombshell at the time. Boston had just won another championship. It was Russell's third season as coach of the Celtics, and his second straight title. His scoring had dropped precipitously—it was under 10 points per game, though it had never really mattered—but he was still averaging 19 rebounds, and his defense was still ferocious. To this day, folks think Russell hung up his Number 6 jersey too soon.

But Russell sensed something inside him had changed. It wasn't his ego. The year Russell retired was the year Lew Alcindor was to enter the NBA as the number-one overall pick in the draft; he hadn't yet assumed the name Kareem Abdul-Jabbar or the mantle of the greatest scoring machine in league history. Alcindor was coming off three successive NCAA championships at UCLA, and was so widely regarded as the best player in the world that Russell was asked, "Don't you want to see how you can do against Alcindor?" Russell bristled and replied, "The question is: How would Alcindor do against me?"

He was defensive, as always. Everything Russell did was defensive. No, you will not score on me. No, you will not get inside my head. No, you have nothing to say to me. And so he couldn't hear those who begged him to play on. He listened to the drum in his own soul, and knew that without the rage, he was ordinary. And ordinary was never what Bill Russell was about.

And now, as we celebrate athletes with riches Russell never dreamed of, he has become the whisper of a memory. The Celtics have had Cowens and Bird, and a few more titles; the league has had Magic and Michael, and astronomic growth, though not without cost. It doesn't seem to be so much about winning anymore. There's too much preening to do—too much yearning to be the man.

Years after Russell was gone, as the story goes, Auerbach walked onto the court at a Celtics practice, and the players were kidding around about who had the best moves, and who had the best shot, and who was the biggest star. And Auerbach waved his hand at them dismissively. "If Number 6 were here," he said, "all you sorry bastards would be shaking in your shoes."

The Coach. In the '70s, the game would change from the one Russell loved. "I tried to treat them like men," he said of his time coaching the Seattle SuperSonics. "And some of them weren't."

JIM BROWN
All-Everything

He'd take off from his three-point stance, moving with power and purpose, take the ball from the quarterback, and burst forward with a brutal confidence, running low to the ground with his head up. And then, at the point of contact, when other runners would cover up or try to fall forward, Jim Brown would explode. Tucking the football tightly to his gut, he'd lower a shoulder toward his tackler, and swing his free arm into his opponent's chest with a stunning forearm shiver. "All you do," said the Giants' feared linebacker Sam Huff, "is grab hold, hang on and wait for help."

For nine seasons, from 1957 through 1965, there wasn't enough help in the world. "For mercurial speed, airy nimbleness, and explosive violence in one package of undistilled evil, there is no other like Mr. Brown," wrote Red Smith. Brown—who lettered in five sports in high school and four at Syracuse University—might have been the most talented all-around athlete of the 20th century. Rather than pursuing multiple sports, he compressed all his talents into football, joined the Cleveland Browns in 1957, and became the best running back in the history of the NFL.

No runner in pro football has done what Brown did for the Browns in those nine seasons. He led the NFL in rushing eight of those years, accumulated 12,312 yards in just 118 games (averaging 104 yards per game for his career), scored 126 touchdowns and gained 5.2 yards per carry, still an NFL career record.

But that doesn't begin to explain the impact that he had on the sport. At 6-foot-2-inches, 230 pounds, he was a fast, intimidating, *angry* runner who delivered as much punishment as he sustained. One Philadelphia newspaperman described him "careening through the Eagles like a runaway taxi in a wax museum."

Though he never wore hip pads, and ran as a marked man throughout his career, Brown never missed a game. After being brought down by gang tackles, he would lie on the ground an extra moment, slowly gather himself up, then gingerly get to his feet. This was his ingenious way of pacing himself; he reasoned that if he moved that deliberately early in the game, by choice, opponents wouldn't detect his fatigue late in the game, when he had to move that slowly.

At the end of the 1962 season, when repeated line plunges cut down his effectiveness, he played a crucial role in a player revolt that got Paul Brown sacked in Cleveland. New coach Blanton Collier installed his option-blocking attack in 1963, sending Brown on more sweeps, and giving him the choice to pick his own holes. He responded by running for a record 1,863 yards and scoring 12 touchdowns.

BROWN:
"ALL YOU DO
IS GRAB HOLD,
HANG ON
AND WAIT FOR
HELP"

NAMATH:
"PRO FOOTBALL'S
VERY OWN
BEATLE"

The next year, he led the Browns to their last world championship of the century.

He was dominant again in 1965, winning his second MVP award and scoring 21 touchdowns. And that's how it ended. On the eve of training camp in 1966, while on the set of *The Dirty Dozen* in London, Brown announced his retirement at age 30. "For all the guys who stayed too long—Joe Louis, Muhammad Ali—I thought it was embarrassing," Brown would say later. "People had sympathy for them, and you should never have sympathy for a champion."

His post-retirement life has been as eventful as his athletic career. There have been numerous charges, but no convictions, of sexual abuse. Yet Brown was undeniably a force for good in urban America. His Black Economic Union helped black-owned businesses in the 1960s. And in the late 1980s his Amer-I-Can Program counseled gangs toward more productive lifestyles. He continued to be outspoken, even threatening an NFL comeback at age 47. "If I became a pawn of society and said the things I was supposed to say as most of your superstars do today, I would be rich and I would be given false popularity. But when history comes down, that ain't nothing. I am a free man within society. I love that."

JOE NAMATH
Broadway

With a quarterback's natural swagger and Sixties sensuality, Joe Namath changed both the structure and climate of pro football. His sleepy-eyed good looks and trademark white shoes made him among the first outright sex symbols in sports—or, as Dan Jenkins put it in 1966, "pro football's very own Beatle." And when he predicted that his Jets would upset the mighty Baltimore Colts in Super Bowl III, then delivered on the claim, he became a legend. Along the way, he fulfilled his ambition "to become known as a good quarterback, not a rich one."

Namath was a three-sport star in high school at Beaver Falls, Pennsylvania, before going to college at Alabama, where he led the Crimson Tide to the national title in 1964, and Bear Bryant called him "the greatest athlete I've ever coached." When the American Football League's New York Jets signed Namath to a three-year contract for $400,000 (twice as large as any pro football contract up to that point), "The Foolish League" forced the NFL toward a merger.

Namath didn't waste any time making his mark on the Big Apple, flaunting both his newfound riches and his playboy image. Whether lounging on the llama-skin rug in his Upper East Side apartment, scrambling through the taverns and clubs of New York City, or marching the Jets down the field in the wide-open AFL, he brought a sense of individualism and style to the game that hadn't existed. In 1967, he explained, "I don't like to date so much as I just like kind of, you know, *run into somethin'*, man." As a quarterback,

Namath matured quickly, and by the late Sixties, Vince Lombardi was describing him as "the perfect quarterback." Adept at reading defenses, he possesseda smooth drop-back and quick, almost instant release. ("He makes the rush obsolete," said frustrated Chief Jerry Mays.) Namath became the first quarterback to pass for more than 4,000 yards in a season, in 1967.

But his impact transcended record books. Like Muhammad Ali in boxing, Namath was on the forefront of a new era of great athletes confident enough to boast of their prowess and talented enough to deliver on those outrageous claims. The Thursday before his 19-point underdog Jets battled the Colts in Super Bowl III, he announced matter-of-factly: "We're gonna win. I personally guarantee it." Three days later he engineered the greatest upset in pro football history, befuddling the Colts by eschewing the Jets long-passing attack in favor of a ball-control game plan, made possible by the way Namath artfully sliced up the Colts' strong-side rotating zone defense. Calling audibles on most plays, he completed 17 of 28 passes for 206 yards, won the MVP award, then marched off the field with a raised "Number One" index finger in the air.

The rest of his career would be marked by injuries (five knee surgeries in all) and off-the-field exploits (Pete Rozelle made him give up his ownership of Bachelors III restaurant, and Namath made a memorable television commercial wearing panty-hose). But the league that Namath surveyed at the end of the century was one largely of his own making.

Celebrity aside, when he was healthy, he was among the most feared players in the history of the game. As Raiders owner Al Davis put it in the late Sixties, "He tilts the field."

SANDY KOUFAX
A Level Beyond

The right leg stabbed skyward as the body rocked so far back the left hand nearly brushed the ground. It was as much ballet as baseball, but just as hitters became transfixed by the acrobatic grace of the windup, Sandy Koufax delivered the pitch. It might be the fastball, dipping, darting and rising while arriving so rapidly it didn't have time for a nickname. Or perhaps the equally nasty curve, which seemed to start its arc from somewhere out in the parking lot. It really didn't matter because, as Hall of Fame slugger Willie Stargell observed, "Trying to hit him was like trying to drink coffee with a fork."

Koufax was in the majors before he was 20 years old and in the Hall of Fame before he was 40. A late bloomer with a 36–40 record in his first six seasons, Koufax hit his stride in 1961, winning 18 games and the first of his four strikeout titles. Injury slowed his momentum in 1962, but Koufax closed his career in classic style, elevating his art to a legendary plane of performance. Averaging more than 300 strikeouts a season while posting a phenomenal 97–27

KOUFAX: "TRYING TO HIT HIM WAS LIKE TRYING TO DRINK COFFEE WITH A FORK"

PALMER: "FOLLOWING PALMER DOWN THE COURSE WAS NOT UNLIKE RUNNING BEFORE THE BULLS AT PAMPLONA"

record, Koufax was virtually unhittable in his final four seasons as he led the majors in every conceivable pitching category in an unprecedented display of pure and total pitching dominance.

He won just 165 games in his career, but Koufax became the youngest Hall of Fame inductee ever, at age 36, in recognition of the extraordinary achievements and condensed brilliance of his unique, injury-shortened career. He was the first three-time Cy Young winner, and the only one to do it when the title of baseball's premier pitcher went to the single hurler judged to be the best of both leagues. In 1963, when he was also league MVP, he became the first unanimous Cy Young selection, embellishing that accomplishment by leading the Dodgers to a World Series sweep of the Yankees. Yogi Berra, after watching Koufax strike out 23 Yankees in 18 innings, said: "It's easy to see how he won 25 games. What I don't understand is how he lost five."

Koufax's spectacular success came with a physical price, as arthritis twisted his pitching arm out of shape, leaving it a full inch shorter than his right arm by the time he retired at age 30, after the 1966 season. But while pain couldn't keep "our Jewish warrior"—as devoted Brooklyn fans rooting from a continent away dubbed him—off the mound, his faith could. He sat out the opening game of the 1965 World Series to observe Yom Kippur, later throwing two shutouts and winning the final game, along with his second Series MVP award. In the regular season that year, he also established the major–league season strikeout record at 382, and threw a no-hitter for the fourth season in a row, this one a perfect game against the Cubs. Ernie Banks summed up both the game and Koufax's career succinctly: "Sandy tried to throw the ball right past us. And he did." —*Michael Point*

ARNOLD PALMER
Leading the Army

He came charging up the last two fairways at Augusta National, making birdies and winning the 1960 Masters like a John Wayne in spikes. Arnold Palmer began changing golf forever that day, making an elitist sport more inclusive, affecting the game far beyond his 60 career victories on the PGA tour.

Over the next half decade, Palmer became the most popular golfer ever. It wasn't just that he won seven major championships between 1958 and 1964. It was *how* Palmer won, the way he looked more like a linebacker than a golfer, and the timing of his ascension, linked forever to golf's emergence on television and to his rival, Jack Nicklaus. Thanks to Palmer, the number of public courses increased dramatically, as golf became popular recreation for truck drivers as well as doctors. He himself became a conglomerate with the help of super agent Mark McCormack, the first athlete to make millions of dollars from his name off the field.

Palmer introduced himself to America by winning the

1958 Masters, an event televised that year for only the third time. By then, some had already taken notice. At a previous Masters, the writer Dan Jenkins wondered aloud who the vacationing longshoreman was. At 5-foot-11-inches, 180 pounds, Palmer had broad shoulders, a slim waist, outsized hands and muscles developed by maneuvering a tractor at the nine-hole course in Latrobe, Pennsylvania, where his father, Deacon, was once the greenskeeper and later head pro.

With his hair tousled and shirttail flapping, Palmer slashed forcefully at the ball, producing low hooks, often dramatic ones from the rough after errant tee shots. He chain-smoked, hitched his pants, took risks with his shots, watching them through squinting eyes. He oozed emotion, bonding with his swelling galleries, "Arnie's Army." "Trying to follow Palmer down the course was not unlike running before the bulls at Pamplona," the writer George Plimpton once said.

It was like that at the 1960 Masters. Trailing Ken Venturi by one stroke, Palmer, using his unconventional knock-kneed stance, sank a 27-foot putt for birdie on the 71st hole. Then he hit a six-iron into the wind, leaving himself a 5-foot birdie putt for victory. "If I ever had to have one putt to win a title," Bobby Jones once said, "I'd rather have Arnold Palmer hit it for me than anyone I ever saw."

Palmer's next big conquest was at the 1960 U.S. Open at Cherry Hills, where he trailed Mike Souchak by seven shots beginning the final round. Palmer drove the par-4 first hole, birdied six of the first seven, shot 65 and won by two strokes.

Soon Nicklaus would come; later Palmer's putting would go. The two developed a rivalry born of respect and envy, Palmer for Nicklaus' talent, Nicklaus for Palmer's popularity.

Palmer led the 1966 Open by seven shots with nine holes left. He squandered the lead, lost a playoff to Billy Casper—and became even more likable, more human. Palmer's popularity was built to last, much like the baseball icon Joe DiMaggio. The two-way flow of love has never subsided, as was apparent after Palmer underwent surgery for prostate cancer in January 1997. Or when he approached the 18th green at his final U.S. Open in 1994 at Oakmont, not far from Latrobe. Applause shook the grounds that day, and Arnold Palmer wept.

—*Mark Rosner*

OSCAR ROBERTSON
The Big O

Oscar Robertson redefined the point guard position the day he moved into the NBA.

With his arrival in 1960, Robertson instantly became the most versatile player the league had seen. At 6-foot-5-inches, 220 pounds, he could shoot, drive, pass, rebound and defend. Not that his domination should have been unexpected: In college, he had averaged 33.8 points, 15 rebounds and seven assists for Cincinnati, becoming the first player in NCAA history to lead the nation in scoring three straight seasons.

ROBERTSON:
"HE CONTROLS
EVERYTHING
OUT THERE"

RUDOLPH:
THE FRENCH
CALLED HER
THE BLACK PEARL

Magic Johnson made the triple-double his personal statistical category during the 1980s, but Robertson invented it. He is the only player in NBA history to *average* double figures in scoring, rebounds and assists for an entire season (1961–62). Robertson scored more points than any guard except Michael Jordan, and ranks third in assists after John Stockton and Johnson. "He controls everything out there, and he wastes the least amount of effort of any player I've ever seen," Celtics coach Red Auerbach once said.

Too big for guards to cover, Robertson patiently took advantage of smaller defenders, dribbling forcefully as he backed opponents toward the basket, reducing the distance of any shot by a few feet, then holding the ball high on his distinctive-looking jumper. "He cradled the ball in his right hand like a waiter carrying a tray of champagne glasses," wrote Robertson biographer Ira Berkow.

For all he accomplished in Cincinnati, Robertson never won an NBA championship during 10 years with the Royals. After failing to mesh with his new coach, backcourt legend Bob Cousy, Robertson was traded to Milwaukee in 1970, at age 31. In his first season with the Bucks, playing with the young Lew Alcindor, Robertson finally won his only title.

Considered a warm person away from the court, Robertson often sulked on it, upset with the imperfection of referees, teammates or himself. The first African-American basketball player at the University of Cincinnati, he was deeply affected by the racism he encountered in distant cities as well as his own. Turned away from the team's hotel during a 1958 road trip to Houston, Robertson had to stay in a college dormitory at Texas Southern. "When a black man breaks a window with a brick, America sees the black race doing it," he said in 1968. "But when a white man gets up on a tower in Texas and starts shooting people, then they say it's an isolated case."

For all his oncourt skills, Robertson's biggest assist came long after his retirement. In 1997, he made headlines again by donating a kidney to his 33-year-old daughter, Tia, saving her life.

—*Mark Rosner*

WILMA RUDOLPH
Grace in Motion

"The only thing I ever wanted when I was a child was to be normal," Wilma Rudolph remembered as an adult. "To be average." But the century's most improbable great athlete was never average. Growing up poor, frail and sickly, the premature baby (weighing 4½ pounds at birth) was stricken with polio at age four, leaving her left leg paralyzed. She learned to walk only with leg braces, suffering bouts of double pneumonia and scarlet fever during a childhood marked by almost constant physical therapy.

Finally able to attend school at age seven, she was able to shed her braces for corrective shoes at eight, and three years later began playing basketball in the backyard. By her sophomore year at Burt High School in Clarksville, Tennessee, she was already an athletic miracle, an all-state basketball player averaging more than 30 points a game. While playing basketball, she was discovered by Ed Temple, the track coach at Tennessee State, who presided over the famed Tigerbelles, the nation's premier track and field program for women. Rudolph fell under Temple's tutelage, and suddenly the legs that had prevented her from being normal helped render her extraordinary. She developed into a tall, graceful beauty, 5-foot-11-inches and 130 pounds, with a serene countenance and a quiet determination forged out of her difficult childhood.

When she burst into the national consciousness, after winning three sprint gold medals at the 1960 Olympics in Rome, she became an overnight embodiment of the American Dream. Running with a smooth fluidity, she exuded an economical grace, and even her name lacked sharp consonant edges. Her beauty and success signaled the end of that old shibboleth that women could not be both athletic and feminine.

With her close-cropped hair, smooth smile and gently searching eyes, Rudolph possessed "a look of mingled graciousness and hauteur that suggests a duchess," wrote Barbara Heilmann in *Sports Illustrated*. That distinctive carriage led to her worldwide celebrity, as crowds around Europe clawed to get a touch of her, going so far as stealing her shoes from her feet. The French called her *La Perle Noire*, the "Black Pearl." To the Italians, she was *La Gazella Nera*, the "Black Gazelle."

In America, she was acutely conscious of being black. When the city fathers of Clarksville wanted to throw her a parade and banquet upon her return from Rome, she insisted that it be integrated. In so doing, Rudolph directly brought about the first integrated public event in the history of Clarksville.

She would retire from track in 1963, secure in her accomplishments, becoming a schoolteacher and an inspiration to thousands of athletes. She died in 1994 of a brain tumor, one of the most loved and revered female athletes ever. In 1989, she told the *Chicago Tribune*, "Believe me, the reward is not so great without the struggle. I have spent a lifetime trying to share what it has meant to be a woman first in the world of sports so that the other young women have a chance to reach their dreams."

GALE SAYERS
The Original "Magic"

His essence is reflected more in the grainy images from a projector than by the record book, though Gale Sayers did produce jarring numbers. He was a five-time All-Pro who set eight NFL records, and at 34 became the youngest player ever inducted into the Pro Football Hall of Fame.

Perhaps the most amazing number was five—the num-

SAYERS: "THE RECORD BOOK AND A THOUSAND FEET OF ACTION FILM"

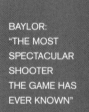

BAYLOR: "THE MOST SPECTACULAR SHOOTER THE GAME HAS EVER KNOWN"

ber of seasons he played before knee injuries took their toll; athletically speaking, he lived fast and died young. "The record book and a thousand feet of action film are all the proof needed of his football greatness," George Halas, the crusty owner of the Chicago Bears, once said.

Yet Sayers wasn't about numbers at all. His career rushing total was only 4,956 yards, and he played in just 68 games over seven injury-plagued years with the Bears, mute testimony that it wasn't what he did but how he did it. With speed and the elusiveness of a bar of soap in the tub, he was Barry Sanders but without the portfolio—and, most sadly, without the benefit of modern orthopedic techniques that could have saved a career ruined by two major knee surgeries.

His nickname was "Black Magic," later just "Magic," because of his supernatural combination of speed and maneuverability. Sayers attributed his edge to how he planted, cutting on his heels rather than the balls of his feet, but this middle son of an Omaha, Nebraska, car polisher wasn't all sparkle and shine. "I hit him so hard I thought my shoulder must have busted him in two," 300-pound Rosey Grier once said. "I heard a roar from the crowd and figured he had fumbled, so I started scrambling around looking for the loose ball. But there was no ball—and Sayers was gone."

As a rookie from Kansas in 1965, he ran for 867 yards and scored 22 touchdowns, an NFL single-season record that stood for a decade and remains the rookie mark. Six of them came on a muddy field against the 49ers, the last on an 85-yard punt return.

It was the knees, finally, that did him in. A submarine tackle by San Francisco's Kermit Alexander in 1968 tore his medial collateral ligament in three places. After a comeback, which defied medical convention, he rushed for a league-leading 1,032 yards in 1969 and earned the Halas Award for courage, which he tearfully dedicated to his teammate and roommate, Brian Piccolo, who at that moment lay dying from lung cancer. Sayers tore up his knee again in 1970, and this time he couldn't come back. The Magic was gone, and before the 1972 season, Sayers retired.

—*Mark Wangrin*

ELGIN BAYLOR
Aviation Pioneer

Long before Michael Jordan claimed the air as his performance space, Elgin Baylor went up and checked out the property. Baylor, after a storied college career at Seattle, joined the Minneapolis Lakers in 1958, bringing to the NBA a rare combination of power, speed, grace, elevation and accuracy. He scored with style, flourishing during an era before the NBA's widespread popularity. Longtime students of the game saw a lineage of regal, fluid athleticism begin with Baylor and extend through Julius Erving to Michael Jordan.

In 1960, the 6-foot-5-inch, 225-pound Baylor scored 71

points against the Knicks. For his 14-year career, he averaged 27.4 points and 13.5 rebounds a game. His legacy, seen in latter-day skywalkers Connie Hawkins and David Thompson, would have been even more prominent had Baylor not spent half of his career hobbled by injuries to both knees. Still, he averaged more points than everyone in NBA history save Jordan and Wilt Chamberlain. And no one Baylor's size, not even Charles Barkley, grabbed more rebounds per game. "Elgin is bull-strong, quick and very daring," teammate Jerry West once said. "I think he's the most spectacular shooter the game has ever known."

Baylor had the skill and agility to advance the ball up court like a guard against pressure defenses. Yet he did not avoid tangling with larger players near the basket. Indeed, he enjoyed competing against the great Celtics' 6-foot-9-inch center Bill Russell, contending for tip-offs, wrestling for rebounds or freezing him with moves and shooting over him. Against smaller opponents Baylor didn't have to bother with fakes. He bullied his way to the basket. "When Baylor gets the ball, the opposition scatters like quail at the sight of a hunter," Jim Murray wrote in 1961. But he never did bag an NBA title. The Lakers, led by West and Baylor, lost to Boston in the Finals five times between 1962 and 1968. After Wilt Chamberlain joined the Lakers, giving them three future Hall of Famers, they lost in the 1969 Finals to Boston and the next year to New York.

Baylor could be as formidable off the court as on, needling teammates, rarely conceding an argument. "Elgin was a motor mouth," teammate Hot Rod Hundley once said. "Elgin never shut up." He did on at least one occasion. In January 1959, his rookie season, the Lakers were in Charleston, West Virginia, for a game against Cincinnati. The hotel clerk looked at Baylor and two other African-Americans on the team and said, "We can't take those three. We run a respectable hotel." Baylor said nothing. But he decided to not play in the game. Hundley, a white man raised in Charleston, tried to dissuade Baylor from his protest. When he finally spoke, Baylor said, "Rod, I'm a human being. I'm not an animal put in a cage and let out for the show." Hundley, understanding the dignity and pride in Baylor, said, "Baby, don't play." —*Mark Rosner*

BOB BEAMON
One Shining Moment

In the light, tense air of Mexico City, at 3:46 p.m., October 18, 1968, in a few seconds of spectacular physical exertion, Bob Beamon performed what many regard as the single most surpassing athletic feat of the century.

Before that moment the wispy-thin, 160-pound national long-jump champion had traced a strange path to Mexico. His father was dead before he was born, his mother died before his first birthday and his stepfather was an ex-convict, so Beamon grew up tough and insecure on the hard streets

BEAMON:
"IT FELT
LIKE A
REGULAR JUMP"

BUTKUS:
"DICK RATTLES
YOUR BRAINS
WHEN HE
TACKLES YOU"

of Jamaica, New York. Passing on a scholarship offer from Southern Cal, he started college at North Carolina A&T, then transferred to Texas-El Paso, but was suspended when he and several teammates refused to compete against Brigham Young University due to the racial policies of the Mormon church.

He arrived at the 1968 Summer Olympics in Mexico City as one of the co-favorites, but the smart money was elsewhere. Beamon didn't seem to have the discipline, didn't even make the customary tick marks on the runway to calibrate his strides in the approach to the takeoff board.

But at the finals, preparing for his first jump, he stood at the beginning of his approach and looked up twice, thinking to himself, "Don't foul." He began uncoiling his long 6-foot-3-inch frame over the 134-foot approach, eventually nearing the limit of his sprinter's speed, before hitting the takeoff block perfectly, exploding out and up above the pit.

"It felt like a regular jump," said Beamon afterward. But the leap itself, along with his perfect sprint, form at takeoff, and splendid extension, created something much more: an instant of pure, unalloyed physical splendor. Jesse Owens, who'd once held the record in the event, remembered watching him in midair and marveling at the flight. Beamon came down with such force that he launched himself right out of the back of pit. There was the long wait to measure the jump, as the optical measuring device, moving toward Beamon's mark in the sand, fell off the end of its rail.

The world record at the time was 27 feet, 4¾ inches, a mark that had been extended just 8½ inches in the previous 33 years. But in an instant, Beamon added nearly two feet to the record, jumping 29 feet, 2½. As Coles Phinizy wrote in *Sports Illustrated*, Beamon "had taken off into thin air in the year 1968 and landed somewhere in the next century." On the sidelines, the reaction ranged from awe to anger. "Compared to this jump, we are as children," said the glum Soviet Igor Ter-Ovanesyan. "I can't go on, we'll all look silly," said defending Olympic champion Lynn Davies, before barking at Beamon: "You have destroyed this event."

For Beamon himself, there could be no second act. He would never reach 27 feet again. But 23 years later, when Mike Powell finally bested Beamon's record, it was the oldest mark in the track and field record book. And his legend would outlive even the record.

DICK BUTKUS
The Madman

They were safe, or should have been, on their team bus after an afternoon of mayhem at Wrigley Field in the late 1960s, but then some impatient driver bumped them from behind in the post-game traffic crunch and one shell-shocked Baltimore Colt couldn't help himself.

"There's Butkus again," came a voice from the rear.

Dick Butkus didn't just hit halfbacks harder, roam the

sidelines better and play with more single-mindedness than anyone else, he got into your head. Facemasks were but a hindrance. If he wanted to stick his finger in your eye, he did. If you retaliated, you might start needing two hands to count to five. "That's dangerous for a guy to do, 'cause I got sharp teeth, heh, heh," he once said.

Madness was his method. With fierce eyes underscored with eye black and a toothy, diabolical snarl, he challenged whole sidelines to fights and called time-out late in one-sided games so he would have more chances to hit somebody. He once got four personal foul penalties in an exhibition game. And a poll of NFL quarterbacks named him the second–most-feared defender in the league—21 years after he had retired.

"Butkus, if he doesn't tackle you himself, you can hear him coming," said Steelers quarterback Terry Hanratty. "You know he's going to be there eventually." Bart Starr was more succinct: "Dick rattles your brains when he tackles you."

The seventh of nine children born to Lithuanian parents on the hardscrabble South Side of Chicago, Butkus was a two-way star at Illinois before joining the Chicago Bears as a first-round draft choice in 1965. At 6 foot 3 inches, 245 pounds, he had the size of a defensive tackle and the speed of a running back. Adolph Schultz may have serendipitously created the middle linebacker spot while playing for Michigan in 1905—he wanted a better view of the offense—but Butkus did for the linebacker prototype what Goddard did for rockets. "If God ever designed a man to be a professional football player," George Halas said, "he had Butkus in mind."

Though he played on only two winning teams in nine years with the Bears, Butkus became the best and most feared middle linebacker in the game, making All-NFL seven times and earning a spot on the NFL's 75th anniversary team. After bad knees drove him to retirement, he became a broadcaster, light beer pitchman and actor, capitalizing on and even mocking his fierce image.

"People feared him, even his teammates feared him," teammate Gale Sayers said. "He hit me as hard in practice as anyone ever did in a game. That's the way he played."

—Mark Wangrin

WILT CHAMBERLAIN
Above the Crowd

Wilt Chamberlain was the first of the giant basketball icons. At 7-foot-1 and 275 pounds, he was the most physically imposing man of his era and, in his prime, the most dominating offensive player of any period. Yet as proficient as he was, the agile Chamberlain could never elude his critics or his nemesis, Bill Russell of the Boston Celtics.

Chamberlain arrived in the NBA in 1959 with a large reputation, having averaged 29.9 points a game during two seasons at the University of Kansas. After a one-year stint with the

CHAMBERLAIN: "NOBODY LOVES GOLIATH"

FOYT: "TALKING TO A.J. WHEN HE'S ANGRY IS LIKE DANCING WITH A CHAINSAW"

Harlem Globetrotters, he became even more prolific as a pro, scoring 37.6 points a game as a rookie with Philadelphia and averaging 50.4 two seasons later, an NBA record that stands today. Chamberlain averaged nearly 40 points a game during his first seven seasons, before he decided to become a passer. In the second phase of his career, he became the only center to lead the league in assists during a season. He still holds rebounding records for a game (55), season (27.2) and career (22.9).

Chamberlain's look—muscular upper body and trademark goatee—was as distinctive as his game. He leaned toward the basket for dunks and finger rolls, and faded away for his famous bank shot from the left side. Chamberlain and the 6-foot-9-inch Russell created the league's first great rivalry. It was a source of frustration for Chamberlain, because whatever team he was on usually lost important games to Russell's Celtics. Despite his accomplishments, Chamberlain was frequently attacked by critics, because his teams rarely met their expectations. "Nobody loves Goliath," said Alex Hannum, one of Chamberlain's coaches.

Goliath had one glaring weakness. He was a pitiful 51 percent career free-throw shooter. But Chamberlain made a remarkable 28 of 32 while scoring his record 100 points against the Knicks in 1962. The game was witnessed by only 4,124 fans in Hershey, Pennsylvania, the gym half full.

Though Chamberlain doubled Russell's scoring average, he was almost always compared unfavorably because Russell's more talented Celtics won 11 NBA titles. Chamberlain won one with Philly (1967) while Russell was playing and another with the Lakers (1972) after Russell retired. Boston coach Red Auerbach, who always infuriated Chamberlain, once said, "Bill was a better player because he played with his head, was more motivated and, most of all, had a bigger heart."

Denied titles, Chamberlain took pride in his prowess elsewhere. In his autobiography, he claimed to have slept with 20,000 women and fought off an attacking mountain lion. But years later, the Russell comparisons still evoked a defensive reaction: "Russell didn't win 11 championships. He played on a team that won 11 championships. I wonder how Russell would have rated if his team hadn't won all those championships."

—Mark Rosner

A.J. FOYT
An Urge to Excel

A.J. Foyt didn't necessarily want to set speed records, although he routinely did so; he just couldn't bear to have anyone finishing in front of him.

"There never has been a driver with such an absolute urge to excel, the absolute necessity to win," said rival Al Unser. The tough-talking Texan with the turbo-charged temper did exactly that, bringing auto racing into the mainstream of American sports while consistently leaving his competition in the rearview mirror.

Foyt was racing roadsters, motorcycles and midget cars competitively in Houston by his teenage years, eventually dropping out of school to devote his full attention to professional racing. In 1961, three years after qualifying in his initial attempt, the 26-year-old Foyt won his first Indy 500 crown, setting a track speed record while nursing his car home with a defective clutch. Repeating the feat with wins in 1964 and 1967, he solidified his claim as the decade's most successful driver. And in 1977, Foyt took yet another victory lap at the Brickyard, becoming the first driver to win four Indy 500s.

Foyt's success ranged far from Indy and ovals. He won the Daytona 500 in 1972, in the process setting a speed record which lasted until 1980. Even more impressive was his 1967 season, when he won his fifth overall USAC crown as well as winning his third Indy championship and co-driving the winning car in Europe's 24 Hours of Le Mans Grand Prix endurance race.

When Foyt wasn't in front he wasn't much fun to be around. His own father said: "Talking to A.J. when he's angry is like dancing with a chainsaw." Unfortunately, the perfectionist Foyt was angry too much of the time. His public exhibitions of rage, which included punching matches with fellow drivers and his own crew, reinforced his reputation as a rugged, no-nonsense competitor with the explosive temper of a man who just couldn't understand why everyone wasn't as totally focused as he was.

Foyt also possessed an obstinate attitude regarding change at a time when new ideas regarding design and technology were radically reconfiguring his sport. Although he frequently appeared to be racing antiques and was seemingly always behind the technological curve, Foyt somehow still consistently managed to be in front of the pack when the checkered flag was waved.

Retiring from driving in 1993 to concentrate on team ownership, Foyt remained a combative and controversial force in racing. His legacy as a relentless and resourceful driving champion is an illustrious one, as was the individualistic approach he brought to racing. When the indomitable Foyt was behind the wheel, it wasn't the power of the engine that mattered most, it was the willpower of the driver.

—*Michael Point*

MARIO ANDRETTI
That Burning Desire

They always used to say, 'Man, if the kid survives, he'll be good,'" remembered Mario Andretti of his early days in racing. "That was music to my ears because I knew what they thought: 'At least he stands on the button, so as soon as he learns how to do it right, he'll really go.' You have to show that burning desire. When you do that, nobody faults you."

As a driver, Andretti's desire and versatility were unsurpassed. He arrived in the United States at age 15, from a

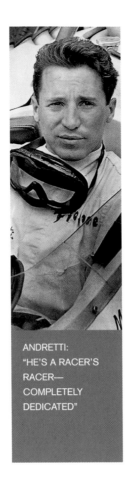

ANDRETTI: "HE'S A RACER'S RACER— COMPLETELY DEDICATED"

displaced persons camp in Italy where he'd dreamed of racing greatness, and by the age of 30, he had won both the Indianapolis 500 and the Daytona 500. Later, he'd go on to win the world driving championship in Formula One, becoming the first person to win Indy, Daytona and Formula One and establishing himself as the most versatile driver in auto racing history.

Squinting under his trademark shiny silver helmet with the blazing red arrow on the crown, the compact, 5-foot-5-inch, 140-pound Andretti excelled on dirt tracks, ovals or road races, and he thrived in any kind of machine, from stock cars to the aerodynamic open-wheel racers on the Indy and Formula One circuits. "Mario is the best all-round driver I've ever had," said Roger Penske in 1977. "He's a racer's racer—completely dedicated, single-minded and passionately competitive."

Andretti's father, Alvise, was a prosperous farm administrator in Montana, Italy, who lost his land in World War II, and wound up in a displaced persons camp in Lucca for seven years. Andretti grew up idolizing Italian Grand Prix champion Alberto Ascari. Providentially, when the family sailed to America in 1955, Alvise Andretti found work at a textile mill near the racing hotbed of Nazareth, Pennsylvania, where Mario and his twin brother, Aldo, discovered American sprint racing. Throughout the 1960s, after Aldo was sidelined by a crash, Mario raced whenever and in whatever he could. In his first full ride on the USAC circuit in 1965, he finished third in the Indianapolis 500 and won the season driving championship. In 1967, he took on the good ol' boys on the NASCAR circuit, and won the Daytona 500.

In 1969, he came to Indy in Colin Chapman's radically redesigned Lotus and sported one of the best cars in prequalifying, but suffered a crash in practice that totaled the car and left him with first- and second-degree burns on his face. Resorting to a back-up car that possessed none of the technical innovations of the Lotus, Andretti qualified in the front row. He matured as a driver in the race—conceding an early lead because his car was overheating, working his way back up the leader board as other racers dropped out with mechanical trouble. On his final lap, before taking the checkered flag in record time, Andretti thought about his "one very long journey from a displaced persons camp in Italy to the top of the world."

In 1977, he went to the Formula One circuit in Europe and, a year later, fulfilled his boyhood dream of winning the Grand Prix title. He clinched the crown in a bittersweet race at the Italian Grand Prix at Monza (teammate Ronnie Peterson died in the race), just miles from his boyhood home. "I don't know if I could ever describe how much it means to me," he said.

He retired in 1994 as the most versatile, and one of the most beloved, racers ever. "No one taught me how to drive," he said. "I've been driving all of my life. When I got to the big time, I asked guys things, but no one would help me much. So I watched guys and I drove. I learned by doing."

BOB GIBSON
"I've Got to Win"

On the mound, Bob Gibson was a vision of economy and precision. "He pitches like he's double-parked," said Vin Scully. There was very little of the cat-and-mouse game with Gibson. He was simply a stalker, eyeing the plate with a look of barely controlled menace.

His competitive edge was so finely honed that he refused to fraternize with players from other teams, even keeping a stony distance at All-Star Games. He once claimed to have played tic-tac-toe with his daughter 200 times without once letting her win. "I've always had to win," he said. "I've *got* to win."

Gibson was born in Omaha in 1935, three months after his father had died. He was one of seven kids raised by his mother, a laundry woman, and he survived a spate of child-hood illnesses to become the first black to play on the base-ball and basketball teams at Omaha's Creighton University.

When Johnny Keane took over as manager of the St. Louis Cardinals in 1961, he put Gibson into his rotation. For the next dozen seasons, he dominated National League hit-ters. He'd retire in 1975 with 251 wins and two Cy Young Awards, the first pitcher since Walter Johnson to record 3,000 strikeouts. During the 1968 season, he was so over-powering—winning 22 games, striking out 268 hitters and sporting a 1.12 ERA—that he helped push the major league rules committee to lower the pitcher's mound in the fol-lowing season, to give hitters an added advantage.

But when the pressure was greatest, in pennant races and World Series, he rose to new realms. In the Fall Classic, he posted seven wins in a row, recorded a 1.89 ERA, strik-ing out more than 10 batters per game. In the 1964 World Series, he won the fifth game in 10 innings, 5–2, over the Yankees. On two days rest, Cards manager Johnny Keane brought him back to start Game 7. Gibson didn't have his best stuff, was suffering from a strained arm, but he still struck out nine men in a 7–5 win. "He pitched the last three innings on guts," Keane said.

Gibson won all three of his starts, including Game 7, in the 1967 Series, to carry the Cardinals past the Boston Red Sox for their second title in four years, solidifying his repu-tation as the era's ultimate big-game pitcher. And he was heroic in the 1968 Series as well, striking out a record 17 Tigers in the opening game, and 10 more in his Game 4 shutout, before losing a Game 7 duel to Mickey Lolich.

Long after Gibson left the game, hitters remembered that scary vision of him on the mound, glaring in toward home plate, determined to succeed on his own terms.

"His ability in baseball," wrote David Halberstam, "did not exist apart from the rest of his being; rather, his ability as a player was an extension of his will as a man. When opposing teams prepared to *battle* Gibson (and that was the right word: battle), they were taking on not just Gibson the pitcher, but Gibson the man."

GIBSON:
"HIS ABILITY AS
A BALLPLAYER
WAS AN EXTENSION
OF HIS WILL
AS A MAN"

HULL:
"THE NHL'S
MOST DRAMATIC
PLAYER"

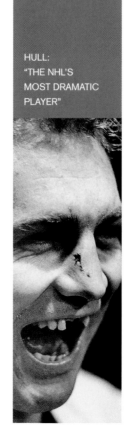

BOBBY HULL
The Golden Jet

Born in 1939, in Point Anne, Ontario, Bobby Hull received his first pair of skates for Christmas in 1942. By 1957, he was a star left wing for the Chicago Black Hawks, with a brisk style and temperament that made him a crowd favorite through-out his 23-year career. He was "a statue come alive from the Golden Age of Greece," gushed a Chicago society columnist, "incredibly handsome even without his front teeth." But "statue" seemed an ill-chosen term: More than his slicked-back blond hair, the Golden Jet's blazing speed—clocked at nearly 30 miles per hour—was the source of his nickname. His trademark rushes, capped by his screaming 118 mile-per-hour slapshot, was one of the most thrilling perfor-mances professional hockey had ever seen. A 1966 *New York Times* headline asserted simply: "Hull's Success Understand-able: Skates Fastest, Shoots Hardest."

Hull played with an almost cheery abandon, his gap-toothed smile in evidence even when heavily shadowed by the game's toughest players. The 22-year-old led the Black Hawks to the Stanley Cup over the Canadiens in 1961, the club's first championship since 1938. By then he had devel-oped one of the sport's first banana blades, and its benefits ultimately forced the league to legislate the degree of cur-vature allowed. Hull claimed that he scored more goals with the wrist shot than any other.

And there were many. In his third season, 1959–60, he tied for the league lead with 39 goals. He scored 30 or more goals in each of the next 16 seasons, leading the NHL seven times. In 1962, Hull became the third player to reach the 50-goal mark—hockey's magic number, and a record originally set by Maurice "The Rocket" Richard.

Near the end of the 1965-66 season, his Roger Maris-like pursuit of 51 (which he achieved four games after becoming the only player to break the 50 barrier twice) was one of the major sports stories of the year. He finished with 54 goals in 65 games, and would lead the league for the next three years.

In 1972, Hull signed a $1.35-million deal—plus a $1-mil-lion signing bonus—with the Winnipeg Jets of the rival World Hockey Association. His defection to the fledgling league gave the WHA instant legitimacy, and marked Hull as "the Joe Namath of hockey." In his first three WHA seasons, he scored 181 goals and won the MVP award twice. He played with the Jets for all seven years of the league's exis-tence, finishing his career back in the NHL with the Hartford Whalers in 1980.

Though he was the NHL's first $100,000 earner and the man who ushered in the big-money era of the '70s, Hull is still best remembered for his speed and his shot. He ended his iron-man run with 610 goals and 560 assists for 1,170 points. "His style of play," wrote E. M. Swift in *Sports Illustrated*, "matched his personality—open, dramatic, uncompromising and utterly joyful." —*David Zivan*

JERRY WEST
The Sharpshooter

Jerry West doesn't hold a patent on the jump shot, but no one in basketball history was consistently better at scoring from the perimeter than the former Los Angeles Laker star of the '60s and early '70s. The renowned coach Frank McGuire stated flatly, "West is the best shooter I've ever seen."

History will note that West is widely considered among the game's four best guards, a class that includes Michael Jordan, Magic Johnson and Oscar Robertson. He became such an icon that a silhouette of him in action—dribble-driving to his left—adorns the NBA logo.

West averaged 27 points a game over 14 seasons, second among guards to Jordan. Often working the middle ground that is so neglected in the current era of three-point shots and dunks, West devastated opponents with his ability to shoot off the dribble with a lightning release. West also used his quickness to drive around defenders who snuggled up to him with hopes of stopping the jumper.

Though he is best remembered as a shooter, he led the league in assists in 1971–72. Average-sized for a guard at the time—6-foot-3-inches, 180-pounds—he used his speed and long arms to become a ballhawking defender (breaking his nose nine times), earning membership to the All-NBA defensive team four times.

In 1969, West became the only player from a losing team to win an NBA Finals MVP. A year later, he hit the legendary shot from beyond midcourt against the Knicks to send their 1970 Game 3 Finals series game into overtime, though New York won that game and went on to win the championship.

Two years after losing to the Knicks, West would get redemption, teaming with Wilt Chamberlain to win his only NBA title, in 1972. He would have more success with championships in the front office. He helped put together Laker teams that won five NBA titles in the 1980s. As executive vice president of basketball operations for the Lakers, he developed a reputation as perhaps the league's shrewdest judge of talent.

Born in Cheylan, West Virginia (population 500), West played basketball because it was something a small-town kid could do by himself. Perhaps because of his modest roots, West, the second pick in the 1960 NBA draft, often doubted his own ability. "I really played out of fear that I was going to fail," West once said. "If we lost, it was always my fault, and that's a terrible burden to carry around with you."

West's talent and drive made him among the most admired players in the league, and were acknowledged at his retirement ceremony in 1974. "The greatest honor a man can have is the respect and friendship of his peers," said the great Celtics center Bill Russell. "You have that more than any man I know."
—*Mark Rosner*

WEST:
"I REALLY PLAYED OUT OF FEAR THAT I WAS GOING TO FAIL"

CLEMENTE:
"WHAT FAMOUS ATHLETE LAST DIED FOR A CAUSE BIGGER THAN HIMSELF?"

ROBERTO CLEMENTE
"To Be Remembered"

Roberto Clemente played the game of baseball with a kind of prideful vengeance. The handsome, dark-skinned Puerto Rican's marvelous game never received the credit it deserved, partly because he didn't play in a media capital, and partly because his passion was so frequently misinterpreted as pure vanity. Clemente used the real and perceived slights as the fuel for his fiery, indomitable spirit. "Baseball survives," wrote Jimmy Cannon once, "because guys like Clemente still play it."

Though Mays, Mantle and Aaron got more headlines, Clemente at his best was in the same class. A 12-time All-Star, he batted over .300 in 13 seasons, amassed 3,000 hits, won four National League batting titles and was the NL MVP in 1966. For all that, his ultimate moment of glory didn't come until the 1971 World Series. At age 37 he led the Pirates back from a 3-games-to-1 deficit to a seven-game win over the Baltimore Orioles, earning MVP honors after hitting .414 with 12 hits in the Series. It was a coming-out party of sorts, as Clemente was finally and publicly regarded as the most complete player in the game.

"The very special thing about Roberto, physically, is his hands," said Tom Seaver. "So very powerful. He stood there, far away from the plate, with that great big long bat, and with those strong hands he controlled it like crazy, hitting pitches on the side of the plate."

To the end, he remained prideful. In the fall of 1972, after the Pirates were eliminated from the playoffs, he complained to friends that he'd been slighted by *Sports Illustrated*, which hadn't put him on the cover after his 3,000th hit. "I want to be remembered as a ballplayer who gave all he had to give," he once said. That line became his epitaph when he was killed in a plane crash on December 31, 1972, on a mission of mercy to help victims of an earthquake in Nicaragua.

After his death, the Baseball Writers Association of America waived the five-year waiting period for the first time since Lou Gehrig's death, and voted Clemente into the Baseball Hall of Fame. On August, 6, 1973, Clemente was inducted along with, among others, his childhood hero, Monte Irvin.

"What famous athlete last died for a cause bigger than himself?" asked Wilfrid Sheed in 1973. "Clemente could sometimes seem like a pest, a nagging narcissist, with only his burningly serious play to deny it. Yet when that plane crashed carrying relief supplies to Nicaragua, we saw what he had meant all along. It was like the old Clemente crashing into the rightfield wall in a losing game: the act of a totally serious man."

Putting It on Ice: Starr's sneak proved the difference in the famed "Ice Bowl."

PRO FOOTBALL
1967 NFL Championship
The Icemen Cometh

At 13 degrees below zero, with 15 mph winds and a minus-48 wind chill, it was the coldest NFL game on record. On December 31, 1967, the two-time defending champion Green Bay Packers met the Dallas Cowboys in a rematch of the previous season's NFL title game. The teams played in brutal circumstances, on a field that really was frozen tundra, since the 750,000-volt, subterranean heating system below the field went out.

Green Bay jumped ahead to an early 14-0 lead, but the resilient Cowboys fought back to within 14-10 at the half. That's where it stood until the beginning of the fourth quarter, when Dan Reeves threw a halfback-option pass past a stunned Packer secondary to a wide-open Lance Rentzel, who went in for a 50-yard touchdown, putting the Cowboys up 17-14. Green Bay's final drive began on its own 32 with 4:50 remaining. After hitting Donny Anderson to convert a third-and-nine, Bart Starr passed again, hitting Chuck Mercein out of the backfield for a gain of 19, down to the Cowboy 11, with 1:11 left. On the next play, Cowboy tackle Bob Lilly bought the designed fake (guard Gale Gillingham pulling as if to lead the classic Packer power sweep), and Mercein darted through the hole Lilly left, bringing the Pack down to the Dallas 3. Anderson ran to the one on the next play, giving Green Bay first and goal with 30 seconds left. After two more plays, the Packers used their last time-out, facing a third and goal still at the one.

Instead of calling a relatively safe pass that could be thrown away and would have left time for a game-tying field goal, Lombardi took an epic gamble. On the sidelines during the timeout Starr told him that a quarterback sneak would work. "Then do it," said Lombardi, "and let's get the hell out of here." Jerry Kramer and Ken Bowman double-teamed Cowboy defensive tackle Jethro Pugh, and Starr knifed through the hole that was left, landing in the end zone with 13 seconds left. The Packers had won the "Ice Bowl," 21–17, giving Lombardi his fifth NFL title. After the game, Lombardi acknowledged that the call was a roll of the dice. "I didn't figure the people in the stands wanted to sit around in the cold any longer," he said. "I do have some compassion, though I've been accused of having none."

GOLF
1960 U.S. Open
■ It was the era of Open Saturday, when the final two rounds of the U.S. Open were played on the same day, testing a man's stamina as much as his golfing skill. As he set out for his final round, on a blazing Saturday afternoon at Cherry Hills in Denver, Arnold Palmer wasn't even on the leader board, standing seven strokes behind leader Mike Souchak and in 15th place. But this would be the day, in Dan Jenkins' words, that "we witnessed the arrival of Nicklaus, the coronation of Palmer, and the end of Hogan." Young Jack Nicklaus, just 20 years old, shot the lowest amateur score ever, a 282. The great Ben Hogan, at 47, made a late charge and had a share of the lead going to the 17th hole, only to falter, finishing in fourth place. But the charismatic chain-smoking Palmer seized the day, drove the green on the 346-yard first hole, birdied each of the first four holes on the way to a 30 on the front nine, and shot a 65, to work all the way back through the field and win his only Open.

PRO FOOTBALL
Super Bowl III
■ "I personally guarantee it," said Joe Namath and, in so doing, the most visible player of the upstart American Football League had raised the stakes of the third Super Bowl, in January 1969, in which the Baltimore Colts of the National Football League were favored by 19 points. Instead, the country saw the first great upset in Super Bowl history, as Namath played error-free football, read the Colt defense perfectly (audibling frequently), and the Jets outplayed the 14-1 NFL champions, en route to a 16-7 win.

BOXING
1964 Clay-Liston
■ There was Sonny Liston, the awesome champ, his neck wrapped with towels, delivering his menacing, dead-end stare at the young challenger. And here was the young, pretty, irrepressible Cassius Clay, staring right back at him, growling, "Chump! Now I got you, chump!" The 7-1 underdog walked into the ring in Miami, on February 25, 1964, confident that his elusiveness would confound a champion who was considered unbeatable. Clay proved his mettle in the early rounds, but got in trouble in the fourth, temporarily blinded by the wintergreen and alcohol mixture that the Liston camp was using for liniment on the champ's sore shoulder. But by the end of the fifth round, Clay's vision cleared and he was back on the attack. In the sixth, he peppered the wearying champ with long-range jabs and crisp left hooks. And before the seventh round, Liston's corner threw in the towel, making Liston the first heavyweight champ to lose his title while sitting on his stool since Jess Willard conceded to Jack Dempsey in 1919. The next day, Clay announced he was changing his name to Muhammad Ali, and a new era began.

COLLEGE BASKETBALL
1966 NCAA Championship Game
■ Texas Western, fielding an all-black starting lineup, knocked off favored Kentucky, featuring an all-white starting lineup, in what many would come to view as a watershed moment, the "Brown v. Board of Education" game in college basketball. The final score, 72-65, was closer than the game itself. The Miners took control early and physically dominated Kentucky. While the game was seen years later as a pivotal moment for blacks in basketball, the racial contrast was barely reported at the time. "I don't think I had my head in the sand or anything," said Texas Western coach Don Haskins. "I just never heard the word quota around here. So I played my best players, who happened to be black."

BASEBALL
1960 World Series
■ The mighty Yankees batted .338 and won Games 2, 3 and 6 by a margin of 35 runs. But at Pittsburgh's Forbes Field, in an unforgettable Game 7, each team took turns pulling off dazzling rallies. The Yankees tied the game in the top of the ninth with two runs, the last on a marvelous baserunning play by Mickey Mantle, who'd singled in the first run. With one out, Mantle at first and pinch-runner Gil McDougald at third, Yogi Berra hit a sharp grounder to first. Rocky Nelson fielded the ball and stepped on the bag, but then Mantle slid back into first, eluding Nelson's late tag, and McDougald scored from third, tying the game at 9-9. Pirate second baseman Bill Mazeroski opened the bottom of the ninth by stroking Ralph Terry's 1-0 slider over the left-field wall to win the game and the Series for Pittsburgh. The Pirates had been outscored 55-27 and had 31 fewer hits in the Series. But for the first time in 35 years, they were world champions.

The Decade of Hardcourt Dynasties

The two great sporting dynasties of the '60s were so dominant and so powerful, they've become synonymous with the word dynasty. Beginning in 1964, **John Wooden**'s UCLA Bruins won the NCAA tournament 10 times in 12 years, including a record seven straight from 1967-73. And in the same era, beginning in 1957, the Boston Celtics were winning 11 out of 13 NBA championships, including a record eight straight from 1959-66. Both teams built their attacks on disciplined, fast-break offenses and pressuring defenses, anchored by dominating big men (**Lew Alcindor**, then Bill Walton for UCLA, and the irrepressible Bill Russell for the Celtics, player-coach for Boston's last two titles of the '60s).

■ **City of Champions.** Los Angeles and Boston had the Bruin and Celtic dynasties, but at the end of the decade, there was no better place to be than New York. Broadway Joe Namath guaranteed, then delivered, the Super Bowl for the Jets in January of 1969. Nine months later, the Amazin' Mets upset the Baltimore Orioles in the '69 World Series. And as workers were cleaning up confetti from that parade, the 1969-70 basketball season was beginning. It would end with Willis Reed and the New York Knicks winning the franchise's first NBA title.

■ **Most Unlikely Champion.** Every year in the NFL playoffs, the networks flash a graphic saying the Oakland Raiders were the first wild-card team to win the Super Bowl. This is technically accurate, but misleading. In 1969, the last year of the American Football League, the Kansas City Chiefs finished 11-3, in second place in the AFL West, but qualified in the league's expanded playoff format. The Chiefs then beat, in succession, the defending world champion Jets, 13-6, at Shea Stadium; the mighty Raiders, 17-7, at Oakland in the AFL's last game; and, finally, the heavily favored Minnesota Vikings, 23-7, in Super Bowl IV in New Orleans. The win was a harbinger of the more complex offenses of the '70s and '80s, and sweet redemption for quarterback Len Dawson and coach Hank Stram, who had been battered by Green Bay in the first Super Bowl.

■ **Close But No Cigar.** In the 1960s, the Dallas Cowboys built a reputation as a model franchise that simply couldn't win the big one. In their seventh season, 1966, they lost the NFL championship game, 34-27, at home to the Packers. A year later, they'd lose the NFL title in the famed Ice Bowl. In both 1968 and 1969, Dallas won the NFL's Capitol Division, only to be eliminated in the first round of the playoffs by Cleveland.

	COLLEGE BASKETBALL	PRO BASKETBALL NBA	ABA	HOCKEY NHL	BASEBALL MLB	COLLEGE FOOTBALL	PRO FOOTBALL NFL
1960	Ohio State	Celtics		Canadiens	Pirates	Minnesota	Eagles
1961	Cincinnati	Celtics		Black Hawks	Yankees	Alabama	Packers
1962	Cincinnati	Celtics		Maple Leafs	Yankees	USC	Packers
1963	Loyola, Ill.	Celtics		Maple Leafs	Dodgers	Texas	Bears
1964	UCLA	Celtics		Maple Leafs	Cardinals	Alabama	Browns
1965	UCLA	Celtics		Canadiens	Dodgers	Alabama (AP) Mich. St.(UPI)	Packers
1966	Texas Western	Celtics		Canadiens	Orioles	Notre Dame	Packers
1967	UCLA	76ers		Maple Leafs	Cardinals	USC	Packers
1968	UCLA	Celtics	Pipers	Canadiens	Tigers	Ohio State	Jets
1969	UCLA	Celtics	Oaks	Canadiens	Mets	Texas	Chiefs

NOTES   **Pro Football:** AFL and NFL signed merger agreement before 1966 season, and played first Super Bowl in the January following that season. Champions are listed in the calendar year of the regular season. **College** Champions are mythical national champion, as voted by sportswriters in the Associated Press poll and by coaches in the United Press International poll. **Pro Basketball:** American Basketball Association began play in 1967-68

When Giants Walked the Sidelines

Vince Lombardi, who had been one of Fordham's famed "Seven Blocks of Granite" linemen, took over the Green Bay Packers in 1959 and in the '60s led them to five NFL championships (and the first two Super Bowl victories). Along the way, he created an aura of football dominance so powerful that the NFL ultimately named its Super Bowl champions trophy after him.

Forty years after he took over in Green Bay, Lombardi's offensive philosophy, simple, power football, relying more on physical superiority and execution rather than trickery or razzle-dazzle, remains a cornerstone of any successful pro offense. Power sweeps are no longer the meat and potatoes of football attacks, but Lombardi's underlying contribution—the superb execution of pulling guards toward the point of attack, and using double-teaming and cross blocks to confuse and exploit the opposition's first line of defense—remain part of football's strategic liturgy.

He was football's most famous taskmaster, torturing his Packers in training camp with his feared grass drills, and treating his players like wayward boys in an orphan home, who needed both mental and moral discipline. "If you cheat on the practice field, you'll cheat in the game," he said, "and if you cheat in the game, you'll cheat the rest of your life."

While Lombardi dominated the sideline, **Red Auerbach** became the most commanding presence in pro basketball arenas. The crafty, inimitable Brooklynite became synonymous with winning, leading his Celtics to nine NBA titles in his last 10 seasons as a head coach. Few coaches ever took greater joy in triumph; Auerbach's traditional victory cigar, lit after a Celtic win was in the bag, was described by Bob Cousy as "the single most arrogant act in all of sports."

One of the ironies is that after Auerbach retired, the Celtics were often associated with great white players— Larry Bird, Dave Cowens, Kevin McHale. Some even suggested that there was a grand plan on Boston's part to remain the whitest team in the league. That conveniently omitted Auerbach's contributions to integrating the NBA. Boston was the first team to draft an African-American player (Chuck Cooper in 1950), the first to field an all-black starting five (1964) and the first to hire a black head coach (Bill Russell, in 1966). "He was no leader of civil rights," said Cousy. "But show him a polka-dotted seven-footer who can dunk and he'll put him on the team. He was completely one-dimensional—his entire life was win."

The Consummate Politician

On January 26, 1960, **Pete Rozelle**, the 33-year-old general manager for the Los Angeles Rams, was named commissioner of the National Football League, a compromise choice selected on the 23rd ballot. At the time, the 12-team league's offices were in suburban Philadelphia, and pro football was still a distant second to baseball in the affections of the American public (a 1961 Gallup poll showed 34 percent of Americans naming baseball as their favorite sport, 21 percent naming football).

The underestimated Rozelle simply revolutionized modern sports over the next decade. Moving the league's offices to New York City, to be closer to the media centers that were integral to the league's health, Rozelle pushed through a visionary revenue-sharing agreement (which allowed small-market franchises such as Green Bay to compete on equal footing with the New Yorks and Chicagos of the league) whose cornerstone was a league-wide television contract that would soon enough become the envy of the entire sports world.

Jack Kent Cooke, who owned the Washington Redskins and entertained the cream of D.C.'s power elite in his owner's box, called Rozelle "as skillful a politician as I have met in my life. His capacity to conjure up agreement is sometimes nothing short of miraculous. He is the consummate politician."

Rozelle understood that the NFL was "selling an experience" to its fan base, a new generation of middle-class workaday Americans who had fewer cares and more disposable income in the postwar years. Rozelle presided over the potentially divisive competition with Lamar Hunt and the American Football League, signing a merger agreement in 1966 that led to a joint draft and the Super Bowl, and the full merger in 1970. In 1968, in another Gallup poll, 36 percent of Americans said football was their favorite sport, while only 21 percent chose baseball.

TOP OF THE NEWS: Every institution in America is being questioned, yet the world of sports continues to grow and college football celebrates its 100th anniversary. A new football league rises up to challenge the NFL and a new basketball league takes on the NBA. By the end of the decade, a Gallup poll shows that pro football has replaced baseball as the most popular sport in the land.

Movies

It's a bad decade for baseball and football movies, but Paul Newman (in his breakthrough role) and Jackie Gleason shine in *The Hustler* and, in 1969, Robert Redford is convincing in **Downhill Racer**. Based on the novel by Walter Tevis, *The Hustler* tells the story of "Fast" Eddie Felson, a pool shark who makes his way across the country, intent on taking down the legendary Minnesota Fats. In *Downhill Racer*, Redford—doing most of his own stunts—plays self-centered American skiing hope Davis Chappellet, who clashes with his coach (Gene Hackman) while fighting for the Olympic gold medal in the downhill. Charlton Heston played an aging quarterback for the New Orleans Saints in 1969's *Number One*, whose main claim to fame was a guest role by Saints head coach Tom Fears.

Reading List

The decade is highlighted by two intimate glimpses into the world of professional football. First there's participatory journalist George Plimpton's **Paper Lion**, a vivid sketch of what a professional football team looks like to an Everyman interloper. The flip side is the view from inside from one of the gladiators, Jerry Kramer's *Instant Replay*, co-written with Dick Schaap. The memoir of a season with the Green Bay Packers presents almost harrowing images of the physical, emotional and psychological toll exacted by training camp, and the long season that follows.

The big baseball book of the decade *is* a big baseball book: Macmillan's *Official Baseball Encyclopedia*, the first definitive statistical history of the sport. Eliot Asinof's *Eight Men Out* provides the truest look at the events leading up to and including the Black Sox scandal in the 1919 World Series. Lawrence Ritter's *In the Glory of Their Times* is the first and best of many books in baseball's oral history.

Two of the most memorable pieces of the decade are in *The New Yorker*. "Hub Fans Bid Kid Adieu," by John Updike, takes the measure of Ted Williams' final game and John McPhee's

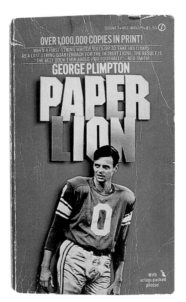

A Sense of Where You Are is an intimate profile of Princeton All-America Bill Bradley that originally ran as a piece in the magazine.

Politics

More than ever before, the real world intersects with sports. Pete Rozelle decides the NFL should go ahead and play games just two days after President Kennedy is assassinated, and is roundly criticized for it. (He later describes the decision to play the games as the biggest mistake of his 29-year career as commissioner.) Five years later, in 1968, the Mexico City Olympics' most incredible athletic feat (Bob Beamon's world-record long jump) is overshadowed by its most compelling statement of protest (John Carlos' and Tommie Smith's raised, black-gloved fists of salute during the playing of the National Anthem). Sports is no longer just an escape, but also a reflection of society.

Television

In an episode of *The Munsters* that first airs April 8, 1965, Herman is showing

How fast must a man go to get from where he's at?

DOWNHILL RACER

ROBERT REDFORD GENE HACKMAN CAMILLA SPARV 'DOWNHILL RACER'

PRODUCED BY RICHARD GREGSON DIRECTED BY MICHAEL RITCHIE WRITTEN BY JAMES SALTER TECHNICOLOR A PARAMOUNT PICTURE

Stats

$50,000
Rights fee CBS paid to telecast 1960 Winter Olympics from Squaw Valley

66
Number of yards Jim Marshall of the Vikings ran, in the wrong direction, for a safety against the 49ers in 1964

1,815
Number of career hits Stan Musial had at home when he retired in 1963

1,815
Number of hits Musial had on the road

$18,000,000
Amount paid in indemnities by the American Football League, to merge with the NFL in 1966

00:50

Amount of time left in New York Jets–Oakland Raiders game November 17, 1968, when NBC cut away to air its Sunday night movie, *Heidi*. Jets were leading, 32-29, when game went off air; Raiders rallied to win, 43-32

112
Record number of games it took Pancho Gonzales to beat Charles Pasarell at Wimbledon in 1969

$40
Price of a season ticket for the Minnesota Vikings in their inaugural season, 1961

Eddie how to hit a baseball when he smacks one that travels eight blocks, hitting Dodgers manager Leo Durocher in the head. Durocher, dazed but impressed, gives Herman a tryout, but the hapless giant inadvertently does $75,000 damage to Dodgers Stadium and terrifies the team, which begs assignment to the minor leagues if Munster is signed.

Fashion

The Denver Broncos get off to an ignominious start with their ill-fated brown and yellow ensemble. Brown helmet, yellow jersey, brown pants and socks with alternating vertical brown and yellow stripes. In August 1962, prior to an intrasquad game, the Broncos throw the socks into a bonfire to celebrate the end of a blighted era.

where in 1963 the Kansas City Athletics introduce gold sleeveless uniforms with green shirts underneath, the first time in nearly 30 years a major-league team has worn anything other than white uniforms for home games. A year later, Chicago White Sox road uniforms change from gray to light blue, and two expansion teams in 1969—the Seattle Pilots and the Montreal Expos—also wear blue road uniforms.

Impressions of the '60s

From ESPN's Charley Steiner:
   The Sixties. The decade of Love. And Haight. And social revolution. And conscience. And gloves.
      ...The gloves worn by Muhammad

> *"Where have you gone, Joe DiMaggio? A nation turns its lonely eyes to you."*
>
> —Paul Simon, singing about lost innocence in *Mrs. Robinson*

All across football there is a move toward more color in football uniforms. The Minnesota Vikings wear purple pants for away games, the Kansas City Chiefs break out fire-engine red pants for road games, and even the stodgy old Pittsburgh Steelers come up with gold accents on the shoulders of their white road jerseys.

   The same trend is seen in baseball,

Ali, who changed only everything about what athletes were supposed to be. An athlete, a showman, a salesman, a social force, a political leader, the conscience of a generation, not because he wanted to be, but was destined to be. A hero of the black inner city and the white college campus. When he put on his gloves, he was an artist in the ring, like no other heavyweight before. Or since.

   ...Tommie Smith and John Carlos made their athletic mark with their feet and their social contribution, wearing black gloves on their clenched fists after Smith won the gold medal and Carlos the bronze in Mexico City. An act of conscience and a call for black power, within months of the murders of Martin Luther King and Robert Kennedy.

   ...And the glove of the lithe center fielder Curt Flood, who told the Cardinals and the Phillies and baseball, hell no, he wouldn't go. Again, an act of conscience. "I do not feel that I am a piece of property to be bought and sold." He would be a martyr for major leaguers forever.

   ...Ali, Smith, Carlos and Flood. Symbols of the Sixties.

   Love and Haight.

1960 **The two-point option** on points after touchdown, in the American Football League.

   EXIT **Friday Night Fights** is canceled by NBC.

1961 **The Los Angeles Angels** (who later move to Anaheim) and **Washington Senators** (who become the Texas Rangers) in baseball.

   The fiberglass pole in pole vaulting.

1962 **Dodger Stadium**, with a 6-3 Dodger loss to the Reds.

   The Houston Colt .45s (who later change their name to the Astros) and the **New York Mets** in baseball.

1963 **The Pro Football Hall of Fame** opens in Canton, Ohio.

   NFL Properties, the licensing arm of the NFL.

   Instant replay, used by CBS during the Army-Navy game.

   EXIT **The Polo Grounds.**

1964 **The Sports Illustrated swimsuit issue**.

   The soccer-style kicker in pro football, with Buffalo's signing of Pete Gogolak of Cornell.

1965 **Indoor baseball**, with the opening of the Astrodome in Houston.

   The International Swimming Hall of Fame in Ft. Lauderdale, Florida.

1966 **The Atlanta Braves,** who move from Milwaukee.

   Black head coaches in the NBA, with the Celtics naming Bill Russell their player-coach.

   Merger agreement between the NFL and AFL, ending six years of player bidding wars.

1967 **The American Basketball Association**, with the Oakland Oaks beating the Anaheim Amigos, 132–129.

   EXIT **The dunk in college basketball.**

   The first Super Bowl, which until 1969 is officially titled the NFL-AFL World Championship Game.

   The Fosbury Flop in the high jump, as popularized by Dick Fosbury.

1968 **The North American Soccer League.**

   The Open Era in tennis, as professionals become eligible for Grand Slam tournaments for the first time.

   The U.S. Hockey Hall of Fame in Eveleth, Minnesota.

   The Naismith Memorial Basketball Hall of Fame, in Springfield, Massachusetts.

1969 **Kansas City Royals**, **Seattle Pilots** (who later became the Milwaukee Brewers), **San Diego Padres** and **Montreal Expos** join major league baseball.

   Divisional play and the League Championship Series in major league baseball.

THE 1970s

Sports moved to center stage, with the Fall Classic ready for prime time and the Super Bowl emerging as an unofficial national holiday. And from the tragedy of Munich to the Battle of the Sexes, its central dramas realized a cultural significance far beyond the arenas and stadiums. It was an age of financial emancipation for athletes, and the best of the best became millionaire celebrities. No one made more money, or was more celebrated, than the irrepressible boxer from Louisville, who spent the decade proving that American lives can have second acts.

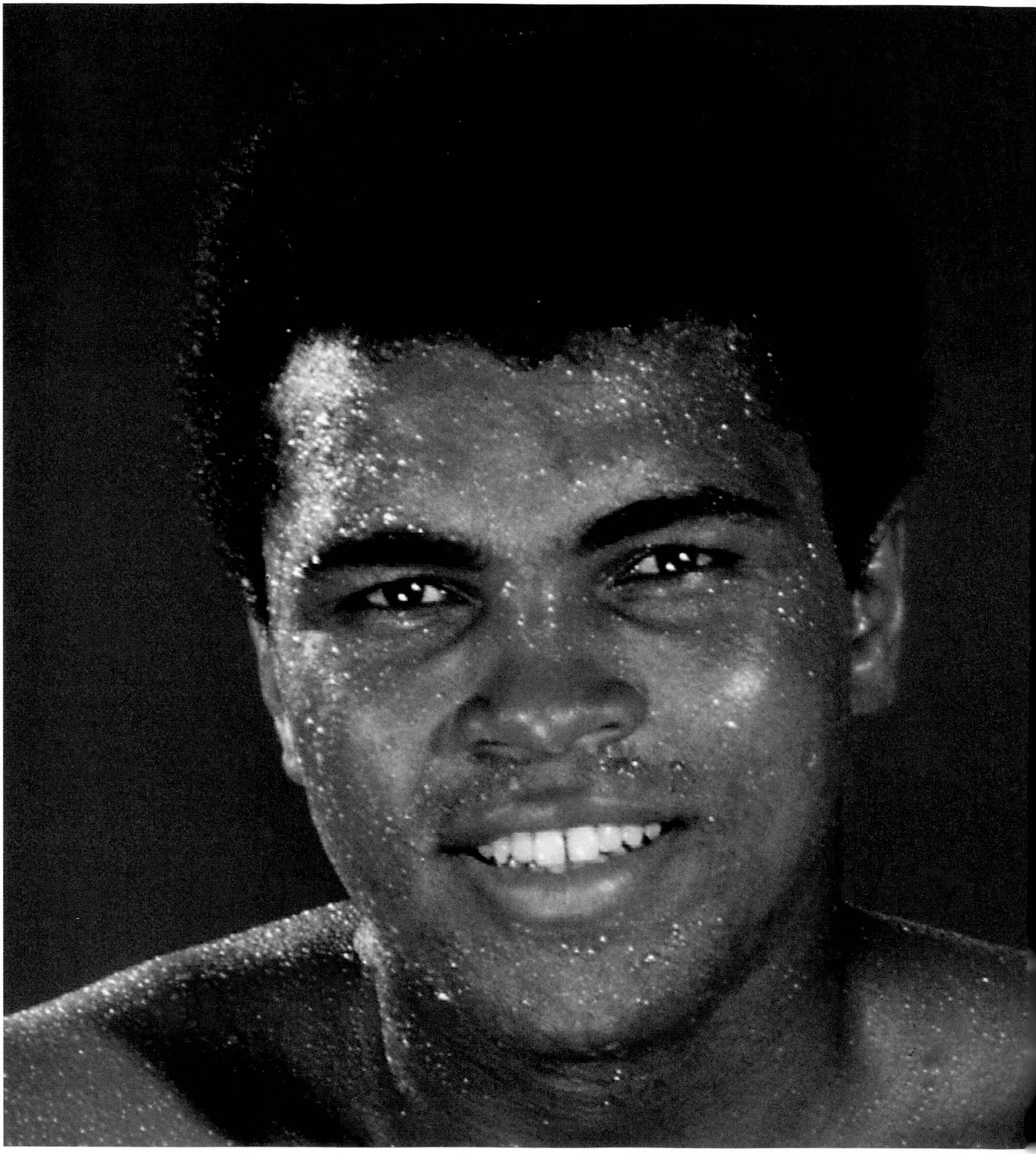

MUHAMMAD ALI By Joyce Carol Oates

The Greatest Second Act

I was determined to be one nigger that the white man didn't get.
—Muhammad Ali, 1970

Boxing was nothing. It wasn't important at all.
Boxing was just a means to introduce me to the world.
—Muhammad Ali, 1983

I N THE 20TH CENTURY, and perhaps most spectacularly in the Seventies, sports has emerged as our dominant American religion. Through the excited scrutiny of the media, our most celebrated athletes acquire mythopoetic status; they are both "larger than life" and often incapacitated for life in the ordinary, private sense. To be a champion, one must only be a consistently better performer than his or her competitors. To be a great champion, like Muhammad Ali, one must transcend the perimeters of sport itself to become a model (in some cases a sacrificial model) for the general populace, an image bearer for an era.

Though he came of age as an extraordinary young boxer in the Sixties, and made his mark as a radical political presence during that decade, it was in the Seventies that Ali achieved greatness. He did so through his unexpected exploits in the ring, but also through the life and image that he projected to the American public. He was a force, not only in sports and popular culture, but in American intellectual life, where, a decade after his famous stance against the Vietnam War, he remained a galvanizing, electrifying figure that proved ceaselessly fascinating to the American literati. Though the decade was marked by Vietnam, Watergate, disco, decadence, and malaise, it was a decade that Ali spanned and encompassed—he did as much as anyone to define the decade. If the Seventies was the Me Decade, then Ali was the Royal Me.

The Seventies, following the inglorious end of the Vietnam War, is our decade of transition—a time of accommodation, healing, and reassessment. Who would have thought that Muhammad Ali's defiant repudiation of American foreign policy, in the mid-Sixties considered virtually traitorous by some observers, would come to be, in the decade to follow, a widespread and altogether respectable political position? Who would have thought that the lone black athlete, like Ali, once ostracized by the media,

PREVIOUS PAGES
Battle Gear.
Ali's Everlast trunks, in which he floated, stung and made boxing history.

Still Pretty.
The People's Champ after a workout in 1970.

would come to be emblematic of the "new" era in which, following Ali's example, athletes like Reggie Jackson (the first major-league baseball player to sport a mustache since 1914) could express (or exhibit) themselves in essentially playful, stylistic, and theatrical gestures that had little to do with their utilitarian function as athletes? Who would have thought that such flamboyant, controversial gestures as Ali's penchant for declaiming poetry and the comical "Ali shuffle" would influence a new generation of blacks? His influence could be felt for decades in music, where rap soared to prominence; in the scathingly funny comic routines of performers like Richard Pryor; in sports, where end-zone dances and home-run trots took on new stylistic embellishments; and above all in basketball, where players like Julius Erving (and later, Michael Jordan) combined extraordinary skill, like Ali, with a personal sense of style? Compare the modest, constrained public personae of Joe Louis, Ezzard Charles, Jackie Robinson of an earlier era in which the black athlete was given to know that his presence was provisional and not a right; his very career was a privilege that might be revoked at any time. Even some of Ali's contemporaries and antagonists, like Joe Frazier and George Foreman, spent some if not all of their careers hewing to these unwritten rules.

The phenomenon of media attention—and hype—accorded every turn of Ali's career was unlike any that preceded, just as the ever-increasing purses paid to professional athletes in our time is a consequence of Ali's role in the public consciousness. Perhaps economic autonomy for athletes in sports like baseball and football would have followed in due course, but not so swiftly in the Seventies (leading to the 1974 strike in football, for instance, and true free agency a few years later in baseball) without Ali's example. Ali is the quintessential "free agent" his much-maligned predecessor Jack Johnson might have been, except for the overwhelming opposition of that era's white racism. And Ali was the Muslim pioneer through whose unwavering example such athletes as Kareem Abdul-Jabbar were allowed to change their names and present themselves explicitly as members of a distinctly non-Christian and non-traditional religion.

VIEWED FROM THE PERSPECTIVE OF THE NEW CENTURY, the Seventies was a traditional period in which, in a sense, a New Era of sports was born. If the celebrity athlete with his astronomical contract is a permanent fixture of American public life, who but Muhammad Ali, once Cassius Clay of Louisville, Kentucky, was his progenitor?

"Styles make fights," Ali's great trainer, Angelo Dundee, said, in reference to his dazzling young boxer's ring performances, but the insight applies to the mass replication of images generally. Ali soon revealed himself as a master of a new, radically iconoclastic style in public life. Though complicated by issues of religion and race and "ego," the essential message of Muhammad Ali in the late Sixties and early Seventies was simple and defiant: *I don't have to be what you want me to be.*

No other athlete has received quite the press—accusing and adulatory, condemning and praising, seething with hatred and brimming with love—that Ali has had. From the first, as the young Cassius Clay, he seems to have determined that he would not be a passive participant in his image making, like most athletes, but would define the terms of his public reputation. As sport is both a mirror of human aggression and a highly controlled, "playful" acting out of that aggression, so the public athlete is a

Prodigy. A 12-year-old Clay strikes a familiar pose in preparation for the Louisville Golden Gloves.

play-figure, at his most conscious and controlled moments an actor in a theatrical event. Ali brought to the deadly serious sport of boxing an unexpected ecstatic joy that had nothing to do with, and in fact was contrary to, his political/religious mission. His temperament seems to have been fundamentally childlike; playing the trickster came naturally to him. "My corn, the gimmicks, the acting I do—it'll take a whole lot for another fighter to ever be as popular as Muhammad Ali," he remarked in an interview in 1975. "The acting begins when I'm working. Before a fight, I'll try to have something funny to say every day and I'll talk ten miles a minute.... I started fighting in 1954, when I was just twelve, so it's been a long time for me now. But there's always a new fight to look forward to, a new publicity stunt, a new reason to fight."

There were years following Ali's refusal to be inducted into the U.S. Army, as a member of the Nation of Islam, when he was one of the most despised public figures in America; even, in State Department terms, a "possible security risk"! Boxing audiences didn't greet him with incantatory chants of "Ah-li! Ah-li! Ah-li!" but with boos. It's rare to encounter an athlete who chooses to be a martyr for a principle; an athlete who has made himself into a figure of racial identity and pride. The issue of race was always predominant in Ali's strategy of undermining an opponent's confidence in himself and, ingeniously, though sometimes cruelly, fashioning himself as the "black" boxer against the "white man's" Negro. Floyd Patterson, much admired by white America, was particularly susceptible:

> *I'm going to put him flat on his back*
> *So that he will start acting black.*

(In fact, Ali didn't put Patterson flat on his back, but humiliated him in a protracted, punishing fight.) Even as the brash 22-year-old contender for the heavyweight title, Ali had dared mock the champion Sonny Liston as an "ugly ol' bear"—an "ugly slow bear"—Liston, who'd so demolished Patterson! Years later, in 1975, Ali would relentlessly taunt Joe Frazier with remarks that would have seemed, from a white boxer, racist:

> *Joe Frazier is a gorilla,*
> *And he's gonna fall in Manila!*

Yet worse (or funnier): "Frazier's the only nigger in the world ain't got rhythm." Frazier, too, was fashioned by Ali into the white man's Negro; the boxer whom whites presumably wanted to win, therefore isolated from the community of blacks. Is this bad sportsmanship on Ali's part, a sly sort of racist tweaking of noses; is it Ali at his purposeful worst, or simply a manifestation of the man's enigmatic nature, the trickster-as-athlete?

Race has long been an American taboo. The very word *nigger* strikes the ear as obscene; in using it, particularly in the presence of whites, blacks are playing (or making war) with the degrading, demeaning historical context that has made it an obscene word, in some quarters at least. (In another context, the word can be a sign of affection. But this context isn't available to whites.) Ali, intent upon defining himself as a rebel in a white-dominated society, would make of every public gesture a racial gesture: defiance toward the white Establishment, alliance with the black community. In doing so, he upped the ante: Years after Selma and Montgomery, MLK and Malcolm X, when white America imagined that it had conceded the point on racial

Student. With Malcolm X in Miami in 1964. Promoters were nervous about the Muslim leader's presence and asked him to distance himself from Ali until after the Liston fight.

equality, Ali kept harping, kept ranting, reminding the country that equality meant not just assimilation but genuine *diversity*. The numerous televised fights of the Seventies always ended with the similar scene: Howard Cosell trying to quiz Ali about strategy or tactics, and Ali initially ignoring him so he could first give his long, grandiloquent thanks to Allah and Muslim leader Rev. Elijah Muhammad. The political issue of serving in Vietnam ("No Vietcong ever called me nigger" was Ali's most pointed defense) would seem to have been secondary to the more pervasive issue of black inequity in America, for which Ali would be spokesman, gadfly, and, if needed, martyr. In his *Playboy* interview of November 1975, Ali said that, following the teachings of Elijah Muhammad, founder of the Nation of Islam, he believed that the majority of whites are "devils" and that he anticipates a separation from white America: "When we take maybe ten states, then we'll be free."

By making race so prominent an issue, Ali provoked a predictably hostile response from the Establishment, including the federal government. Though forbidden to leave the United States, he would be exiled within it; as a black Muslim he would be "separate" from the white majority. Indeed, among public celebrities of the America 20th century only Charlie Chaplin and Paul Robeson, persecuted by right-wing politicians in the 1950s for their "Communist" principles, are analogous to Ali. The black athletes Jackie Robinson and Arthur Ashe, in their very different ways—Robinson in integrating major league baseball and Ashe in his activist phase in the public cause of AIDS education—acquired a profound cultural significance apart from their sports, yet were never controversial figures like Ali. Considering the protracted violence of the Sixties, the assassinations of public figures, and frequent killings and beatings of civil-rights activists, it seems in retrospect miraculous that Muhammad Ali, the self-declared "nigger that the white man didn't get," didn't provoke violence against himself.

Ali rode the crest of a new wave of athletes—competitors who were both big and fast.... Ali had a combination of size and speed that had never been seen in a fighter before, along with incredible will and courage. He also brought new style to boxing.... Jack Dempsey changed fisticuffs from a kind where fighters fought in a tense defensive style to a wild sensual assault. Ali revolutionized boxing the way black basketball players changed basketball today. He changed what happened in the ring, and elevated it to a level that was previously unknown.

—Larry Merchant

THE EXTRAORDINARY CAREER OF ALI is one of the longest, most varied, and sensational of boxing careers. Like Joe Louis, Sugar Ray Robinson, and Archie Moore, among few others in so difficult and dangerous a sport, Ali defended his title numerous times over a period of many years; he won, he lost, he won and he lost, beginning brilliantly in 1960 as an Olympic gold medalist and ending, not so brilliantly, yet courageously, in 1981. What strikes us as remarkable about Ali is that, while as the brash young challenger Cassius Clay he'd been ready to quit his first title fight, with Sonny Liston, in an early round (with the complaint that something was in his eye), he would mature to fight fights in the 1970s that were virtually superhuman in their expenditure of physical strength, moral stamina, intelligence, and spirit: the long, grueling, punishing fights with Joe Frazier (which, in turn, Ali lost, and won, and won); and the famous Rope-a-Dope upset of champion George Foreman in Zaire in 1974, which restored Ali's title to him. Never has a boxer so clearly sacrificed himself in the finely honed, ceaselessly premeditated practice of his craft as Ali.

"I'm a *BAD* man!" Clay exults after Liston refused to answer the bell for the seventh round. "I shocked the world!" The next day he would shock the world again, changing his name to Muhammad Ali.

F. Scott Fitzgerald's cryptic remark, "There are no second acts in American lives," would seem to be refuted by the example of Ali; dazzling as he was as a young boxer, he becomes more interesting in his second phase as a boxer no longer young, forced to rely upon superior intelligence and cunning in the ring, as well as the potentially dangerous ability to "take a punch"; bringing to bear against his hapless opponents some of the psychic warfare we associate with actual warfare—that is, the wish to destroy the opponent's spirit before the body is even touched.

"Float like a butterfly, destroy like a viper" might have been a more accurate metaphor for Ali in his early professional fights, from 1960 through '67. Not until the emergence of Mike Tyson at an even younger age in the mid-eighties would a young heavyweight boxer make such an impact upon his sport as this Olympic gold medalist who turned pro after 108 amateur bouts. Born Cassius Marcellus Clay in Louisville, Kentucky, on January 17, 1942, grandson of a slave but reared in a comfortable, supportive black middle-class environment, the young Cassius Clay was like no other heavyweight in history: massive, perfectly proportioned, a Nijinsky with lethal fists and a demeanor both in and out of the ring that might be called inflammatory. By instinct, Clay knew that boxing is, or should be, entertaining. Boxing is, or should be, *drama*. From the campy pro wrestler Gorgeous George, he'd learned that people will buy tickets to see a boxer lose as well to see a boxer win. Calling attention to oneself, cartoon-and-comic-book style, is a way of calling attention to the fight, and to box-office revenue. The early disdain of boxing experts for the "The Mouth" is certainly understandable in the light of boxing's tradition of reticent champions (like Louis); a boxer should speak with his fists, not his mouth. With adolescent zest, predating the insouciance of the black rap music, Cassius Clay repudiated all this.

> This is the legend of Cassius Clay, / The most beautiful boxer in the world today.
> He talks a great deal and brags indeed / Of a muscular punch that's incredibly speedy.
> The fistic world was dull and weary, / With a champ like Liston things had to be dreary.
> Then someone with color, someone with dash, / Brought fight fans a-runnin' with cash.
> This brash young boxer is something to see / And the heavyweight championship is his destiny.

And much, much more.

Of course, the young boxer's arrogant verbosity and pre-fight antics were more than balanced by his ring discipline and boxing skill. From the first, Clay attracted media attention as much for his style as for his victories. What was unique about Clay in the 1960s? Even after his wins against such well-known veterans as Archie Moore and Henry Cooper (whose face Clay savagely bloodied in a bout in England in 1963), the eccentricies of Clay's style aroused skepticism and sometimes alarm in commentators. A. J. Liebling described this bizarre heavyweight as "skittering…like a pebble over water." He held his gloves low, as a boxer is trained not to do. He leaned away from his opponent's punches instead of slipping them, as a boxer is trained to do. He feinted, he clowned, he shrugged his head and shoulders in odd ways, even as he danced in a sort of sidelong way. He performed a "shuffling" movement to distract opponents and entertain spectators. In the words of Garry Wills, Clay "carries his head high and partly exposed so that he can see everything all the time…whips his head back just enough to escape a punch without losing sight of his man." In Hugh McIlvanney's prophetic words, the young boxer seemed to see his life as a "strange, ritualistic play" in which his hysterical rantings were required by "the script that goes with his destiny." Norman Mailer wrote extensively and with romantic passion of the young boxer as a

The Stand. Ali in 1967, the day before he would refuse induction in the army and be robbed of the prime of his boxing career. Angelo Dundee said, "We never saw Muhammad Ali at his best."

"six-foot parrot who keeps screaming at you that he is the center of the stage. 'Come and get me, fool,' he says. 'You can't, 'cause you don't know who I am. You don't know *where* I am. I am human intelligence and you don't even know if I'm good or evil.'"

Consider the first, shocking title fight with Sonny Liston (shocking because the seven-to-one underdog Clay won so handily, and the seemingly unbeatable champion ignominiously quit on his stool after six rounds): The younger boxer simply out-boxed, out-punched, out-danced, out-maneuvered, and out-psyched his older opponent. What an upset in boxing history, on February 25, 1964! This fight is fascinating to watch, like a dramatized collision of two generations/two eras/two cultures: a fairy tale in which the audacious young hero dethrones the ogre exactly according to the young hero's predictions.

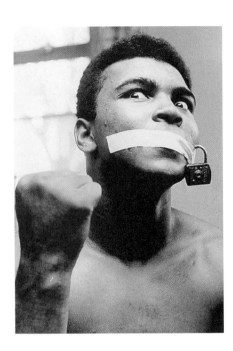

YET WHAT CONTROVERSY FOLLOWED when Cassius Clay announced that he was changing his debased "slave" name to "Muhammad Ali"; he'd been converted to the black militant Nation of Islam (more generally known as the Black Muslims) and was "no longer a Christian." With remarkable composure, the young athlete who'd seemed so— what other word but *young* best described him?—if not *adolescent, juvenile*—was publicly and courageously re-defining himself as *black*. As, three years later, he would yet more provocatively define himself as a conscientious objector who refused to be inducted into the U.S. Army to fight in Vietnam, with the punitive result that he would be stripped of his title and license to box in the United States. (Interesting if sobering to note that the majority of white publications, including even *The New York Times,* as well as television commentators, refused throughout the 1960s to acknowledge Ali's new, legal name. Might it have been the quixotic hope that in refusing to sanction "Ali" in the media, his allegiance to the Nation of Islam, if not to blackness itself, might simply fade away?)

Between February 1964 and his ascension to heavyweight champion in April 1967, when he was forced into an involuntary exile, Ali successfully defended his title nine times. Widespread white disapproval of his new identity didn't discourage boxing fans from attending his spectacular fights.

Soon afterward, Ali's early dazzling career would come to an abrupt end. Increasingly controversial as a result of his public commitment to the Nation of Islam (which was regarded by many whites and some blacks as a black-racist cult), Muhammad Ali drew a maelstrom of censure when, in April 1967, he refused to be inducted into the U.S. Army and, besieged by the media, uttered one of the classic, incendiary remarks of that incendiary epoch: "Man, I ain't got no quarrel with the Vietcong." He would be found guilty of "knowingly and unlawfully refusing induction" in a federal court in Houston, Texas, and given, by an elderly white judge, the stiffest possible sentence: five years in prison and a $10,000 fine. (Ali's mentor, Elijah Muhammad, served just three years for urging his followers to resist the World War II draft.) There would be years of appeals, enormous legal bills, and continued controversy, but Ali would spend no time in jail. Nor would he be allowed to box in the prime of his fighting life, a melancholy loss acknowledged by Angelo Dundee—"We never saw Muhammad Ali at his best." Not only did boxing commissions refuse to sanction the undefeated heavyweight champion to box, but the State Department, in a repressive tactic bringing to mind the persecutions of Charlie Chaplin and Paul

Roaring Again. After his exile, Ali returned as loud as ever, but not as fast. The charisma, however, was unaffected by the layoff.

The First Superfight. At right, Ali on the ropes against Joe Frazier in their first fight, 1971 in Madison Square Garden. The champion Frazier would knock Ali down in the 15th and retain his title.

Robeson in the Fifties, revoked Ali's passport so that he couldn't fight abroad.

Then, in 1970, with fairy-tale logic, as the Vietnam War wound down—a bitter and yet unresolved episode in our history—and the tide of public opinion shifted against the military, the U.S. Supreme Court overthrew Ali's 1967 conviction and he was reinstated as a boxer. Like a rogue elephant exiled to the periphery of his world yet always conscious of and always uneasily observed by that world, Ali returned in triumph—almost!—to reclaim his title.

The return also presaged a period of black cultural domination of both sports and society, with Ali as touchstone and catalyst. In Thomas Hauser's oral history of Ali, Julian Bond described his return fight against Jerry Quarry in 1970 as "like nothing I've ever seen. The black elite of America was there. It was a coronation… and the style of dress was fantastic. Men in ankle-length fur coats; women wearing smiles and pearls and not much else."

I N THE SEVENTIES BELONG ALI'S GREAT FIGHTS, and to say that they were unanticipated is not to disparage the younger boxer but to extol the older. In the intensely fought, physically exhausting fights with Joe Frazier and George Foreman, Muhammad Ali proved himself a great, and not merely a gifted and charmed, athlete. After three and a half years of not boxing, though only 29, Ali was conspicuously slower and knew better than to dance away from his opponent; he would have to compensate for his lost agility with sheer boxing (and punching) technique; he would have to train to take, and not exclusively give, punishment. That this was a deliberate strategy is important to note.

"I don't train like other boxers," said Ali in a 1975 interview. "For instance, I let my sparring partners try to beat up on me about eighty percent of the time. I go on the defense and take a couple of hits to the head and the body, which is good: You gotta condition your body and brain to take those shots, 'cause you're gonna get hit hard a couple of times in every fight. Meanwhile, I'm not gonna beat up on my sparring partners.… If I kill myself punching at them, it'll take too much out of me. When you're fightin' as much as I have lately, you're supposed to be boxin' and doin' something every day, but I can't dance and move every day like I should, because my body won't let me. So I have to stall my way through."

If this sounds like a recipe for disaster, it was also, for Ali, in the short run at least, a recipe for success. Indeed, it is the game plan for the remainder of Ali's career, the strategy that would win him two of his epic fights with Joe Frazier and the legendary Foreman fight in which, miraculously (or so it seems) the younger, stronger, and seemingly more dangerous Foreman would punch himself out on Ali's stubborn body in eight rounds, to relinquish the heavyweight title another time to Ali. As Ali's doctor at that time, Ferdie Pacheco, said: "Ali discovered something which was both very good and very bad. Very bad in that it led to the physical damage he suffered later in his career; very good in that it eventually got him back the championship. He discovered that he could take a punch."

And take punches Ali did, for the next six years.

The great, extravagantly publicized matches of this period of Ali's career belong with the great sports events of all time. Frazier–Ali I (1971, which attracted more viewers than any boxing match in history), Ali–Frazier II (1974), Ali–Frazier III (1975), and Ali–Foreman (1974) would seem to inhabit an archetypal realm of the spirit that

Rumble in the Jungle.
In Kinshasa, Zaire, Ali pulled off one of the great upsets in boxing history, outsmarting George Foreman with his famed "rope-a-dope" strategy.

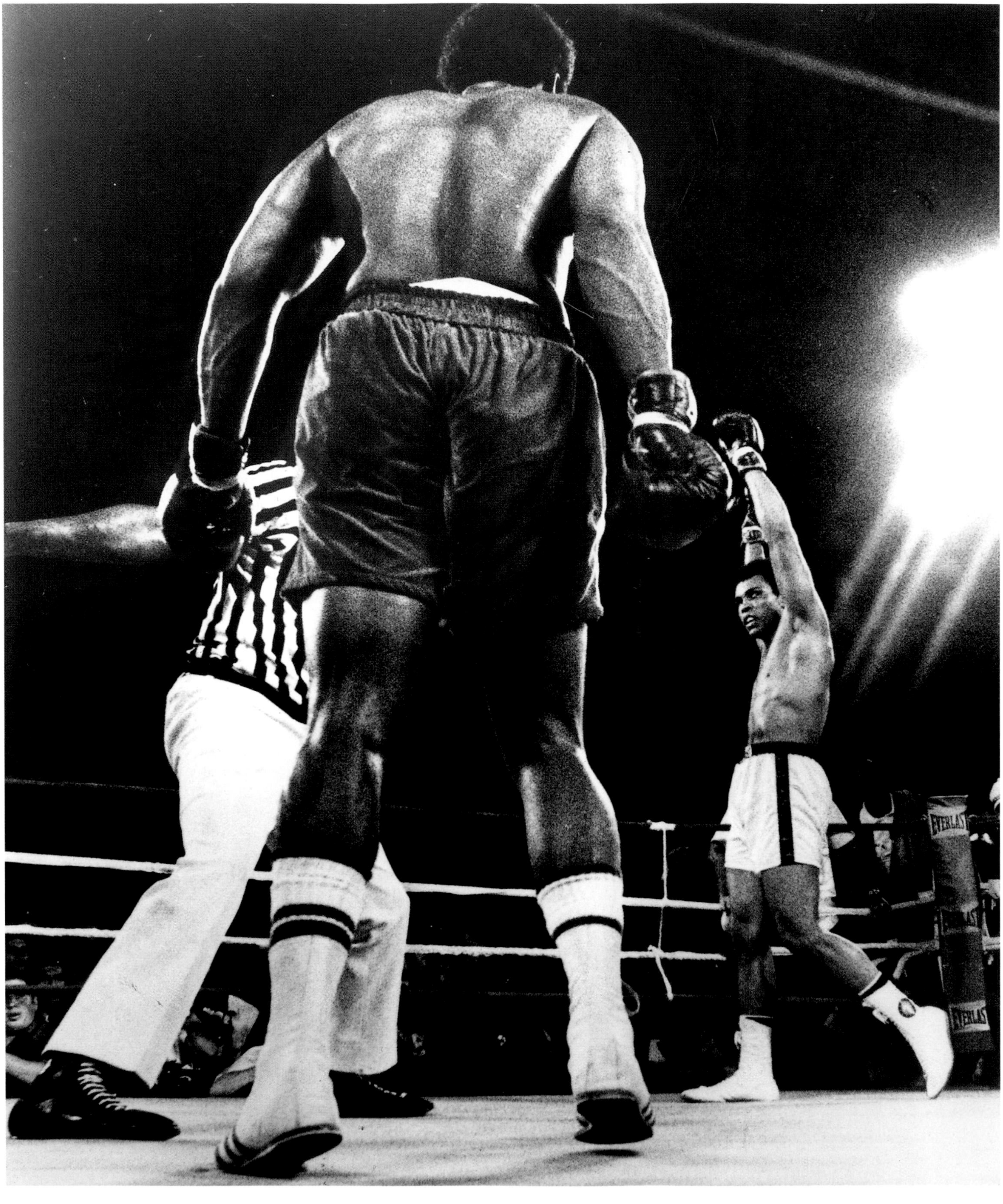

transcends most sports events. The perilous, cathartic heights of Greek and Shakespearean tragedy come to mind when we consider these draining fights in which even the winners are irrevocably altered. (After 14 rounds of "The Thrilla in Manila" with Frazier in 1975, Ali, the winner, nonetheless described the experience "like death. Closest thing to dyin' that I know of.") Not surprisingly, these epic boxing matches excited media interest and drew to Ali's camp numerous commentators, some of them famous themselves (like George Plimpton, Norman Mailer), who would spend more than a month in Zaire for the Ali–Foreman fight. (See the Academy Award–winning documentary *When We Were Kings* and Norman Mailer's highly stylized coverage, *The Fight.*) Not just Ali's stoical courage as an athlete, but Ali's ingenuity drew such attention. For even the aging Ali was a meta-athlete who conceived of his public appearances as theater, not merely, or wholly sport; Ali was a superb athlete, but he was also a superb actor, exhibiting "Ali" to the acclaim of millions.

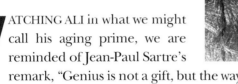

WATCHING ALI in what we might call his aging prime, we are reminded of Jean-Paul Sartre's remark, "Genius is not a gift, but the way a person invents in desperate circumstances." There is something of the con man in Ali, and his game is to make us want to believe in his indestructability, even as, perhaps, Ali doesn't, or can't, believe in it without qualification himself. Consider the Foreman fight. In *When We Were Kings*, Foreman is repeatedly "dissed"; he is the opponent whom we are invited to scorn, because he is not Ali, our hero. (In a sense, there is room for only one boxer in the ring, if that boxer is Ali. He won't play fair in seeking an audience's attention.) As in the fairy tale of heroes and villains, Foreman, for all his gifts, is the villain. Even as we watch this astonishing fight between an aging Muhammad Ali and a young and vigorous George Foreman, reputedly one of the hardest-hitting heavyweight punchers of all time, we are mystified: How did Ali do it? Granted even his superhuman will, how did his body withstand such repeated, relentless blows? The Rope-a-Dope strategy is the very triumph of purposeful masochism; yet such triumph inevitably carries with it irretrievable loss. (Would Ali have wished to win over Foreman had he been able to anticipate his physical and mental deterioration—his "Parkinsonianism"—of later years?) Wittily titled the "Rumble in the Jungle," as if it were but a cartoon or comic-book event, this fight, which returned his title to him, surely contributed to Ali's taking into his body a year later the "closest thing to death."

Following these remarkable fights, Ali would exult in being again "King of the World"—"The Greatest." He had secured his position as the most famous athlete of the Seventies, and perhaps of all time. He had traded his health, it would develop, but such a trade would perhaps have seemed worth it at the time. Unlike the only undefeated heavyweight champion in history, Rocky Marciano, Ali fought worthy opponents, most of them younger than himself.

On Top Again. Ali had conjured up another great victory, through a combination of his innate talent, his intelligence and the sheer force of will. "Now you see me, now you don't," he'd written. "George thinks he will, but I know he won't."

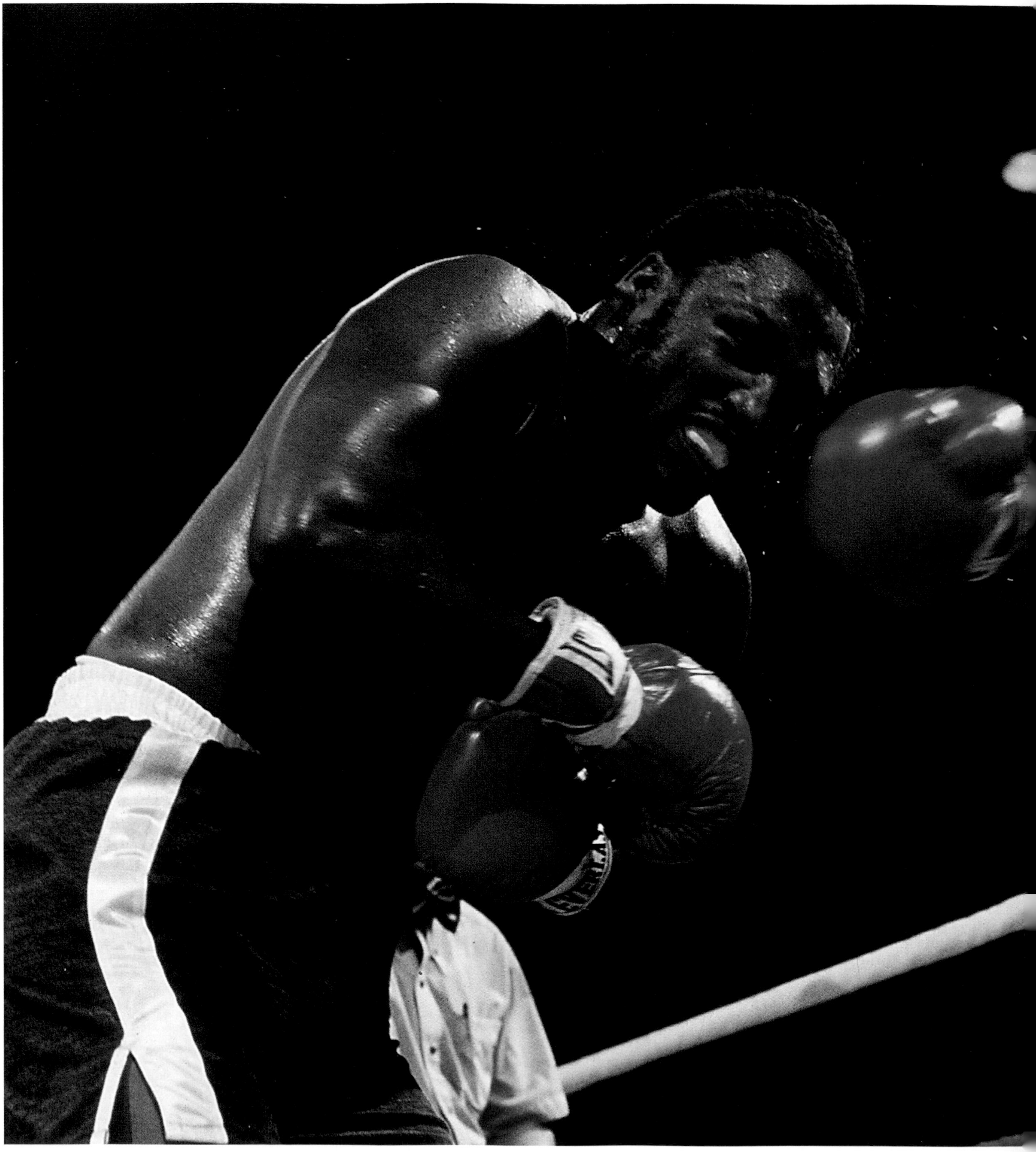

The Thrilla in Manila.
What Ali would call his "toughest fight," the third match against Frazier, took a severe physical toll on both men. "Closest thing to dyin' I know of."

He would defend his hard-won title several times, against such opponents as Chuck Wepner, Ken Norton (who would break his jaw), Jimmy Young (who would break his eardrum), and Earnie Shavers; unexpectedly, he would lose on points to the young Leon Spinks (with only seven pro fights to his credit) in 1978. Though Ali would beat Spinks in their rematch, and announce his retirement, he would be unable to resist returning to the ring; two years later, he would be beaten decisively, and painfully, by his former sparring partner Larry Holmes. By this time Ali was 38 and long past his prime; his career had in effect ended with the 1978 loss to Spinks.

Yet, like many another former champion (Louis, Ezzard Charles, Ray Robinson, Ray Leonard, Roberto Duran, et al.), Muhammad Ali would continue to fight, if not to box with any degree of his former talent. His final match, sanctioned not in the United States but in the Bahamas, in crude, unprofessional surroundings (a cowbell was used in place of a defective ring bell), was with a mediocre 28-year-old Trevor Berbick, who easily outscored a slow, plodding Ali on points. For there is a point at which even the ingenuity of desperation fails. (Berbick would have the distinction in 1986 of being spectacularly floored in the second round of his title defense by boxing's new prodigy, Mike Tyson, who would formally end the "post-Ali era.")

As the English sportswriter Hugh McIlvanney noted, "Graceful exits are rare in professional boxing, but few great champions have gone out more miserably than Muhammad Ali." But even in the waning years of his career he would be an emblem of the courage and stoicism of the aging athlete, so much a part of our contemporary scene. (Ironically, it would be Ali's old opponent George Foreman who would return to the ring as a "mature" boxer and captivate, in another era, the attention, and affection, of millions of viewers.)

AND SO, 25 YEARS AFTER THE FIRST FRAZIER FIGHT that ushered in his most glorious athletic era, a nation saw Muhammad Ali—who once seemed an image of discord, embodying all that was disconsonant about the modern urban multicultural American experience— holding the torch at the Atlanta Olympic Games, a sainted symbol of healing. We remembered the bluster in a different way, celebrating it even as it is so absent from the present-day Ali persona, still playful but largely muted by Parkinson's. At the same time, Ali is deadly serious about his mission as a member of the Nation of Islam; there is nothing playful or trickster-like about his commitment to the Muslim faith ("Muslims…live their religion—we ain't hypocrites. We submit entirely to Allah's will").

So there has always been something enigmatic about Clay/Ali, a doubleness that suggests a fundamental distinction between public and private worlds: And what a testimony is Ali's career of nearly three decades to the diversity of media attention! In our time, in his sixth decade, long retired from the sport that made him famous and from adversarial politics that made him notorious, Ali now enjoys a universal beneficence. He has become an "American icon" known through the world; a brand name symbolizing "success." He remains a Muslim but no longer belongs to the Nation of Islam; he no longer makes pronouncements of a political nature. He has become a megacelebrity divorced, like all such celebrities, from history; a timeless mass-cult contemporary of Elvis Presley and Marilyn Monroe.

He who was once the icon-breaker is now an icon.

Back in the Homeland.
Ali in Africa for the Foreman fight in 1974. As Ali mingled among the Zairians before the fight, Bundini Brown shouted, "The King has come home to reclaim his crown."

JACK NICKLAUS
The Golden Bear

Winning breeds winning," Jack Nicklaus once said. "You learn how to win by winning. As long as I'm prepared, I always expect to win." The most prolific winner of major championships in the history of the game, and the dominant golfer of the postwar era, Nicklaus won 20 major titles and finished in the top five of 56 Grand Slam championships.

His game was a marvel of power and intuitive skill. The drugstore owner's son from Columbus, Ohio, shot 51 for nine holes during his first round of golf as a 10-year-old. He qualified for the U.S. Open at 17, won the U.S. Amateur at 19, and at age 22, slayed Arnold Palmer—and his Army—in the playoff for the 1962 U.S. Open. Ignoring the taunts of the partisan gallery ("Miss it, Jack!"), Nicklaus coolly shot a 71 to win his first professional major. "That was it," Palmer would say later. "If I could have stopped that big dude out there, I might have held him for five years. But he just took off."

As Nicklaus matured, he became the game's most awesome hitter off the tee, gobbling up par 4s, routinely reaching par 5s in two. It was after he shot a record 271 at the Masters in 1965 that Bobby Jones remarked: "Palmer and [Gary] Player played superbly, but Nicklaus played a game with which I am not familiar."

What the golf world was witnessing was the most sustained exhibition of Grand Slam excellence in history. No other man has won each of the four professional majors twice; Nicklaus has won each at least three times. From that 1962 Open through the 1981 PGA, a span of 79 majors, Nicklaus finished in the top 10 of 61, and the top five of 51. Come Sunday, the Golden Bear was almost always in the hunt.

As amazing as his consistency was his mid-career transformation, from the tubby "Fat Jack," 225 pounds of crew-cut ungainliness, to—with a diet and a longer hairstyle—the svelte, even sexy Golden Bear of the 1970s.

But what truly endeared Nicklaus to the crowds was his grace under pressure and his towering sense of sportsmanship. He was a competitor so fierce that he avoided forging close friendships on the tour, yet so uniformly gracious in defeat that opponents often found it unnerving. After sinking a treacherous five-footer on the last hole of the 1970 Ryder Cup, he picked up Tony Jacklin's marker, conceding him his two-footer and ensuring the first tie in the 42-year history of the competition. "I don't think you would have missed that putt," Nicklaus told Jacklin, "but in these circumstances, I would never give you the opportunity." Nicklaus lived the ideal—both consummate competitor and sportsman.

And that's why the crowds grew to revere him. When he

NICKLAUS: "THE REMARKABLE COMBINATION OF POWER AND FINESSE"

AARON: "AN ANGRY PERSON IS NOT A SUCCESSFUL PERSON"

made his final glorious run, shooting a 30 on the back nine at Augusta in 1986 ("maybe as fine a round of golf as I've ever played"), to come from off the leader board to win his sixth Masters, at age 46, the response wasn't just warm, it was rapturous. By then he'd become not just a living legend, but also—having designed and built more than 100 courses himself—the First Gentleman of Golf.

"I never thought anyone would ever put Hogan in the shadows, but he did," said Gene Sarazan. "Nicklaus has the remarkable combination of power and finesse, and he is one of the smartest guys ever to walk the fairways. And he has been an extraordinary leader. What more is there to say? Jack Nicklaus is the greatest competitor of them all."

HANK AARON
Slaying the Dragon

If Babe Ruth was around today, he wouldn't be able to walk the streets. He'd be on every other commercial," observed outfielder Gary Sheffield on the 25th anniversary of Henry Aaron's record-breaking 715th home run. "But you don't see Hank Aaron on any commercials, and he can walk around without getting noticed." Recognition was never what Aaron sought. His achievements piled up almost as quietly as he stood in the batter's box. And it may take the passing of another generation—who now will see the Henry Aaron Award bestowed each year on the major league's top hitter—to afford him the iconic status he deserves.

There has never been a question, however, about the respect afforded by opposing pitchers. "He's the toughest in the league," said Sandy Koufax, who gave up Aaron's 1,000th hit. "Just Bad Henry. There's no way you can pitch him when he's hot." Usually, he was. Aaron was a paragon of consistency, hitting at least 20 home runs for 20 straight seasons, from 1955 through 1974, and hitting .305 for his career. He holds more major-league records than any other player, including total bases (6,856), extra-base hits (1,477), RBIs (2,297) and, of course, home runs (755).

Of course, one number outshines the rest, the "white man's record," as some called it, that he shattered on April 8, 1974. Aaron had finished the 1973 season with 713 home runs, one shy of Ruth's record. Atlanta Braves owner William Bartholomay wanted Aaron to sit out the 1974 season opener in Cincinnati, but commissioner Bowie Kuhn ordered him into the lineup. Aaron calmly belted the first pitch he saw for number 714. Four days later in Atlanta, Aaron took a fastball by Dodgers pitcher Al Downing over the left-field wall and into history. Rounding second, he barely acknowledged the fans who came onto the field to touch him in his greatest moment. Commissioner Kuhn was not even present.

Ruth's record was not the first barrier Aaron had overcome. Born February 5, 1934, into poverty in Alabama, Aaron made his way through the minor leagues, becoming the first black player in the Class A South Atlantic, or "Sally" League, in 1953. He won the batting title that season with a .362 average and led the Jacksonville Tars to the pennant. Despite his success, Aaron's early batting technique was highly unconventional. From his sandlot days, Aaron hit cross-handed, batting righty with his left hand on top of the grip. And he hit off his front foot, which should have diminished his power.

Aaron had switched to the conventional grip by the time he broke camp with the Milwaukee Braves in 1954. He had been close to a deal with the New York Giants, where Aaron would have been in a lineup with Willie Mays, and for years Leo Durocher loudly regretted losing the young prospect. On September 23, 1957, the 23-year-old crushed a two-run homer—which Aaron decades later said was probably his most memorable—that brought Milwaukee its first pennant. He finished the season with 44 homers, 132 RBIs and a .322 average. In a seven-game series against the Yankees, Aaron led the Braves to the 1957 World Championship, hitting safely in each game and going 11 for 28 (a .393 average), with three homers, seven RBIs and 22 total bases.

"I have been misunderstood by a lot of people, simply because I don't talk a lot," Aaron said once. "And when I do talk, people think I am an angry person. I'm not an angry person, because I feel that an angry person is not a successful person." Aaron's success was acknowledged by his 1982 induction, on the first ballot, into the Hall of Fame. Still, he remains undervalued. During the 25th anniversary celebrations, *Atlanta Journal-Constitution* columnist Terence Moore noted something "strange" in the festivities, that, for all Aaron's towering accomplishments, it often seemed that we had only just discovered him.   —*David Zivan*

BILLIE JEAN KING
The Pioneer

When Billie Jean Moffitt was growing up in Long Beach, California, her firefighter father pointed her toward tennis, having judged softball not sufficiently ladylike. By age 12, she'd decided what she wanted to do with her life. "If I ever become a great champion," she vowed to herself, "I'll change tennis." She would change more than that, becoming the single most important figure in the explosion of women's sports in America.

The irony is that the spark of King's feminism ultimately came from her ex-husband, Larry King. While both were attending Los Angeles State University in the early 1960s, he pointed out the injustice of their comparative conditions. He had received an athletic scholarship and financial aid, as the last member of a six-man tennis team, while she—ranked in the top five in the world—received no aid. Years after they'd divorced and Billie Jean had publicly acknowledged her lesbianism, she still credited King with "waking me up to what it means to be a feminist."

KING:
"IF I EVER BECOME A GREAT CHAMPION, I'LL CHANGE TENNIS"

ORR:
"WHEN HE GOES BY MY BENCH, I TURN AWAY SO I WON'T HAVE TO WATCH"

That awareness first manifested itself in her play on the court, where she won 20 Wimbledon titles, including six singles crowns. "When in doubt, she charged," wrote Sally Jenkins, "and with that philosophy she shifted the spectrum of female possibilities from the decorative to the active."

But as important, King was in the forefront on virtually every important gender-equity issue in sports in the 1970s. She argued for equal prize money at Grand Slam championships; risked her career to help start the first women's professional tour; became the founding president of the Women's Tennis Association; and founded the Women's Sports Foundation and *WomenSports* magazine. With Larry King, she created the concept of World Team Tennis, and turned it into a professional league. And at the apex of WTT in the mid-Seventies, she became the first woman to coach professional male athletes.

But King is a feminist icon largely because of the 1973 Battle of the Sexes, an athletic footnote but a cultural milestone, in which she defeated the 55-year-old ex-pro (and avowed "male chauvinist pig") Bobby Riggs, in a hype-heavy, glitz-drenched, nationally televised Astrodome challenge match that could only have occurred in the 1970s. "This is a culmination of a lifetime in the sport," King said after the straight-sets win. "Tennis has always been reserved for the rich, the white, the males—and I've always been pledged to change all that."

On that night in Houston, with the hopes of an entire gender resting on her shoulders, King simply dominated Riggs. "Ridiculous as this may sound," wrote Grace Lichtenstein, "her victory helped validate the idea that women could hang in there, not just on the tennis court, but on the job or in the home. It was proof not so much of physical prowess, but of mental toughness. Feminists had not yet reached out to the masses. Billie Jean reached out, grabbed them by the hair and made them take notice."

BOBBY ORR
Too Good to Be True

Historians mark the dawn of the modern age of professional hockey as 1967, when the NHL expanded from six teams to 12. In fact, it began a year earlier, when Bobby Orr took the ice for the Boston Bruins, and took the game to a broader audience across America. Orr didn't just dominate the game, he altered it. To say he was the greatest defenseman ever is to miss the central point—he changed the position, turned it into one of both defense *and* attack. The only defenseman ever to lead the NHL in scoring, Orr had the creative genius to open the game up in ways previously thought impossible.

A ferocious penalty killer with consummate puck-handling skills, he was one of the fastest skaters in the league, with a keen passing eye and a low, lethal slap shot. Rather than passing to center ice, Orr often would gather the puck, sweep behind his own goal, and begin one of those daring, trademark end-to-end rushes, the puck on his stick throughout, thrilling crowds and demoralizing opponents. "When he goes by my bench," said Leafs coach Punch Imlach, "I turn away so I won't have to watch."

The grandson of an Irish professional soccer player, and the son of an NHL prospect who passed up an offer from the Bruins so he could fight in World War II, Orr grew up in the harbor town of Parry Sound, Ontario. By age 12, he had been discovered by the Bruins, who got his services for their junior-league affiliate at age 14. Four seasons later, at the youngest permissible age in the NHL, Orr joined the Bruins, and commenced to revolutionize the sport.

He was named the league's outstanding defenseman eight times. He had the speed to catch up to odd-man rushes and a willingness—cherished by teammates making a fraction of his salary—to surrender his body to block shots.

In his fourth season, 1969–70, he became the only player in NHL history to win four individual season trophies: the Hart (most valuable player), Ross (as league scoring leader), Norris (outstanding defenseman) and Smythe (playoff MVP). In that dream season, Orr led a physical, talented band of Bruins to their first Stanley Cup title in 29 years, sealing the finals sweep of St. Louis with an overtime goal later voted the greatest moment in league history. Sweeping across the front of the Blues' goal, Orr put a shot between the legs of goalie Glenn Hall, and was tripped just after releasing it. The famous picture of the moment—a horizontal, airborne Orr, already celebrating the victory in flight—remains the most indelible image of the Bruins legendary Number 4.

Even at the height of his powers, he exuded a sense of earnest, small-town goodness. In 1970, a teammate groused that Orr was spending too much time and money on charity work. It turned out that his big problem was his knees. By the mid-Seventies, six knee operations had gotten the best of Orr, reducing him, in the words of one sportswriter, to a "Mickey Mantle on skates." His wife, Peggy, spoke of nights when Bobby would bend his knees to sit down "and you could hear the loose pieces of bone knocking around in there."

The Bruins, afraid of his condition, declined to offer him a big contract, and he signed with the Chicago Black Hawks in 1976. He played the shanks of two seasons with Chicago before surrendering to the inevitable.

"What's Orr's best move?" said Gordie Howe. "I'd say his best move is putting on those skates. He plays the funny kind of game; he doesn't let anyone touch the puck."

KAREEM ABDUL-JABBAR
Sky's the Limit

When the game was on the line and Kareem Abdul-Jabbar's team needed a basket, there was never any question where the ball was going. Abdul-Jabbar's high-arcing sky hook wasn't simply basketball's most reliable shot. "It's the

ABDUL-JABBAR: "YOU HAVE TO HAVE THAT WEAPON TO ALLOW YOU TO GO BEYOND AGE, INJURIES AND DEFENSE"

greatest weapon of one person who's ever been an athlete in any sport," Lakers coach Pat Riley once said.

The 7-foot-2-inch Abdul-Jabbar scored more points during the regular season and playoffs than anyone in NBA history. Many of them came with the elegant, unblockable sky hook; no athlete was ever identified more by one characteristic of his game. "You have to have that weapon," said Riley, "to allow you to go beyond age, injuries and defenses."

Indeed, Abdul-Jabbar played until he was 42, leading the Lakers to five NBA titles in the 1980s (after winning one earlier with Milwaukee) and receiving six MVP awards, more than any other player in NBA history. His career was prolonged by yoga, proper diet and an increasingly savvy playing style. When Abdul-Jabbar was named *Sports Illustrated's* Sportsman of the Year in 1985, Denver coach Doug Moe suggested that Kareem, at age 38, was playing the best basketball of his career.

In his 1983 autobiography, *Giant Steps*, Abdul-Jabbar suggested that Chamberlain "brought the big man from clod to controlling factor." Abdul-Jabbar was the next step in the evolution of the center.

Born Lewis Ferdinand Alcindor Jr., he was a national celebrity while attending Power Memorial High School in New York, winning 71 consecutive games. Alcindor then went off to UCLA, solidifying the dynasty of coach John Wooden, serving as a bridge between the Walt Hazzard–Gail Goodrich and Bill Walton eras. Alcindor made a stunning debut in 1965 by scoring 31 points as the UCLA freshman team easily defeated the two-time defending national champion varsity. He then led the Bruins to an 88–2 record and three straight NCAA titles, earning the outstanding player award at the Final Four each time. He averaged 26.5 points and 15.5 rebounds in college.

One day during practice, Wooden noticed that the trajectory of his prize freshman's hook shot was too flat. He instructed Alcindor to use more arc. With that, the sky hook was born.

But other lessons were more painful for him. His experiences with racism in New York, Los Angeles and the South turned him against white people, at least as a group, he wrote in *Giant Steps*. That left him remote, alienated and disinclined to represent the United States in the 1968 Olympics. He stayed home. Within three years, he became a Muslim, changing his name to Kareem Abdul-Jabbar in 1971.

"Kareem lives a life with a moat around it," Jim Murray once wrote during the Laker years. But by the early 1980s, Abdul-Jabbar began connecting more with fans and even with reporters, whom he had avoided much of his career. When he broke Chamberlain's NBA record for field goals, fans of the rival Boston Celtics gave him a long standing ovation. "I found out there are a lot of nice folks out there," Abdul-Jabbar told writer Gary Smith in 1985. "I've become a familiar face, not a creature from a distant planet."

—*Mark Rosner*

JULIUS ERVING
Doctor's Orders

Dr. J was a secret, a myth, an urban legend—the traveling circus that never came to your town. In the renegade American Basketball Association of the 1970s, Julius Erving became the last American sports superstar to gain that status without the benefit of widespread national television exposure. The legend of the Doctor grew through breathless press clippings and word of mouth.

With his mushrooming Afro and wispy goatee, sporting the mod stars-and-stripes uniform of the New York Nets, the Doctor was in fashion. And his game was a glimpse into basketball's future, the catalyst for the transition between the low-post game dominated by hulking centers to one of fluid motion and athleticism, in which graceful, multidimensional players could do it all. When he won the NBA Most Valuable Player award in 1981, he was the first non-center in 17 years to do so. Over the next 17 seasons, 13 of the winners were non-centers.

Erving's game was playground artistry, founded on the cement courts in Hempstead, Long Island, in the 1960s. "As a kid, I played a lot of one-on-none," he recalled. He developed a repertoire of moves he would fully unleash in the Rucker Park summer league, where word of *the Doc-tah* first spread. He'd gotten the nickname at Roosevelt High in Hempstead, from his friend Leon Saunders (teammate Willie Sojourner added the initial in the pros). After two years at the University of Massachusetts, he signed with the Virginia Squires in 1971. He was an instant hit in the fledgling league and led the ABA in scoring during his second season, after which Nets owner Roy Boe brought him back home to Long Island to play for the Nets in Nassau Coliseum, just minutes from where Erving grew up.

Lithe and fast, at 6-foot-7-inches, 200 pounds, with huge, size-11 hands, Erving dominated with his superb court presence and elusive jumping ability. And he seemed to rise to the occasion in big games, especially the 1976 ABA finals, where he averaged nearly 40 points a game to vanquish a favored Denver team, whipping Nugget defensive stalwart Bobby Jones in the process. "He destroys that adage that I've always been taught," said Jones. "That one man can't do it alone."

"It's all psychological," Erving said later. "If we're down a few points and I'm fast-breaking toward the hoop, I'll sometimes decide that the time has come to get freaky. It gets the crowd up and our team up and it gets me up. Because of the excitement we'll often start to defend better, to make good plays, and to pull ahead."

Though Erving's electric presence helped force the merger prior to the 1976–77 season, he never played an NBA game with the cash-strapped Nets, who sold him to the Philadelphia 76ers days before the season opener. He led the Sixers to the NBA Finals three times, in 1977, 1980 and

ERVING:
"I'LL SOMETIMES DECIDE THAT THE TIME HAS COME TO GET FREAKY"

PETTY:
"A TEAM MAN WILL WIN MORE THAN AN INDIVIDUALIST"

1982, but they lost each time. The ring finally came a year later; after signing free-agent Moses Malone from Houston, the Sixers plowed through the 1983 playoffs, losing only a single game. By that time, Erving was an elder statesman in the NBA, revered by fans and courted by marketers who were as attracted to his smooth off-court demeanor as his explosive on-court abilities.

Erving retired in 1987, after becoming the first non-center to score 30,000 points in the pros. He worked in the Philadelphia front office, and later became the executive vice president of the Orlando Magic in 1997. During his career and after it, he remained among the most respected figures in basketball history. "I never heard anybody knock him or express jealousy," said all-pro Dominique Wilkins. "Never one negative word. I can't name you one other player who has that status."

RICHARD PETTY
King Richard

Richard Petty grew up in a racing family and became the greatest and most beloved stock-car racer ever. The molasses-tongued backwoods gentleman from Level Cross, North Carolina, was a study of laid-back lankiness in wraparound shades, while he dominated the Grand National/NASCAR circuit for most of his 34 seasons as a driver, winning 200 races, seven Daytona 500s and seven driving championships. When asked which accomplishment he was most proud of, he replied, "Still being alive."

Born in 1937, Petty grew up with the sport, learning it at the hand of his father, Lee Petty, a NASCAR legend in his own right who won the first Daytona 500, in 1959. From the age of 12, Richard worked in the pits for Lee's crew, and after graduating from high school, he attended business school. Richard was a departure from the hell-bent, lead-footed moonshine runners of legend. He learned early in his career that it was "more important to be smooth than flashy," and while he was an aggressive driver, he was always among the most controlled on the circuit. Petty became the biggest winner in NASCAR by understanding his car's limitations and by picking his spots carefully. No one was better at the subtle art of drafting, tucking in behind a competitor and saving fuel by gliding in the "clean air" behind an opponent's car, then slingshotting past him at a crucial moment. "When Richard sneaks in behind you, you can hardly feel it," said A. J. Foyt, who carried on a spirited rivalry with Petty.

Following his father's example, Richard treated the NASCAR circuit as a family business. His brother Maurice built his engines; his cousin Dale Inman was his crew chief. "I'm a team man," he said. "And in the long run, a team man will win more than an individualist." The Pettys were an innovative group, the first team on the NASCAR circuit to use a roll bar in a car, to use two-way radios for car-to-pit communication, to develop a nylon window screen and to use a helmet cooler, circulating fluids around the driver's head during the race. Later, Richard's son Kyle joined the circuit. "I've had some good luck during my career," Richard Petty said. "I had the good fortune to grow up with the sport and have my daddy to watch and learn from. Then I raced with some of the greats and they taught me a lot. And maybe I taught them a few things, too."

Whether in a Plymouth, Dodge, Oldsmobile or Buick, Petty drove with the number 43 emblazoned on the side of his car—his father, Lee, used to drive Number 42. Even after becoming a legend, Petty seemed unaffected by his stardom, forever his father's son. "I don't know anything about greatness," he once said. "That's for others to decide. My daddy was a race driver, so I became a race driver. If he'd been a grocer, I might have been a grocer."

O.J. SIMPSON
Juice

Before 1994, when O. J. Simpson stood charged with the murder of his ex-wife, Nicole Brown Simpson, and her friend Ronald Goldman, he was better known as one of pro football's two or three greatest running backs.

Though it's easy in retrospect to say that Simpson always tried a bit too hard to be easygoing, the fact remains that America embraced him as it had few other black athletes before. In the 1970s, he was breaking records, running through airports for Hertz (as the first black celebrity to be featured in a national corporate ad campaign), and deflecting praise to his offensive line. In less than a decade, he'd become the single most popular figure in American team sports—a black hero of racial neutrality whom white kids adored. In a mid-'70s poll of grade-schoolers, commissioned by *Ladies Home Journal*, Simpson was voted the nation's most admired figure, by both boys *and* girls.

On the field, from his first game at Southern Cal in 1967, he represented a quantum leap into the next wave of physical evolution at his position. Taller, stronger and heavier than most running backs of the period, he was also faster than virtually all his peers, a Sixties anomaly who would become the prototype back of the next generation. "Simpson was not only the greatest player I ever had, he was the greatest player anyone ever had," said USC coach John McKay. In addition to winning the Heisman in 1968, Simpson led the Trojans to a national title in 1967, thanks to his memorable 64-yard touchdown run to beat crosstown rival UCLA, 21-20.

Drafted by the abysmal Buffalo Bills with the first pick of the 1969 draft, he languished for three years in pass-oriented offenses. But Lou Saban arrived in 1972 and quickly realized that he shouldn't be using the game's best running back as a decoy. The change took: Simpson led the NFL in rushing in Saban's first season, then broke Jim Brown's all-time single-season rushing record in the second, finishing

SIMPSON: "HE WAS THE GREATEST PLAYER ANYONE EVER HAD"

CONNORS: "I HATE LOSING MORE THAN I LOVE WINNING"

with 2,003 yards in 14 games. He might have been even better in 1975, when he accounted for 2,243 yards running and receiving, scored 23 touchdowns and led the league's most prolific offense, running behind his offensive line, dubbed the "Electric Company," because they "turn on the Juice."

For all his power, Simpson was a spectacularly elusive back, stepping lightly, sensing tacklers from his blind side, spinning away at the last instant. And he was tough. "Sooner or later, no matter how hard you make it for him, O.J. will beat you," said one opposing coach. "Eight, 10, 20 carries, no matter how much muscle you lay on him, he does not discourage. He has brought back to pro football the Jimmy Brown dimension—the great running back who actually gets tougher the more tired he seems to be."

That was the case in 1973, when he broke Brown's season record with a 200-yard performance in the season finale against the Jets. With snow swirling around the field and his blue pants muddied from the Shea Stadium turf, Simpson kept bursting through holes, skating over the treacherous surface, and into the record book. "I was in the locker room all by myself right before the game ended," he recalled. "I started walking around thinking how I couldn't wish to be anything more or anyone else. I was part of the history of the game. If I did nothing else in my life, I'd made my mark."

Twenty-one years later, he'd go on trial and become a talisman of overexposed media celebrityhood. The irony was that the murder charge only served to obscure the mark he'd made on the game, and those vivid images of his playing days seemed a long way off.

JIMMY CONNORS
The Art of War

Besides being the most prolific winner in men's tennis history, Jimmy Connors is the pivot on which tennis' past turned into its future. When he was dominating the majors in 1974, storming his way to Wimbledon and U.S. Open titles, he was the original punk rocker of sports, a talented brat whose vulgarity was matched only by his power and energy. His celebrated romances, first with Chris Evert and later with *Playboy* centerfold Patti McGuire, made headlines. His battling style ushered in a more aggressive game, and he revolutionized the backhand, becoming the first to use a two-fisted shot not merely as a resource but as a lethal weapon.

The game looked, sounded and felt different in Connors' hands. With his tautly strung, steel-suspension T-2000 racket, he led the tennis equipment revolution away from wood and into lighter, stronger materials. In contrast to the graceful court movements of the previous generation of talented Australians, his game was a brashly kinetic American charge, more boxing than ballet. On the service return, he was a charging bull, reacting to the ball's motion in an instant, hitting it on the rise. "Serving to him is like pitching to Hank

Aaron," said John Newcombe. "If you don't mix it up, it's going out of the ballpark." With the added power of the two-fisted stroke, he had the ability to add torque to his return, sending service rockets blistering back across the net at frightening speeds.

Connors would win a men's record 109 tournaments, as well as eight major singles titles, including the U.S. Open five times (the only player to do so on all three surfaces—grass, clay and hardcourt). Though others won more major titles or dominated for longer periods, no one else played the game with more verve or passion than Connors. "I hate losing more than I love winning," he said in 1976.

He was proof that some champions aren't born so much as made. His mother, a divorced teaching pro named Gloria Connors, was his coach, tutoring him on the low-rent public courts in Belleville, Illinois. "Jimmy was taught to be a tiger on the court," she recalled. "When he was young, if I had a shot I could hit down his throat, I did. And I'd say, 'See, Jimmy, even your mother will do that to you.'"

When Connors arrived on the pro circuit out of UCLA in 1972, he had already perfected his brash, combative on-court style, which could alienate fans and opponents alike. Even between points, he moved to an internal rhythm—blowing on his hands out of habit as much as necessity, constantly tugging up his shirtsleeves to free his shoulders for the severe arm motions to follow, habitually shifting his weight back and forth while waiting to receive a serve. Connors' shots were hit flat and violently, leaving less margin for error than any great player in history.

But by the end of the 1970s, topspin was enjoying a renaissance, and Connors' time seemed over. He was vanquished in two Wimbledon finals by Bjorn Borg, and later outflanked by younger players like John McEnroe and Ivan Lendl. But he continued battling, rebuilt his game and in the early Eighties, won Wimbledon again and the U.S. Open twice more. In 1991, after 20 years on the tour, he was the grand old man at the U.S. Open, the "people's champion" who staged a series of heart-stopping late-night rallies on the raucous center court at Flushing Meadow, advancing to the semifinals in a fortnight-long display of crafty gamesmanship, veteran composure and the same raw, viper intensity that he introduced two decades earlier. "What Jimmy has is what we'd all kill for," said Ilie Nastase that fall. "Just one more time." Connors made the most of it.

SECRETARIAT
"Too Much Horse"

As the big chestnut colt came around the final turn at Belmont Park, headed for immortality, the grandstand rising in a lunatic roar, his jockey, Ron Turcotte, was struck by another sound: silence. No thundering hooves behind him. By that point, Secretariat was all alone, no horses even close enough to eat his dust, rumbling to what veteran turf writer

SECRETARIAT: "THE GREATEST PERFORMANCE BY A RACEHORSE THIS CENTURY"

Whitney Tower called the "greatest performance by a race-horse in this century."

It was the 1973 Belmont Stakes, the culminating performance in a classic three-act play in which Secretariat become the first Triple Crown winner since Citation a quarter century earlier. Since 1948, seven colts had won the Kentucky Derby and Preakness, only to falter at the Belmont Stakes. There was much pre-race speculation about whether Sham, who'd finished second in the first two Triple Crown races, was better suited to the longer distance at the Belmont. But in the final race, with history in the balance, Sham wasn't a factor. Despite—or perhaps because of—all the publicity and pressure, the horse nicknamed "Big Red" (just like Man o' War) went out and tore up Belmont, winning the race in record time, and by an astonishing 31 lengths.

While the nation did not discover Secretariat until that spring, there had been clues of greatness for some time. Born of thoroughbred royalty—the son of the '57 Preakness winner Bold Ruler out of the prodigious dam Something-royal—the colt seemed special from an early age.

"He was wonderful-looking, almost too pretty to be good," said Penny Chenery Tweedy, his owner during his racing career. Weighing 1,154 pounds fully grown, and sporting the blue-and-white checkerboard silks of Meadow Stable, he developed a remarkable physique—his broad, powerful chest gave him a massive lung capacity, his heart was 2½ times the size of a standard thoroughbred, and he had the muscular hindquarters of the best speed horses. He had won the Eclipse Award for Horse of the Year as a two-year-old (and of course would do so again as a three-year-old).

The Triple Crown journey began on the first Saturday in May, as Secretariat set a track record in the Kentucky Derby, at 1:59⅖, running each quarter mile of the mile-and-a-quarter race faster than the previous.

But two weeks later, in the Preakness at Pimlico Raceway in Baltimore, there were still people who thought the horse could be beat. Laffit Pincay, aboard Sham, had come close in the Derby and, whipping his mount around the final turn at the Preakness, was convinced he might overtake Secretariat in the stretch. "It wasn't until I noticed that he never cocked his stick that I thought I might be in trouble," said Pincay.

At the Belmont, where Secretariat went off as a 1–10 favorite, he took the lead so clearly by the final turn that Turcotte was able to check the infield board as he went by the eighth pole. "Then I set my horse down for the only time in the race," he said. "We both must have wanted the record—and we got it." His time of 2:24 was the fastest mile and a half ever run on a dirt track anywhere in the world.

"It was as though, like a brilliant jazz musician, he was making the whole thing up as he went along," wrote Secretariat's biographer, William Nack, "improvising something different for each race. All Turcotte had to do was hang on. He knew better than to interfere: *Quiet, genius at work.*"

MARK SPITZ
Alone in the Water

His teammates at the Santa Clara Swim Club used to watch the scene with mute wonder. As the teenage Mark Spitz prepared for an event, his father, Arnold, would give him a pep talk: "There are eight guys in that pool for the race, but only one is a winner. The others are bums." The younger Spitz grew up obsessed with the idea that proving himself a winner would bring him love, adulation and fame. Paradoxically, he became both the greatest American swimmer in history and something of an athletic afterthought. He was an Olympic hero never truly embraced by the American public.

He certainly worked hard enough in pursuit of his goal. The son of a steel-company executive who instilled in him a single-minded devotion ("Swimming isn't important; winning is," said Arnold Spitz), Mark developed into a gifted, prickly loner who set a raft of world records swimming under the legendary coach George Haines as a schoolboy in Santa Clara, then led Indiana University to four straight national championships. His celebrated flame-out at the 1968 Summer Games in Mexico City—where he predicted six gold medals but won gold only in a pair of relays—set the stage and raised the stakes for the 1972 Olympics.

By the time of the Munich Games in 1972, Spitz looked the part of the California-bred sporting hero: lithe and well-muscled, with high cheekbones, dancing eyes and a dashing mustache. Beyond the looks, he was an athletic anomaly blessed with the ability to flex his legs *forward* at the knee, inestimably adding thrust to his legwork beneath the surface and perfectly complementing his long upper arms, ideal for a swimmer.

"I want to win at Munich and then quit," he said prior to the 1972 Games. "I never swam for glory, only the satisfaction of being recognized the best in the world." Spitz would succeed spectacularly, winning gold medals in all seven events he entered in Munich. He opened with the 200-meter butterfly and dominated from the start, setting a world record and winning by more than two seconds. And on it went—the 100 butterfly, the 100- and 200-meter freestyle, and three relay races (the 4x100 freestyle, the 4x200 freestyle and the 4x100 medley relay), setting world records in every event. The closest call came in the 200-meter freestyle, where he trailed fellow American Steve Genter at the final turn, but passed him in the end. At the medal ceremony, a jubilant Spitz waved his shoes at the crowd and the television cameras. Perhaps it was this graceless gesture, but more likely it was the tragedy of 11 Israelis murdered by Palestinian terrorists that overshadowed the entire Games, and Spitz's accomplishments. For whatever reason, his athletic success never translated to public acceptance, and when he attempted an ill-fated comeback at 39, he seemed curiously unfulfilled—a great athlete who could never fully enjoy his greatest triumph.

SPITZ:
"ONLY ONE
IS A WINNER"

BLANDA:
"MORE PRIDE
IN WINNING THAN
ANYONE I'VE
EVER MET"

GEORGE BLANDA
The Old Man

In 1970, George Blanda was well on his way to a Hall of Fame career that would conclude with 236 touchdown passes, 335 field goals and an NFL record 2,002 points scored and 26 years of service. But then came that magic fall, which turned him from a star into a national icon.

The man Johnny Unitas used to jokingly refer to as "my boyhood hero" was the hale and hard-bitten son of a Youngwood, Pennsylvania, coal miner. Blanda began as a blocking back in the single-wing at Kentucky, before Bear Bryant arrived and put him under center, as a T-formation quarterback. Drafted by the Bears in 1949, he fought for time as a quarterback (starting from 1952–54), but he was more valued as a kicker, nailing every extra point he attempted from 1951–56. When the Bears asked him to go to full-time duty as a kicker before the 1959 season, he retired and went into the trucking business in Chicago.

But wooed by the nascent AFL's Houston Oilers in 1960, Blanda enjoyed a renaissance. In the first six seasons of the AFL, he threw 148 touchdown passes, leading Houston to the first two league titles. After the 1961 AFL title game, the AP was already referring to him as "the ageless George Blanda."

In 1970, the first year of the merger, the 43-year-old Blanda began the season as the backup to Daryle "The Mad Bomber" Lamonica in John Madden's wide-open Raider attack. The Raiders opened with a sluggish 2–2–1 start, but in the sixth game of the season, Blanda came in for an injured Lamonica in the first quarter, throwing three touchdown passes to beat Pittsburgh. The next week, against archrival Kansas City, he came on to lead a late drive and kick a game-tying 48-yard field goal with three seconds left. A week later, he replaced Lamonica against Cleveland, and threw a game-tying touchdown and kicked a game-winning field goal in the last two minutes. Over the next two weeks, he threw a late game-winning touchdown against Denver, and kicked the winning field goal with four seconds left to beat the Chargers. On five consecutive Sundays, Blanda had emerged from the bench, pulled his battered silver helmet over his shaggy gray hair, and rallied the Raiders to four wins and a tie. He went from the sports pages to the front pages, hailed as an icon of over-40 vitality. The dream season earned him the AP Male Athlete of the Year award. Oakland lost the AFC title game, but Blanda nearly rallied them one more time, against the Colts.

In 1973, at age 46, Blanda scored 100 points. The end came in 1976, a month before his 49th birthday, when Raiders coach John Madden cut him. "George was a grizzly, the toughest competitor I've ever seen," Madden wrote later. "He had more pride in winning than anyone I've ever met." When he left the game, Blanda held the career scoring record for the Raiders. And the Oilers. And the Bears.

JR Superstar: Rodgers emerged from the '71 classic ragged but victorious.

COLLEGE FOOTBALL

As Good As It Gets

The scene was Thanksgiving Day 1971 in Norman, Oklahoma, and the long-awaited, much anticipated showdown between No. 1 Nebraska and No. 2 Oklahoma. At stake was an unbeaten season, Orange Bowl berth, Big 8 title and shot at the eventual national championship. The 9–0 Sooners, with their lethal wishbone triple-option attack, were ranked No. 1 in scoring offense. The defending national champion Cornhuskers were 10–0, and ranked No. 1 in scoring defense. Back and forth across Owen Field they went, in a splendidly played game. When Oklahoma double-teamed wingback Johnny Rodgers, Nebraska used I-back Jeff Kinney, who ran for 174 yards. When Nebraska bottled up lightning bug halfback Greg Pruitt, OU's Jack Mildren threw two touchdown passes and ran for 131 yards.

The difference, ultimately, was Rodgers. His skittering first-quarter punt return, featuring a full 360-degree opening spin and a gorgeous cutback move to break free, gave Nebraska the early lead. And then, late in the fourth quarter, with OU ahead 31–28 and Nebraska facing a third-and-eight at the Oklahoma 46, Jerry Tagge scrambled and threw a low pass to Rodgers, who dropped to one knee and caught it for a crucial first down. Kinney scored five plays later, and then it was left to Rich Glover and the vaunted NU defense to hold. But Oklahoma nearly struck again; Mildren found Jon Harrison alone on a deep route (NU defensive back Joe Blahak fell down), but overthrew him, and Nebraska finally shut the Sooners down.

It was the zenith of the Big 8's power. After Nebraska routed new No. 2 Alabama, 38–6, in the Orange Bowl, the Big 8 trio of Nebraska, Oklahoma, and Colorado finished 1-2-3 in the final Associated Press poll. "It was the best team I ever coached and the only close game we had, and we played some pretty good football teams," said Nebraska coach Bob Devaney.

PRO FOOTBALL

1971 Divisional Playoff, Miami vs. Kansas City

■ It was a bad year for turkey dinners. One month to the day after the Nebraska-Oklahoma epic, the Miami Dolphins battled the Kansas City Chiefs in a Christmas Day playoff game that would become the longest in the history of the NFL. After Miami scored to tie the game at 24 in the last two minutes, Kansas City's Ed Podolak (who would gain 350 all-purpose yards on the day) ran the ensuing kickoff back to the Miami 22. But Jan Stenerud's attempt at the game-winner went wide, sending the game to overtime. And in the first overtime period, his 42-yarder was blocked by Miami's Nick Buoniconti. Finally, halfway through the sixth period, Garo Yepremian kicked the 37-yard game winner, after 22 minutes and 40 seconds of extra time. It was a changing of the guards for the two franchises. Miami would play in the next three Super Bowls, winning two. The Chiefs, who'd won three AFL titles in the Sixties, wouldn't return to the playoffs for 15 years.

GOLF

1977 British Open

■ At the usually windy Ailsa course at Turnberry, the sun shone and conditions were perfect for the rising young gun Tom Watson to stake his claim to king of golf against the old pro, Jack Nicklaus. Playing together, both men shot 65 in Friday's third round, breaking away from the rest of the field, and were paired up again on Saturday. Nicklaus led by two with just six holes left, but Watson birdied 13 and then nailed a 60-foot putt from off the green on 15 to tie it again. At the 16th tee, Watson looked over to Nicklaus and said, "This is what it's all about, isn't it?" And Nicklaus, smiling, said, "You bet it is." On 17, Watson's marvelous three-iron put him on the green in two, and Nicklaus' approach went awry. Watson nailed his birdie putt to take a one-stroke lead onto the final hole, where both men birdied. Watson posted his second straight 65, to finish at 268 and demolish the tournament record by eight strokes; Nicklaus broke it by seven. After walking off with his arm around Watson, Nicklaus was gracious as ever at the trophy ceremony. "I gave you my best shot," he said to Watson, "and it just wasn't good enough. You were better."

BOXING

1975 Ali-Frazier III

■ It was billed as "The Thrilla in Manila," the third and final battle between Muhammad Ali and Joe Frazier. It turned out to be among the greatest fights ever, a classic contrast of fighting styles, and two great heavyweights fighting desperately on a grand stage. While Ali dominated the early rounds, the implacable Frazier fought back in the middle going. At the beginning of the seventh round, Ali walked to the center of the ring and said, "Old Joe Frazier! Why, I thought you were washed up." "Somebody told you wrong, pretty boy," replied Frazier, and the battle resumed. Ali was in deep trouble in the 10th, but fought his way out of it. Frazier, moving slower, absorbed some tremendous punishment in the 12th, and Ali ended the 13th by connecting on nine unanswered blows. In the corner before the 15th, Frazier trainer Eddie Futch called it off, unwilling to see his man hurt more. Afterward, Ali sounded like exactly what he was—a man who'd survived a war. "It was like death," he said. "Closest thing to dyin' I know of."

PRO BASKETBALL

1970 NBA Finals

■ The classic series between the Knicks and Lakers, which featured Jerry West's last-second 55-footer to send Game 3 into overtime, seemed to swing in Game 5, when Willis Reed went down with a strained thigh muscle. He sat out Game 6, and with no one in the middle to stop Wilt Chamberlain, the Lakers blew out New York, with Wilt scoring 45. Reed was doubtful for Game 7, and didn't come out for warm-ups. But moments before the tip, with his leg heavily bandaged and shot with painkillers, Reed moved gingerly out of the locker room and onto the floor. The Madison Square Garden crowd exploded and, if anything, got even louder when Reed scored the Knicks' first two baskets of the game. Those were his only points in 27 minutes, but his inspiration was huge. Uplifted by Reed's gritty play and Walt Frazier's clutch performance (35 points, 19 assists), the Knicks played a complete game to win, 113–99. "The Captain showed us something that night," said Cazzie Russell. "His mere presence, the way he kept going, it made us play harder."

BASEBALL

1975 World Series

■ It was a tense, contentious classic well before Game 6, when Boston's Carlton Fisk willed that 12th-inning homer fair, to win the game and send the Series to the limit. After Fisk's homer pierced the Boston night, the Red Sox faithful returned for Game 7, convinced that the Curse of the Babe was finally set to end. But Cincinnati's Joe Morgan, who'd won Game 3 with a 10th-inning single, would disappoint Boston again, chipping a ninth-inning go-ahead single in the Series finale to score Ken Griffey and bring the Reds their first title in 35 years.

The Lawyer for the Defense

Shortly before the end of the '71 regular season, Montreal called up a gangly, 6-foot-4, 215-pound, minor-league goaltender named **Ken Dryden**, who'd spent much of the season in legal studies at McGill University. Dryden led Montreal through a storybook playoff run, knocking off Boston (which had boasted the league's top four regular-season scorers) in the quarterfinals. "He's an octopus," grumbled Phil Esposito after one Bruin loss.

A year later, the Canadiens laid the groundwork for the rest of their '70s dominance. New coach Scotty Bowman, hired away from his GM job at St. Louis, brought the team together and healed the French-English rift that had existed under Al MacNeil. And the Canadiens dealt to get the first pick in the entry draft, selecting Quebec right winger Guy Lafleur.

The Canadiens, with Bowman, Dryden and Lafleur, won five more Stanley Cups, before Dryden retired after the 1979 season to practice law (and Jacques Lemaire and Yvan Cournoyer also hung up their skates). Those teams also included defensive

stalwarts Guy Lapointe and Larry "Big Bird" Robinson, and numerous offensive fireworks. But Dryden, who won five Vezina Trophies during his eight full seasons in the league, was the glue. "Ken might lose one game, but he rarely lost two in a row," said Bowman. "Oh, he was so consistent."

■ **City of Champions.** The Pittsburgh Pirates, with Willie Stargell playing a big role both times, won the World Series in 1971 and 1979, but no one called Pittsburgh "the city of champions" until the Steelers started winning, paying off beloved owner Art Rooney for his decades of suffering.

The key to the Steelers rise was Chuck Noll, who'd played for Paul Brown in the '50s, coached under Don Shula in the '60s, and learned plenty from both men. Noll's Steelers, built through a succession of terrific drafts, were defensive terrors, led by Joe Greene and the famed linebacker corps of Jack Ham, Jack Lambert and Andy Russell. On offense, Noll stuck with the slow-developing Terry Bradshaw, who eventually helped the Steelers win four Super Bowls in the '70s. Throughout, Noll maintained a low-key self-assurance that was infectious. As running back Rocky Bleier once said, "Chuck's the only guy I know who bought a plane before he took flying lessons."

	COLLEGE BASKETBALL	PRO BASKETBALL NBA	ABA	HOCKEY NHL	WHA	BASEBALL MLB	COLLEGE FOOTBALL		PRO FOOTBALL NFL
1970	UCLA	Knicks	Pacers	Bruins		Orioles	Nebraska (AP)	Texas (UPI)	Colts
1971	UCLA	Bucks	Stars	Canadiens		Pirates	Nebraska		Cowboys
1972	UCLA	Lakers	Pacers	Bruins		A's	Southern Cal		Dolphins
1973	UCLA	Knicks	Pacers	Canadiens	Whalers	A's	Notre Dame (AP)	Alabama (UPI)	Dolphins
1974	N.C. State	Celtics	Nets	Flyers	Aeros	A's	Oklahoma (AP)	Southern Cal (UPI)	Steelers
1975	UCLA	Warriors	Colonels	Flyers	Aeros	Reds	Oklahoma		Steelers
1976	Indiana	Celtics	Nets	Canadiens	Jets	Reds	Pittsburgh		Raiders
1977	Marquette	Trail Blazers		Canadiens	Nordiques	Yankees	Notre Dame		Cowboys
1978	Kentucky	Bullets		Canadiens	Jets	Yankees	Alabama (AP)	Southern Cal (UPI)	Steelers
1979	Michigan State	SuperSonics		Canadiens	Jets	Pirates	Alabama		Steelers

NOTES **Pro Basketball:** American Basketball Association disbanded after 1975-76 season; NBA absorbed four ABA teams into the NBA. **Hockey:** World Hockey Association disbanded after 1978-79 season; NHL absorbed WHA teams into the NHL. **College football:** Champions are mythical national champions, as voted by sportswriters in the Associated Press poll and by coaches in the United Press International poll.

Legends of the Fall—and Winter

They were already legends when the Seventies began, but during the decade **John Wooden** and **Paul "Bear" Bryant** proved that they were still on top of their game.

Wooden was perhaps the most cerebral coach ever, a man who preached the value of discipline in an age that glorified spontaneity. He never told his team to beat its opponent, but simply to play the best it could possibly play within its own abilities. It's a testament to his wisdom and leadership skills that he reached such disparate personalities as Kareem Abdul-Jabbar and Bill Walton. His persona, of the teacher who fostered a nearly ascetic striving for goodness ("Make each day your masterpiece"), struck deep in the players who played for him.

They, in turn, made Wooden a legend and UCLA the greatest college basketball power ever. The Bruins won 10 national championships for Wooden over a 12-year period, including seven straight from 1967-73. On the best of these teams, the Bruins weren't playing other teams so much as they were battling Wooden's private concept of perfection. In that seven-year title span that UCLA's teams were so dominant, the practices were more competitive than the actual games. Bill Walton described the practices as, "Two hours of nonstop basketball, at the highest level, with the greatest players and with the master sitting there, critiquing everything, never letting a single error go unnoticed or uncriticized, yet always pointing out the positive things and building the team for the championship moment."

Bear Bryant didn't just speak wisdom, he growled it—in a low rumble. "Don't do a lot of coaching just before the game," he said. "If you haven't coached them by 14 minutes to two on Saturday, it's too late then."

Bryant "coached them" as well as anyone, and while he'd reached retirement age during the Seventies, his Alabama Crimson Tide won one consensus national title, and a share of two others during the decade. The most memorable came after the 1978 season, when the Tide beat No.1 Penn State, 14-7, with a fourth-quarter goal-line stand in the Sugar Bowl.

"Football has never been just a game to me," Bryant wrote in his memoirs. "Never. I knew it from the time it got me out of Moro Bottom, Ark. … All I had was football. I hung on as though it was life or death, which it was."

He coached at Maryland, Kentucky and Texas A&M, before returning to Alabama, his alma mater, in 1958, where he remained for 25 seasons, winning 232 games and six national championships, ultimately winding up as the winningest coach in major-college football history.

Not a technical innovator so much as a commanding, intimidating, natural leader, Bryant willed his teams to victory, always able to recruit a bit more effectively than his foes, practice a bit harder, devise game plans a bit smarter and, in short, inspire his troops to play a bit better. "No coach ever won a game by what he knows," Bryant once said. "It's what his players have learned."

COACHING WISDOM

"I've always felt that the most important word in the English language is no. You can always change no to yes, and that makes everybody feel good. But it's hard to change yes to no. I've always tried to tell kids that if you're in doubt about anything, say no."

—Indiana basketball coach Bobby Knight

"A school superintendent I once worked for told me, Don't ever force a guy to tell you, No. If it's really important to you and you might get a no, don't force the issue. Walk away."

—Houston Oilers coach Bum Phillips

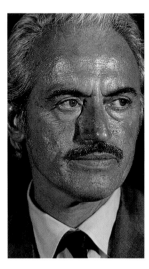

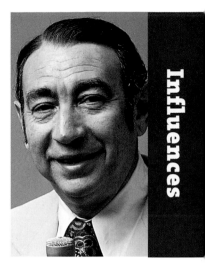

Troublemakers

When the sports explosion of the Seventies came, no man played a bigger part in it than **Marvin Miller**, executive director of the Major League Baseball Players Association.

Miller was the Moses of the baseball players union, taking a group of well-paid employees who essentially had few rights, and turning them into the most powerful union in American labor, which enjoyed what well could be the most rapid salary increases in any industry in world history.

In the mid-'70s, through his shrewd work in interpreting the contracts of Jim "Catfish" Hunter, Andy Messersmith and Dave McNally, he achieved something heretofore unknown in baseball: true free agency. The average player's salary tripled between 1976 and 1980, and by the mid-'90s, the average major leaguer was earning one million dollars a season, while the best of them were making 10 times as much. As *Sports Illustrated's* Tom Verducci wrote, "Having established for the players both purpose and freedom, [Miller] is the association's George Washington and Abraham Lincoln rolled into one."

Miller won the players' loyalty by telling them what could be. **Howard Cosell** gained his notoriety telling it like it was. While Miller was intense and private, Cosell was bombastic and self-aggrandizing, but so often he was right.

He came onto the sports world decrying the clubby collegiality of "jockspeak" and the empty platitudes of most television sportscasters. Cosell was the leading force in television for covering sports as news—as part of the world, not divorced from it. For his efforts, he often upstaged the event he was covering, and in a *TV Guide* poll in the mid-'70s, he was voted at once the most-liked and least-liked sportscaster in the country. His presence turned *Monday Night Football* from a novelty into an event, making the unlikeliest of sports announcers a prime-time star.

"In a country that has been shot through with perjury at the highest level, Cosell maintains a blunt and frequently painful honesty that is all the more shocking because it comes in the otherwise bland arena of sports," wrote Robert Daley in *The New York Times Magazine* in 1974. "He persistently infuriates those who think sports and religion are the same, and he defies those who advocate blandness in TV journalism."

What Miller and Cosell shared in common was the belief that sports shouldn't only reflect America but lead it, serving a small model for a country trying to live up to its ideals.

TOP OF THE NEWS: As Watergate unravels a presidency, the old rules of professional sports are falling apart. Both baseball and football stage major work stoppages, and by the end of the decade, a few players are true free agents, and some of them have become millionaires.

Reading List

It is, arguably, the true golden era for sports journalism. Within a five-year period, from 1970-74, there is Dan Jenkins' best-selling novel *Semi-Tough*; Jim Bouton's locker-room tell-all *Ball Four*; Roger Kahn's reminiscence of *The Boys of Summer*; Roger Angell's elegant *The Summer Game*; Robert W. Creamer's definitive biography *Babe: The Legend Comes to Life*; Robert Peterson's *Only the Ball Was White;* William Brashler's vivid novel *The Bingo Long Traveling All-Stars and Motor Kings*; Leo Durocher's autobiography *Nice Guys Finish Last*; Pete Axthelm's street basketball memoir *The City Game*; Pete Gent's gritty football novel *North Dallas Forty*; and Roy Blount, Jr.'s journal about a season with the Pittsburgh Steelers, *About Three Bricks Shy of a Load*.

The end of the decade includes a pair of worthy basketball books: Bill Bradley's ruminative *Life on the Run*, and the often acerbic *Second Wind*, by Bill Russell (and Taylor Branch). And there's a new magazine. In 1979, the Washington Post Co. tests a new monthly sports magazine, *Inside Sports*, which opens to rave reviews, but is sold off within two years of its April 1980 national launch, re-emerging in the mid-'80s with scaled-down ambitions and budget.

Movies

The first—make that only—classic hockey movie is *Slap Shot*, starring Paul Newman as Reggie Dunlop, the aging player-coach fo the Charleston Chiefs, a struggling minor-league team that seems destined for extinction at the end of the season. The profane, funny film captures the sounds and sentiments of the hockey locker room with humor and credibility, and includes terrific on-ice action, as directed by George Roy Hill (*The Sting*).

Burt Reynolds, who played football at Florida State, stars in two football films: *The Longest Yard*, about a group of prison inmates playing a team of guards; and *Semi-Tough*, Michael Ritchie's

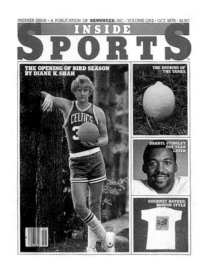

PREMIER ISSUE • A PUBLICATION OF **NEWSWEEK** INC • VOLUME ONE • OCT. 1979 • $1.50

INSIDE SPORTS

THE OPENING OF BIRD SEASON BY DIANE K. SHAH

THE SOURING OF THE YANKS

DARRYL STINGLEY ONE YEAR LATER

GOURMET HATRED, BOSTON STYLE

(extremely) loosely adapted screen version of Dan Jenkins' novel. The NFL won't authorize its teams' involvement with the making of *Semi-Tough*, but does cooperate with the makers of *Black Sunday*, a movie about terrorists who want to set off a bomb at the Super Bowl. The worst sports movie of the decade might be the tennis drama *Players*, about which the critic Leonard Maltin writes, "There's something wrong with any movie where Pancho Gonzales gives the best performance."

Fashion

The Pirates begin the decade as the first team to wear double-knit polyester uniforms, and end it sporting uniforms from a Japanese manufacturer with mix-and-match pants and jerseys that come in black, gold, white, and white with yellow pinstripes and black trim. In '71, the Orioles experiment with all-orange uniforms; in the middle of the decade, Cleveland occasionally wears all-red uniforms; and in '79, the Phillies sport—on one occasion—all-burgundy uniforms. For most teams, the default road color goes from the traditional gray to an eggshell light-blue. But none of these developments prepares anyone for the assault on the senses that the **Houston Astros** perpetrate in 1975, unveiling jer-

seys with horizontal stripes (in varying thicknesses) of orange, red and yellow.

In basketball, mod is the word. The ABA's Floridians are decked out in burnt orange and pink, and the Atlanta Hawks experiment with pea green. In the college ranks, Marquette coach Al McGuire has Jule Campbell, better known as the editor of *Sports Illustrated*'s annual swimsuit issue, design the pullover jerseys that they wear during the 1976-77 season when they win the national championship.

Politics

Jack Kemp, who starred with the Buffalo Bills in the Sixties, wins a U.S. House of Representatives seat there in 1970. In 1978, Bill Bradley wins a U.S. Senate seat in New Jersey, where he was an All-American at Princeton before playing with the New York Knicks.

Television

TV embraces tear-jerker sports stories. First there's *Brian's Song*, the story of Brian Piccolo's friendship with Gale Sayers, starring James Caan and Billy Dee Williams. *It's Good to Be Alive*, based on Roy Campanella's autobiography, premieres with Paul Winfield in the starring role. There's also *Something for Joey*, about Heisman winner John Cappelletti.

35
Consecutive games won by Toledo University, 1969-1971, whose quarterback Chuck Ealey helped lead the team to the third-longest winning streak of the century in college football, snapped in 1971 by Tampa University

3:21
Elapsed time, in hours and minutes, of the 1971 Christmas Day divisional playoff game between the Miami Dolphins and Kansas City Chiefs, which—at 82:40 of game time—was "The Longest Game Ever Played"

27
Number of wins notched by Steve Carlton for the Phillies in 1972, the most ever for a pitcher with a last-place team

Secretariat's time in winning the 1973 Kentucky Derby, still the fastest ever

$175,000,000
Cost to build Louisiana Superdome in 1975

6,856
Number of career total bases for Hank Aaron, 722 ahead of the second-highest total, by Stan Musial

26
Record number of consecutive losses suffered by the Tampa Bay Buccaneers through December 4, 1977

Playing Games

It's an interactive decade. There's the continued popularity of electric football, whose plastic-mounted players are pulled inexorably toward the center of a metallic vibrating field. **Super Toe** is all about the kicking game, coming with a set of goal posts and yardage markers. And Sure-Shot Baseball (or Hank Aaron

Baseball, in some versions) has jump ramps for the marble-sized batted ball to take off on. Then there's the simple, modern classic: Nerf ball, Nerfhoop—every bedroom is an arena.

Sounds

Anything is possible in the Seventies. The one-hit act Johnny Wakelin & The Kinshasa Band performs "Superman—Muhammad Ali," who is also celebrated in Billy Joel's "Zanzibar" ("Ali dances and the audience applauds"). Meanwhile, good ol' boy Charlie Daniels sings the praises of a racecar driver—and not even a NASCAR regular—in his Top 10 story-song "Uneasy Rider" ("Mario Andretti would have sure been proud/ of the way I was moving when I passed that crowd"). Cheech & Chong immortalize Tyrone Shoelaces and Basketball

Jones, while Frank Sinatra records the nostalgic Joe Raposo–penned "There Used to Be a Ballpark."

One of Bob Dylan's best compositions of the decade is "Hurricane," an intense 8½-minute account of the plight of middleweight contender Rubin "Hurricane" Carter, convicted of murder in New Jersey. The publicity surrounding the song raises public clamor for a retrial, but Carter is found guilty again. Twelve years later, the indictments are excused and he's finally freed.

Impressions of the '70s

From ESPN's Dan Patrick:

I grew up in the 1970s in Cincinnati, which had not yet been designated a small market. Those teams were not only a pleasure to follow, they were the last of their kind. They had Pete Rose, Joe Morgan, Johnny Bench, Tony Perez and George Foster. That's at least four Hall of Famers. When you add Dave Concepcion, Ken Griffey and the pitching staff, you have what may be the greatest National League team of all time.

In 1976, the Reds swept the Yankees to win their second World Series in a row. Later that year, the

Andy Messersmith decision made sure that a team like the Big Red Machine would never form again, especially in a town—excuse me, "market"—the size of Cincinnati. Except for Bench, all of those great Reds players eventually left for other teams, back when that was unusual for guys heading to Cooperstown.

In 1999, Ken Griffey Jr. and Alex Rodriguez have no chance of finishing their careers together as Seattle Mariners. And that's fine. Progress is progress. But I'm glad I got to see those Reds before free agency, or free-market capitalism, or whatever it was, made that kind of team impossible to keep together. Somehow I think my 1970s memories of those Reds will age better than my Floridian nephew's recollections of the 1997 Marlins.

> *"Fans are the only ones who really care. There are no free-agent fans. There are no fans who say, 'Get me out of here. I want to play for a winner.'"*
>
> **—columnist Dick Young, on modern sports**

1970 · **Monday Night Football**, as the Cleveland Browns beat Joe Namath and the New York Jets, 31-21.

1971 · **The Virginia Slims Tour**, for women tennis pros.

The Fiesta Bowl, with Arizona State beating Florida State, 45–38.

Baseball helmets required of all players.

Night baseball in the World Series, as Game 4 of the Pirates-Orioles series is broadcast in prime time.

1972 · **Freshmen in college sports**, after the NCAA rules them eligible for varsity competition.

The World Hockey Association.

1973 · **The designated hitter**, in the AL, with the Yankees' Ron Blomberg drawing a walk, the first DH plate appearance.

The National Track and Field Hall of Fame in Charleston, West Virginia

1974 · **A black manager in the major leagues**, as Frank Robinson is hired by the Cleveland Indians.

The World Football League.

The New Orleans Jazz join the NBA.

The Kansas City Scouts and **Washington Capitals** of the National Hockey League.

1975 · **EXIT** **The World Football League.**

Sudden-death overtime, for regular-season games in the NFL.

The dunk, in a popular return, to college basketball.

1976 · **EXIT** **The American Basketball Association,** when the Indiana Pacers, Denver Nuggets, San Antonio Spurs and New York Nets are absorbed into the NBA.

EXIT **The College All-Star Game in football.**

Giants Stadium, luring the New York Giants out of their own state, into New Jersey.

The Seattle Mariners and **Toronto Blue Jays**.

1977 · **The high-five,** first executed by Los Angeles outfielder Glenn Burke, who was on deck when Dusty Baker hit his 30th homer to give the Dodgers their record fourth player to reach that plateau.

Women drivers in the Indianapolis 500, when Janet Guthrie qualifies.

1978 · **Two more wild-card berths,** in the National Football League.

Indoor soccer, with the formation of the Major Soccer League.

The three-point goal in the NBA, first scored by Chris Ford of the Celtics.

1979 · **EXIT** **The WHA,** when the Winnipeg Jets, Edmonton Oilers, Hartford Whalers and Quebec Nordiques are absorbed into the NHL.

ESPN goes on the air.

THE 1980s

It was morning in America, and the decade began with a miracle in Lake Placid. Before it was over, sports fans would witness a resurrection in pro basketball and the rise of the The Great One in hockey. With America moving to more traditional values, there couldn't have been a better time to celebrate the grit and persistence of baseball's most revered throwback, the hard-charging man chasing Ty Cobb's record. But upward mobility and material consumption carried a price, and no one would pay for it more dearly than the man they called Charlie Hustle.

The Price You Pay

G REED IS GOOD. GREED "WORKS." Gordon Gekko said it in *Wall Street*. But Pete Rose lived it every day. At first he thrived on that unconscious motto. Eventually he overdosed on it. Ultimately he fell from grace because of it.

When the 1980s began, Rose was a flawed but powerfully appealing man. By decade's end—after glory, wealth, dishonor, addiction to gambling, five months in jail, and lifetime banishment from baseball—he hardly seemed a human being at all but, rather, a symbol of his era, as well as a victim of it.

Rose was greedy for everything. He wanted to get more hits, have more World Series rings, make more money, be more famous, have more women, win more bets, stiff more bookies, tell more jokes, have more clubhouse buddies, and just generally have more fun than any full-grown kid on the planet. With a roll of $100 bills big enough to choke a racehorse stuffed in the pocket of his skintight polyester slacks, the guy with the square head and the Prince Valiant haircut basically got everything he ever lusted for. Sadly, nobody ever told Pete the corollary to "Greed works." Greed is hollow.

For more than 30 years, the world not only indulged, but encouraged Rose in his protracted pursuits of teenage kicks. Everything that was most delightfully bumptious, funny, and generous about him was praised in headlines. He was all that. Everything that was overbearing, undereducated, dishonest, and comically nouveau riche usually received a wink and a laugh.

After all, somebody has to live in the biggest god-awful tract mansion in that gated,

PREVIOUS PAGES
In his Element.
Rose never seemed more at home than when he was on the job, wearing his Reds helmet.

Rose Is a Red.
"He is Cincinnati," said Sparky Anderson upon Rose's return to the Reds in 1984. "He's a Red."

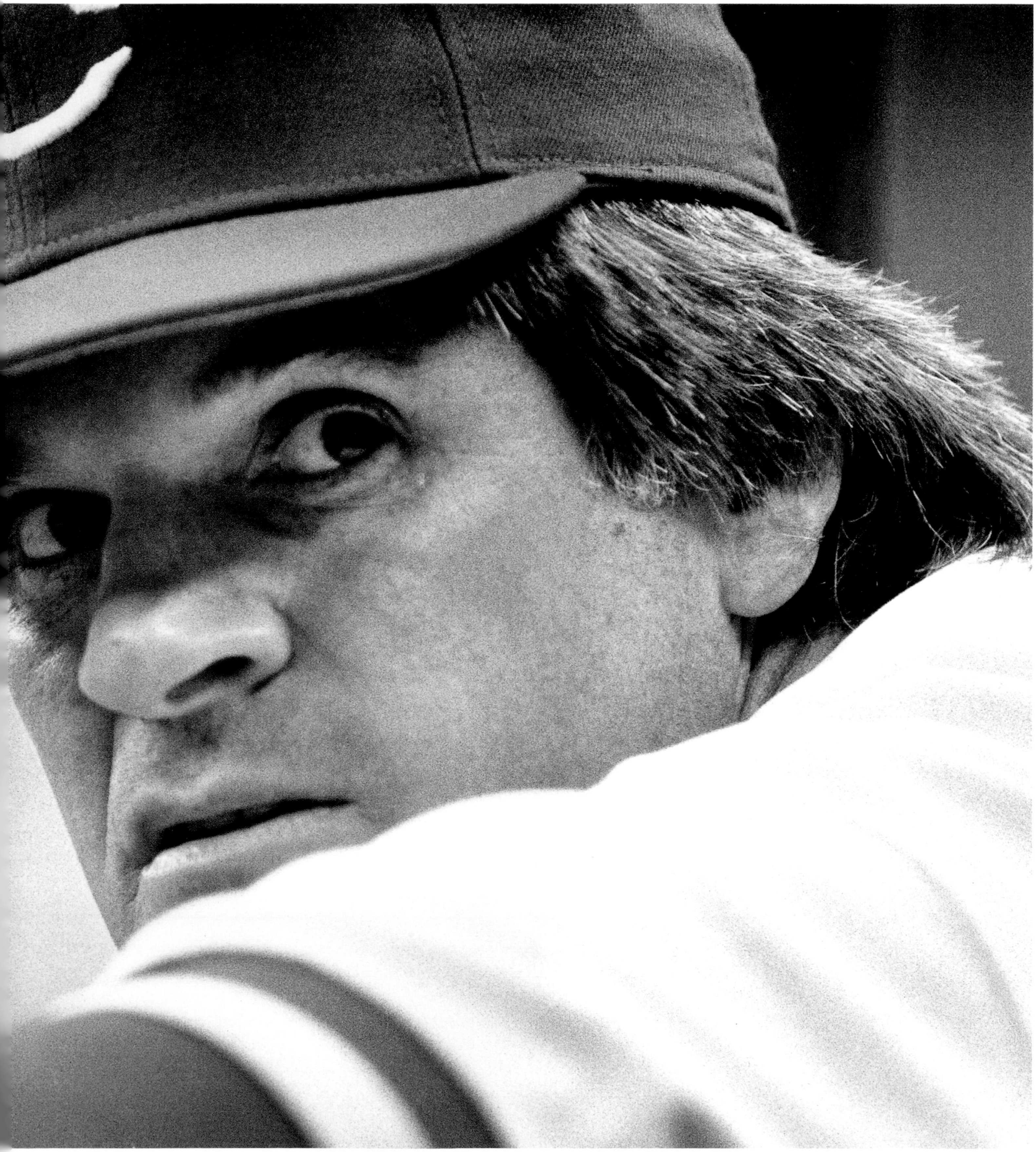

treeless "community" on American Dream Drive. Somebody somewhere has to believe the boy with the most toys and the girl with the biggest breasts is the winner. Why not Pete? When he was finally taken to jail, the photo caption might as well have said, "Arrested Adolescence."

Perhaps no athlete could have encapsulated the immaturity, energy, charm, excess, conspicuous consumption and corrupted innocence of the decade more than the ballplayer known as Charlie Hustle; for Rose was truly the king of the hustlers—in the best and worse sense.

Hit Men.
Rose with, from left, Bobby Tolan, Johnny Bench and Alex Johnson in 1969, when all were hitting above .300. "He seems to have an obligation to hit," said Lou Brock.

ON THE FIELD, he dealt in the most solid currency—true, hard-won accomplishment. In uniform, he knew who he was. Every word that left his mouth was rich with authority and identity. Off the field, he was often lost, secretly lonely, and surrounded by sycophant losers. Gambling became the metaphor for a counterfeit private life. Away from baseball, he progressively became addicted to the thrill of something-for-nothing in a sleazy wise-guy demimonde where nothing, ultimately, meant anything.

Did Rose mimic his age or, as it sometimes seemed, was he actually a step ahead of his time, even in his vices? What is a manager who gambles on his own team if not the baseball equivalent of an inside trader? Once, Rose gave every Reds coach a truck as a postseason gift. Ah, trickle-down economics.

Who but a Master of the Universe would give his mistress a necklace inscribed, "To My Rookie of the Year"? As for paying all his taxes: Come on, man, who pays taxes on an autograph show? But then, until Rose and his ilk came along, who'd have been crass enough to charge kids for an autograph?

Whatever his sins, Rose will always be one of the most largely drawn figures that his sport has ever seen. Eventually Rose will probably be pinned to the wall of baseball history—like some rare bug in a museum—by three sharp-pointed facts, none of them as solidly unequivocal as they appear at first glance.

First, in 24 seasons, an All-Star at four different positions, he had more base hits than any player ever, breaking Ty Cobb's record of 4,191 in 1985 and finishing with 4,256. That's not quite an accurate picture of Rose the player. He was great, but never close to the greatest of his time. Singles-hitting leadoff men who lack speed and have no true defensive position are not the highest form of baseball life. Once, asked if he belonged on an All-Time baseball team, Rose said, "Yeah. I'm the utility man."

Next, three years after retiring, this player who had symbolized the sport for years was banished from the game and kept out of the Hall of Fame, perhaps forever. According to the commissioner of baseball, Rose had broken the number-one taboo in his sport: gambling on the game itself, including his own team's games. That's not quite the whole picture, either. Was he an out-of-control, over-his-head-in-debt habitual gambler? Absolutely. Were several of his friends crooks, drug dealers and almost comical small-time thugs? Yup. Did he gamble on baseball? Very likely. Did he bet as much as $2,000 a game on his Reds (always to win, never to lose)? Probably. But did the Dowd Report absolutely prove he bet on *baseball*? Maybe not quite.

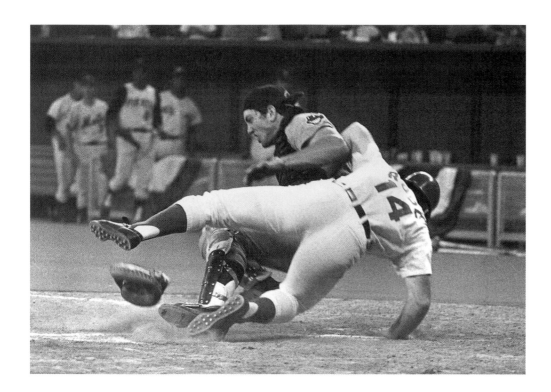

F INALLY, IN 1990, THE HIT KING WAS SENT TO JAIL for tax evasion, just like Al Capone. Even that put the worst face on Rose's misdeeds. The income on which he ducked paying taxes was only about three percent of his total income. He'd *paid* 12 times as much as he avoided. How does that level of deceit compare to the national average? How many corporate raiders of the Eighties never served a day for shenanigans that scammed millions and got thousands fired? Of course, by the time Rose got caught, the public was ready to see somebody get roasted on their own bonfire of the vanities.

Rose's worst punishment, however, is that our appreciation of him as a person and ballplayer is likely to fade, perhaps even disappear, with time. Shoeless Joe Jackson has been compressed by the decades into five words: "Say it ain't so, Joe." Rose is such a convenient caricature of the Eighties that we may misplace the person underneath the records and the scandals.

Under the pressure of society-wide disgrace, that person may no longer exist. But he did once. Forget for a moment the lost soul of the Dowd Report. Instead, remember the man who knew exactly who he was from the instant he walked through the door marked "Players Entrance" until he left it once again. Rose would not evoke such sad memories now if, once, he had not stood for so much that was full of life.

Pete Rose was part of the *best* of his time, too. Oh, how he sold it. And we were ready to buy.

In the 1980s, Rose was an incessant focus of national attention, a symbol of American heroism, an ambassador for his sport, a one-man traveling show of capitalist self-promotion and, in the end, the ultimate poster boy for self-delusion, self-indulgence and self-destruction.

In the 1960s and 1970s, he was mostly just a helluva ballplayer.

For the first 16 seasons, and 3,164 hits, of his career, Rose played for his home-

Charlie Hustle.
Barreling into Ray Fosse
for the winning run in
the 1970 All-Star Game.

Key Cogs in the Machine. With Joe Morgan in the Reds' locker room in 1976. "The standard-issue white hero, Johnny Bench, never joined their inner circle of 'outsider' coolness."

town Reds. From his first day, veterans on his own Reds despised him. Who runs to first base on a walk? Only a showboat who's trying to attract attention to himself. That's not hustle. It's what baseball has always called "false hustle." Of course, in the Eighties, copping an edgy attitude that gained you credit for absolutely everything you did, even leaving the bat on your shoulder for ball four, suddenly fell under a new modern rubric: marketing.

Fans in opposing cities booed him, too.

Interestingly, only blacks on the Reds befriended Rose in his early years. He never forgot it. His rapport with African-American and Latin-American players was absolutely genuine. He, along with Joe Morgan and Tony Perez, were the emotional core of the Reds, while the standard-issue white hero, Johnny Bench, never joined their inner circle of "outsider" coolness.

In his prime, which lasted from 1963 through 1979, Rose slashed the ball to every corner of the park from both sides of the plate. From a crouched, defiant stance, Rose would glare at the pitcher while screwing his batting helmet down on his head as though twisting a grapefruit on an old-fashioned juicer. Though he always bragged about being "the first $100,000 singles hitter," Rose actually had almost exactly 60 extra-base hits every season, and sometimes as many as 16 home runs.

As for Rose's defense, it was much like his managing in the late Eighties. No one remembers it. He was functional, adequate and nondescript—except for that attitude thing. As a first baseman, after catching the routine third-out throw, Rose punctuated thousands of meaningless innings with a feisty, swaggering spike of the ball back toward the mound. The gesture seemed to say, "Take that, foul foes." Or "Well done, my teammates." In retrospect, it seems to say, "Look at me."

B Y THE TIME ROSE FINISHED HIS FIRST TOUR in Cincinnati after the 1978 season, he was an apparent lock on the Hall of Fame and a central historical place as the leadoff man on perhaps the greatest team ever (the 1975 Reds). When free agency finally arrived in 1976, it seemed as if Rose had spent his whole life preparing for just such a bidding contest for himself.

On the first day of spring training in 1979, the Philadelphia Phillies gathered to begin their 96th consecutive season without a World Series title. They were also about to start their first season with Pete Rose. It wouldn't take them long to find out why he—more than Tony Perez, Joe Morgan, or Johnny Bench—had been at the emotional core of the Big Red Machine in Cincinnati which won four National League pennants in the Seventies.

Larry Bowa, Philadelphia's scrawny, scrappy shortstop, assumed he'd be the initial Phil to walk through the clubhouse door. That was his badge of pride. Since the day Rose signed, the two players had bragged about who'd show up in Clearwater first. After all, Rose considered himself the all-time hardworking, hard-nosed, run-to-first-base-on-a-walk overachiever.

Both men had been together in Las Vegas, but Bowa returned to Florida early to make sure he'd keep his word. At midnight, just hours before the Clearwater gates were scheduled to open, Bowa got a call from Rose, who was in Vegas. "You win. You'll be there before me," said Rose over the phone as the slot machines jangled as background music.

When Bowa wandered into the Phils' deserted clubhouse at 7:40 A.M.—twenty minutes earlier than ever, just to make sure—who was standing by Bowa's locker, all dressed in new Phillie garb, but a red-eyed, grinning Rose.

"Jesus, it ain't fair," wailed Bowa.

Rose had grabbed an all-night nonstop flight from Vegas to Tampa, landing, as Rose put it, "about two minutes late, at 5:23 A.M. I figured I'd wander out to the park…didn't have nothin' else to do."

That day, the Phils clubhouse was reborn. Within an hour, Bowa had figured out his retaliation. He got the Phils' fitness wizard, huge Gus Hoefling, to get Rose in a wrestler's throat hold. "That's it," cheeped Bowa. "Turn the son of a bitch into an $800,000-a-year vegetable."

Childishness, camaraderie, obsession with success, and a certain level of what-the-hell recklessness are absolutely essential to most great baseball teams. Rose took the locker room—the locker room of a relentless, driven champion—with him everywhere he went. It was the only tone of voice, the only stance toward work and toward other people, which he understood. And he understood it perfectly. That's why he

Always On the Go. His trademark headfirst slide. "If you play an aggressive, hustling game, it forces your opponents into errors," he said. "It helps you at every level but is perhaps most important when you get to the majors. The good major league teams don't make many mistakes, so by playing aggressively you've got a much better chance to make the error happen."

played in six World Series. And that's why he had a record of which he was even prouder than his 4,256 hits.

"I've played in more winning games than any player in history," he told me. "It's not in the record book. I figured it out myself."

"Pete Rose makes me look in the mirror," said the Phils' future Hall of Famer Mike Schmidt, who'd played most of his career on losers. "If what he's giving is a hundred percent, then my hundred percent must be coming up short."

JUST BY BEING HIMSELF, usually at full volume, Rose defined a whole jock ethos. Everything—from the way he negotiated a contract to the time of day he reported for work to the kind of jokes he told—defined an approach to baseball. It was also a proven Winner's Way, as he'd be glad to tell you.

Hard as it may be to realize now, the America of 20 years ago was intoxicated by that single word—winner. We'd lost in Vietnam, humiliated ourselves in Watergate, and watched as inflation-adjusted returns in the stock market went down by more than 50 percent over the previous dozen years. In many ways, Americans felt humbled and poor—unaccustomed emotions. Rose was the delicious antithesis of all that "malaise." He was the old, tough, self-reliant, potent American prototype who scattered infielders like candlepins. Rose knew he had something to sell.

On that February day when Rose became a Phillie, he had recently signed the biggest free agent contract in baseball history ($3.2 million for four years) despite being 37 years old. Soon every free agent would understand how to play this coast-to-coast game of Up the Ante. But Rose was the first athlete to master it. In each town Rose played one team off against the others, saying how much he'd love to be a (fill in the name of your favorite team). Of course, being a businessman, he'd just have to take the high bid. How could you ask him to do otherwise? But, remember, deep down, he'd really *love* to be a …

This modus operandi, devoid of any sense of corporate or civic loyalty, became standard operating procedure throughout much of America in the Eighties. The hot "talent," from Wall Street to Silicon Valley, went to the high bidder with the best stock option plan and the most executive perks. Perhaps Rose helped set that tone of unashamed self-interest. Just as American companies had never apologized for enormous profits, Rose showed the line of reasoning that a successful employee could use to wrest a salary that had heretofore been considered almost obscene.

"If you always give your best, then, hell, man, you deserve what you get. Go ahead and enjoy it," said Rose in his tasseled Gucci loafers, open-neck silk shirt, gold medallion, diamond-studded Rolex, and collar-length hair.

Finally Rose chose the Phillies, bragging, "I got so much money that if you stacked up all the cash, a show horse couldn't jump over it." Why Philadelphia? "If I can win the World Series for the *Phillies,* I can do *anything,*" he said.

One year later, in 1980, the Phils did indeed win the first World Series in their history.

In baseball, at least, the winner-take-all culture was already being born. Who cared if Merv Rettenmund had to pinch-hit for the minimum salary? Or got released if he asked for a raise? Not Pete. Did Merv lead the league in hits? Did he put the fannies in the seats? Hell, no. Pete did. So pay up.

The Hit King. Celebrating with Reds owner Marge Schott, above, after the record-breaking hit, right, against the Padres in 1985. "I'm just like everybody else," he'd taken to saying. "I have two arms, two legs and 4,000 hits."

The Promised Land.
Joining the Philadelphia Phillies, he led them to their first world championship in their 97 seasons of existence. Slugger Mike Schmidt called him "the most likable arrogant person I've ever met."

Yet Rose, to his credit, was also an almost ideal teammate—as long as you remembered that Pete was the superstar and that, ultimately, any locker room banter could be settled with a joke about the size of his wallet. No rookie's problem was too small for him to hear. No player knew the first names of more groundskeepers around the league. "Pete prefers the little people," said his manager Sparky Anderson.

By the late Seventies, all Rose's hard work and open-handedness toward any player who needed help—be it with cash or a batting tip—seemed to come back to him like bread on the water. When he got his 3,000th hit in 1978, then followed it up with a 44-game hitting streak later that summer, Rose had reached icon status, even among other veteran players.

While Rose respected baseball's "little people" and showed them both deference and, often, real concern, he definitely did not want to be one of them himself. Rose loved a world of double standards for superstars. At Studio 54, the velvet ropes were dropped for the cool dudes and the hot chicks. Special rules for special people. Pete grasped the Eighties code perfectly: Close the deal, get the perks. And no questions asked.

"The Reds have covered up scrapes for Pete his whole career," Orioles general manager Hank Peters once told me, long before Rose's image was tarnished. "He's always been in some little jam…but people never seem to hold it against him." Would such trivialities have been held against John Merriweather at Salomon Brothers? In Liar's Poker, did anybody ever call Pete's bluff?

As his fame grew, Rose began to assume that he could get away with anything as long as he did it with Pete Rose insouciance. One day at the White House, Rose smuggled in a "Hustle Makes It Happen" T-shirt and a bottle of "Pete!" chocolate drink to give to President Jimmy Carter, as well as a $9.95 Pete Rose watch for first daughter, Amy. Before Carter could utter two sentences, Pete had handed him the cheap watch.

"We thought we'd frisked Pete at the door," an aide told me, mentioning the T-shirt and chocolate drink. "But he had the watch in his side pocket."

P ERHAPS THE WORST BREAK OF ROSE'S CAREER was the peculiar *timing* of his popularity. Between 1965 and 1979, he was truly a great player, hitting .300 on 14 occasions in those 15 seasons and getting 200 hits 10 times. He led the league in either batting average, hits, doubles, or runs scored 17 times. He did it all while switching from second base to the outfield to third base to first base. Wherever the team needed him, that was the position he played.

Yet, superb as he was, Rose was never beloved until he got old. As his baseball skills inevitably eroded, his social polish, humor, and salesmanship improved. Once hated by many fans as a burr-cut redneck hard-ass who sometimes played dirty, Rose gradually became the Symbol of the Game. By 1975, he was *Sports Illustrated*'s Sportsman of the Year. (The runner-up was O.J. Simpson.) In 1978, Rose's hitting streak put him in the national spotlight every day for two weeks. Helping the Phils to the Series in 1980 and '83 solidified his status. But the ultimate sanitizing and glorification of Rose did not reach its apotheosis until 1985 when he became the Hit King.

Press, players, fans—we were all guilty of aiding and abetting Rose in losing his grip on reality. The common sense and modesty that most people have had beaten into them in their 20s, and which even haughty ballplayers gain in their 30s as they lose their skills, Rose was able to postpone indefinitely. At ages when players traditionally gain humility, Rose was learning pride.

Often Pete was so perfect, even in his brazen imperfections, that we couldn't resist him. Why even try? He was that rarest celebrity—someone absolutely authentic. No amount of native craftiness or self-promoting guile could have led him to the tone of voice—perfect baseball pitch—that inhabited every quote that came out of his mouth.

Once, at his daily streak press conference, Rose suddenly volunteered: "After I catch Wee Willie Keeler, I gotta pass Sidney Stonestreet. You know, he hit in 48 straight. Betcha never heard of Sidney Stonestreet. That's 'cause I just made him up. He played for the Rhode Island Reds in the Chicken Coop league. With a name like that, I figure he musta been an old-timer. I gotta have something between Keeler and DiMaggio to shoot for, and I think Ol' Sidney's gonna be a lotta help."

We'll never know whom Rose would have invented with an unknown 51-game hitting streak. What details of Stonestreet's life would Pete have concocted? My guess was that Sidney'd have a third gonad.

The Manager. Even on the bench, he had a thirst for action. After allegations of betting came out, he said, "I'd be willing to bet you, if I was a betting man, that I have never bet on baseball."

The next day, Rose quipped, "They say the odds are 91-to-1 on me catching DiMag. Anybody know how I can get a bet down on me?" Not 90-to-1, mind you, but 91-to-1—the *real* odds. Straight from a bookie?

More than any of our games, in baseball we see the players' faces every day. Because we've heard or read their words for years, we feel we know them like family. So we care. We can't help it. After so many seasons, nobody felt as much like old-shoe family as Pete.

The night his streak was stopped, he ripped two line drives at Atlanta third baseman Bob Horner. As he jogged past the rookie, Rose cracked, "Kid, will you go some place? I ain't learned to curve 'em around you yet."

After the game was done and the streak dead, Rose showed a sense of loss only once. "I wanted to see what it would have been like to get up in the Fifties. Not so much to break DiMaggio's record but just for the experience, just to know the feeling."

Finally, long after the game, at two o'clock in the morning, Rose was drowning his sorrows—with a glass of milk at an all-night lunch counter with a half dozen fans. Rose was up, demonstrating plays from the game. "So that's Pete Rose," said one middle-aged man. "My God, he's just like he seems. Now, that's a star."

Nobody loved that word *star* more than Rose. He poured himself into the role, as though his barely formed soul were a liquid that could take the reassuringly solid shape of that five-pointed vessel.

ROSE'S "MATERIAL BOY" VIEW OF THE WORLD was widely held, though sometimes it dressed in more respectable intellectual garb. For example, Edward Bennett Williams, owner of the Orioles and perhaps the most famous trial lawyer in the country, called this approach "competition living." Everything was a game. You played your hardest, win or lose, whether the arena was a courtroom, national politics (where Williams was a prominent Democrat), or the ball field. Then, for an encore, you did it all over again. Sisyphus might shake his head—if his neck weren't too stiff from pushing that rock up the hill every day.

For Rose and Williams—and millions of others Americans, it often seemed— there was nothing better than The Game. Sometimes, there was nothing *except* the game. Under all the Eighties striving there often seemed to lurk a profound shallowness, a lack of imagination, a desperate need to fill time with tangible accomplishments. Even the term *trophy wife* was born.

Perhaps nothing frightened the Competition Liver more than the end of the game; the thought of retirement was, in a way, worse than the idea of death itself. To keel over on the job—what was so bad about that? When Oriole manager Earl Weaver retired voluntarily as the age of 53, Williams was stupefied. How could a man who was still hailed as the best manager in the sport simply quit? Why? Because, Weaver said, he had enough money not to work. That was why. He preferred to play golf with his friends, have dinners with his wife, visit his grandchildren, grow his tomatoes, and "watch the sun go down, but not always behind the left-field fence."

For Rose, like Williams, who died in harness, hollowed out by cancer but billing hours to the last, the idea of the Last Game was profoundly disturbing. If you live for the Action, what must the thought of a lifetime of relative inaction do to the gears of your nature? One day Rose gazed at the field during batting practice. Then in his mid-40s and still playing almost every day, he'd achieved a sublime

The Verdict.
Bart Giamatti, delivering the news of Rose's lifetime ban, which he called "the sad end of a sorry episode. One of the game's greatest players has engaged in a variety of acts which have stained the game, and he must now live with the consequences of those acts."

weatherbeaten ugliness. The wrinkles in his face were so deep that the sweat, when it poured down, looked like the rain running down the bark of a tree. Pete, what are you looking at so hard?

"The older you get, the days are coming to an end, so you want to enjoy them," he said. "You can't bear to give one away…not even one…. Everything's real vivid these days. I kind of look at things from the inside and the outside at the same time."

Perhaps a wise person would have seen Rose's problems coming that very day, that minute. After he finally caught Ty Cobb—after no team wanted him anymore, his crowd-drawing appeal dissipated—what was he going to do with Time? Where would he find his Action?

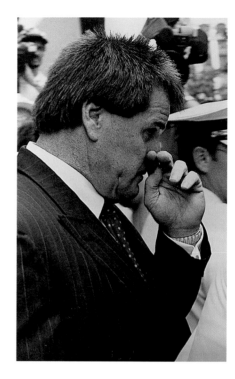

A CTUALLY, ROSE'S OLD FRIENDS, like Sparky Anderson, could tell you. Pete would be at the racetrack more and more. Or watching sports on TV, deeper and deeper into the night. The devil must have invented cable TV with Rose specifically in mind. It let him watch games and place bets virtually around the clock. And it helped prevent his active mind from ever alighting on a thought, a book, or an aspiration that was not connected to sports.

Rose's greatest night and his worst were perhaps the same: September 11, 1985. That evening he finally caught Cobb. In retrospect, it's also the precise moment when the rest of his life began to look as empty of goals, as bereft of suitable consuming competitions, as it had looked rich previously. When his sliced single into left field landed on the crappy old fake turf of Riverfront Stadium, Rose went from having a sublime, energizing, almost superhuman quest to having no quest at all.

Perhaps, as he stood on first base and cried, he knew that what he'd termed the Big Knock was actually the end of something. "I cried when my father died and tonight," said Rose, who adored his tough jock dad and modeled his whole youth around pleasing his old man, who actually died young, barely in his 40s.

"I looked up in the sky and started thinking about my father. I thought I saw him there. And right behind him was Ty Cobb," said Rose, quickly sensing how to turn the sentimental, sappy moment into another marketable Rose quip. "Regardless of what you think, Ty *is* up there."

Sometimes, the quotes in baseball are almost too prescient to credit. After his 4,192nd hit, Rose was asked to sum up his feelings. He could have turned the question any way he saw fit. Yet he chose to comment on his whole future, as though he'd already anticipated it. "A lot of people will remember me for tonight," he said. "There are a lot of things you can remember me for, not all of them good. You can remember me for a divorce…for a paternity suit. I know what I've accomplished. I really can't worry about it."

After that, the ride was downhill for Rose. He probably knew it would be. His gambling and his debts had been growing for years. After his divorce from his first wife, Karolyn, in 1980, the people who surrounded him were often trash. Was he punishing himself for squandering the love of a woman who was often referred to as "the best thing that ever happened to Pete"?

Perhaps, to a certain temperament, Rose's frightening descent might seem as fascinating as the upward arc of his career. In a letter, John Keats once wrote, "What shocks the virtuous philosopher delights the chameleon Poet. It does no harm from

The Aftermath.
In 1990, after being sentenced on tax evasion charges. "I am very shameful to be here today in front of you," he told the judge. "I lost my dignity, I lost my self-respect, I lost a lot of dear fans and almost lost some very dear friends."

Local Hero. Though public sentiment across the country was turning against Rose, some fans in Cincinnati remained blindly loyal.

its relish of the dark side of things any more than from its taste for the bright one."

Perhaps the public has relatively little of that amoral chameleon Poet in its disposition. Seven months of headlines, followed by tawdry details about Rose's gambling problem, were enough to sate almost everyone. Who was really surprised? Rose had always been so open about his tacky tastes.

For 30 years America had cheered Rose for remaining childlike. He was selfish but charming. Vain but joyous. Shallow but shrewd. Crude but funny. Prone to the vices but honest about it. Oblivious to society's conventions but also mythically large. Why would a common man—given such overwhelming behavioral reinforcement by the public— ever change?

We celebrate heroes when they accomplish tasks that demand that they go beyond normal human limits. Then we are shocked when they act as though normal human limits do not apply to their private conduct. "I can, because I'm different." Won't those same words—full of hubris—tempt a person into mischief on a hundred other occasions?

Sadly for Rose, his final act of the decade was a quintessential Eighties turn: the addict in denial. Everybody in America seemed to know what was happening to Rose except Pete himself. He alone didn't get it.

Baseball wanted Rose to confess. To everything. Then the game could forgive him. It was that simple. Admit your problem. Get kicked out of the sport for a while. Get yourself fixed. Get reinstated. Why, baseball had so many reformed cocaine addicts in the Eighties that they could probably have formed a team in each league. Then, no doubt, they'd have met in the Series. Confession, tears, and rehabilitation were practically a national agenda.

But Rose couldn't admit his problem. He lied to investigators, stonewalled and threatened legal action. He played it like Don Corleone. So baseball got tough right back. Rose wasn't bigger than the game. He had to lose.

Finally, a deal was struck. Rose signed an agreement which "permanently bans him from baseball." In return, baseball did not reach any formal finding that Rose had bet on baseball games—despite a 225-page report with seven volumes of added material. In short, Rose signed away his future so that he did not have to face his problem, fix it, or admit what it had led him to do.

"The banishment for life of Pete Rose from baseball is the sad end of a sorry episode," said comissioner Bart Giamatti, a former president of Yale. "One of the game's greatest players has engaged in a variety of acts which have stained the game, and he must now live with the consequences of those acts....There is absolutely no deal for reinstatement. That is *exactly* what we did *not* agree to." Then, in what Rose considered a profound stab in the back, Giamatti added that he personally believed Rose had bet on baseball.

B ASEBALL GOT RID OF ROSE FOREVER. All Rose got was the right to keep playing the role of the tough guy who'd beaten the rap on a technicality. "To think I'm going to be out of baseball for a very short period of time hurts," said Rose the day he was banned. The sports world shook its head in disbelief. Didn't he get it? Not then. And not now. A decade later, Rose, who has a sports radio show and owns a restaurant, is still frozen in 1989. Periodically he talks about reinstatement or the Hall of Fame. He might as well lecture the wind. Hasn't he internalized the fact yet that, a week after he was banned, Giamatti died of a heart attack?

That day Rose's chances died, too. As they probably should have. His distinction of being the only human being on baseball's "permanently ineligible" list is not about legalities or hair splitting. It's not about whose name is on what betting slip or whose testimony is truth or lies. It's about right and wrong. Rose still doesn't understand that he was wrong. And that in the broadest and deepest sense, he got what he deserved. Not for what he did. But for refusing to take responsibility and pay the price for what he did. Of course, the bookies say Rose was famous for welching on his debts.

Denial is a strange devil. A nation eventually digests its collective experience and moves on, dealing with what's best and worst in its nature and its past. Sometimes individuals can't do it. They get locked at a point in history—their own personal history—and can't get unstuck. That's Rose.

In 1997, he made the papers again. A dealer in Las Vegas accidentally gave Pete too many chips. Rose walked out and wouldn't give them back. Such unregenerate behavior is just one more illustration of why Rose evokes so much empathy, but so little sympathy.

With each passing year, most of the legends in sports—those that define an era for us—seem more vivid and valuable. They remain pertinent. With each passing year, Pete Rose makes himself seem more irrelevant. He has not moved on with us but, rather, remains an unevolved prisoner of his past.

Yes, arrested, again.

Fleeting Triumph. With Padres first baseman Steve Garvey smiling behind him, Rose responds to the Riverfront Stadium crowd after breaking Cobb's record.

WAYNE GRETZKY
The Great One

The best player in the history of hockey never looked like much of a hockey player. He was smallish (just under 6 feet, about 180 pounds), relatively weak, was never a fast skater, and lacked a powerful slapshot. Yet Wayne Gretzky, with that utterly average body, became one of the most dominant athletes in the history of North American team sports.

Statistically, his accomplishments defy the imagination: He was both the greatest passer *and* greatest goal scorer in NHL history. After 14 years in the league, he stood at the top of both the career and single-season records for goals, assists and scoring. He also won four Stanley Cups and a record nine Hart Trophies as the league's MVP. But his greatest feat, quite simply, was that he saved hockey. Gretzky joined the NHL at a time when it was without a national television contract and most of its teams were losing money; his excellence and charisma forced the sport back onto the front pages as one of the "Big Four." In the celebrity-crazed world of the Eighties and Nineties, Gretzky was nothing less than the sport's ambassador, the only face in hockey that registered outside the world of sports. The sport was uniquely blessed, in that they had a star of superhuman abilities as well as flawless character.

Growing up in Brantford, Ontario, Gretzky was skating at age two, learning the fundamentals of hockey under the keen eye of his father, Walter, a telephone repairman with Bell Canada. He built a homemade rink in his family's backyard and ran the tyke through drills before he was in preschool. "Skate to where the puck is going to be, not to where it is," Walter stressed. Wayne dominated the pee-wee ranks, left home to play for a junior-league team at 14, and in 1978, at age 17, signed a contract with the Indianapolis Racers of the World Hockey Association. Eight games into his rookie season, the struggling franchise sold his contract to the Edmonton Oilers where, despite doubts about his size, he proved an instant sensation. The next year, 1979, Edmonton was one of four franchises merged into the NHL, and Gretzky started reshaping the league. He would win the Hart Trophy in each of his first eight seasons, lead the league in scoring 10 times and top the league in assists each of his first 13 seasons. "He passes better than anybody I've ever seen," Bobby Orr said.

Snaking through defenders with a kind of slouchy elusiveness, the big Number 99 on his back exaggerating his slight frame, Gretzky proved remarkably durable. And it was in those subtle, ineffable skills—the sense of a teammate coming down the wing out of the corner of an eye, the fraction of a second the puck is on a stick blade on a touch pass,

GRETZKY: "SKATE TO WHERE THE PUCK IS GOING TO BE, NOT TO WHERE IT IS."

MONTANA: THAT HARD GLEAM OF INDOMITABLE WILL

the silent reading of a carom that would leave a defender flailing helplessly—that set Gretzky apart.

"He has an enormous sense of patience," said the Canadiens' great goaltender, Ken Dryden. "Everybody has a moment of panic, but Gretzky's comes so much later than other players'. When he comes down the ice, there's a point when the defenseman thinks: He's going to commit himself one way or the other now. When that moment passes and Gretzky still hasn't committed, the whole rhythm of the game is upset, and suddenly a player becomes open who wasn't open a moment before."

After winning the four Stanley Cups in Edmonton, he was traded to the Los Angeles Kings in 1988, and helped hockey break through to the Sun Belt and West Coast. After a brief stint in St. Louis, he went to the New York Rangers before the 1996-97 season. A year later, he accumulated his 1,851st assist, which meant that even if Gretzky had never scored a goal, he'd still be the league's all-time leading scorer. At age 38, in 1999, he recorded five assists in a game. When he retired at the end of the season with 2,857 career points, the NHL retired the No. 99 with him.

"Gretzky sees a picture out there that no one else sees," said Bruin executive Harry Sinden. "It's difficult to describe, because I've never seen the game he's looking at."

JOE MONTANA
State of Grace

In Joe Montana's ice-blue eyes there was a calmly sinister resolve that went beyond *cool*. It was the implacable stare borne of a lifetime of being told he wasn't good enough. Great quarterbacks who've been discarded or treated disrespectfully early in their careers (Hall of Famers Johnny Unitas and Len Dawson also fit the description) emerge with that hard gleam of indomitable will, a grace under pressure that can seem eerie to opponents and teammates alike. "It's almost like he does it in the third person," said teammate Randy Cross. That composure helped make Montana the best quarterback of his generation.

Though he lacked the chiseled physique and cannon arm of the prototype passers of the era, Montana won a national championship at Notre Dame and four Super Bowls for the San Francisco 49ers. After 13 seasons with the 49ers and two more with the Kansas City Chiefs, he retired with the highest passing-efficiency rating and lowest interception percentage in NFL history. But he would be best remembered for his otherworldly cool in the most pressing moments of the biggest games. "He's got this resourcefulness, this something that's hard to put into words," said his coach, Bill Walsh. "He won't choke. Or rather, if he ever does, you'll know everyone else came apart first."

That special quality—later dubbed "Montana Magic"—was there for everyone to see at an early age. Growing up in the coal town of Monongahela, Pennsylvania, he threw three perfect games in Little League baseball, and received a basketball scholarship offer from North Carolina State. Instead, he chose Notre Dame, where he worked his way up from the seventh-string quarterback on the depth chart, gaining a reputation for impossible comebacks and leading the Irish to the 1977 national title.

But Montana's "measurables" were inferior, and so scouts graded him down in the 1979 NFL draft. At just over six feet, 197 pounds, he appeared spindly, couldn't throw the deep ball well and couldn't even manage a spiral on his short passes. But San Francisco, where Walsh was constructing an innovative controlled passing attack, chose him in the third round, the 82nd pick in the draft. In his second year, Montana won the starting job; in his third, 1981, he toppled the team of the 1970s, the Dallas Cowboys, with his off-balance touchdown throw to Dwight Clark to win the NFC championship game. Two weeks later, Montana won the first of his four Super Bowls.

Montana's most memorable performance came in Super Bowl XXIII, the one title game in which he didn't win the MVP (it went to Jerry Rice, who caught 11 of Montana's passes for 215 yards). Trailing the Bengals 16–13, the 49ers got the ball on their own 8-yard line with 3:10 left. "I heard somebody screaming, 'We got 'em!'" recalled Bengals reciever Cris Collinsworth. "I yelled, 'Will you see if Number 16 is in the huddle?' He said, 'Yeah.' I said, 'Then we haven't got 'em.'"

His 1993 exit from San Francisco was bittersweet, but his final two years for the Chiefs showed that he still had that touch. Even at the end, opponents were still marveling at his steely resilience. "Joe Montana is not human," said Collinsworth. "I don't want to call him a god, but he's definitely somewhere in between."

CARL LEWIS
The Athlete

LEWIS: "HE WAS THE BABE RUTH AND MICHAEL JORDAN OF OUR SPORT"

With four gold medals around his neck and all his challengers spectacularly vanquished, Carl Lewis must have felt a little like Alexander the Great as he looked down at the mere mortals surrounding his perennial perch at the top of the awards podium at the 1984 Olympics in Los Angeles. Lewis, who had run faster and leapt farther than any human on the planet, appeared to have no more worlds to conquer as his only true competition was gravity and time itself. So, the supremely confident Lewis set out to defy both the pull of the earth and the tick of the clock. And he did.

Lewis was quite simply the greatest track & field athlete of all time. "He was the Babe Ruth and Michael Jordan of our sport," proclaimed Pete Cava of the U.S. Track Federation. Lewis won gold medals in four Olympics, and might have won five without the American boycott of the 1980 Games. When he overcame all odds to win his final medal at age 35, he had earned 10 Olympic medals, nine of which were gold.

His success between Olympics was just as overwhelming, as he also served as a high-profile catalyst for the advent of a modern golden age of track & field. "You always tried harder when Carl was competing," said sprinter Leroy Burrell. "Part of it was the natural urge to win, but a lot of it was because you didn't want to get embarrassed."

Despite the medals he won and records he set in running events, Lewis regarded sprinting as just a way to improve his long jumping—as if it needed improvement. Beginning in 1981, Lewis amassed 65 consecutive long-jump victories, going a full decade without losing. When he added the 1988 long jump Olympic gold medal to his collection, it was the first time anyone had successfully defended the title. That achievement soon paled in importance, as Lewis repeated the feat in 1992 at Seoul and again in 1996 in Atlanta.

His outspoken nature, incessant self-promotion and flamboyant yet very private personal life set Lewis apart. It also undermined his efforts to achieve in his home country the pervasive popularity he enjoyed internationally. Maligned and misunderstood, often with transparent malice, Lewis nevertheless insisted on doing things his own way. Lewis stayed clean in a dirty sport, even when the chemically enhanced Ben Johnson taunted him in temporary victory, and made himself the first great athlete of the new era of open professionalism in track & field. "He had to invent what a professional track & field athlete is," said Olympic high jumper Dwight Stones, adding "the person who tries to invent something invariably gets a lot of heat for it."

But Lewis' ultimate invention was himself. And anyone who witnessed the incredible rush of the finely focused and perfectly tuned Lewis in full stride, eyes fixed on a record-breaking horizon, couldn't help but agree with his University of Houston coach Tom Tellez, who said, "He's the greatest athlete I've ever seen."
—*Michael Point*

EARVIN "MAGIC" JOHNSON
The Star of Showtime

JOHNSON: HE "TURNED THE CITY GAME INTO PART OF THE CULTURE OF MIDDLE AMERICA"

When Earvin "Magic" Johnson dribbled out of Michigan State and into the Los Angeles Lakers' backcourt, he began rearranging the way a basketball team looks and plays, removing the distinctions between positions. At 6-foot-9-inches, he was basketball's first triple threat—the tallest man ever to play point guard in the NBA, yet with skills so diverse that he also worked at forward and center.

When Johnson arrived in 1979, most fans viewed the NBA as a collection of individualists straight off the playground. But Magic changed all that. High-stepping downcourt on a fast break, smiling all the while, he made the game more fun, more accessible than it had been in years. With a deft assist from his rival Larry Bird, Johnson turned the city game into part of the culture of Middle America, emphasizing the timeless appeal of teamwork.

Though a great soloist, the point guard preferred to blend

in with the Lakers' accomplished "Showtime" band of stars. He made the triple-double—double-figure production in points, rebounds and assists—part of the American lexicon, achieving it 136 times in a career that yielded five NBA titles for the Lakers during the 1980s. He was so versatile that when teammate Kareem Abdul-Jabbar missed Game 6 of the 1980 NBA Finals against Philadelphia, the rookie filled in at center with 42 points, 15 rebounds and seven assists, carrying off the Finals MVP trophy and the title in what was the most memorable game of his pro career.

Johnson popularized another term—coast-to-coast—as he grabbed rebounds and dribbled to the other end for lay-ins. He made look-away passes that could slip through a knothole; spinning, juking moves while shifting the ball from hand to hand; and an almost flat-footed, shot-put jumper that looked like it belonged to the last kid picked in gym class. He also had an uncanny knack for slipping through defenses. Bird's recollection of one Johnson play evoked many others: "I can still see him in my head, coming upcourt, faking right, faking left, then pulling it back and laying it in."

Then came November 1991, when Johnson made an impact beyond the basketball court, announcing his retirement because he had tested positive for HIV, the virus which causes AIDS. In *The Fort Worth Star-Telegram*, Jim Reeves wrote, "AIDS came home to our neighborhood today. It pulled up a chair, sat down in our midst and began shaking hands." Indeed, Johnson put a celebrity's face on the virus, starting a national dialogue that would eventually lead to widespread acceptance and a greater understanding of those who live with it. NBA players who had feared their proximity to Johnson during his brief return for the All-Star Game and the Olympics in 1992 readily welcomed him during another short-lived comeback in 1996. After Johnson came back to win the MVP award at the 1992 All-Star Game, his mother, Christine, spoke up among all the hugs and said, "You don't have to be afraid of him."

—*Mark Rosner*

MARTINA NAVRATILOVA
Changing the Game

Raised on clay courts outside of Prague, her first big tennis tournament canceled on the day the Soviet tanks rolled into Czechoslovakia in 1968, a young Martina Navratilova always dreamed about a life in America.

She finally visited the States as a 16-year-old prodigy in 1973, and defected at the U.S. Open in 1975. Though she was clearly a supreme talent, Navratilova's early years were maddeningly inconsistent, marked by flashes of brilliance and stunning lapses of self-destruction. She trained poorly, relying on her natural ability to see her through, and lived on a steady diet of Big Macs and other fast food (ballooning to 167 pounds in 1976). She'd win one major, then collapse

NAVRATILOVA:
"SHE WAS GIVING
100 PERCENT
OF HERSELF TO
TENNIS"

HEIDEN:
"HE GAVE THE
MOST DOMINANT
PERFORMANCE
IN THE HISTORY OF
MANKIND"

in the next. "She goes from arrogance to panic, with nothing in between," said tennis impresario Ted Tinling.

But in 1981, she met and hired former women's college basketball great Nancy Lieberman as trainer, and finally began to hone her vast talents. Not merely an aggressive player who used the whole court, Navratilova brought a new level of power to the women's game with her lethal first serve and hard, precise volleys. Her sharp features and wire-rimmed glasses gave her an intense professorial look, and she was a burden to prepare for—a left-hander with power and exquisite court sense. Her game literally forced other women on the tour to change their approach. "Ten years ago," said Chris Evert in 1985, "you didn't have to be a great athlete—you just had to be a great tennis player. Then along came Martina, and the way she worked with the weights, the way she was watching everything she was eating—she was giving 100 percent of herself to tennis, and that inspired the women players."

Navratilova went 90–3 in 1982, 86–1 the next year and 78–2 in 1984, running off winning streaks of 74 and 54 matches in the process. She won six straight Wimbledons from 1982–87, then won her record-breaking ninth singles title (one more than Helen Wills Moody) at the All-England Club in 1990. She retired with 18 Grand Slam singles titles, 31 doubles titles and seven mixed doubles titles, a total just six short of Margaret Smith Court's record 62. In the process, she got the best of one of sport's classic rivalries, her dramatic serial duels with Evert that produced some of the best tennis anywhere. Navratilova won 43 of their 80 matches and, most important, went 10–4 against Evert in their Grand Slam finals. "There has never been a rivalry like it in women's sports," wrote Frank Deford. "You could even leave out the qualifying gender and be correct."

Inevitably, perhaps, her sexuality would become an issue. But here, too, Navratilova set new standards. Few world-class athletes had ever publicly acknowledged homosexuality, but Navratilova came out at the height of her career, and in doing so, defused an issue that had for too long been hidden in the shadows. She retired as an adored sports legend, admired for her candor and grace as well as her furious, dominating game.

ERIC HEIDEN
True Gold

As an orthopedist practicing in California at the end of the century, Eric Heiden would introduce himself to patients or associates and get a crooked eyebrow in return.

"Wasn't there a speed skater by that name?" would be the comeback, and the easygoing man with the still-boyish smile and salt-and-pepper hair would nod and say, Yes, there was.

Once upon a time, Eric Heiden wore sunglasses and a hood when he competed in a sport that normally got about as much exposure as a nun's navel. Not that he didn't like it that way. "I don't want them to put me on a pedestal," he said. "I want to stay just the way I am now. I'd really be uptight if people were praising me and stuff like that."

Those were the words uttered by this straightforward son of a Wisconsin doctor in February 1980, minutes after completing a show of dominance never before seen in Olympic history. Mark Spitz had won seven gold medals in the 1972 Munich Olympics and Jesse Owens had won four in track & field in Berlin 1936, but none had ever matched what Heiden did at Lake Placid. Five events, five individual gold medals and five Olympic records. Wearing a skintight gold suit, Heiden won sprints, zipping to wins in the 500- and 1,000-meters. He won the middle distance, the 1,500. He owned the endurance events, his will prevailing over searing lungs and thighs, to win the 5,000 and 10,000.

Marathoner Bill Rodgers compared it to a runner winning all the distances from the 400 meters to the 10,000. "Eric has done the impossible," he said. The night before the 10,000, Heiden was in the crowd as the U.S. team, featuring several of his former Wisconsin Badger hockey teammates, stunned the heavily favored Soviet Union. He overslept the following morning, rushed to the rink, and with no time to warm up, he still broke the world record by six seconds.

"He gave the most dominant performance in the history of mankind in an Olympic competition, and he got jobbed by a lucky hockey team," said television announcer Keith Jackson. "What he did in 1980 was one of a kind, and we'll probably never see it again."

Actually, Heiden preferred being overshadowed, and was less impressed with his own feats. "Heck, gold medals? What can you do with them?" he said. "I'd rather get a nice warmup suit. That's something I can use. Gold medals just sit there."

It wasn't just talk. Heiden had an opportunity to cash in on his success, but the 1980 Sullivan Award winner, as the nation's top amateur athlete, chose to endorse only a handful of products. He consistently steered clear of the type of public-relations blitz afforded Olympic heroes Spitz and Bruce Jenner.

"Whenever I think of those guys, I don't like what they did," Heiden said. "They just sold themselves. It's like everyone owns a little piece of you."

Heiden remained his own man and charted his own course. He retired from speed skating soon after the Olympics, focusing on competitive bicycle racing—he won the U.S. Pro Cycling Championship in 1985—before a scary crash in the 1986 Tour de France prompted him to quit and focus on his studies at Stanford Medical School.

He didn't lace up his speed skates at all after 1980, satisfied with his signal accomplishment and the accompanying memories. "Maybe if things had stayed the way they were, and I could still be obscure in an obscure sport, I might want to keep skating," he said after winning the fifth and final Olympic gold. "I really liked it best when I was a nobody."

—*Mark Wangrin*

BIRD:
HE REALLY DID
MAKE EACH
OF HIS
TEAMMATES
BETTER

LARRY BIRD
Bird of Prey

From the moment he walked out on the court, wiping his hands dry on the soles of his sneakers, Larry Bird looked less like a star basketball player than anyone of his generation. Pale-skinned, with a mop of unruly blond hair, a weak chin and a hawklike nose, he appeared ungainly at first. But the proof was on the floor, where the 6-foot-9-inch forward possessed an otherworldly sense of court awareness and a mastery of basketball's subtlest skills. He was the living embodiment of one of basketball's oldest clichés: He really did make each of his teammates better.

In 1974, he left his hometown of French Lick, Indiana (pop. 2,351), and headed to the 33,000-student campus of Indiana University to play for Bobby Knight. But within a month, the homesick Bird returned home, working on a sanitation department garbage truck and coping with a short, acrimonious marriage and his father's 1975 suicide. In nearby Terre Haute, Indiana State University kept calling. And it was at this obscure school in the middling Missouri Valley Conference that the Bird legend—gorgeous passer, dead-eye shooter, amazing work ethic—was born. In his senior season, he swept the player-of-the-year awards while leading the largely unseen Sycamores to the No. 1 ranking. In the 1979 NCAA tournament, undefeated Indiana State marched all the way to the national championship game, before falling to Earvin "Magic" Johnson and Michigan State, in what remains the highest-rated college basketball telecast ever.

Joining the bottomed-out Celtics in 1979 (Red Auerbach had craftily drafted him a year earlier, signing him before the 1979 draft), Bird led a 32-game turnaround in his rookie year, and captured his first pro title a season later. In the mid-Eighties, he would win three consecutive MVP awards and two more titles, the sweetest one coming in the 1983–84 season, when the Celtics beat Magic and the Lakers in seven games.

As the Bird-Magic rivalry reinvigorated a moribund NBA, his race—what *The Boston Globe*'s Bob Ryan called his "undeniable whiteness"—became a cultural flashpoint, sent up by Spike Lee in two films. The issue wouldn't go away, even in moments of Bird's greatest brilliance, like the dagger-to-the-heart steal of Isiah Thomas' inbounds pass that won Game 5 of the 1987 Eastern Conference Finals (which led Thomas to grumble, after the series, that if Bird were black, he'd be "just another good player"). But the wisest basketball heads understood that Bird's unique game transcended questions of race. "It's hard to look at a white man and see black," said Magic Johnson. "But when I look at Larry, that's what I see. I see myself."

Bird's bad back forced him to retire in 1992, though he took a victory lap in Barcelona with the Dream Team. Five years later, the consummate team player became the consummate player's coach, nearly toppling the Bulls' dynasty in his first season on the Indiana Pacers bench. Seeing his flat, cool courtside manner, fans couldn't help but recall the indelible vision of Bird in his playing days: the cold-blooded killer standing on the perimeter—ball in hand, eyes surveying the scene, small mouth coldly impassive—ready to do more damage. "Ninety-nine percent of the players in this league will take the final shot at the buzzer if the game is tied," Bird once said. "But be down one or two and no one will. And my teammates, they *wanted* me to take those shots. That means a lot; that's worth everything."

WALTER PAYTON
Sweetness

With tremendous muscle control and balance—he could walk the width of a football field on his hands—Walter Payton ran like a drum major, straight-legged and on his toes, and used the phenomenal strength in his buttocks, thighs and hips to make percussion his instrument.

Given a choice between running out of bounds or turning into a defender, the man whose gloved-fit CB handle was "Mississippi Maniac" would lower his shoulder and play demolition derby. "Why let the guy who's going to hit me get the easiest and best shot?" Payton rationalized.

It often wasn't a fair exchange, even against 300-pound defensive linemen, because few football players were ever more physically gifted than Payton. Chicago Bears running backs coach Fred O'Connor once took a look at the 5-foot-10-inch, 205-pounder and said, "God must have taken a chisel and said, 'I'm gonna make me a halfback.'"

"I figure it's similar to trying to rope a calf," Vikings defensive back Bobby Bryant said of stopping the Hall of Famer. "It's hard enough to get your hands on him, and once you do, you wonder if you should have."

Nicknamed "Sweetness" in college because of his moves, the former Soul Train dance contest winner couldn't sit still, talking on the phone one minute, playing the drums the next, driving one of his nine cars around the block the next, just for something to do.

"He must be the reincarnation of a Great White Shark," said his older brother Eddie, who returned kicks for the Detroit Lions. "If he stops moving forward, he will die."

Payton graduated from Jackson State in only 3½ years, at age 20, and was the fourth player taken in the 1975 draft, by the lowly Chicago Bears. For 13 seasons he didn't stop moving forward, setting NFL rushing records for single-game (275 yards vs. the Vikings in 1977) and career (16,726) yardage. He often made holes where there were none—he didn't run behind a Pro Bowl lineman in any of his first 10 years, until the 1985 season that ended with a Super Bowl championship.

Despite his affinity for contact, Payton missed only one game in his career—a coach's decision because of an ankle

PAYTON:
"YOU LIVE LIFE BECAUSE YOU LOVE IT"

MOSES:
"THE DAY I FEEL NICE AND RELAXED WILL BE THE DAY I KNOW THE STREAK IS IN DANGER."

sprain his rookie year that Payton insists he could have played on. He flippantly referred to off-season arthroscopic surgery on both knees after the 1983 season as "my 11,000-yard checkup."

A prankster who would perk up team meetings with a barrage of firecrackers, Payton was all business on the field. Down by the goal line, he was virtually unstoppable, launching from behind the line of scrimmage and leaping over the struggling mass of linemen for touchdowns. He could catch passes and block better than nearly all of his peers, and one assistant coach joked that he didn't mind interceptions because it gave him a chance to see Payton tackle somebody. Bobby Beathard, the respected NFL personnel director, acknowledged that Payton "may be the most complete player who ever played in the NFL."

"He follows the code—the old gladiator's code" said Jim Brown, the man whose career rushing record he broke.

"I'm like the Marines," Payton said. "Put me in to do the hard work."

After retiring in 1987, Payton raced cars on the Road America circuit and became a successful businessman. In 1999, he revealed he was battling a rare liver disease (primary sclerosing cholangitis) and had been put on the transplant list. He vowed to take his usual uncompromising approach. "It's just like football," he said. "You never know when or what your last play is going to be. You just play it and play it because you love it. Same way with life. You live life because you love it. If you can't love it, you just give up hope."
—*Mark Wangrin*

EDWIN MOSES
An Era Unto Himself

It is never just one thing. When an athlete dominates a sport for as long and as completely as Edwin Moses did, it's inevitably a confluence of factors, not simple physical superiority. In 1976, the year Moses won his first Olympic gold medal in the 400-meter intermediate hurdles, it was obvious that he had a physique uniquely suited to the event. "His size and speed; his base, the ability to carry the stride; his 'skim,' what we call the measurement of the stride over the hurdle—he had it all," said Dr. Leroy Walker, the coach of the 1976 U.S. team. So Moses was blessed, but the staggering record that he began a year later would have been impossible were it not for his other extraordinary gifts, especially his unflappable composure and his cerebral vision, his ability to both raise hurdling to an art and reduce it to a science.

The son of a Dayton, Ohio, school principal, he was a college sophomore—attending prestigious Morehouse College on an academic scholarship—when he broke the world record and won gold in Montreal. Soft-spoken and reserved by nature, Moses created an aura of distance about himself, with his dark aviator glasses, his rawhide necklace, his taciturn manner and the hooded sweatshirts he wore while warming up. In 1977, he commenced the most amazing streak in track history, winning 122 consecutive races, 107 of them finals. As the streak mounted, Moses became one of the biggest names in track, taking a previously obscure event and putting it on center stage, where he seemed the only featured player. His opponents were clearly in awe of him, but what kept Moses going was his perfect understanding of the event and his fear of failure. "It still feels like I'm being led to my execution 15 times a year," said Moses in 1984. "The day I feel nice and relaxed is the day I'll know the streak is in danger."

Before 1976, it was customary for world-class runners to take 14 strides between hurdles, then increase to 15 or 17 as fatigue set in over the last 200 meters. Moses took 13 strides throughout the race, a feat that one rival coach swore was impossible before he saw it. Many criticized Moses for being aloof, for not using a coach, for not signing with one of the country's major track clubs—but the wise old track coaches understood his genius, his grasp of the mathematical absolutes of the event. "Edwin's knowledge of the event is so infinite as to make any coach superfluous," said Walker. "All Ed needs is somebody to hold the watch."

He missed his second gold in 1980, when the U.S. boycotted the Moscow Olympics, but was still invincible at Los Angeles in 1984, winning again without truly being challenged.

The man with the astounding 9-foot, 9-inch running stride saw his record streak come to an end 9 years, 9 months and 9 days after his previous loss, when Danny Harris shaded him in Madrid on June 4, 1987. Three months later, in his last great triumph, the 31-year-old Moses dug deeper and won the event again at the World Championships.

He would dabble in other sports—a certified pilot since 1981 and a part-time scuba diver, Moses flirted with bobsledding in the early Nineties—but his interests always turned to the 400 IM, an event had become synonymous with his name. "I'm hoping that streak will stand for a long time," said Moses in 1996. "That it will be my mark on the sport, my legacy."

LAWRENCE TAYLOR
"I Eat Quarterbacks"

Lawrence Taylor didn't just dominate the game, he altered it. The man they called LT "changed the way defense is played, the way pass rushing is played, the way linebackers play and the way offense blocks linebackers," said John Madden. The 6-foot-3-inch, 240-pound terror was the dominant defensive player of the 1980s, defining the position of "rush linebacker" for years to come.

The son of a Williamsburg, Virginia, shipyard worker, Taylor wasn't even a major-college prospect coming out of high school. Before North Carolina's staff saw him on film

TAYLOR:
"THEN I GO BACK TO THE REST OF THE WORLD, AND THAT'S WHERE THE TROUBLE STARTS"

MARINO:
"HE'S A PASS RUSHER'S NIGHTMARE"

and recruited him, his only other scholarship offer had come from Richmond. This created a fiercely proud and fiercely motivated player (if not student) who was exquisitely self-conscious about the image he projected. He refused to answer to "Larry" in high school, because he didn't think the name sounded tough enough. And in college, where he barely survived academically, he began developing a reputation as a hard drinker and wild driver. But on the field, he played in a controlled rage. After being chosen second overall by the New York Giants in the 1981 draft, he announced at his first New York City press conference, "I like to eat quarterbacks in the backfield."

First as his defensive coordinator, then as a head coach for the New York Giants, Bill Parcells created schemes in the 3–4 defense in which Taylor could wreak havoc. He moved all around the line, confusing blocking schemes and torching game plans with a vicious, marauding style. From the weakside linebacker spot, paired against a blocker trying to stop him in his space, his combination of speed and strength made him nearly unstoppable. And once he got to the passer, he had a pioneering tomahawk strip move—his right arm swiping down on a quarterback's arm the instant before contact—that forced numerous fumbles and spawned many imitators.

Even as he was winning two Super Bowls, going to 10 straight Pro Bowls and amassing 142 sacks, Taylor was living a double life. "Sunday is a different world," he once said. "It's like a fantasy world which I'd rather live in. Then I go back to the rest of the world and that's where the trouble starts." After entering detox in 1986, he was suspended for substance abuse again in 1988. Twice after his 1993 retirement, he was arrested for trying to buy crack cocaine from an undercover cop.

He would be remembered as perhaps the greatest outside linebacker in NFL history and, just as clearly, as a lost soul. Or as his close friend and teammate Beasley Reece once said, "The thing I remember best that he said to me is, 'It's tough being LT.' People just don't know."

DAN MARINO
The Arm

When Dan Marino was growing up, four blocks away from the campus of the University of Pittsburgh, his father played catch with him in the backyard, teaching him to throw the football from his ear, rather than taking the traditional full windup that most young quarterbacks learn.

On the strength of that strong arm and his devastatingly fast release, Dan Marino went on to become the most prolific quarterback in NFL history. Hobbled by knee injuries later in his career, Marino was still a maddeningly elusive target. "He's a pass rusher's nightmare," complained the Bills' Bruce Smith. "He's got good protection, which is bad enough. But he never holds onto the ball long enough to let you get your hands on him." Marino would engineer more fourth-quarter comebacks than any quarterback in NFL history, developing a mystique that affected players on both teams. "In that situation, he throws darts," said the Bills' Darryl Talley. "It's unfair."

At 6 feet 4 inches, 212 pounds, with the quickest release since Joe Namath, he was the living embodiment of the prototype NFL quarterback. Marino stood tall in the pocket, his intense eyes peering out over his modified birdcage facemask, eerily similar to one that Namath used to wear.

The pros saw him coming from his freshman year in college. After leading Pittsburgh to three straight 11–1 seasons, Marino went into the 1982 season as a favorite for the Heisman Trophy, a national championship and a high draft pick. But the Panthers dipped to 9–3, and Marino threw only 17 touchdown passes, amid rumors of stubbornness, drug use and immaturity.

The whispers took a toll. When the 1983 draft came around, six quarterbacks were drafted in the first round. John Elway was predictably first, but four other quarterbacks—Todd Blackledge, Jim Kelly, Tony Eason and Ken O'Brien—were selected before Marino. With the 27th pick, Don Shula, coming off a Super Bowl loss to Washington, instantly snapped up Marino for the Dolphins.

He was starting by the sixth game of his rookie season, and led the Dolphins to seven wins in nine games, en route to becoming the first rookie quarterbackever to start in the Pro Bowl. The next season, Marino put up the sort of mindbending numbers that could be the standard against which quarterbacks are compared well into the next century. In leading the Dolphins to a 14–2 mark in 1984, he threw for an NFL record 48 touchdown passes (breaking the old mark by 12), and 5,084 yards, averaging nine yards per attempt. When the 49ers frustrated Marino with a 4–2–5 alignment in Super Bowl XIX, Miami fell, 38–16.

The end of Marino's dream season seemed a mere prelude for a career full of Super Sundays. But though he would go on to hold the NFL career record for touchdowns, passing yards, attempts and completions, the century would end without Marino ever returning to a Super Bowl.

By the twilight of his career, he was as immobilized as Namath was in his later days, but courageously carried on in search of that ring, driven by his competitiveness and that rifle arm. His left leg was protected by a Lenox Hill derotation brace (originally designed for Namath in the 1970s), and his right leg featured braces on both the knee and his ankle. Walking on or off the field, Marino looked every bit the battered gladiator. "I put my head down when he walks," said Dolphins trainer Ryan Vermillion. "It's horrible. When he plays, he looks a lot better."

And yet Marino soldiered on, one of the NFL's classic warriors, searching for that elusive title, earning both the respect and admiration of his opponents. "There couldn't have been a better passer ever," said Bruce Smith. "Playing him twice a year is like playing DiMaggio all the time."

EVERT: "SHE'S THE ULTIMATE PROFESSIONAL"

CHRIS EVERT
A Whole Woman

She arrived on the scene at age 16 at the 1971 U.S. Open, the embodiment of all-American femininity with a coolly detached veneer that belied her girlish features. She fought off six match points to win her second-round match, marching all the way to the semifinals. Over the next 18 years, Chris Evert became the most respected, most recognized and, ultimately, most revered female athlete in the country.

But at the beginning, even Evert herself doubted whether beauty and athleticism could mix. She was raised on a steady diet of baseline bashing by her tennis-pro father, Jimmy Evert, on the hard-baked clay courts of Fort Lauderdale. At age 15, she upset No.1 Margaret Court. A year later at Forest Hills, she was christened America's sweetheart, and cultivated an image—ribbon in her pony-tailed hair, nails freshly painted, lacy frills on her bloomers, pompom socklets peeking out of her shoes—of a dashing damsel who just happened to be carrying a racket, and happened to know what to do with it. "I never felt like an athlete," she said of those early years. "I was just *someone who played tennis matches*. I still thought of women athletes as freaks, and I used to hate myself, thinking I must not be a whole woman."

But Evert already possessed a champion athlete's mental toughness. "She won't carry anyone and she'll never tank a match," said Bud Collins in the 1970s. "She's the ultimate professional." Her consistency was unmatched: She retired with a .900 winning percentage (1,309-146), the best in the history of professional tennis. She was ranked in the top four in the world for 18 straight years, won at least one Grand Slam tournament for 13 straight years, and advanced to the semifinals in 52 of the 56 majors in which she played, including the first 34.

While others had better individual strokes, or more exciting all-court games, Chrissie had her nerves of steel. "I realize that a lot of fans think my game is boring," she said. "But this is the game I played to win. Losing hurts me. I was always determined to be the best." In 1974, she took her trademark two-fisted backhand to a Wimbledon title and the No.1 ranking, and was part of the "Love Doubles" match with brash men's No.1, Jimmy Connors. Their engagement was off by the U.S. Open that year, but other high-profile romances would follow, including a marriage to fellow pro John Lloyd, which ended in an amicable divorce.

In the late Seventies, when Martina Navratilova rose to No.1, Evert's own notions of training began to change. Realizing she had to become a better athlete to contend with Navratilova, she upgraded her training regimen. Their long-running rivalry—with Navratilova holding a 43–37 lead overall, 10-4 in Grand Slam finals—was the best in tennis and maybe all of sport. And the vulnerability she exhibited in her matches against Navratilova humanized Evert, turning her again into the fan favorite of her early years. Her most satisfying Grand Slam wins might have been her last two—tense, three-set battles that she took from Navratilova at the 1985 and 1986 French Opens. When she retired after a quarterfinal loss to Zina Garrison at the 1989 U.S. Open, it marked the end of an era, leaving both players in tears.

"Her legacy is that we might have a few charming, sporting players down the line because people remember Chris," said tennis eminence Ted Tinling. "She's a great role model—for the image she projects and for her backhand. I think there must be a million kids playing who wouldn't have played if they had defensive backhands. All the kids can attack on both wings now, and that wouldn't exist if it hadn't been for Chris."

BO JACKSON
"Keepin' Myself Busy"

For a while in the late 1980s, the age-old argument about the identity of the world's greatest athlete was moot. Bo Jackson, the bulky, chiseled speedster from Bessemer, Alabama, was running wild. Others have played two professional sports for longer periods of time, but no one, not even Jim Thorpe, approached Jackson's excellence at the highest levels of the two reigning national pastimes. From 1987–90, he spent his summers as one of the most feared hitters in the American League for the Kansas City Royals. And in the fall, he became perhaps the most feared runner in the NFL for the Los Angeles Raiders.

Eventually, Jackson's versatility would become a staple of American popular culture (through the "Bo Knows" shoe ad campaign). The country was fond of the soft-spoken Jackson because, unlike so many other athletes with attitude, there was nothing calculated about his demeanor. At Auburn, where he won the Heisman Trophy in 1985, he was so shy that he couldn't speak in the first person without stammering, and he had a nervous habit of chewing soda straws—literally going through dozens a day. Chosen first in the 1986 NFL draft by the Tampa Bay Buccaneers, who offered him a $4.6–million package, Jackson instead signed a minor-league deal with the Royals. A year later, after a meteoric rise to the majors that showed flashes of brilliance, he signed with the Raiders, to pursue his "hobby" of pro football after the baseball season.

He became a force in both sports. He was the All-Star Game MVP in 1989, but long before then, he was generating his own lore—a 461-foot homer off Nolan Ryan, a stunning throw from the warning track to home plate on the fly to nail a runner in Seattle. The manchild seemed able to do whatever he wanted—breaking bats over his knee in frustration after strikeouts, and not just scaling but actually *running up* outfield walls. In 1990, playing at Yankee Stadium, he hit home runs in his first three at-bats before injuring himself in the field. He was out of action for two months, but came back to hit a homer in his first at-bat. "Bo's got

JACKSON: "BO'S GOT MAYS' TALENT, AND HE'S GOT MAYS' MAKEUP."

LOUGANIS: "NOBODY COMBINES ALL THE ELEMENTS LIKE GREG DOES"

[Willie] Mays' talent, and he's got Mays' makeup," said Royals manager Billy Gardner.

In football, he was undoubtedly the fastest running back in the game. His 91-yard touchdown run against the Seattle Seahawks in 1987 was a revelation of speed, and part of a 221-yard game that is still the record for *Monday Night Football*. But in a 1991 playoff game against Cincinnati, Jackson suffered a serious hip injury that ended both his careers. He'd never play football again, and would return as a shell of his former self in baseball, eventually undergoing hip-replacement surgery and retiring after the 1994 season.

America wondered what might have been, but Jackson himself had no regrets. "I can probably say, if I wanted to be in the baseball Hall of Fame, I could have been easily," he said. "If I wanted to be in the football Hall of Fame, I could have done that, too. But I can say also that I wouldn't go back and change a thing. Nobody waits for you to hit your last homer, score your last touchdown. You have to grow up. You have to move on."

Others hang on long after their talent is gone, but Jackson's time was done. And Bo knew that, too.

GREG LOUGANIS
Profile in Courage

It always looked easy when Greg Louganis left the diving board: the height, the rotation, the alignment and the entry. From a distance it was all elegance and grace, but up close you could hear the grunting and appreciate the power.

"What is it that Nureyev, the dancer, says? 'We try to create the illusion that we're doing nothing when we're really working,'" said Ron O'Brien, his longtime coach. "That's what Greg has been able to take out of dance and put into diving. He can create the illusion."

Louganis won 47 national AAU titles, six world championships and five Olympic medals, four of them gold. He won from the 10-meter platform and the three-meter springboard, often having clinched the competition before his final dive.

Darkly handsome with a 44-inch chest over a 28-inch waist, Louganis was Hollywood hunky. He stood 5-foot-9-inches, weighed 160 pounds with seven percent body fat and possessed preternatural strength and flexibility. Even his bow legs were a benefit, allowing him an opening to look for the water while maintaining the required tight tuck.

"There are people who get into the water cleaner, with less splash, and there are people who spin faster, like some of the acrobatic Chinese divers," said 1976 springboard gold medalist Phil Boggs. "But there's nobody who combines all the elements like Greg does. He's the state of the art in diving."

Born to unwed 15-year-olds in San Diego in 1960, Louganis was adopted when he was nine months old by an El Cajon, California, couple. Seeking the approval of an authoritarian father—and to avoid the teasing of classmates, who called him "nigger" because of his Samoan heritage and made fun of his dyslexia— Louganis moved from dancing lessons to gymnastics before finding his love in diving. As an 11-year-old diving in a junior national meet he caught the eye of two-time U.S. diving gold medalist Sammy Lee. "When I first watched him, I said to myself, 'My God, that's the greatest talent I've ever seen,'" recalled Lee, who became his coach.

At the Montreal Olympics in 1976, the wide-eyed 16-year-old chased Italian diving legend Klaus Dibiasi down to the last dive in the platform event before settling for the silver medal, prompting Dibiasi to say, "Next Olympics, I watch you."

The U.S. boycott kept Louganis from diving in Moscow in 1980, but he came back in Los Angeles in 1984 to easily win gold in the platform and springboard. He duplicated the double in Seoul four years later in one of the most dramatic performances of the Games.

Late in the springboard qualifying, Louganis hit his head during a reverse 2½ somersault from a pike position. Five stitches closed the wound, but Louganis was badly shaken, less because of the wound itself than because he was HIV-positive, something only a handful of his closest friends knew. Summoning his legendary powers of concentration, he somehow held himself together to win the springboard finals 20 hours later and the platform later in the week.

Though he had long come out to his close friends and family, outside the inner circle his sexuality was the subject of whispers. Louganis retired from diving in 1988 and proclaimed his homosexuality at the 1994 Gay Games in New York City. A year later his autobiography was published. In *Breaking the Surface* he openly discussed being gay, living with AIDS and his several attempted suicides.

"It's been so difficult with the secret, and asking people to keep the secrets," Louganis said. "I was feeling like a fake."

That illusion broken, Louganis said he began feeling more comfortable about himself and his role in redefining diving greatness. "Being gay and being in sports isn't supposed to mix," Louganis said. "I think I proved that wrong."

—*Mark Wangrin*

JACKIE JOYNER-KERSEE
Second to None

By the time Jackie Joyner-Kersee won her third Olympic gold medal in 1992, her second in the hepathlon, people weren't calling her the world's greatest female athlete anymore. "She's the greatest multi-sport athlete ever, man or woman," said 1976 Olympic decathlon gold medalist Bruce Jenner.

The prideful, strong-willed Joyner-Kersee is America's most decorated female track & field performer (with three Olympic golds, a silver and two bronze medals) and perhaps the premier female athlete of all time. Only Babe

JOYNER-KERSEE: "ALL WE EVER WANTED WAS TO BE RESPECTED FOR WHAT WE WERE TRYING TO DO"

Didrikson's feats compare with Joyner's wide array of talents, and Babe's dominance came in a much less competitive era for female athletes.

At the Seoul Olympic Games in 1988, Joyner-Kersee pulled off a stirring double. She set a world record in the heptathlon, the seven-event female counterpart to the decathlon, and won the gold medal in the long jump. To win Olympic gold in a multi-event test like the heptathlon—comprising the 100-meter hurdles, shot put, high jump, 200 meters, long jump, javelin and 800 meters—and then have the talent, to come back and win an individual medal was thought to be impossible in the modern age of track & field. Until Joyner-Kersee did it.

The people who knew her best were the least surprised. Born in 1962 in a small shack across the street from a pool hall and liquor store on the gritty streets of East St. Louis, Illinois, she was named after First Lady Jacqueline Onassis because, in the words of her grandmother, "this little girl will be the first lady of something." Growing up with a strict mother determined to keep her out of trouble, channeling all her energies to sports and studies, she earned a scholarship to UCLA, where she was a four-year starter in basketball, as well as a champion long jumper. It was at UCLA where she met assistant coach Bob Kersee, who helped her realize her potential in the heptathlon and later became her husband.

Throughout the late Eighties and early Nineties, Joyner-Kersee was the grand dame of American track and field's extended first family. Her brother Al Joyner won Olympic gold in the triple jump in 1984; her sister-in-law, the late Florence Griffith Joyner, won three Olympic gold medals; and Bob Kersee coached a stable of Olympic-caliber athletes.

Jane Fredericks, the nation's previous heptathlon champion, viewed Joyner-Kersee's ascendance with appreciation. "Hers was a real talent, not a forced one," Fredericks said. "She wasn't driven to compensate for some bitterness or character failing. She felt good about herself. She had a sense of purpose."

And people felt good about her. After conjuring up one last victory—at the Goodwill Games in 1998—Joyner-Kersee returned to East St. Louis for a victory lap at a farewell meet. "All we ever wanted was to be respected for what we were trying to do," she said of the female athletes of her era. "I think that's what's happening now. Now people are accepting us and saying that it's okay."

Raising the Flag: After the comeback, everyone believed in miracles.

HOCKEY
Miracle at Lake Placid

The Cold War was burning hot, American hostages were still in Iran, the President said the country was suffering from "a malaise," and in Lake Placid, New York, a young United States hockey team was trying to do the impossible—defeat the Soviet Union in the medal round of the 1980 Winter Olympics. It was a game that no expert gave the collection of American amateurs a chance to win. The Soviets were regarded as the best team in the world, and they'd routed the U.S. squad 10–3 in a Madison Square Garden exhibition 13 days previous. But the Americans had been a team of destiny in Lake Placid, earning a surprise tie with Sweden in their opener after pulling their goalie, then upsetting powerful Czechoslovakia, 7–3, en route to qualifying for the four-team medal round. Before the game against the Soviets, U.S. coach Herb Brooks told his squad, "You were born to be players. You were meant to be here. This moment is yours."

The U.S. team seized that moment. The heavily favored Soviets jumped out to 1–0 and 2–1 leads, but a rebound goal by Mark Johnson in the final second of the first period gave the U.S. new hope. More important, it prompted Soviet coach Viktor Tikhonov to remove legendary goalie Vladislav Tretiak in favor of the less experienced Vladimir Myshkin. The Soviets went up, 3–2, in the second period, but the U.S. evened it again in the third, on a Johnson power-play goal. With the pro-U.S. crowd creating a deafening din, the Americans pushed for the winner. It came off the stick of team captain Mike Eruzione, who put a wrist shot through a screen to beat Myshkin. After the U.S. held on for the 4-3 win, pandemonium reigned in Lake Placid and around the country. But the U.S. locker room was a scene of stunned, grateful glee. "It was absolutely quiet," said Steve Janaszak, the Americans' reserve goaltender. "Some guys were crying a little. You got the idea that the game wasn't over yet, because no one is ever up a goal on the Russians when a game is over. No one really believed it."

Two days later, in the finale against Finland, the U.S. finished their task, scoring three goals in the third period to beat the Finns, 4-2, and win the gold medal.

TENNIS
1980 Wimbledon Gentlemen's Final

■ John McEnroe came to Britain as a marked, despised man, McNasty to the Fleet Street press. His behavior during the Wimbledon fortnight didn't change anyone's mind. But his play in the final caused McEnroe's detractors to see the heart and brilliance beneath the surly exterior. Facing Bjorn Borg, attempting to become the first man in 74 years to win five straight men's singles title at Wimbledon, McEnroe jumped out to a quick lead, taking the first set, 6–1. After Borg rallied to win the second and third sets, 7–5 and 6–3, the two went to a tiebreaker in the fourth set. What ensued was a mini–drama of such high suspense, it would go down as the most memorable tiebreaker ever. Five times, Borg had match point, but each time McEnroe battled back. After 22 minutes, McEnroe took a Borg serve and rocketed it back crosscourt. Borg mishit his drop volley—and McEnroe had prevailed in the tiebreak, 18–16. "I say to myself, I have to forget," said Borg later. "I have to try to win." And displaying the resolve of one of the great champions, he fought on, finally breaking McEnroe in the 13th game, then holding serve to win the fifth set, 8–6, and the match. McEnroe exited to cheers and greater appreciation—and he'd win three of the next four Wimbledon titles.

GOLF
1986 Masters

■ All across the back nine on that Sunday, golfers stood over their shots, steadied themselves, and then… were jerked out of their concentration by explosions of sound. These weren't your typical Sunday charge roars, they were Golden Bear Roars, and they meant that Jack Nicklaus, 46 and left for dead as a contender in majors, was scorching the back nine, rocketing up the leader board to challenge for another green jacket. Nicklaus had been playing well all week (his son Jackie was caddying for him), but opened the final round six strokes back. Shooting a 30 on the back nine, he passed Seve Ballesteros, Greg Norman, Tom Watson, and Bernhard Langer, turning back the clock for his sixth Masters title, gaining the decisive one-stroke margin when he drilled his third straight birdie, on 17. "I will never forget the ovation we received on our walk up to the 18th green that day," he said later. "It was deafening, stunning, unbelievable in every way. Tears kept coming to my eyes, and I had to tell myself a number of times to hold back my emotions, that I still had some golf to play."

PRO FOOTBALL
1981 NFL Playoff San Diego at Miami

■ The San Diego Chargers, with the most explosive offense of the Eighties, were already ahead 24–0 when Dolphins coach Don Shula pulled starter David Woodley in the second quarter, installing veteran Don Strock. The game was 24–10 when the Dolphins struck with some high school razzle-dazzle on the last play of the first half. Strock hit wideout Duriel Harris on a buttonhook, who then pitched to Tony Nathan on the old hook-and-lateral trick play. Nathan ran untouched into the end zone and Miami was within seven at the half. In the back-and-forth second half, San Diego rallied late, when Dan Fouts overthrew Kellen Winslow but connected with James Brooks. Winslow came up big later, blocking a late field goal attempt to send it into overtime. At 13:52 of overtime, Charger Rolf Benirschke kicked the winning field goal, 41-38. The game's hero was Winslow, the Chargers' tight end, who caught 13 passes for 166 yards.

COLLEGE FOOTBALL
1984 Orange Bowl

■ Two years to the day after the Chargers-Dolphins game, the Orange Bowl was the site of another classic. Nebraska entered the 50th Orange Bowl ranked No. 1 in the country and undefeated, with the most potent offense of the postwar era, paced by "the triplets," the skill-position trio of quarterback Turner Gill, Heisman Trophy–winning I-back Mike Rozier and wingback Irving Fryar. The Miami Hurricanes were 12-point underdogs, but had the advantage of playing in their home stadium. Stifling Nebraska's option game, and picking apart an overmatched Cornhusker secondary, Miami jumped out to a 17-0 lead. NU's rally started with its famed "Fumbleroosky" play, with Dean Steinkuhler running it in from 19 yards out. After NU tied it at 17, Miami jumped back out to a 31–17 lead, with Bernie Kosar throwing for two touchdown passes. But in the fourth quarter, Gill led the Huskers back again, and NU converted a fourth-and-eight, with Gill pitching to Jeff Smith, who ran 24 yards for a touchdown with 48 seconds left, to bring Nebraska within one. And at that moment, with a national title just an extra point away, Nebraska coach Tom Osborne chose instead to go for the win, a move as daring as it was honorable. But Gill's pass to Smith in the end zone was deflected, and Miami had won its first national championship.

Walsh Brings the Blueprint

When the decade began, there was no mystique surrounding the San Francisco 49ers. They were simply another struggling team, one with a storied tradition but no trophies. Since debuting in the All-America Football Conference in 1946, the 49ers had never won a league championship. Enter **Bill Walsh**, who left Stanford to coach the 49ers in 1979. After he inherited a 2-14 club, he installed a new offense and revamped the 49ers' scouting system. And in his first draft, in 1979, he spent a No. 3 draft choice on Notre Dame quarterback **Joe Montana**. With that, the 49ers embarked on a run that would bring them five Super Bowl titles in 14 seasons, raise them to the level of the NFL's elite glamour franchises, and change the face of modern football strategy. At the end of the century, their run of excellence was still alive.

But the '80s were their decade. In Walsh's third season, San Francisco advanced to the Super Bowl (thanks to the Montana-engineered 89-yard drive at the end of the NFC championship game, which ended with "The Catch," Dwight Clark's famous fingertip touchdown reception, to beat Dallas). Montana would post a 4-0 record in Super Bowls, as San Francisco won titles fol-

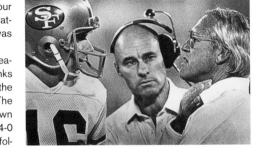

lowing the '81, '84, '88 and '89 seasons. Their West Coast offense, built on a controlled passing game that stressed pass-route options and the ability to gain yards after the catch, became the most successful offense of the '80s, and the most imitated offense of the '90s. Walsh brought a serene sense of organization and confidence to the 49ers. Though he left after the third Super Bowl title, a scintillating 20-16 win over Cincinnati, the system was in place. George Seifert took over in 1989, and won a Super Bowl in his first season as an NFL head coach. Eventually, Montana would give way to Steve Young, but the 49ers just kept winning.

■ **Long Island Reign.** The New York Islanders joined the NHL in 1972 and, under coach Al Arbour and general manager Bill Torrey, took their lumps in the early seasons. Building carefully through the draft, they grew into a balanced, potent power and, as the '80s began, they took over the NHL, winning four consecutive Cups. With Bryan Trottier centering to right wing sharpshooter Mike Bossy, the Islanders were an offensive power still able to play a physical game. The great Denis Potvin anchored the defense, and nasty goaltender Billy Smith (the first player taken in the '72 expansion draft) was the last line of defense. "I wish everyone who played hockey could know the feeling of winning the Stanley Cup," said Trottier. "You win it once and you get greedy. You want to keep on winning it."

	COLLEGE BASKETBALL	PRO BASKETBALL NBA	HOCKEY NHL	BASEBALL MLB	COLLEGE FOOTBALL	PRO FOOTB... NFL
1980	Louisville	Lakers	Islanders	Phillies	Georgia	Raiders
1981	Indiana	Celtics	Islanders	Dodgers	Clemson	49ers
1982	North Carolina	Lakers	Islanders	Cardinals	Penn State	Redskins
1983	N.C. State	76ers	Islanders	Orioles	Miami, Fla.	Raiders
1984	Georgetown	Celtics	Oilers	Tigers	Brigham Young	49ers
1985	Villanova	Lakers	Oilers	Royals	Oklahoma	Bears
1986	Louisville	Celtics	Canadiens	Mets	Penn State	Giants
1987	Indiana	Lakers	Oilers	Twins	Miami, Fla.	Redskins
1988	Kansas	Lakers	Oilers	Dodgers	Notre Dame	49ers
1989	Michigan	Pistons	Flames	Athletics	Miami, Fla.	49ers

NOTES **College football**: Champions are mythical consensus national champions as voted by sportswriters in the Associated Press Poll, and by coaches in the United Press International poll.

CEOs for the Hardcourt

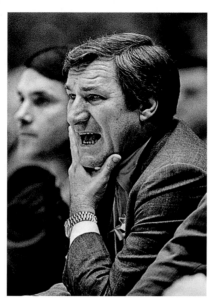

With his Armani suits, slicked-back hair, and fondness for inspirational catch-phrases, **Pat Riley** was the perfect embodiment of the '80s executive as basketball coach. He was a hardcourt corporate raider who preached the joys of hard work and seemed uniquely able to motivate modern athletes to play within a system that provided both structure and flexibility.

In November 1981, he took over a Los Angeles Lakers team that was rife with dissension, and coached them to four titles in the Eighties, placing them in the NBA Finals in seven of the next eight seasons. Riley was always conscious of motivating the troops. He seized on LA's soft image in 1985, pushing the Lakers toward a seven-game win in their rematch with Boston. And after the Lakers won the title in 1987, Riley guaranteed that they'd become the first team to win repeat championships since the Celtics of the late '60s. He was criticized in some corners for putting undue pressure on his team, but the guarantee served a larger function—it provided the team, seeking its fifth world title of the decade, a new focus and motivation—which they used to fulfill his guarantee. "Coaching is an interactive relationship whereby it's my job to elicit a response in order to get a result, which is to win," said Riley in 1993.

At the college level, **Dean Smith** accomplished many of the same things, with a lighter touch and less expensive suits. In 1961, Smith took over a North Carolina basketball team reeling from recruiting violations, and turned it into the toast of Tobacco Road. Along the way, he built up a reputation as one of the consummate gentlemen of college basketball. There would be no chair throwing, no scandals, almost all of his players would graduate, and the Tar Heels would almost always be in the running for a national title. In his 36 years coaching the Tar Heels, they went to the NCAA Tournament 27 times, advanced to 11 Final Fours (more than any coach save John Wooden), and won national championships in 1982 and 1993.

"He had a style that no one's ever going to copy," said Duke coach Mike Krzyzewski. "To be that smart, that psychologically aware, that good with X's and O's, with that system, and to always take the high road, that just isn't going to happen again."

The Salesman

It would be wrong to suggest that **David Stern** saved the National Basketball Association. Though the league's reputation was at its all-time low at the beginning of the '80s, help was already at hand. The arrival of Earvin "Magic" Johnson and Larry Bird, and the renewal of the pitched Lakers-Celtics rivalry, helped to jump-start interest, and when Michael Jordan arrived in 1984, it hardly took a genius to figure out how the league might expand its appeal.

Still, Stern was a crucial figure in the league's history because the NBA's fourth commissioner was instrumental in maximizing the league's newfound '80s popularity. By the end of the decade, the league whose very existence was being questioned in 1980 was clearly the hottest professional sports league in America. And Stern earned much of the credit, as well as being named the Associated Press "Executive of the Decade" for the '80s.

In 1978, Stern joined the league under commissioner Larry O'Brien as full-time general counsel, and by 1980, he'd been promoted to executive vice president of business and legal affairs. Before succeeding O'Brien in 1984, Stern helped to broker the revolutionary labor agreement that gave the owners a salary cap in exchange for guaranteeing players 53 percent of gross revenues. In doing so, he averted a strike and brought the acrimonious players and owners together. "All the teams were islands unto themselves," said one NBA staffer. "What Stern did was take the islands and turn them into a continent."

Under Stern, the league became conscious about being both a sports *and* entertainment entity. Tapping into the hip-hop generation, the league's marketing arm took advantage of the NBA's broad-based fan demographic, more racially diverse than baseball and younger than football. The Stern era brought the NBA draft lottery, which served the dual purpose of heightening interest in the league's college player draft and in discouraging teams from tanking at the end of the season. In 1984, the All-Star Game became an All-Star Weekend, adding a slam-dunk contest, a legends game (later changed to a rookie game) and a three-point shooting contest.

In the post-Jordan era, the underlying assumption of the NBA's marketing philosophy, promoting the league's personalities rather than its competition, was still open to debate. But Stern's NBA was ahead of the curve in the '80s, and the NBA owed much of its success to his canny, balanced leadership. As Orlando executive Pat Williams put it, "David Stern can sell an anvil to a drowning man. He can sell a pogo stick to a kangaroo."

TOP OF THE NEWS: No one escapes the Bonfire of the Vanities: There are drug busts in the Olympics, steroid abuse in pro football, point shaving in college sports and greed in virtually every arena. But in the upwardly mobile decade, there are still some superstars—Gretzky, Magic, Bird, Montana—able to transcend all that.

Movies

"Get a hit, Crash."

"Shut up."

The best baseball movie of the decade is Ron Shelton's gritty, finely observed **Bull Durham**, the romantic comedy about a philosophical career minor leaguer, played by Kevin Costner, who tutors an up-and-coming young pitcher (Tim Robbins) "with a million-dollar arm and a five-cent head." The rising young star, Ebby Calvin "Nuke" LaLoosh, is getting schooled off the field by the baseball-loving "friend of the game," Annie Savoy (played smartly by Susan Sarandon). Shelton, who spent five years in the minors, gets all the details just right. The decade's other gem is John Sayles' adaptation of Eliot Asinof's *Eight Men Out*, which faithfully recreates the Black Sox scandal of 1919. John Cusack, as Buck Weaver, steals several scenes. Sayles plays the writer Ring Lardner.

In *Hoosiers*, Gene Hackman stars as an aging coach with one last shot at redemption. Based on the story of a small-town Indiana school that advanced to the state championship basketball game against a big-city prep power, the film was both a critical and commerical hit. David Anspaugh's picture features a strong supporting performance by Dennis Hopper, as an alcoholic fan and father.

Playing Games

Daniel Okrent writes *Nine Innings*, a microscopic examination of a single regular-season baseball game, between the Baltimore Orioles and the Milwaukee Brewers. But he'll get more attention for inventing Rotisserie League Baseball, the armchair game that creates dream teams with real players' statistics. This launches a small industry of fantasy (and football, golf, hockey, basketball, NASCAR) leagues, magazines, books, and statistical services.

Reading List

In 1986, Bill James publishes his magnum opus, **The Bill James Historical Baseball Abstract**, a dense, readable, illuminating history of the game that breaks new ground in both statistical analysis and hot-stove inspiration (in

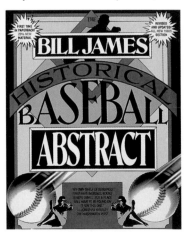

addition to providing never-before published statistical information on Hall of Famers, James also names the ugliest player of each decade).

John Feinstein spends *A Season on the Brink* with Indiana basketball coach Bobby Knight, emerging with a complex portrait of a driven man. And Daniel Okrent edits *The Ultimate Baseball Book*, among the most-lavishly-praised books of its kind. John Thorn and Pete Palmer publish the first edition of *Total Baseball*, the book that will eventually displace Macmillan's *Baseball Encyclopedia* as the official statistical history of the major leagues.

Politics

A jury rules against the NFL in an anti-trust suit brought by the Los Angeles Coliseum Commission and the Oakland Raiders, paving the way for the club to move to L.A. The ruling rocks Pete Rozelle and the NFL, and sets the stage for moves by the Cleveland Browns, Los Angeles Rams and Houston Oilers in the decade ahead. But in 1986, the NFL wins one for losing. The Second Circuit Court of Appeals upholds a New York jury ruling for the United States Football League in its $1.7 billion anti-trust suit against the NFL, but awards the USFL only $1 in damages. By anti-trust law, the damages are automatically trebled, to $3.

Sounds

Rap music embraces sports culture. In "The Message," the seminal, issue-oriented hit by Grandmaster Flash & The Furious Five, a singer complains that he "can't even watch the game/Or the Sugar Ray fight." In 1983's "Basketball," rapper Kurtis Blow sings praises to scores of hoops stars ("I used to go to dinner, then take the girls/To see Tiny play against Earl the Pearl"). And on the title track Public Enemy's 1987 debut album *Yo! Bum Rush the Show*, lead singer Chuck D raps about his crew "rushin' like the

THE SUPER BOWL SHUFFLE*
THE CHICAGO BEARS SHUFFLIN' CREW

Bears in the 46."

As the Chicago Bears roll unimpeded to Super Bowl XX, they cut sports' first music video, **"The Super Bowl Shuffle."** In uniform, several of the team's stars groove and rap about their dominance. Walter Payton sings, "They call me Sweetness and I like to dance/ Running the ball is like making romance."

Earlier in the decade, in "Cadillac Ranch," Bruce Springsteen evokes the mythic early days of stock-car racing, singing about "Junior Johnson runnin' through the woods of Caroline." Steve Earle tells about a high school football star in "No. 29," and Nils Lofgren pre-

sents a portrait of the inner lives of two championship prizefighters in the melodrama "No Mercy."

Fashion

The excesses of the '70s are mostly forgotten, as baseball starts a move back toward more traditional styles. The button-up jersey makes a return to popularity, after the decade-long dominance of the double-knit pullover. The pacesetter is the Atlanta Braves who, in 1987, switch from their modern style back to the traditional jersey, with a tomahawk on the front, that they'd last worn 25 years earlier, as the Milwaukee Braves.

In track, Florence Griffith Joyner sports six-inch nails and a series of one-legged unitards during the 1988 Olympic Track & Field Trials in Indianapolis. Later, she designs new uniforms for the Indiana Pacers.

Impressions of the '80s

From ESPN's Kenny Mayne:
You're thinking I picked the last year of the decade because that's as far back as my memory goes. There's something to that. But there's more to the notion that what **Joe Montana** did in the Super Bowl of 1989 speaks to the entire decade.

The story goes that Joe took the huddle to start the winning drive, paused, and said, "Look, there's John Candy." Either Candy had a sideline pass or Joe had even better vision than we all thought. Maybe the whole thing is apocryphal. Either way, its legend illustrates the calm Montana brought to a huddle, brought to a play.

Candy's out of sight now. Joe's seeing end zone. Snap of the ball, look off the helpless defense. The head turns back to the left. John Taylor breaks on his post move. The ball's already there. "As a kid that's what you did in your backyard," said Montana. "You dreamt of that happening, winning a Super Bowl by throwing a TD pass. But the funny thing is our backs lined up wrong. Had they blitzed from my front side, I wouldn't have been protected."

I miss John Candy. I miss Joe's cool.

> 'm going to write a book—How to Make a Small Fortune in Baseball. *You start with a large fortune."*
>
> —Philadelphia Phillies owner Ruly Carpenter

Debuts and Exits

1980 **The Dallas Mavericks** join the NBA.

EXIT **The United States**, and 63 other nations, from the 1980 Summer Olympics in Moscow, protesting the Soviet invasion of Afghanistan.

The Senior PGA Tour.

1982 **Tear-away jerseys in college football.**

1983 **The U.S. Olympic Hall of Fame** in Colorado Springs.

Overtime for regular season games in NHL reinstated for first time since 1942, with five-minute time limit (rather than 20).

The United States Football League, designed to avoid direct competition with the NFL by playing its games in the spring.

1984 **The Soviet Union**, and 13 other Eastern bloc nations, from the 1984 Summer Games in Los Angeles, citing the "gross flouting" of Olympic ideals by the U.S. Olympic Committee.

EXIT **The Colts from Baltimore**, as the franchise moves to Indianapolis under cover of darkness.

1985 **EXIT** **The North American Soccer League.**

The 45-second shot clock, in college basketball.

EXIT **The United States Football League** After winning $3 from the NFL in an anti-trust suit.

1986 **Instant replay in the NFL.**

The three-point field goal in college basketball.

Women in pro basketball, with the debut of Nancy Lieberman with the United States Basketball League's Springfield Fame, in a 122-107 win over Staten Island.

1988 **The Miami Heat** and **Charlotte Hornets** in the NBA.

The first African-American referee in NFL history, when Johnny Grier leads a crew onto the field September 4.

Night games at Wrigley Field for the first time in its 74-year history.

A two-point conversion for the defense in college football, if it returns a blocked extra-point kick or a two-point conversion attempt to the opposite end zone.

The catcher's helmet, required in the major leagues for the first time.

The Minnesota Timberwolves and **Orlando Magic** in the NBA.

1989 **EXIT** **The use of kicking tees for field goals** and extra points in college football.

THE 1990s

You couldn't avoid it — sports had become big business; so contentious that it often seemed bent on self-destruction. Baseball's labor squabbles shut down the 1994 World Series and, four years later, the NBA nearly lost an entire season. But in the midst of all the hype, bombast and commercial tie-ins, sport's grandest jewels shone as brightly as ever. Six times during the decade, when cynics complained that sports had lost its soul, Number 23 carried his team through a triumphant June, proving again that the heart of a champion is timeless and transcendent.

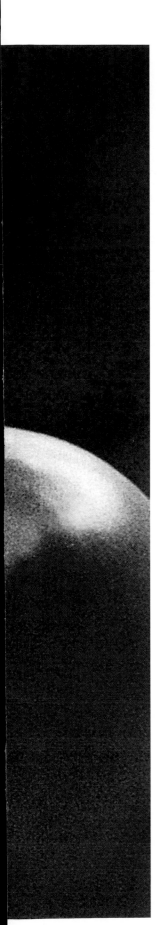

The Head and the Heart

TO WRITE ABOUT MICHAEL JORDAN IS TO STAND UPON a mountain of press clips and pretend they don't exist. At the end of a century that made sports a global, 24-hour, overanalyzed, zealously professional, obsessively marketed, and extravagantly played commodity, Jordan's career is the culmination of a long journey. Which means his every eyelash flutter has been photographed, catalogued, annotated, footnoted, and e-mailed by somebody at some time.

So I will not be so foolish as to attempt to topple or even torch that mountain. It's too large for me to push and I lack the fuel to incinerate it completely. Instead I offer two discreet little essays—one on Jordan's head, the other on his heart—that I lay atop the mountain as it awaits some yet unseen 21st-century bonfire.

Michael Jordan's Head

One way to understand Michael Jordan's impact on his era is to gaze at the man's head. Not his brain, mind you—that wonderful muscle that conceived and executed feats of unparalleled athleticism—but the smooth brown casing that surrounds it. Jordan's head didn't start out bald. As a college boy at North Carolina and a young pro on the selfish, undisciplined mid-Eighties Chicago Bulls, Jordan sported the low, round Afro that was one African-American fashion option of the period—the other being the greasy, defiantly lower-class Jheri curl.

There was nothing noteworthy about Jordan's head then, except perhaps a rapidly receding hair line that seemed to destine him for premature baldness. Jordan and

PREVIOUS PAGES
Prime Number. Jordan's Number 23 became an icon of excellence for the '90s. When he returned temporarily wearing Number 45, the picture didn't look right—he seemed heavier and less graceful.

The Look. His wide smile and sly eyes lit up when the stakes were the highest. And in six Finals, Jordan's Bulls were 24-10.

The First Sign.
Jordan, as a freshman, sinks the winning shot in the 1982 NCAA championship game against Georgetown. Patrick Ewing, in the lane, had found his nemesis.

his peers were trapped in a lackluster time for black style. Unlike the gloriously majestic though difficult to manage H-bomb Afros that had given Kareem Abdul-Jabbar and Julius "Dr. J" Erving such panache, the ensuing epoch ushered in a scaled-down brand of black hair that was either pedestrian or deeply heinous, like Michael Jackson's notorious curls. (God knows the terrible turn American culture would have taken if Jordan had adopted a hairstyle that ruined countless sofas, shirts, and bedsheets with its noxious lubrication.) Around 1987, Jordan abandoned the pretense he wasn't going bald, thankfully didn't call the Hair Club for Men, and instead began a new era in American style.

Now, the bald black dome as cultural signifier had been championed before. Early in the century the look was associated with the brilliant, boastful, bodacious heavyweight Jack Johnson, a man so infamous and reviled that after his decline no prominent Negro sported a well-waxed, bald-head look for two generations. It wasn't until the confident Afro-Americans of the 1970s that the bald look resurfaced with the deep-voiced balladeer Isaac Hayes, aka "Black Moses," leading the way.

The sharp blade of Jordan's barber gave his era a fresh definition of what a masculine hero looks like. In the process, Jordan finally buried the anachronistic Afro and squeezed away the last of those scary curls, and gave black men a new benchmark of pride. I know that's a lot of weight to place on anyone's head—especially one without hair. But I'm not through. With all due seriousness, I submit that Jordan isn't Jordan, the most internationally recognized American athlete since Muhammad Ali, without that decision to shed.

Sure, Jordan's still a great athlete with hair—he beat Georgetown as a college player with a head full of the stuff—but he's not the same icon. Imagine his Nike ads, his instantly recognizable "Jump Man" logo, the design on his cologne bottle, or the countless beauty shots of Jordan if he'd lingered in the bald-or-not-to-be-bald netherworld that his worthy adversary Clyde Drexler lingered in far too long. Blessed with a wonderfully symmetrical skull and rich milk chocolate skin, Jordan's head, like Babe Ruth's paunch and Bill Russell's goatee, is intrinsically linked to his sporting achievement and off-court persona.

The ripple effect of Jordan's razor blade was to transform a dull period in style into a new time full of bald, bad, beautiful black men. In large part this was because the look created a nice trey of benefits—it was sexy to women, intimidating to men, and simple to maintain. Jordan's golf buddy, Dream Team teammate and future Hall of Famer Charles Barkley, was a clear (and shining) benefactor of the Jordan effect. It should be noted, however, that Barkley's bald head worked more as a confirmation of Barkley's villainy than his heroism.

In the wider world, black men of all strata, from the British folk rocker Seal, to the Ralph Lauren model Tyson Beckford, to embattled rap star Tupac Shakur, adopted the bald look in search of the sensuality, toughness, and magnetism it bestowed on Number 23. Certainly it wasn't for everyone. My three-year run as a Jordan wannabe will not enhance anyone's memories of the Nineties. Nor will the dome of the earnest but profoundly misguided white center Matt Geiger, who, for all his waxing and shaving, will never be as macho as even Mr. Clean.

Jordan's head gave all of us everyday people a chance to share something with him, to look in the mirror in the morning and feel somehow linked to him in a way that buying his latest sneaker couldn't. Yet this fun and, admittedly, whimsical connection to Jordan means nothing without the heart that gave his head meaning.

Michael Jordan's Heart

Excellence is not a word bandied about much in the Nineties. Marketing and its cousin, market share, stand alongside *millennium, technology,* and, of course, *Internet* as the buzz words of the age. Size matters immensely. Not size as in power forwards or centers but as in the portfolios of Bill Gates and Jordan's good buddy Phil Knight. In the Nineties we loved being dwarfed by the magnitude of a person's pocketbook, since we are so rarely daunted by the greatness of their genius. Of that mountain of Jordan clips referred to earlier, at least one side is formed of inky pages documenting his wily agent, heavenly salary, and bountiful endorsement dollars.

Yet nobody in this age of buccaneer deal making has questioned Jordan's right to

Jordan's Head, Before.
Sure, Jordan's still a great athlete with hair, but he's not the same icon.

every damn dollar. This is because he gave America something it so desperately craved and so rarely received, soul-satisfying artistry and undiluted excellence. In an age of hype (and commensurate disappointment) Jordan delivered and delivered and delivered. Six times in the Nineties he was champion of the National Basketball Association, anchoring the truest dominance of any sport since Bill Russell's Celtics of the Sixties.

In the Eighties Larry Bird's Celtics won three and Magic Johnson's Lakers took five, but during the half dozen seasons of the Nineties that Jordan started with the Bulls, the franchise hung a championship banner after each one. Those matching sets of three titles included the 1995–96 campaign when they won a record-breaking 72 games in the regular season. It is in the inauguration of that second Bull run, circa 1995 to 1998, that I believe Jordan's case for off-the-chart greatness is best made.

The first championship run was very different from the second, just as two halves of a decade usually elude facile linkages. The Horace Grant–Scottie Pippen–Bill Cartwright–John Paxson–B. J. Armstrong team always seemed vulnerable, like they were only one or two defensive stops by the opponent from defeat. Before the Bulls' breakthrough in 1991, the bullying Detroit Pistons, led by baby-faced assassin Isiah Thomas, Joe Dumars, and a gang of long-limbed enforcers (Bill Laimbeer, John Salley, James Edwards, and the then black-haired Dennis Rodman) damaged the bodies and psyches of Jordan and his then slender sidekick Pippen.

Once the brutal Motor City squad was finally vanquished, the Bulls, toughed and battle tested, engaged in pitched wars with the gifted Cleveland Cavaliers, the hard-nosed New York Knicks and a series of Western Conference foes. Jordan scared you when you played these Bulls, but you always sensed that he was carrying them on his back; any slippage on his part—and sudden excellence on yours—and you'd have the rings. Perhaps I thought this because I was a needy Knick season ticket holder in deep denial. Despite Pat Riley's power suits and Anthony Mason's glowering game, the Knicks, and every other franchise, were destined to be bridesmaids. If Jordan had won only those three titles, he'd still be one of the greatest to play the game, and one of its truest winners.

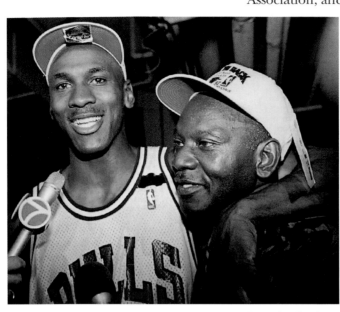

His Father's Son. Above, James Jordan, constantly at his son's side during the early years of his pro career, celebrates the Bulls' second world title, in 1992. His father would live to see only one more championship.

The Air Up There. In his first years as a pro, Jordan's physical prowess was so fresh, and his Bulls teammates so inferior, some perceived him as a selfish show-boat (right). But as he willed his teammates toward the first of six titles, he revealed himself as a great leader.

YET IT'S WHAT HAPPENED IN THE PERIOD BETWEEN TITLES three and four that made the man into as close to a contemporary myth as this cynical time can muster. For it is one thing to win; it is another to face tragedy and ridicule and to win again. We now enter the dark time.

It began on July 23, 1993, just weeks after championship number three, with Michael's father, James Jordan, returning home from a wedding in Wilmington. A little tired, he pulled his red Lexus 400 to the side of Highway 74 to take a nap. Days later his body was found dumped in a nearby river. He'd been shot dead by a slug from a .38 pistol. This was the kind of monstrous, life-altering tragedy all too common across the contemporary American landscape. That it happened to the family of a sports superstar didn't make it any more horrifying, just infinitely more public. Jordan had often called his father his best friend.

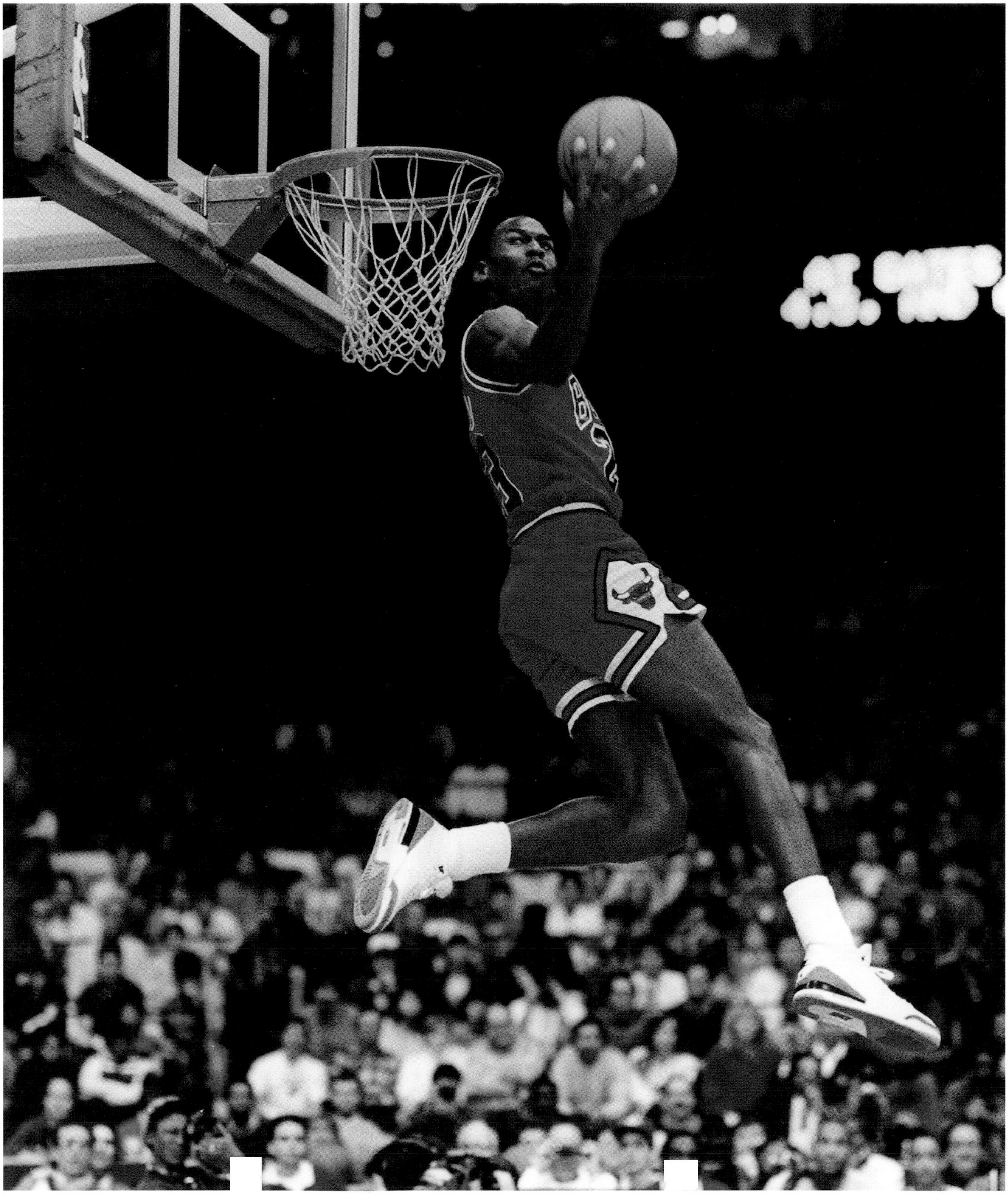

The bond was apparent at the many games and appearances James Jordan accompanied his son to.

The hollow, lonely feeling that descended upon Jordan and his family following the murder led him to a radical and, ultimately, unsatisfying decision. His retirement from the NBA at 30, though clearly premature, was understandable because of all he'd attained in the game—seven consecutive scoring titles (tying Wilt Chamberlain) and three straight championships—and because of the incalculable sense of loss.

Tragedy turned to curiosity when Jordan announced he was trading in sneakers and shorts for cleats and gloves. That no one laughed—though many snickered—when he announced he was going to pursue a baseball career in the White Sox's minor-league system is a testament to the respect he'd earned. Even that most judgmental group in the nation, callers to sports-talk radio shows, mostly bit their tongues. That his competitive fire still burned was evident as fans watched him chase fly balls and struggle with the strike zone. Thankfully, his batting average, never above .258 in two minor-league campaigns, speaks to the futility of his ballyard play and the inevitability of his return to the hardwood. (This cartoonish career turn was appropriately immortalized in the animated film *Space Jam*.)

Trading in Sneakers for Cleats.
"That his competitive fire still burned was evident as fans watched him chase fly balls and struggle with the strike zone."

MICHAEL JORDAN RETURNED TO HIS TRUE CALLING on a March Sunday afternoon in Indianapolis, but Number 23 was nowhere in sight. He wore Number 45 in that game and for the rest of the regular season, retiring his original number because it was what his father had seen him play in last. To the fans it was a beautiful gesture that came from the heart. To his rivals in the NBA it was a sign, perhaps, that this was a new Jordan, one not quite as invincible as the old one.

Even after dropping "a double nickel" (in Spike Lee's words), or 55 points, one spring night in New York, Number 45 often seemed rusty and lacking in NBA stamina. Almost two years away from a sport in which the level of athletic ability is constantly rising appeared an eternity. In the 1995 playoffs, Chicago faced the brash, hip-hop happy Orlando Magic, a team stocked with new jack stars, from the mammoth center Shaq O'Neal, to the multitalented guard Penny Hardaway, to the long-range sharpshooters Dennis Scott and Nick Anderson.

Most problematic for the Bulls was the presence of Horace Grant, their once crucial power forward, who fled to Orlando for free-agent millions. In the addition and subtraction classes of free-agent–era pro sports, Grant didn't simply make the Magic smarter and wiser, his absence made the Bulls softer and meeker. Throughout the six-game series Grant killed the Bulls with put backs and jump shots, while the younger players, particularly the trash-talking Anderson, attacked Jordan like he was a pauper, not a prince. The most memorable and symbolic play of the series happened in the fourth quarter of game one, when Anderson picked Jordan's pocket, a steal which led to a crucial dunk and a crushing defeat. It looked like a new dynasty had emerged, and it didn't wear red and black. Piling it on after Game 1 and throughout the Magic's four wins to two defeats of the Bulls, Anderson and his teammates taunted Jordan about the rust in his game. (Although, fittingly, Anderson would endure his own trial in the Finals, missing four free throws that would have won Game 1 versus Houston.) Jordan had

Anderson's cruel critiques ringing in his ears all the summer.

Was his reign now truly over? With his champion's mantle now rudely pulled down, was he now just good and no longer great?

That summer Jordan made three crucial decisions: He decided to wear number 23 full-time again after first putting it back on during the losing Orlando series; he supported the Bulls' decision to sign the tenacious, troubled rebounder Dennis Rodman; and he recommitted himself to the game, coming back with his old endurance and increased upper-body strength, testimony to his re-ignited fire. In this new phase Jordan refurbished his game. The tongue still hung out and, of course, the bald head still glistened, but the tomahawk dunks were less frequent, replaced by a deadly fade-away jumper that was his new money shot. This weapon was now employed to break the spirit of the Starks, Millers, and Hawkins he faced. Slightly more earthbound yet still lethal, Jordan played the 1995–96 season as if all of his previous accomplishments in the sport were at stake.

Following the tragedy of his father's death and the farce of his baseball career came the redemptive final act of this drama on June 16, 1996, on the floor of Chicago's United Center. As the buzzer sounded on Chicago's 87–75 victory over

A Lonely Triumph. On Father's Day 1996, Jordan's Bulls clinched their first title since his return. Remembering his father, he clutched the game ball at the end of the clinching victory. It was an act not of jubilation but of immense sorrow.

the Seattle SuperSonics, giving them their fourth title of the Nineties, Jordan wrestled the ball out of the hands of guard Randy Brown. It was not an act of jubilation but immense sorrow. Sprinting and twisting through the celebrating crowd, Jordan arrived in the relative sanctity of the Chicago dressing room (relative, since there was an NBC crew on hand) to lie on the floor and cry for the father that wasn't

there. Adding even greater poignancy was the fact that this particular June 16 wasn't just Game 6 of the NBA Finals—it was Father's Day.

This was a key image of the era, and one for the ages. After a career of on-court highlights and poised on-camera appearances to hawk products, here was Michael Jordan, emotionally naked, overwhelmed by a mix of grief and satisfaction beautiful in its truth. In a era of scripted outrage from pundits on 24-hour cable, when hyped-up controversy breeds suspicion of emotional displays and tabloid television cameramen can turn a family's grief into a visual cliché of a family's tears, Jordan's action was as pure and spontaneous as Nineties media-saturated culture ever saw.

This was far from the end of Jordan. More titles, more commercials, more calculated imagery, and more vacillating retirement talk would add layers to Jordan's personal mountain of ink. But it was this series of events involving death, retreat, redemption, and real emotion that, to quote the philosopher C. L. R. James's lovely cricket metaphor, lifted Jordan beyond the boundary of the game itself and, in fact, beyond the world of style and celebrity he was central to.

His second and, hopefully, final retirement before the lockout-shortened 1999 season was as well timed as any jump shot. Like Jim Brown, Bill Russell, and a few other of the century's best, Jordan left the game a winner, his career not tarnished, like that of Willie Mays or Muhammad Ali, by memories of lackluster final years.

THOSE BEMOANING BASKETBALL'S FATE WITH JORDAN GONE—specifically those writers still tossing newspaper columns on that bonfire of clippings—acted as if number 23 hadn't just refined the game, but actually invented it. The game will go on without him. Every day, kids of all ages lace up their sneakers and pull up their socks in search of companionship, exercise, and fleeting moments of transcendence. And, if some of the older kids are lucky and they go to the right gym on the right day, they may end up on Jordan's side in a pick-up game. Away from the lights and the money and the hype, they'll be just like him—seeking the competition and the fleeting perfection of sport. At the end of the century, as one hundred years ago, that quest is what truly endures.

PREVIOUS PAGES
The Last Shot. His series winner in 1998 at Utah—his final shot as a professional—will only increase the size of his legend in the decades to follow.

The Eternal Competitor.
Seeking the fleeting perfection of sport.

PETE SAMPRAS
Heart of a Champion

It was Pete Sampras's blessing to develop into the most supremely skilled men's tennis champion since the Open Era began in 1968, possessing an all-court game of power and elegance that evoked the Australian champions of the 1960s. But it was Sampras' curse to develop this beautiful game in the Nineties, at a time when a good portion of the audience believed that "Image Is Everything." Because of that, the best tennis player since Rod Laver spent much of his triumphant decade having to answer questions about his on-court persona, or lack thereof. "I do have a personality," he insisted at one point. "The people that know me know that."

So did the people who knew tennis. For the really odd part of the bland Sampras rep was this: The incontrovertible proof of his grit, charisma and character was out there on the court for anyone who was paying attention. Sampras wasn't just the most gifted athlete to play tennis—with smooth, flowing strokes and an almost balletic sense of form on the court—he also developed into one of the game's bravest battlers.

In the 1995 Australian Open, after his coach Tom Gullikson left prematurely because of an illness later diagnosed as a brain tumor (he'd die a year later), the distracted Sampras fell behind two sets to love against Jim Courier. He fought back to even, but began weeping on the court during the fifth set over the stress of the long fortnight and the illness of his friend and mentor. Sobbing openly, he defeated Courier, 6–3, in the fifth set. The next year, at the 1996 U.S. Open, he battled Alex Corretja in one of the most memorable matches of the decade. Seized by cramps, vomiting twice during the final set, Sampras fought off one match point with an ace, and prevailed, 9–7, in the tiebreaker to win a four-hour, nine-minute war that revealed the heart of a champion. Three days later, he won the title.

Sampras burst into the national consciousness as the youngest male winner ever of the U.S. Open, capturing the 1990 Open at 19 years, 28 days, ripping through Ivan Lendl, John McEnroe and Andre Agassi in the last three rounds, winding up with 100 aces in the tournament. But it took a while for him to develop into the world's best player. He was uncomfortable with the pressure in the years following the Open win, and it wasn't until his U.S. Open loss to Stefan Edberg in the 1992 finals that his attitude changed. "It made me realize just how bad it feels to lose a Grand Slam final," he said. "How the only player that people care about is the one who gets his name engraved on the trophy." Over the next six years, Sampras won 10 more Grand Slam titles and lost only one final (the 1995 Australian, to Agassi).

SAMPRAS:
"I DO HAVE A PERSONALITY. THE PEOPLE WHO KNOW ME KNOW THAT"

RICE:
"JERRY HADN'T HAD A WHITE COACH, SO THERE WERE DOUBTS"

And if some fans still didn't appreciate the genius of his game, his opponents surely did. "He has this way of keeping at arm's length the issues that could threaten his love for the game and his dedication to it," said Boris Becker. "That says a lot about his pure passion as a tennis player. And it makes life as a tennis player easier for him."

JERRY RICE
Those Beautiful Hands

Gloster Richardson, a fine NFL wide receiver whose own hands sported Super Bowl rings with the Chiefs and Cowboys, was the pass receivers coach at Mississippi Valley State when a lanky, quiet kid named Jerry Rice arrived in 1980. After a few practices Richardson knew he'd seen something special. "They're just beautiful," Richardson said of Rice's hands. "Real soft, real quiet. Always right on time. He doesn't need to use his body to catch the ball. His hands are just a gift."

That gift, and a fanatical determination to improve his game, would make Rice perhaps the greatest wide receiver in NFL history. By the end of the century he would own the receivers wing of the NFL record book. He would eventually break all the career records—most catches, most yards, most touchdowns—for receivers. Along the way, Rice bridged two eras of 49er excellence, serving as the go-to guy for both Joe Montana and Steve Young.

Rice first earned scouts' attention as the featured wideout in Archie "Gunslinger" Cooley's run-and-gun "Satellite Express" offense at Mississippi Valley State, where he set 18 Division I-AA records grabbing passes from Willie Totten. But the Delta Devils' passing attack was a technical marvel, and some NFL personnel people suspected that it wasn't Rice so much as the system he played in. "A lot of scouts thought we just lined up and ran deep," said Cooley. "What it all meant was that Jerry hadn't had a white coach, so there were doubts."

Not among the 49ers. Bill Walsh, who'd been intrigued with Cooley's attack for years, was so sold on Rice, he traded up to the 16th spot in the 1985 draft—one selection ahead of Tom Landry and the Dallas Cowboys, who would have taken him 17th. Within two seasons, he'd become the best receiver in the NFL, a strong, elusive wideout who was dangerous because of his uncanny ability to get open and then gain yards after the catch.

On the biggest stage, Rice had his biggest games. In three Super Bowl appearances—all 49er wins—he caught 28 passes for 512 yards and seven touchdowns. His 11-catch, 215-yard performance against Cincinnati in XXIII earned him an MVP award (and he was the irresistible decoy on Joe Montana's game-winning touchdown pass to John Taylor). A year later, his silky post-pattern touchdown catch at the end of the first half opened the floodgates in the 49ers' 55–10 blowout of the Denver Broncos. And in Super Bowl

XXIX, Rice's 44-yard touchdown on the third play of the game, after the Chargers spent two weeks focusing on keeping him from the big play, signaled that the rout was on.

"He just gets so *open*," said Montana, straining for a way to articulate it. "He has the knack of knowing when to break, when to use his speed." Seattle's Steve Largent, who would see Rice break his touchdown record, was amazed by his subtleties. "Little things like body leans and head movements, the things a lot of guys who have great physical ability won't do. Other guys will say, 'I'm faster' or 'I'm better than this defender.' But Jerry does them both."

BONNIE BLAIR
"A Tough Chick"

The woman who humbled the mighty East German speed-skating machine at Calgary in 1988 stood 5-foot-5-inches, looked like a buffed Holly Hunter in head-to-skate Lycra, and readily conceded, "I can cry at the drop of a hat."

She ate peanut butter and jelly sandwiches before her Olympic races, was sponsored by the Champaign, Illinois, Policeman's Benevolent Association and had an unassuming, fresh-faced appeal. She was everybody's girl next door—if they lived next to a Navy Seal boot camp.

"It's hard to describe Bonnie Blair," said one-time U.S. teammate Mary Docter. "She's just a tough chick."

Blair, showing more grit than a belt sander, won five Olympic gold medals, more than any other female American. Typically self-effacing, she laughed off the suggestion she was born to be a speed-skating phenomenon, noting she was seven years younger than her next oldest sibling.

"I was an accident," she said. Yet it was not serendipity that led to her dominance. Blair's introduction came to the speed-skating world via the loudspeaker at a meet where her father had taken some of her five older siblings—four of whom would hold national titles—to compete. "The Blairs have another skater," the voice on the loudspeaker said. At age two she began skating, wearing shoes inside the skates to make up for her tiny feet, and was racing by five. "I can't even remember learning how to skate," she said. "It comes almost as naturally to me as walking."

In 1984, at age 19, she made her first Olympic team, finishing eighth in the 500 and getting a taste of what she needed to win at that level. "I used to be lazy," she would later say. "I could always come up with excuses for skipping a workout. I hadn't reached the point where I was a student of the sport."

Unable to win strictly on physical power, like her Eastern European rivals, Blair had to rely on technique and heart. Her explosive starts and tight, low crouch allowed her to maximize her speed. "She's smooth, graceful—it's almost like she's floating over the ice," said former U.S. coach Mike Crowe. "She's quiet, too. There's not a lot of ice flying, and when she puts her foot down, it's solid—no wiggles at all."

BLAIR:
"IT COMES
ALMOST AS
NATURALLY TO
ME AS
WALKING"

LEMIEUX:
"HE'LL MAKE
YOU LOOK LIKE
A COMPLETE
IDIOT"

Blair won the 500 meters in a world-record 39.10 seconds and finished third in the 1,000 in Calgary. Always skating before a vocal group of family and friends dubbed "Blair's Bunch," she swept the sprints in Albertville in 1992 and Lillehammer in 1994, to become the first U.S. athlete to win the same event in three consecutive Olympics.

With the medals came the perks—a Kellogg's Corn Flakes box, a street named for her back in her hometown of Champaign and special vanity license plates (GOLD X5) from the governor of Wisconsin (where she by then lived and trained). But Blair remained unfazed. "Bonnie doesn't know she's a celebrity," said her mother, Eleanor. "She sees herself as a regular person."
—*Mark Wangrin*

MARIO LEMIEUX
The Second Coming

In the early 1980s, while Mario Lemieux was dominating Canadian junior hockey, his agent convinced him to wear jersey number 66, inviting comparisons to the incomparable Wayne Gretzky, whose 99 then adorned the backs of most hero-worshipping kids in Canada. But it is a mixed blessing at best to be compared to the Great One, and it took Lemieux a long time to elude Gretzky's awesome shadow. But by the time he finished his career, jersey number 66 was a hockey icon as well.

Growing up in a working-class neighborhood in Montreal, Lemieux was groomed for hockey from an early age. His father, a retired construction worker, left the front door to the family house open in the winter, allowing ice to build up on the front hallway carpet, where he taught Mario and his two older brothers to skate. As a junior, Lemieux developed a reputation as a brilliant, petulant prodigy who amazed fans with his 133-goal, 282-point season (in 70 games) in 1983-84, then alienated them by passing up an invitation to the World Junior Championship.

Selected first in the 1984 draft by the Pittsburgh Penguins, Lemieux joined a woeful franchise desperately in need of a savior. He was an immediate star: He scored a goal on his first shot during his first shift of his first game in the NHL, and won the Calder Trophy as rookie of the year. At 6-foot-4-inches, 210 pounds, Lemieux was larger than virtually any other center in the league, but also possessed a remarkable blend of speed and stickhandling ability. "If you go at Mario like a madman, he'll make you look like a complete idiot," said Boston's Ray Bourque. But the premature comparisons to Gretzky rankled some observers, who rapped Lemieux for an apparent lack of intensity, his inability to carry the mediocre Penguins into the playoffs, even his soft-focus good looks.

Then came 1987's Canada Cup, and all that changed. Playing right wing to Gretzky's center on a dream line of Canadian stars, Lemieux scored 18 points in nine games, including game winners in the last two games of the best-of-three finals series against the Soviet Union. He returned to the NHL a certified star, with more confidence and a new-found sense of purpose, winning his first scoring title and first MVP trophy in the 1987–88 season. That began a six-year run in which Lemieux was the most dominant player in hockey, leading the Penguins to two Stanley Cup titles and averaging more than two points per game for the span.

In January 1993, Lemieux was diagnosed with Hodgkin's disease and underwent debilitating radiation treatments. He was weakened the following season, then took the entire 1994–95 season off to rehabilitate before returning hero-ically, winning scoring titles in each of his final two seasons. Though he retired prematurely in 1997, Lemieux finally was recognized as Gretzky's lone peer, if not his equal. "He revolutionized this game, as Gretzky did," said Rod Brind'Amour of the Flyers. "We all owe him a lot." Hockey paid him the ultimate respect, waiving the customary three-year waiting period in inducting him into the Hockey Hall of Fame.

DEION SANDERS
A Man in His Prime

It was draft day 1989, and Deion Sanders sat on the couch in his then-agent's house in Winnetka, Illinois, encased in gold chains and attitude, devilishly playful, reveling in the adulation of being the fifth pick in the NFL draft. "I'm going to ask for so much money," he boasted to an ESPN audience, "the Falcons are going to have to put me on layaway!"

It wasn't the first time in his athletic career that Sanders' words and attitude would distract from his immense skills, and it wouldn't be the last. The three-sport natural in high school and college developed his "Prime Time" persona at Florida State, where he showed up for his final regular-season game in a limousine, sporting a top hat and tails. What made this self-promotion tolerable was Sanders' perfor-mances—he created his own hype, then lived up to it. He was the first man to play in both a Super Bowl and a World Series, and the first to score an NFL touchdown and hit a major-league homer in the same week.

As a baseball player, Sanders was forever a work in progress, never able to master the finer nuances of hitting. But he worked assiduously at all aspects of his game, and by 1997—his last in the majors before playing football full-time—he routinely tormented opposing pitchers, stealing 56 bases in 115 games.

But on the football field, he was a wonder. Though his let-it-all-hang-out look was peculiar—hand towel flapping from his waistband, chinstraps hanging from his helmet, gloves applied loosely, their Velcro flaps flying free—his skills were never less than exceptional. His quick jam move at the snap could shut down receivers instantly, and in an era of liberal-ized passing rules, the man who once ran a 4.2 40-yard-dash *in shoulder pads* was the ultimate cover cornerback, despite

SANDERS: "HE'S LIKE YOUR NEXT-DOOR NEIGHBOR"

JOHNSON: "I LIVE FOR THAT VERY MOMENT IN THE BLOCKS"

his dubious tackling skills. His closing speed was so other-worldly that, after a few seasons, quarterbacks rarely threw to his side, and virtually never threw his way on out patterns. Leaving the Falcons in 1994, he then led San Francisco to the Super Bowl. A year later, he signed a $35-million deal with the Cowboys and helped them win their third Super Bowl title of the decade. Sanders was a dominant force on defense, and could occasionally break games open offen-sively as a situational receiver, or on special teams as a kick returner.

By 1998, he'd given up the gold chains and become a born-again Christian, preaching the Lord's gospel and speaking out against his past transgressions. But even when he was strutting his stuff across the national stage as the most flamboyant athlete of his time, there was a sense that even Sanders didn't quite believe his own shtick.

"People think he's cocky and arrogant, but when you sit with him on a bus, he's like your next-door neighbor," said Joe Oliver, his teammate in Cincinnati during his last baseball season. "He's not different, he's not arrogant, he's not into himself. He's just a confident guy who believes in his ability."

MICHAEL JOHNSON
Heir to the Throne

Michael Johnson carried the handwritten card as inspira-tion. Its message wasn't so novel—the author wrote that the tightly muscled sprinter ran straight up, with a quick, com-pact stride reminiscent of Jesse Owens—but the signature at the bottom was. It belonged to Ruth Owens, Jesse's widow.

Publicly, Johnson modestly dismissed such comparisons, saying he had not even approached the accomplishments of the hero of the 1936 Olympics. Privately, he embraced them. Owens had won four gold medals in one Olympics, something no other track athlete had done. At Atlanta in 1996, Johnson also wanted to do something no one had done—become the first man to win the 200- and 400-meter dashes in one Olympics. Getting the card from Ruth Owens meant pressure. And Johnson loved pressure.

"I crave it," Johnson said. "I live for that very moment in the blocks when you may win, but you don't know, and now you're going to find out." Deep inside, Johnson knew the answer, for he rarely left anything to chance. Growing up in Paul Johnson's frame house in the Oak Cliff section of Dallas meant being prepared. For everything. Even before they were teenagers, Michael and his four siblings were regularly quizzed by their father on not only what they want-ed to be when they grew up, but on how they would afford the insurance when they bought their first homes.

His answer almost certainly did not include making millions as a sprinter. In high school the man whom oppo-nents would later call Superman wore horn-rimmed glasses, a pressed white shirt and a tie to class every day. On the track he wasn't much more imposing.

"I'd be lying if I said I thought Michael was going to be a world-class sprinter," said coach Clyde Hart, who recruited Johnson to Baylor University. "I don't think anybody did." Hart soon learned of Johnson's work ethic and attention to detail, which includes recording each workout in a journal, almost down to each stride. While most sprinters "guesstimate" the position of their blocks, Johnson brings a tape-measure and aligns them to the sixteenth of an inch. "He measures everything," said his agent, Brad Hunt.

The preparation paid off in Atlanta. Leg injuries cost him a shot at gold in Seoul in 1988, and food poisoning kept him out of a 200 final he was expected to dominate in Barcelona, but the 6-foot-1-inch, 185-pounder accomplished the historic double in the Centennial Games. Running in custom-made gold shoes and with his customary stoicism, Johnson took advantage of a scheduling change arranged specifically for him to complete the grinding sweep with ease, winning the 200 in a stunning world record time of 19.32, and with the largest winning margin since Owens.

When Johnson saw the time on the stadium scoreboard, he let out a scream of disbelief, and later fell prone on the track. Awed, bronze medalist Ato Bolden turned toward Johnson and bowed. "Nineteen point thirty two? That's not a time—it sounds like my dad's birth date," Bolden said.

Cognizant that his gold medal was forged by the heat of his self-imposed pressure, Johnson said, "I know a lot of people say when they succeed, suddenly it's like throwing off a huge weight, but I enjoy it so much. Well, not like it's exactly fun, not birthday-party fun, but I love it so, I do."

With his performance in Atlanta, Johnson supplanted the then-soon-to-be-retired Carl Lewis as the greatest American track athlete and lived up to his comparisons to Owens, an accomplishment made even greater by the fact that he didn't run the sport's sexiest event.

"Traditionally, the 100-meter guys have always been the fastest guys," Johnson conceded. "But since I came along, I've changed a lot of the rules of sprinting."

—*Mark Wangrin*

BARRY SANDERS
A Little Genius

Even if he wasn't destined to become the NFL's all-time leading rusher late in 1999 or early in the 2000 season, Barry Sanders would still be a legend, because he's the first running back since Gale Sayers who truly had to be seen to be believed.

Sayers himself said as much: "Thurman Thomas is a great back. Emmitt Smith is a great back. But I would pay to watch Barry Sanders play. He turns me on." Jim Brown called him a "little genius," and Walter Payton, watching Sanders run in his rookie year of 1989, said flatly, "He's better than I was. I was never that good."

The soft-spoken, devoutly religious fireplug from Wichita,

SANDERS: "THE BEST EVER TO MAKE SOMETHING OUT OF NOTHING"

Kansas, backed up Thurman Thomas for two years at Oklahoma State before bursting into headlines with an out-of-nowhere season in 1988. Sanders rolled up high school numbers—2,628 rushing yards and 39 touchdowns—against major college opposition, then ran off with the Heisman Trophy and into the pros.

Picked third overall by Detroit in the 1989 draft, Sanders signed a contract three days before the regular season started, then ran for 71 yards on nine carries in the first quarter of the season opener. He quickly quieted critics who wondered if his 5-foot-8-inch, 203-pound body could withstand the punishment of the pro game. Sanders was a compact, tightly coiled ball of lightning-fast muscle, capable of mind-boggling cuts and fakes, yet still strong enough to break tackles the old-fashioned way.

"People who hit him around those thunder thighs just bounce off," said one scout. "He's like a Walt Disney deer bouncing through the forest." Or, as coach Mike Holmgren put it, Sanders "is the best ever to make something out of nothing. The best."

He ran for more than 1,000 yards in each of his first 10 years in the league (with more yards in the second five than the first five). In 1997, he rushed for 2,053 yards, the second-highest single-season total in NFL history. But Sanders never was surrounded by the supporting cast that eventually coalesced around Payton in Chicago. He seemed destined for the same fate in football as befell Ernie Banks in baseball—to become an all-time great who never got to the sport's biggest stage.

Along the way to greatness, he earned his peers' ultimate respect. A study in quiet, sturdy pride, the taciturn Sanders spanned and spurned two generations of end-zone dances—from the "Ickey Shuffle" to the "Dirty Bird"—yet remained the consummate professional, living by the old coach's credo: "Act like you've been there before." At the end of those thrilling touchdown runs, Sanders would slow to a trot, heave a big sigh, look at an official with his placid, serene eyes, and gently toss him the football.

His World: Woods exults after sinking the putt that broke the Masters record.

GOLF

The Masters Meets the Future

Coming to the most hallowed grounds in American golf in 1997, with a media posse lying in wait, and all the pressure of great expectations on his 21-year-old shoulders, Tiger Woods responded with the best major tournament performance of the century. After his par on the 18th Sunday, he had his first green jacket, the Masters had a new tournament record, the majors had their first black champion ever and a new era had dawned in golf.

Woods shot 40 on the front nine Thursday, steadied himself with a swing adjustment prior to 10, and then proceeded to shoot the next 63 holes in 22-under par, finishing 18-under, to break Jack Nicklaus' and Ray Floyd's tournament record. Woods won by 12 strokes, the largest margin in a major since Old Tom Morris won the 1862 British Open by 13 strokes. "He's more dominant over the guys he's playing against than I ever was over the ones I played against," said Nicklaus. "He's so long, he reduces the course to nothing. Absolutely nothing."

Playing his first major as a pro, Woods was an awesome sight; his driving average of 323 yards was 25 yards beyond anyone else in the field. After being paired with him Saturday, when Woods increased his three-stroke lead to nine strokes, Colin Montgomerie brought a hangdog expression to the press tent and said, "There is no chance. We're all human beings here. There's no chance humanly possible." Tom Watson, a two-time winner, said, "He's a boy among men. And he's showing the men how to play."

After completing the 72nd hole, Woods rushed into an embrace with his father, a retired army colonel who had devoted much of his life to teaching his son how to play the game. Then, in a weekend when golf's lily-white past confronted its future, Tiger Woods spoke about the black players who had struggled before him. "I wasn't the pioneer," he said. "Charlie Sifford, Lee Elder, Ted Rhodes—those are the guys who paved the way. All night I was thinking about them, what they've done for me and the game of golf. Coming up 18, I said a little prayer of thanks to those guys." Walking to Butler Cabin to accept his green jacket, Woods saw Elder, who in 1975 became the first black to compete at the Masters. He stopped to embrace him, and to give thanks.

BASEBALL

1991 World Series

■ It was the worst-to-first series. Both the Braves and Twins had finished last in their divisions in '90, then turned it around in '91 to advance to the World Series. The Twins took the first two games at the homer-hanky-waving Metrodome, while the Braves tomahawk-chopped their way back, sweeping three games in Atlanta. With the Braves hoping to close it out in Game 6, Kirby Puckett capped a magnificent game with the winning homer in the bottom of the 11th. He'd already singled, tripled, stolen a base, driven in a run with a sacrifice fly and made a spectacular catch against the wall in center. But Game 7 topped it, with the Braves' John Smoltz and the Twins' Jack Morris throwing blanks. Bobby Cox went to his bullpen to get out of jams in the eighth and ninth, but Morris continued scrapping along, pitching 10 shutout innings. Dan Gladden doubled to open the bottom of the 10th. After a sacrifice and two walks loaded the bases, pinch-hitter Gene Larkin hit a drive to left-center to win the Series. It was the most tightly contested Fall Classic ever, featuring five one-run games, three of which went to extra innings.

COLLEGE BASKETBALL
1992 East Regional Final

■ Kentucky's Sean Woods nailed the shot with 2.1 seconds remaining in overtime, sending his teammates bounding off the bench, and much of Kentucky into a jubilant uproar. The Wildcats, it seemed, had knocked off the defending champion Duke Blue Devils. But amid the din at the Spectrum, Duke coach Mike Krzyzewski huddled with his players and opened with this message: "Okay, we're gonna win the game." Then he walked each player through his assignment in basketball's equivalent of the Hail Mary play: Grant Hill would throw the inbounds pass some 75 feet, it would go to Christian Laettner, who'd be cutting toward the Duke free-throw line. It all went as scripted: Laettner caught the ball, dribbled once, faked right, twirled left and threw up a sweet, arcing fallaway jumper that was in midair as the buzzer sounded and swished through the nets an instant later, giving Duke a 104-103 narrow escape, en route to becoming the first repeat national champion in 19 years. "I felt like I was watching Robert Redford in *The Natural*," said Hill of Laettner, who was 10-for-10 from the field (with one three-pointer) and 10-for-10 from the free-throw line, finishing with 31 points for the game. Afterward, Krzyzewski said, "I think we've all been part of one of the great games ever."

PRO FOOTBALL
1992 Buffalo-Houston Wild-Card Playoff

■ The Buffalo Bills had lost the last two Super Bowls and staggered into the playoffs after the 1992 season, losing a 27-3 season finale in Houston to the Oilers. The next week, in the first round of the playoffs, the Oilers visited Buffalo and picked up where they left off. It was 28-3 at halftime and, after Bubba McDowell returned an interception 58 yards two minutes into the second half, Houston was up 35-3 and many of the Rich Stadium faithful were heading for the exits. They missed the greatest comeback in NFL history. Quarterback Frank Reich, who at the University of Maryland had rallied the Terps from a 31-0 deficit to beat Miami, revived the Bills' offense, and they scored 28 points in 11 minutes. Late in the fourth quarter, Reich hit Andre Reed on a touchdown pass for the third time in the half, and the Bills went up 38-35. Though Warren Moon rallied Houston back for a field goal to send it to OT, the Oilers played like they were still in shock. Nate Odomes intercepted Moon early in overtime, and Steve Christie's 32-yard kick won the game. "We fight," said Bills linebacker Darryl Talley, "until they take the last breath out of us."

Great Performances

■ Mark McGwire caught the ghosts of Babe Ruth and Roger Maris, and stayed just ahead of Sammy Sosa, setting baseball's all-time single-season home-run record, by blasting 70 in 1998. McGwire's and Sosa's summer-long race for the record provided some much needed healing to a sport still suffering from the scars of the 1994 strike. It also left the game with another round number to aim at—a mythic figure that looked as imposing as Babe Ruth's 60 homers did in 1927... Their games were one-sided affairs, but few who watched will forget the original Dream Team, the collection of NBA stars who dominated the 1992 Summer Olympics.

Bull Run

After spending much of the late '80s knocking on the door, the Chicago Bulls finally broke through in the '90s. The incomparable **Michael Jordan** raised his game, of course, but he entered the decade as the best player in the league. It was Jordan's ability to conjure performances from his teammates that helped push Chicago to the top. **Scottie Pippen**, branded as soft in the Bulls' playoff losses to the Detroit Pistons, came into his own as one of the league's best all-round players. Even Dennis Rodman toned his act down, or at the very least altered it enough to stick around, when he became a teammate of Jordan's in 1995. From the 1990-91 season through his announced retirement in 1999, Jordan played six full seasons with the Bulls, and they won the NBA title each time, and each of those NBA Finals series ended within six games. Along the way, they built a tremendous psychological advantage over the rest of the league. "Sometimes you can build a team and have a great team that could be a championship team," said Heat coach Pat Riley, "and you never win a championship because you had the misfortune of being born at the same time that Jordan went through his run."

Phil Jackson presided over it all, and succeeded in winning six titles as a coach by prodding his players with an accessible synthesis of an ex-player's empathy, Zen philosophy, and a background in psychology.

■ **Close But No Cigar.** In another generation, the Buffalo Bills might have been embraced as lovable, tenacious heroes, like the Brooklyn Dodgers of the early '50s. But in an era so preoccupied with winning above all else, it was inevitable, perhaps, that one of the most successful franchises of the decade would also become one of the most ridiculed. There was no shame, only anguish, in the 20–19 "wide right" loss to the New York Giants in Super Bowl XXV, when Scott Norwood's kick pulled outside the uprights. But the Bills, led by Jim Kelly and Thurman Thomas' potent "K Gun" offense, and a stout defense anchored by Bruce Smith, kept winning the AFC and coming up short in the Super Bowl. The 37–24 loss to Washington in XXVI is best remembered for Thomas misplacing his helmet at the beginning of the game. By the time the Bills fell in the next two Super Bowls to Dallas, by scores of 52–14 and 30–13, the losses were taking their toll. After he retired from the Bills three seasons later, head coach Marv Levy said, "The depth of anguish I felt after every loss over the past few years has begun to reach an intensity that the thrill of victory couldn't overcome."

	COLLEGE BASKETBALL	PRO BASKETBALL NBA	HOCKEY NHL	BASEBALL MLB	COLLEGE FOOTBALL		PRO FOOTBALL NFL
1990	UNLV	Pistons	Oilers	Reds	Colorado (AP)	Georgia Tech (UPI)	Giants
1991	Duke	Bulls	Penguins	Twins	Miami, Fla. (AP)	Washington (USA)	Redskins
1992	Duke	Bulls	Penguins	Blue Jays	Alabama		Cowboys
1993	North Carolina	Bulls	Canadiens	Blue Jays	Florida State		Cowboys
1994	Arkansas	Rockets	Rangers	CANCELED	Nebraska		49ers
1995	UCLA	Rockets	Devils	Braves	Nebraska		Cowboys
1996	Kentucky	Bulls	Avalanche	Yankees	Florida		Packers
1997	Arizona	Bulls	Red Wings	Marlins	Michigan (AP)	Nebraska (USA)	Broncos
1998	Kentucky	Bulls	Red Wings	Yankees	Tennessee		Broncos
1999	Connecticut	Spurs	Stars				

NOTES **Baseball:** On Sept. 14, 1994, with no hope to reach a labor agreement to end the 34-day-old players strike, owners called off the remainder of the regular season and the entire postseason.
College football: Champions are mythical consensus national champions as voted by sportswriters in the Associated Press poll, and by coaches in the United Press International poll in 1990. Coaches poll supervised by USA Today from 1991-96, and by USA Today/ESPN since 1997.

Experience Necessary

Nebraska coach **Tom Osborne** entered the '90s branded a hidebound traditionalist unable to win the big games, or change with the times. When he retired after the 1997 season, it was as one of the most successful college football coaches ever, and the first since Frank Leahy in the '40s to win three national championships in four seasons. Osborne won more games in his 25 years at the helm of Nebraska than any college football coach in any 25-year span. "He is the most consistent person I've ever known—in every phase of life," said Turner Gill, his quarterback in the '80s and assistant coach in the '90s. And unlike most of the college game's sideline legends, Osborne saved his very best for last: Nebraska went 60-3 over his last five seasons, though the title in 1995 was clouded by charges that he had been too lenient with stars Christian Peter and Lawrence Phillips, both of whom faced criminal charges. On the field, the same power option offense that was judged hopelessly passé by experts at the dawn of the decade proved to be an innovation by the end of it. The key? Two gifted quarterbacks (Tommie Frazier, 1992-95, and Scott Frost, 1996-97) and a perfection in execution not seen on the major-college level since the days of John Wooden's basketball dynasty at UCLA.

While Osborne demonstrated the value of stolid persistence, **Scotty Bowman** succeeded by being persistently contrary. "He goes his own way," said Detroit defenseman Anders Eriksson. "He has his own ideas, and he really makes players be on the edge all the time, so they do their best and play as a team." When that Red Wing team hoisted its second straight Stanley Cup in 1998, it was the eighth time Bowman had coached an NHL champion, tying him with his old mentor, the Canadiens' legendary coach Toe Blake.

Bowman coached 26 winning teams in 27 seasons, brought the Blues to three Stanley Cup finals, won the Cup five times in Montreal, once in Pittsburgh and twice more in Detroit. By the end of the century, many considered him to be the greatest hockey coach ever. "He teaches things that make you a winner," said Red Wings assistant coach Barry Smith. "You learn details, the defensive side of the puck, don't cheat the game, play hard both ways, short shifts, a team mentality, and those kinds of things. Things that will help you win because that takes care of almost all situations."

COACHING WISDOM

"Certainly we should have a lot of coaches who are African-Americans. However, don't tell me as a Polish coach that I can't coach a kid from the inner city. I can coach anybody."

—Duke basketball coach Mike Krzyzewski

"This is private enterprise. The fans are entitled to the best product I can put on the field every Sunday, week in and week out, year in and year out if I'm lucky. How I put that product out there is my damn business."

—New York Jets coach Bill Parcells

Influences

Carrying the Torch

From the first day he took over as commissioner of the National Football League in 1989, **Paul Tagliabue** knew that he would receive none of the credit for the league's future successes, but all of the blame for any setbacks. It was his privilege and curse to succeed the most successful commissioner in American sports history, Pete Rozelle, at the end of Rozelle's 29-year tenure, which perfectly paralleled the game's ascension to its clear standing as the nation's favorite spectator sport.

And though he would inevitably be seen as a caretaker commissioner, and perceived to be less of a visionary than his basketball counterpart, NBA commissioner David Stern, Tagliabue's record at the end of the decade was unassailable.

In 1998, there was the signing of the richest sports (or entertainment) contract in television history, a stunning eight-year, $17-billion deal that guaranteed each NFL franchise $75 million a year in television revenue alone.

But while the league's revenues had quadrupled since Tagliabue took over, Tagliabue's biggest accomplishment was on the labor front. The NFL was the only major sport to go through the decade without a work stoppage, and in 1998, the league and the NFL Players Association extended their contract through 2003. "He's not the most public-relations-oriented guy, but he is a guy who is willing to go out and take a task on and deal with it," said Gene Upshaw, head of the NFLPA. "I've learned one thing through the years that he's been commissioner: If he's not involved in it, it's not going to get solved. It's just that simple."

But there was a limit to Tagliabue's powers, as franchise moves out of Houston, Los Angeles and Cleveland made clear. He did act immediately after the Browns left Cleveland, guaranteeing the city that it would be able to keep the team's history, name and colors, and promising that an NFL franchise would be in Cleveland by the beginning of the 1999 season. The Browns were back in place on September 12, 1999, opening their second NFL era against the arch-rival Pittsburgh Steelers.

It was a tribute to Tagliabue's abilities as both a diplomat and an architect that he was able to increase the NFL's profitability, while still stemming the tide of commercialism sweeping through major sports. Though NHL rinks were clogged with advertisements and major league baseball was considering selling ad space on player uniforms, the NFL remained relatively free of on-field advertisements. Tagliabue, who'd learned at the hand of Rozelle, long ago understood that the most important product the league had to sell was the National Football League itself.

TOP OF THE NEWS: The stars (and the supporting actors) are millionaires, and when baseball goes on strike in 1994, even the President seems powerless to solve the problem. In the Nineties, the world of sports has become part of America's entertainment industry and, for better or worse, the entertainment industry has become part of American sports—time-outs will never be the same

Movies

The decade's two best sports movies are documentaries. *Hoop Dreams*, directed by Steve James, follows a pair of inner-city Chicago youths, both with dreams of NBA riches, through their high school basketball careers. Leon Gast's Oscar-winning *When We Were Kings* is the ambitious documentary about the scene surrounding 1974's Ali-Foreman "Rumble in the Jungle" in Zaire, which Gast shot on the spot, then spent more than two decades trying to finish. It's worth the wait.

"There's no crying in baseball," warns Tom Hanks, a boozy ex-major leaguer hired to manage a women's team in *A League of Their Own*. The affecting comedy about the World War II–era glory days of the All-America Girls Baseball League was a hit at the box office, and renewed interest in the nearly-forgotten women's league, which sprang up during the manpower shortage in World War II.

While desperately trying to get the go-ahead for his long-planned Jackie Robinson biography, Spike Lee shoots *He Got Game*, starring the Milwaukee Bucks' Ray Allen as a coveted high school recruit whose convict father (Denzel Washington) wants him to go to the state university.

Reading List

The decade begins with the ambitious launch of **The National Sports Daily**, edited by Frank Deford. The daily tabloid newspaper devoted solely to sports breaks new ground, breaks a few stars to a national audience (Norman Chad, Charles Pierce), but goes under within 18 months, unable to accomplish the basic goal of all newspapers—get the West Coast box scores in the next morning's edition.

Harvey Penick's Little Red Book: Lessons and Teachings from a Lifetime in Golf, co-written by the legendary Austin golf instructor and Bud Shrake, is a surprise smash, eventually becoming the best-selling sports book ever. Pulitzer Prize winner Jim Murray publishes his autobiography in 1993. H.G. Bissinger's *Friday Night Lights: A Town, a Team, and a Dream* comes out in 1991, the tale of the mythic power of high school football in west Texas. Two important oral histories are published: Thomas Hauser's *Muhammad Ali: His Life and Times* is assembled with the cooperation of the champ; and Terry Pluto's *Loose Balls* chronicles the turbulent history of the ABA.

Alex Rodriguez, Kobe Bryant, Kordell Stewart, and Eric Lindros grace the cover of the first issue of **ESPN, The**

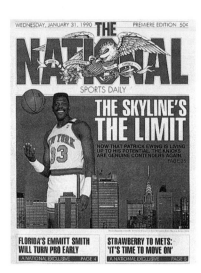

Magazine, which begins publishing as a biweekly in March 1998. Sporting an oversize format and an irreverent look, *ESPN* wins a National Magazine Award for design in its first year.

Sounds

From Hammer's "Too Legit to Quit" to the debut album by Hootie and the Blowfish, athletes start appearing in videos. Some are singing and making their own, led by Deion Sanders ("Must Be the Money"), Shaquille O'Neal ("Shaq Diesel") and Chris Webber (*Too Much Drama*). Meanwhile, in "High Tech Redneck," George Jones paints a picture of a country Superfan who watches "Football, baseball, NASCAR, too/ A picture-in-a-picture and it's all in view."

Playing Games

The sports game-playing world has gone 64-bit, with 3-D graphics, artificial intelligence, and sound effects. The industry leader is John Madden Football, which sells 11 million copies in its first 10 years on the market. The success of that game spawns countless arcade/strategy simulations in baseball, basketball, and hockey, making the sports video game market big business.

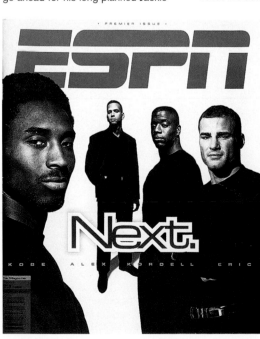

Fashion

Even as some teams are moving toward a more traditional, classic uniform style (the Indians and Jets), there is a powerful force that seems to put a '90s spin on the garish uniforms of the '70s. The Toronto Raptors enter the NBA in 1995 featuring a uniform with a huge cartoon dinosaur. The Tampa Bay Devil Rays begin play in 1998 with the team name across their jerseys in various colors, like a mood ring.

For the second decade in a row, basketball shorts get longer and baggier. The University of Michigan's **Fab Five** follows the lead of Michael Jordan, and the rest of college basketball (with the exception of Bobby Knight's staunchly retrograde, tastefully short shorts-wearing Indiana Hoosiers) follows suit.

Politics

Both J.C. Watts, who quarterbacked at Oklahoma, and Steve Largent, who was a wide receiver at Tulsa, are voted into the U.S. House of Representatives in Oklahoma in 1994.

Impressions of the '90s

From ESPN's Stuart Scott:
The decade ended like the decade began. The best one-on-one player in basketball, the guy who could take any-

"You could write a column starting, 'Sandy Koufax yesterday…' and two million readers would swear it was the greatest column ever written if you never wrote another word. If you wrote a column about whales in the Pacific, you'd better be good. If you wrote a column about Arnold Palmer, you didn't even need verbs in all the sentences."

—Jim Murray on the enthusiasm of fans

one on the planet off the dribble, being the most prolific scorer in the NBA. Right there, the similarities between Michael Jordan and **Allen Iverson** end, right? Sure. Iverson wears baggy shorts off his rear end, wears enough gold to give Fort Knox a run, wears cornrows in his hair, and is publically disliked by some NBA veterans. Seems to me, though, there was this other dynamic "can't-nobody-guard-me" guy who came into the league in 1984. Wore baggy shorts, wore a lotta gold, had a bald head before bald heads were chic, was frozen out during an All-Star Game by some NBA veterans. Michael Jordan took sports toward the end of the century by not adhering to what the establishment had set up. Allen Iverson takes sports into the next century by doing the same. They both have game; they just prove you can have game … on your own terms.

1990 The International Boxing Hall of Fame in Canastota, New York.

Two more wild-card playoff berths, in the NFL.

1991 The new Comiskey Park, with a 16-0 White Sox loss to the Tigers.

A black driver at the Indianapolis 500, when Willy T. Ribbs qualifies.

EXIT Asterisks in baseball records.

1992 Oriole Park at Camden Yards, which becomes the model for a new wave of retro-styled, baseball-only parks.

Pro basketball players in the Olympics.

EXIT Instant replay in the NFL.

1993 The Colorado Rockies and Florida Marlins in major league baseball.

1994 The wild card in major league baseball.

EXIT The 1994 World Series.

EXIT Boston Garden.

1995 Vancouver Grizzlies and Toronto Raptors join the NBA.

Jacksonville Jaguars and Carolina Panthers join the NFL.

The World League of American Football, based in Europe, and later renamed NFL Europe.

1996 Overtime tiebreakers in college football.

EXIT Cleveland Browns, who move to Baltimore and become the Ravens, with the city of Cleveland retaining rights to team name, colors and memorabilia.

The American Basketball League for women.

1997 The Women's National Basketball Association.

Interleague play in baseball's regular season.

1998 The Tampa Bay Devil Rays and Arizona Diamondbacks in major league baseball.

The Nashville Predators join the NHL.

EXIT The American Basketball League.

1999 The "challenge" system of instant replay, in the NFL.

EXIT Tiger Stadium, Milwaukee County Stadium, and the Kingdome.

The Atlanta Thrashers join the NHL.

The new Cleveland Browns join the NFL.

ACKNOWLEDGMENTS

THAT'S MY NAME ON THE BOOK JACKET, but the truth is that *ESPN SportsCentury* is an example of book publishing at its most collaborative. Twenty-seven different writers worked on the book, another dozen people were involved in its design and production, and scores of others contributed in one capacity or another along the way.

One of my favorite things about this book was that it gave me the opportunity to work with several authors I've long admired. David Halberstam, writing the introduction, delivered an essay with his usual passion and intelligence. Roy Blount, Jr. and Robert W. Creamer, whom I've been bothering on a regular basis for the past five years, consented to more pestering. And Gerald Early, Nicholas Lemann, Wilfrid Sheed, Dick Schaap, Tony Kornheiser, Joyce Carol Oates, Thomas Boswell and Nelson George contributed original essays, on subjects often close to their hearts. (Kornheiser's essay on Bill Russell was typically personal; as a 12-year-old, in 1963, his letter praising Russell was published in *Sports Illustrated*—so he's been thinking about the man for much of his life.) Friends and colleagues Michael Point, Mark Rosner, Mark Wangrin and David Zivan delivered valuable pieces as well, each writing 10 short biographical sketches on some of the century's greatest athletes.

The clean, vibrant design is the work of the team at WBMG, Walter Bernard and Milton Glaser's legendary design shop in Manhattan. Art director Irene Vandervoort created a structure that smoothly incorporated the complex collection of editorial elements. But the indefatigable Vandervoort did more than merely design the book—she literally put it together, serving as my New York conduit for all editorial page flow and, at different times during the book's yearlong gestation, acting as photo researcher, copyeditor, proofreader, fact-checker and diplomat. It's her book as much as it is anyone's.

Bernard and Glaser shaped the book's overall look, and devised the concept of the artifact photographs that open each chapter (for which Matthew Klein took the striking shots). The book also profited from Nancy Eising's input; she created a practical way to realize my eccentric vision of running logos of every champion in every major sports league for every year of the century. Kate Gilbert, Maura Mathews and Nigel Cruickshank gave their support along the way. And photo researcher Kristine Gentile Smith was an invaluable help, tracking down not only hundreds of pictures, but also hard-to-find board games, logos, newspapers and magazines.

The ever-patient and helpful staff at Hyperion Books was remarkably accommodating, with support, expertise and, crucially, extra pages. Vice president and publisher Martha Levin played an active role in acquiring our all-star lineup of writers, and was involved every step of the way. Hyperion managing director Bob Miller oversaw the book's complicated creation, and editor Gretchen Young guided it to its conclusion. Anne Cole and Jennifer Morgan were constantly accessible and helpful, and Linda Prather, David Lott and Vincent Stanley guided us through the numerous production questions that arise in a project of this scale. Greg Wade of Color Associates provided his meticulous expertise with color separations.

Then there's the cast of thousands at ESPN. The "worldwide leader in sports" comes at you in waves, like the Prussian army—except they're on your side. Executive editor John Walsh is a wonderful leader and a gifted editor. He also, famously, gets things done. It was his vision that made the book possible. Walsh's assistant, the omnicompetent Grace Gallo, somehow stays on top of everything. Mark Shapiro, the coordinating producer of ESPN's exhaustive SportsCentury documentary series, still managed to find time to give us all the help we needed, and bailed me out of numerous photo crises. His assistant, Cindy Luciani, was always helpful (and, as far as I can tell, always at work). Nick Acocella and Frank Pizzichillo did yeoman research work, excavating mountains of material on everything from hot dogs to the Heidi game. Rick Genovese and Barbara Sheldon helped process our numerous photo requests, and Steve Buckheit and Gentry Kirby helped locate the artifacts.

Chris Berman wrote the eloquent foreword, and 10 other ESPN anchors—Mike Tirico, Karl Ravech, Linda Cohn, Robin Roberts, Rich Eisen, Bob Ley, Charley Steiner, Dan Patrick, Kenny Mayne and Stuart Scott—took time out of their busy schedules to share their impressions of the century. The book is better for it. Steve Bornstein made sure the ambitious project came off, and Sharyn Taymor, director of ESPN Enterprises, worked out the myriad details, as did Judy Fearing and Dick Glover.

Special thanks are due Larry Schwartz. He saved me from myself hundreds of times. As a copyeditor, he's one of the best—reading sympathetically yet skeptically, seeing beyond the accumulation of facts to question the larger truths as well. Howie Schwab gave the book a close, helpful, late read and, along with Schwartz and Steve Hirdt of the Elias Sports Bureau, provided numerous solutions for the back-page feature, The Final Score. Also helping along the way were Kevin Mihaly, John Hassan, Gary Hoenig and Crowley Sullivan.

Finally, several friends and loved ones came through when I needed them most. Rob Minter and Brian Hay generously shared remnants of their personal collections for the Time Capsule sections. Kevin Lyttle and Hay read parts of the manuscript, and weighed in with useful suggestions. Bill James, hard at work finishing his own book, provided tie-breaking judgments in the latter stages. Then there's my close friend and secret weapon, Pat Porter, without whom I've been unable to finish anything of consequence since my college yearbook. He read through the book twice, and provided countless incisive edits and comments. I also want to thank Sloan Harris, my agent and friend in the business; and Rick Pappas, for his infinite generosity and legal guidance.

A lot of people worked long hours on this project, so I'm hardly the only one with domestic IOUs to repay. But I'm especially grateful to my wife, Danica Frost, who flew solo for long stretches during the first four months in the life of our son, Miles. Now I think I need to set a good fatherly example and go clean my room.

MJM
St. Louis, June 1999

CREDITS

Photographs, Paintings and Artifacts

ABC: 27
Allsport: 192 (bottom), 226 (bottom), 251 (bottom), 281, 283 (bottom), 285 (bottom)
AP/Wide World Photos: 10-11, 65 (left), 69, 104, 110, 112, 113 (top 3), 125 (right), 130, 135, 138, 140 (bottom), 141, 148, 168 (top), 170, 191 (top), 195 (bottom), 198 (bottom), 201 (bottom left), 203, 209, 230, 250 (bottom), 260, 271, 283
Archive Photos: 26, 125 (left), 133, 151 (bottom), 169 (top), 173 (left), 210, 270, 282
Archive Photos/The Sporting News: 140 (top), 142 (top), 195 (top)

The Baltimore Sun: 154, 165
George Bellows/Collection of the Whitney Museum of American Art, NY: 24
Bruce Bennett: 75 (right), 250 (top)
Vernon J. Biever: 199
The Boston Celtics: 176-177
Brown Brothers: 36, 37, 39, 40-41, 44, 46, 47, 50 (top & bottom), 84, 87, 89, 114, 120, 121 (top), 143 (bottom), 149 (right)
Clive Brunskill/Allsport: 277 (top)
E. Buk: 57-58
Duane Burleson/Allsport: 285 (top)

The Caren Archive: 42, 43
Rich Clarkson: 173 (right), 229
Tami L. Chappell/Archive Photos: 272
Coca-Cola: 28, 29
Charles M. Conlon/The Sporting News/Archive Photos: 81
Corbis: 38, 40, 48, 49, 51, 53 (left), 61, 62, 63, 66, 67, 68, 71 (top), 72 (bottom), 73, 88, 90, 92 (bottom), 93 (bottom), 94, 95, 97 (left), 97 (right), 102, 105, 106, 107, 111, 116, 117, 118 (top), 118 (bottom), 119 (top), 119 (bottom), 121 (bottom), 122, 127 (bottom), 134, 136, 137, 138-139, 142 (top), 144 (top), 144 (bottom), 145 (top), 145 (bottom), 146, 147, 149 (left), 159, 162, 166 (bottom), 167 (top), 168 (bottom), 169 (bottom), 172, 178, 180, 181, 182, 183, 184, 186, 188, 189, 193 (top), 193 (bottom), 194 (top), 194 (bottom), 196, 200, 201 (top left), 201 (top right), 211, 216, 217, 222 (top), 222 (bottom), 225 (bottom), 227, 228 (top), 231 (top left), 231 (bottom left), 236-237, 238, 239, 240, 242, 244, 245, 246, 247, 251 (top), 252 (bottom), 254 (bottom), 255 (top), 257 (bottom), 261 (center), 261 (right), 263 (bottom), 268, 276, 278 (top), 279 (bottom), endpapers
Culver Pictures: 20 (top), 82

The Daily News: 127 (top)
Jonathan Daniel/Allsport: 266-267
Frank Deford: 284 (top)
Tony Duffy/NBC/Allsport: 258

Malcolm Emmons/NFL: 157, 158
ESPN: 284 (bottom)
The Everett Collection: 98 (top), 126 (top), 151 (top), 202 (bottom), 262 (top)
Everlast: 204-205

Steve Fenn/ABC: 259
FPG: 2-3, 34-35

Mike Gershman: 4-5

Barry Halper Collection: 128-129, 234-235
Brian Hay Collection: 233
Lewis Hine/Courtesy George Eastman House: 22

Institute of Texan Cultures, San Antonio, Texas: 85
International Boxing Hall of Fame: 32-33
International Tennis Hall of Fame: 167 (bottom), 223 (top)
Walter Iooss, Jr.: 185

Jed Jacobsohn/Allsport: 277 (bottom)

Fred Kaplan/NFL: 228 (bottom)
Allen Kee/NFL: 279 (top)
Heinz Kleutmeier: 241

Lamar University: 103
Mitchell Layton/Duomo: 278 (bottom)
Neil Leifer: 8-9, 12-13, 14-15, 25, 206, 213, 215, 218-219, 220-221
Ken Levine/Allsport: 23
Don Levy/Capitol Records: 263 (top)
Library of Congress: 108-109, 113 (bottom)

Alex G. Malloy Collection: 55 (top)
Bob Martin/Allsport: 252 (top)
Fernando Medina/NBA: 274-275
Gjon Mili/Life Magazine: 115
Milwaukee Journal Sentinel: 192 (top)
Rob Minter Collection: 76 (top), 99

National Baseball Hall of Fame Library: 30, 72 (top), 74, 75 (left), 83, 92 (top), 124, 132, 249
NFL: 31, 59, 64, 65 (right), 70, 123, 126 (bottom), 143 (top), 150 (bottom right), 156, 160, 164, 171, 190 (bottom), 283

Marc Okkonen: 232
Ottawa Senators: 96

Hy Peskin/FPG: 175 (bottom)
Petersen Publishing: 150 (top left)
Photo File: 71 (bottom), 254 (top), 255 (bottom), 257 (top)
Rich Pilling/MLB Photos: 243
Pittsburgh Pirates: 190 (bottom)
Popperfoto/Archive Photos: 208, 212
Patrick Porter Collection: 262 (bottom)

Dick Raphael: 166 (top)
Ken Regan/Camera 5: 149 (center), 191 (bottom), 197 (top), 253
Art Rickerby: 197 (bottom)
Robert Riger/NFL: 6-7, 161
Ring Magazine: 98 (bottom)
Wen Roberts: 224 (top), 261 (left)
George Rose/Gamma Liaison: 20 (bottom)

Tom Sarrow: 75 (middle)
Larry Schwartz Collection: 232 (top)
Sears, Roebuck Catalog: 54
Tim Shaffer/AP/Wide World Photos: 280
Bill Smith/NBA: 273
The Sporting News: 76 (bottom)
Sports Illustrated: 174, 231 (top right)
Sports Museum of New England: 100-101, 152-153
Sports Nostalgia Research: 269
Ted Streshinsky/Corbis: 187
Ozzie Sweet: 223 (bottom)

Tony Tomsic: 163, 164, 190 (top), 226 (top), 248
Transcendental Graphics: 53 (right), 91, 132
Tony Triolo: 231 (top center)

David Wells Collection: 79-80
Bruce Whitehill (The Big Game Hunter): 77, 175 (top)

UIUC University Archives: 93 (top)
University of Michigan: 55 (bottom)

Yale University: 52

Contributing Writers

Roy Blount, Jr. is the author of *Be Sweet: A Conditional Love Story*, the novel *First Hubby* and 12 other books. He was once a senior writer for *Sports Illustrated*.

Thomas Boswell is a sports columnist for *The Washington Post*, where he's worked since 1969. He is the author of seven books, including *Time Begins on Opening Day*, and writes for several national magazines.

Robert W. Creamer is the author of several books, including *Babe: The Legend Comes to Life*, a biography of Babe Ruth that was published in 1974 and remains in print today. For more than 30 years he was a writer and editor with *Sports Illustrated*.

Gerald Early is the author of *The Culture of Bruising: Essays on Prizefighting, Literature and Modern American Culture*. He is the Merle Kling Professor of Modern Letters at Washington University in St. Louis.

Nelson George is the author of several books, including *Hip Hop America*, *The Death of Rhythm & Blues* and *Elevating the Game: The History and Aesthetics of Black Men in Basketball*.

David Halberstam is the author of sixteen books, including *The Best and the Brightest*, *The Breaks of the Game* and *Summer of '49*. He has received every major journalistic award, including the Pulitzer Prize.

Tony Kornheiser has been a sportswriter for 30 years at *Newsday*, *The New York Times* and *The Washington Post*. He currently writes a column at the *Post* and does a daily radio show on ESPN.

Nicholas Lemann is a staff writer for *The New Yorker*. He is the author of four books, most recently *The Big Test: The Secret History of the American Meritocracy*.

Michael MacCambridge is the author of *The Franchise: A History of Sports Illustrated Magazine*. Before that, he worked for eight years as a columnist at the *Austin American-Statesman*.

Joyce Carol Oates is the author of *On Boxing*, and most recently, the novel *Broke Heart Blues*. She is a professor of humanities at Princeton University.

Michael Point, the former baseball columnist for the *Austin American-Statesman*, has written about contemporary culture for a variety of publications since 1975.

Mark Rosner has covered college and pro basketball, golf and numerous other sports for the *Austin American-Statesman* since 1983.

Dick Schaap has written and collaborated on a number of well-known sports books, including *Instant Replay*, *Bo Knows* and *I Can't Wait Until Tomorrow 'Cause I Get Better Looking Every Day*. He is the host of ESPN's *The Sports Reporters*.

Wilfrid Sheed is a novelist and essayist, and the author of *My Life As A Fan* and *Baseball and Lesser Sports*. He has written for *The New Yorker*, *Sports Illustrated* and numerous other publications.

Mark Wangrin has written for the *Austin American-Statesman* for 15 years, where's he covered two Summer Olympic Games, five years of pro football, and a wide range of college sports.

David Zivan is an associate editor at *Chicago* magazine, and has written for *Inside Sports*, *TriQuarterly* and *Music, Inc.*

The Final Score

Wilt Chamberlain's **100** points ▪ No. **99**, Wayne Gretzky ▪ The Drive, John Elway's **98**-yard march ▪ Don Larsen's **97**-pitch World Series perfect game ▪ Ty Cobb's **96** stolen bases ▪ Cal Ripken's **95**-game errorless streak at shortstop ▪ The baseball strike of '**94** ▪ Chris Webber calls timeout in the '**93** NCAA title game ▪ San Francisco goes **92** yards to win Super Bowl XXIII ▪ Mike Tyson's **91**-second knockout of Michael Spinks ▪ Grover Cleveland Alexander's **90** shutouts ▪ Billy Cannon's **89**-yard punt return to beat Ole Miss ▪ UCLA's **88**-game win streak in basketball ▪ Bill Bradley's **87** points in the Final Four ▪ Cary Middlecoff's **86**-foot putt at The Masters ▪ Sugar Ray Robinson's **85**-0 amateur record ▪ Jimmy Connors' **84** Wimbledon match wins ▪ North Carolina State upsets Houston in '**83** ▪ "With the **82**nd selection, the San Francisco 49ers draft Joe Montana" ▪ Sam Snead's **81** career PGA tournament wins ▪ The **80**-match rivalry between Martina Navratilova and Chris Evert ▪ Emlen Tunnell's **79** career interceptions ▪ The century's last Triple Crown winner, Affirmed in '**78** ▪ No. **77**, Red Grange ▪ Teemu Selanne's **76** goals as a rookie ▪ Ali vs. Frazier in the '**75** Thrilla in Manila ▪ Marcus Allen's **74**-yard Super Bowl touchdown run ▪ The Bears' **73**-0 title game rout of the Redskins ▪ Ricky Williams' **72** career touchdowns at Texas ▪ Nebraska-Oklahoma in '**71** ▪ Mark McGwire's **70** home runs ▪ The Amazin' Mets of '**69** ▪ Mexico City in '**68** ▪ Earl Webb's **67** doubles in a season ▪ Sammy Sosa's **66** home runs ▪ "**65** Toss Power Trap" ▪ O.J. Simpson's **64**-yard run to beat UCLA ▪ Tom Dempsey's and Jason Elam's **63**-yard field goals ▪ Margaret Court's **62** major championships ▪ Roger Maris' **61** homers ▪ The Last **60**-Minute Man, Chuck Bednarik ▪ Orel Hershiser's **59** consecutive scoreless innings ▪ Miami, Florida's **58**-game home winning streak ▪ Cal's **57**-yard kickoff return to beat Stanford ▪ Joe DiMaggio's **56**-game hitting streak ▪ Eddie Robinson's **55** seasons coaching Grambling ▪ Willie Mays' catch in '**54** ▪ Ben Hogan's three majors in '**53** ▪ Gordie Howe, playing in the NHL at age **52** ▪ Bobby Thomson's homer in '**51** ▪ Maurice Richard, and the first **50**-goal season ▪ Rocky Marciano's **49**-0 career record ▪ Doug Flutie's **48**-yard "Miracle in Miami" pass ▪ Oklahoma's **47**-game winning streak in football ▪ The Bears' **46** defense ▪ The Houston Colt .**45**s ▪ Bill Walton's **44** points in the NCAA finals ▪ Car No. **43**, Richard Petty ▪ No. **42**, Jackie Robinson ▪ Jack Chesbro's **41**-win season ▪ Ernie Nevers' **40**-point game ▪ Barry Sanders' **39**-touchdown season at Oklahoma State ▪ Don Budge's Grand Slam in '**38** ▪ The **37**-foot Green Monster ▪ Harvey Haddix retires the first **36** batters ▪ Washington's **35**-point second quarter in Super Bowl XXII ▪ Northwestern's **34**-game losing streak ▪ The Lakers' **33**-game win streak ▪ No. **32**, Jim Brown ▪ Secretariat's **31**-length win in the Belmont Stakes ▪ Bobby Jones' Grand Slam in '**30** ▪ "Harvard Beats Yale, **29**-29" ▪ Alabama's **28** bowl victories ▪ Dean Smith's **27** NCAA tournaments ▪ Baseball's longest game, **26** innings ▪ Joe Louis' **25** successful title defenses ▪ The Yankees' **24** World Series titles ▪ No. **23**, Michael Jordan ▪ Jerry Rice's **22**-touchdown reception season ▪ The Orioles' 0-**21** start ▪ Jack Nicklaus' **20** majors ▪ The Black Sox scandal of '**19** ▪ Mickey Mantle's **18** World Series homers ▪ The Dolphins' perfect **17**-0 season ▪ Citation's and Cigar's **16**-race win streaks ▪ Hank Aaron's **15** thirty-homer seasons ▪ Dick "Night Train" Lane's **14**-interception season ▪ Bob Gibson's **13**-shutout season ▪ The Packers' **12** NFL championships ▪ Byron Nelson's **11** consecutive tournament wins ▪ Nadia Comaneci's perfect **10** ▪ Carl Lewis' **9** Olympic gold medals ▪ The Celtics' **8** straight NBA titles ▪ Nolan Ryan's **7** no-hitters ▪ Kareem Abdul-Jabbar's **6** MVPs ▪ Carl Hubbell's **5** consecutive All-Star Game strikeouts ▪ The **4** Horsemen of Notre Dame ▪ No. **3**, Babe Ruth ▪ Gene Sarazen's double-eagle **2** ▪ "We're No. **1** !"